Microsoft®

MCSE
Training Kit

Microsoft®
Windows® 2000
Network Infrastructure
Administration

PUBLISHED BY
Microsoft Press
A Division of Microsoft Corporation
One Microsoft Way
Redmond, Washington 98052-6399

Library of Congress Cataloging-in-Publication Data
MCSE Training Kit—Microsoft Windows 2000 Network Infrastructure Administration / Microsoft Corporation.
      p. cm.
   ISBN 1-57231-904-6
   ISBN 0-7356-1130-0
   1. Electronic data processing personnel--Certification.   2. Microsoft
software--Examinations--Study guides.   3. Microsoft Windows (Computer file)   I.
Microsoft Corporation.
  QA76.3 .M33453   2000
  005.7'13796--dc21   00-024946

Printed and bound in the United States of America.

5 6 7 8 9   QWTQWT   5 4 3 2 1 0

Distributed in Canada by Penguin Books Canada Limited.

A CIP catalogue record for this book is available from the British Library.

Microsoft Press books are available through booksellers and distributors worldwide. For further information about international editions, contact your local Microsoft Corporation office or contact Microsoft Press International directly at fax (425) 936-7329. Visit our Web site at mspress.microsoft.com. Send comments to *tkinput@microsoft.com.*

For Microsoft Press
Acquisitions Editor: Jeff Madden
Project Editor: Michael Bolinger

For Training Associates, Inc.
Project Manager: Dave Perkovich, MCT, MCSD
Subject Matter Expert: Sean Chase, MCT, MCSD
Graphic Artist/Multimedia Developer: Stephanie Polhamus

Part No. 097-0003285

Contents

About This Book

Welcome to the *MCSE Training Kit—Microsoft Windows 2000 Network Infrastructure Administration*. This book will teach you how to plan your network infrastructure around features supported by Windows 2000. Issues such as network protocol and services are introduced and compared based on the requirements of your organization. This includes using the Internetwork Packet Exchange/ Sequenced Packet Exchange (IPX/SPX)-compatible protocol to integrate with Novell NetWare. The primary focus of network protocols throughout this book is Transmission Control Protocol/Internet Protocol (TCP/IP) because it is the Internet-standard protocol and is the best choice for enterprise networks. You will learn how to utilize, manage, and configure the TCP/IP protocol and use features such as NetBIOS, WINS, DHCP, and DNS. You will also learn how to configure, manage, and troubleshoot routing and remote access, including setting up virtual private networks (VPNs).

Note   For more information on becoming a Microsoft Certified Systems Engineer, see the section titled "The Microsoft Certified Professional Program" later in this chapter.

Each chapter in this book is divided into lessons. Most lessons include hands-on procedures that allow you to practice or demonstrate a particular concept or skill. Each chapter ends with a short summary of all chapter lessons and a set of review questions that test your knowledge of the chapter material.

The "Getting Started" section of this chapter provides important setup instructions that describe the hardware and software requirements to complete the procedures in this course. It also provides information about the networking configuration necessary to complete some of the hands-on procedures. Read through this section thoroughly before you start the lessons.

Intended Audience

This book was developed for information technology (IT) professionals who need to design, plan, implement, and support Microsoft Windows 2000 on enterprise networks, or who plan to take the related Microsoft Certified Professional exam 70-216.

Prerequisites

This course requires that students meet the following prerequisites:

- Knowledge of the fundamentals of current networking technology is required.
- Knowledge and experience administering Windows NT 4.0 networks is recommended.
- Successful completion of the MCSE Training Kit—Microsoft Windows 2000 Server is recommended.

Reference Materials

You might find the following reference materials useful:

- Microsoft Windows 2000 Server Resource Kit
- Windows 2000 Server Help
- Windows 2000 white papers and case studies, available online at *http://www.microsoft.com/windows2000/guide/server/overview/*

About the CD-ROM

The Supplemental Course Materials compact disc contains a variety of informational aids that may be used throughout this book. This includes an online version of the book, Internet Explorer 5, and media files that assist in demonstrating the information conveyed in the course topics. For more information regarding the contents of this CD-ROM, see the section titled "Getting Started" later in this introduction and the README.TXT file included in the root directory of this CD-ROM.

The multimedia presentations supplement some of the key concepts covered in the book. You should view these presentations when suggested, and then use them as a review tool while you work through the material. A complete version of this book is also available online with a variety of viewing options available. For information about using the online book, see the section "About the Online Book" later in this introduction.

Features of This Book

Each chapter opens with a "Before You Begin" section, which prepares you for completing the chapter.

▶   The chapters are then broken into lessons. Whenever possible, lessons contain practices that give you an opportunity to use the skills being presented or to explore the part of the application being described. All practices offer step-by-step procedures that are identified with a bullet symbol like the one to the left of this paragraph.

The "Review" section at the end of the chapter allows you to test what you have learned in the chapter's lessons.

Appendix A, "Questions and Answers," contains all of the book's questions and corresponding answers.

Notes

Several types of notes appear throughout the lessons.

- Notes marked **Tip** contain explanations of possible results or alternative methods.
- Notes marked **Important** contain information that is essential to completing a task.
- Notes marked **Note** contain supplemental information.
- Notes marked **Caution** contain warnings about possible loss of data.

Conventions

The following conventions are used throughout this book.

Notational Conventions

- Characters or commands that you type appear in **bold lowercase** type.
- *Italic* in syntax statements indicates placeholders for variable information. *Italic* is also used for book titles.
- Names of files and folders appear in Title Caps, except when you are to type them directly. Unless otherwise indicated, you can use all lowercase letters when you type a filename in a dialog box or at a command prompt.
- Filename extensions appear in all lowercase.
- Acronyms appear in all uppercase.
- Monospace type represents code samples, examples of screen text, or entries that you might type at a command prompt or in initialization files.
- Square brackets [ ] are used in syntax statements to enclose optional items. For example, [*filename*] in command syntax indicates that you can choose to type a filename with the command. Type only the information within the brackets, not the brackets themselves.
- Braces { } are used in syntax statements to enclose required items. Type only the information within the braces, not the braces themselves.

- Icons represent specific sections in the book as follows:

Icon	Represents
	A multimedia presentation. You will find the applicable multimedia presentation on the course compact disc.
	A hands-on practice. You should perform the practice to give yourself an opportunity to use the skills being presented in the lesson.
	Chapter review questions. These questions at the end of each chapter allow you to test what you have learned in the lessons. You will find the answers to the review questions in the Questions and Answers section at the end of the book.

Keyboard Conventions

- A plus sign (+) between two key names means that you must press those keys at the same time. For example, "Press ALT+TAB" means that you hold down ALT while you press TAB.

- A comma (,) between two or more key names means that you must press each of the keys consecutively, not together. For example, "Press ALT, F, X" means that you press and release each key in sequence. "Press ALT+W, L" means that you first press ALT and W together, and then release them and press L.

- You can choose menu commands with the keyboard. Press the ALT key to activate the menu bar, and then sequentially press the keys that correspond to the highlighted or underlined letter of the menu name and the command name. For some commands, you can also press a key combination listed in the menu.

- You can select or clear check boxes or option buttons in dialog boxes with the keyboard. Press the ALT key, and then press the key that corresponds to the underlined letter of the option name. Or you can press TAB until the option is highlighted, and then press the spacebar to select or clear the check box or option button.

- You can cancel the display of a dialog box by pressing the ESC key.

Chapter and Appendix Overview

This self-paced training course combines notes, hands-on procedures, multimedia presentations, and review questions to teach you how to design, implement, administer, configure, and troubleshoot a Windows 2000-based network. It is designed to be completed from beginning to end, but you can choose a customized track and complete only the sections that interest you. (See the next section, "Finding the Best Starting Point for You," for more information.) If you choose the customized track option, see the "Before You Begin" section in each chapter.

Any hands-on procedures that require preliminary work from preceding chapters refer to the appropriate chapters.

The book is divided into the following chapters:

- The "About This Book" section contains a self-paced training overview and introduces the components of this training. Read this section thoroughly to get the greatest educational value from this self-paced training and to plan which lessons you will complete.

- Chapter 1, "Designing a Windows 2000 Network," introduces you to the primary network protocols and services for planning a network infrastructure.

- Chapter 2, "Implementing TCP/IP," explains how to install and configure the TCP/IP network protocol.

- Chapter 3, "Implementing NWLink," explains how to install and configure the NWLink IPX/SPX-compatible network protocol. IPX/SPX is typically used on a Novell NetWare local area network (LAN), and NWLink provides you with a way to interoperate with NetWare networks.

- Chapter 4, "Monitoring Network Activity," explains how to use the Network Monitor application that comes with Windows 2000.

- Chapter 5, "Implementing IPSec," explains how to enable, configure, and monitor IPSec, and how to customize IPSec policies and rules.

- Chapter 6, "Resolving Network Host Names," gives an overview of the various methods of name resolution available to TCP/IP.

- Chapter 7, "Implementing Domain Name System (DNS)," explains how DNS is used to resolve host names on your network and across the public Internet. Microsoft Windows 2000 includes an enhanced version of DNS.

- Chapter 8, "Using Windows 2000 Domain Name Service," explains how to work with DNS zones. This includes implementing a delegated zone, and configuring zones for dynamic updates. You will also learn how to configure a DNS server to work as a caching-only server, and how to monitor DNS server performance.

- Chapter 9, "Implementing Windows Internet Name Service (WINS)," explains how WINS is used to resolve host names on your network. You will also learn how to identify the primary components of WINS, install and configure WINS, and troubleshoot WINS on Windows 2000.

- Chapter 10, "Implementing Dynamic Host Configuration Protocol (DHCP)," explains how DHCP is used to manage and configure client computers on your network from a central Windows 2000 server. You will learn how to identify the primary components of DHCP, install and configure DHCP on both a client and server, and troubleshoot DHCP.

- Chapter 11, "Providing Your Clients Remote Access Service (RAS)," explains how to implement Remote Access Services to provide your clients the ability to access network resources from the road or their home. You will learn how to implement secure connections with techniques such as VPNs.

- Chapter 12, "Supporting Network Address Translation (NAT)," describes the network address translation (NAT) protocol, which allows a network with private addresses to access information on the Internet through an IP translation process. You will learn how to configure your home network or small office network to share a single connection to the Internet with NAT.

- Chapter 13, "Implementing Certificate Services," explains the concepts of certificates, which are fundamental elements of the Microsoft Public Key Infrastructure (PKI). You will learn how to install and configure certificates.

- Chapter 14, "Implementing Enterprise-Wide Network Security," describes the security features of Windows 2000 and how to implement as secure a network as possible.

- Appendix A, "Questions and Answers," lists all of the review questions from the book, showing the suggested answer.

- The Glossary lists and defines the terms associated with your study of implementing and administering a Windows 2000 network infrastructure.

Finding the Best Starting Point for You

Because this book is self-paced, you can skip some lessons and revisit them later. But note that you must complete the setup instructions in this chapter before you can perform procedures in the other chapters. Use the following table to find the best starting point for you.

If You	Follow This Learning Path
Are preparing to take the Microsoft Certified Professional exam 70-216, *Implementing and Administering a Microsoft Windows 2000 Network Infrastructure*	Read the "Getting Started" section and follow the setup procedures in the "Setup Instructions" section. Then work through Chapters 1 through 14 in order.
Want to review information about specific topics from the exam	Use the "Where to Find Specific Skills in This Book" section that follows this table.

Where to Find Specific Skills in This Book

The following tables provide a list of the skills measured on certification exam 70-216, *Implementing and Administering a Microsoft Windows 2000 Network Infrastructure*. The table provides the skill and where in this book you will find the lesson relating to that skill.

Note Exam skills are subject to change without prior notice and at the sole discretion of Microsoft.

Installing, Configuring, Managing, Monitoring, and Troubleshooting DNS in a Windows 2000 Network Infrastructure

Skill Being Measured	Location in Book
Install, configure, and troubleshoot DNS	
Install the DNS Server service	Chapter 7, Lesson 4
Configure a root name server	Chapter 7, Lesson 2
Configure zones	Chapter 8, Lesson 1
Configure a caching-only server	Chapter 8, Lesson 2
Configure a DNS client	Chapter 7, Lesson 2
Configure zones for dynamic updates	Chapter 8, Lesson 1
Test the DNS Server Service	Chapter 8, Lesson 2
Implement a delegated zone for DNS	Chapter 8, Lesson 1
Manually create DNS resource records	Chapter 7, Lesson 5
Manage and monitor DNS	**Chapter 8, Lesson 2**

Installing, Configuring, Managing, Monitoring, and Troubleshooting DHCP in a Windows 2000 Network Infrastructure

Skill Being Measured	Location in Book
Install, configure, and troubleshoot DHCP	
Install the DHCP Server service	Chapter 10, Lesson 1
Create and manage DHCP scopes, superscopes, and multicast scopes	Chapter 10, Lesson 2
Configure DHCP for DNS integration	Chapter 10, Lesson 3
Authorize a DHCP server in Active Directory	Chapter 10, Lesson 4
Manage and monitor DHCP	**Chapter 10, Lesson 5**

Configuring, Managing, Monitoring, and Troubleshooting Remote Access in a Windows 2000 Network Infrastructure

Skill Being Measured	Location in Book
Configure and troubleshoot remote access	
Configure inbound connections	Chapter 11, Lesson 2
Create a remote access policy	Chapter 11, Lesson 2
Configure a remote access profile	Chapter 11, Lesson 2
Configure a VPN	Chapter 11, Lesson 4
Configure multilink connections	Chapter 11, Lesson 5
Configure Routing and Remote Access for DHCP integration	Chapter 11, Lesson 6
Manage and monitor remote access	**Chapter 11, Lesson 7** **Chapter 14, Lesson 1**
Configure remote access security	
Configure authentication protocols	Chapter 14, Lesson 2
Configure encryption protocols	Chapter 4, Lesson 3 Chapter 14, Lesson 2
Create a remote access policy	Chapter 11, Lesson 2 Chapter 14, Lesson 2

Installing, Configuring, Managing, Monitoring, and Troubleshooting Network Protocols in a Windows 2000 Network Infrastructure

Skill Being Measured	Location in Book
Install, configure, and troubleshoot network protocols	
Install and configure TCP/IP	Chapter 2, Lesson 3
Install the NWLink protocol	Chapter 3, Lesson 4
Configure network bindings	Chapter 3, Lesson 4
Configure TCP/IP packet filters	**Chapter 2, Lesson 3**
Configure and troubleshoot network protocol security	**Chapter 5, Lesson 2** **Chapter 14, Lesson 2**
Manage and monitor network traffic	**Chapter 4, Lesson 2** **Chapter 14, Lesson 3**

Installing, Configuring, Managing, Monitoring, and Troubleshooting Network Protocols in a Windows 2000 Network Infrastructure *(continued)*

Skill Being Measured	Location in Book
Configure and troubleshoot IPSec	
Enable IPSec	Chapter 5, Lessons 1 and 2
Configure IPSec for transport mode	Chapter 5, Lesson 3
Configure IPSec for tunnel mode	Chapter 5, Lesson 3
Customize IPSec policies and rules	Chapter 5, Lesson 3
Manage and monitor IPSec	Chapter 5, Lesson 4

Installing, Configuring, Managing, Monitoring, and Troubleshooting WINS in a Windows 2000 Network Infrastructure

Skill Being Measured	Location in Book
Install, configure, and troubleshoot WINS	**Chapter 9, Lessons 1-4**
Configure WINS replication	**Chapter 9, Lesson 4**
Configure NetBIOS name resolution	**Chapter 9, Lesson 1** **Chapter 9, Lesson 2**
Manage and monitor WINS	**Chapter 9, Lesson 3** **Chapter 9, Lesson 4**

Installing, Configuring, Managing, Monitoring, and Troubleshooting IP Routing in a Windows 2000 Network Infrastructure

Skill Being Measured	Location in Book
Install, configure, and troubleshoot IP routing protocols	
Update a Windows 2000-based routing table by means of static routes	Chapter 2, Lesson 4 Chapter 11, Lesson 4
Implement demand-dial routing	Chapter 11, Lesson 2
Manage and monitor IP routing	
Manage and monitor border routing	Chapter 2, Lesson 4 Chapter 11, Lessons 1 and 7
Manage and monitor internal routing	Chapter 2, Lesson 4 Chapter 11, Lesson 6
Manage and monitor IP routing protocols	Chapter 2, Lesson 4 Chapter 11, Lessons 1 and 7

Installing, Configuring, and Troubleshooting NAT

Skill Being Measured	Location in Book
Install Internet Connection Sharing	Chapter 12, Lesson 2
Install NAT	Chapter 12, Lessons 2 and 3
Configure NAT properties	Chapter 12, Lesson 3
Configure NAT interfaces	Chapter 12, Lesson 3

Installing, Configuring, Managing, Monitoring, and Troubleshooting Certificate Services

Skill Being Measured	Location in Book
Install and configure Certificate Authority (CA)	Chapter 13, Lesson 2
Create certificates	Chapter 13, Lesson 2
Issue certificates	Chapter 13, Lesson 2
Revoke certificates	Chapter 13, Lesson 3
Remove the Encrypting File System (EFS) recovery keys	Chapter 13, Lesson 3

Getting Started

This self-paced training course contains hands-on procedures to help you learn about implementing and administering a Windows 2000 network infrastructure. To complete these procedures, you must have the following:

- One computer running Windows 2000 Server

There are a few exercises in this book that require two computers. Using a second computer is required to meet the lesson objectives. If you have only one computer, read through the steps and familiarize yourself with the procedure as best you can.

It is recommended that you set up the server on its own network so you do not inhibit your production network or affect other users in your existing domain. However, it is possible to use your existing network with your server.

Caution   Several exercises may require you to make changes to your servers. This may have undesirable results if you are connected to a larger network. Check with your network administrator before attempting these exercises.

Hardware Requirements

Each computer must have the following minimum configuration. All hardware should be on the Microsoft Windows 2000 Hardware Compatibility List (HCL). The latest version of the HCL can be downloaded from the hardware compatibility Web page at *http://www.microsoft.com/hcl/default.asp*.

- 32-bit 166 MHz Pentium processor
- 64 MB memory for networking with one to five client computers; 128 MB minimum is recommended for most network environments
- 2 GB hard disk
- 12X or faster CD-ROM drive
- SVGA monitor capable of 800 × 600 resolution (1024 × 768 recommended)
- High-density 3.5-inch disk drive, unless your CD-ROM is bootable and supports starting the setup program from a CD-ROM
- Microsoft Mouse or compatible pointing device

Software Requirements

You will need a copy of the Microsoft Windows 2000 Server software.

Setup Instructions

The following information is a checklist of the tasks that you need to perform to prepare your computer for the lessons in this book. If you do not have experience installing Windows 2000 or another network operating system, you may need help from an experienced network administrator. As you complete a task, mark it off in the check box. Step-by-step instructions for each task follow.

- [ ] Create Windows 2000 Server setup diskettes
- [ ] Run the Windows 2000 Server Pre-Copy and Text Mode Setup Routine
- [ ] Run the GUI mode and gathering information phase of Windows 2000 Server Setup
- [ ] Complete the installing Windows networking components phase of Windows 2000 Server Setup
- [ ] Complete the hardware installation phase of Windows 2000 Server Setup

Note   The installation information provided will help you prepare a computer for use with this book. It is not intended to teach you installation. For comprehensive information on installing Windows 2000 Server, see the *MCSE Training Kit—Microsoft Windows 2000 Server,* also available from Microsoft Press.

Installing Windows 2000 Server

To complete the exercises in this course, you should install Windows 2000 Server on a computer with no formatted partitions. During installation, you can use the Windows 2000 Server Setup program to create a partition on your hard disk, on which you install Windows 2000 Server as a stand-alone server in a workgroup.

Complete the following procedure on a computer running MS-DOS or any version of Windows with access to the Bootdisk directory on the Windows 2000 Server installation CD-ROM. If your computer is configured with a bootable CD-ROM drive, you can install Windows 2000 without using the Setup disks. To complete this exercise as outlined, bootable CD-ROM support must be disabled in the BIOS.

Important   This procedure requires four formatted 1.44-MB disks. If you use diskettes that contain data, the data will be overwritten without warning.

▶   **To create Windows 2000 Server Setup diskettes**

1. Label the four blank, formatted 1.44-MB diskettes as follows:
   - Windows 2000 Server Setup Disk #1
   - Windows 2000 Server Setup Disk #2
   - Windows 2000 Server Setup Disk #3
   - Windows 2000 Server Setup Disk #4
2. Insert the Microsoft Windows 2000 Server CD-ROM into the CD-ROM drive.
3. If the Windows 2000 CD-ROM dialog box appears prompting you to install or upgrade to Windows 2000, click No.
4. Open a command prompt.
5. At the command prompt, change to your CD-ROM drive. For example, if your CD-ROM drive name is E, type **e:** and press Enter.
6. At the command prompt, change to the Bootdisk directory by typing **cd bootdisk** and pressing Enter.
7. If you are creating the setup boot diskettes from a computer running MS-DOS, a Windows 16-bit operating system, Windows 95, or Windows 98, type **makeboot a:** (where A: is the name of your floppy disk drive), then press Enter. If you are creating the setup boot diskettes from a computer running Windows NT or Windows 2000, type **makebt32 a:** (where A: is the name of your floppy disk drive), then press Enter. Windows 2000 displays a message indicating that this program creates the four setup disks for installing

Windows 2000. It also indicates that four blank, formatted, high-density floppy disks are required.

8. Press any key to continue. Windows 2000 displays a message prompting you to insert the disk that will become the Windows 2000 Setup Boot Disk.

9. Insert the blank formatted diskette labeled Windows 2000 Server Setup Disk #1 into the floppy disk drive and press any key to continue. After Windows 2000 creates the disk image, it displays a message prompting you to insert the diskette labeled Windows 2000 Setup Disk #2.

10. Remove Disk #1, insert the blank formatted diskette labeled Windows 2000 Server Setup Disk #2 into the floppy disk drive, and press any key to continue. After Windows 2000 creates the disk image, it displays a message prompting you to insert the diskette labeled Windows 2000 Setup Disk #3.

11. Remove Disk #2, insert the blank formatted diskette labeled Windows 2000 Server Setup Disk #3 into the floppy disk drive, and press any key to continue. After Windows 2000 creates the disk image, it displays a message prompting you to insert the diskette labeled Windows 2000 Setup Disk #4.

12. Remove Disk #3, insert the blank formatted diskette labeled Windows 2000 Server Setup Disk #4 into the floppy disk drive, and press any key to continue. After Windows 2000 creates the disk image, it displays a message indicating that the imaging process is done.

13. At the command prompt, type **exit** and then press Enter.

    Remove the disk from the floppy disk drive and the CD-ROM from the CD-ROM drive.

▶ **To run the Windows 2000 Server Pre-Copy and Text Mode Setup routine**

Note   It is assumed for this procedure that your computer has no operating system installed, the disk is not partitioned, and bootable CD-ROM support, if available, is disabled.

1. Insert the disk labeled Windows 2000 Server Setup Disk #1 into the floppy disk drive, insert the Windows 2000 Server CD-ROM into the CD-ROM drive, and restart your computer.

    After the computer starts, Windows 2000 Setup displays a brief message that your system configuration is being checked, and then the Windows 2000 Setup screen appears.

    Notice that the gray bar at the bottom of the screen indicates that the computer is being inspected and that the Windows 2000 Executive is loading, which is a minimal version of the Windows 2000 kernel.

2. When prompted, insert Setup Disk #2 into the floppy disk drive and press Enter.

    Notice that Setup indicates that it is loading the HAL, fonts, local specific data, bus drivers, and other software components to support your computer's motherboard, bus, and other hardware. Setup also loads the Windows 2000 Setup program files.

3. When prompted, insert Setup Disk #3 into the floppy disk drive and press Enter.

   Notice that Setup indicates that it is loading disk drive controller drivers. After the drive controllers load, the Setup program initializes drivers appropriate to support access to your disk drives. Setup might pause several times during this process.

4. When prompted, insert Setup Disk #4 into the floppy disk drive and press Enter.

   Setup loads peripheral support drivers, like the floppy disk driver and file systems, and then it initializes the Windows 2000 Executive and loads the rest of the Windows 2000 Setup program.

   If you are installing the evaluation version of Windows 2000, a Setup notification screen appears informing you that you are about to install an evaluation version of Windows 2000.

5. Read the Setup Notification message and press Enter to continue.

   Setup displays the Welcome To Setup screen. Notice that, in addition to the initial installation of Windows 2000, you can use Windows 2000 Setup to repair or recover a damaged Windows 2000 installation.

6. Read the Welcome To Setup message and press Enter to begin the installation phase of Windows 2000 Setup. Setup displays the License Agreement screen.

7. Read the license agreement, pressing Page Down to scroll down to the bottom of the screen.

8. Select I Accept The Agreement by pressing F8.

   Setup displays the Windows 2000 Server Setup screen, prompting you to select an area of free space or an existing partition on which to install Windows 2000. This stage of setup provides a way for you to create and delete partitions on your hard disk.

   If your computer does not contain any disk partitions (as required for this exercise), you will notice that the hard disk listed on the screen contains an existing unformatted partition.

9. Make sure that the Unpartitioned space partition is highlighted and then type **c**.

   Setup displays the Windows 2000 Setup screen, confirming that you have chosen to create a new partition in the unpartitioned space and informing you of the minimum and maximum sizes of the partition you might create.

10. Specify the size of the partition you want to create (at least 2 GB) and press Enter to continue.

    Setup displays the Windows 2000 Setup screen, showing the new partition as C: New (Unformatted).

Note   Although you can create additional partitions from the remaining unpartitioned space during setup, it is recommended that you perform additional partitioning tasks after you install Windows 2000. To partition hard disks after installation, use the Disk Management console.

11. Make sure the new partition is highlighted and press Enter.

You are prompted to select a file system for the partition.

12. Use the arrow keys to select Format The Partition Using The NTFS File System and press Enter.

The Setup program formats the partition with NTFS. After it formats the partition, Setup examines the hard disk for physical errors that might cause Setup to fail and then copies files to the hard disk. This process will take several minutes.

Eventually, Setup displays the Windows 2000 Server Setup screen. A red status bar counts down for 15 seconds before Setup restarts the computer.

13. Remove the Setup disk from the floppy disk drive.

Important   If your computer supports booting from the CD-ROM drive and this feature was not disabled in the BIOS, the computer will boot from the Windows 2000 Server installation CD-ROM after Windows 2000 Setup restarts. This will cause Setup to start again from the beginning. If this happens, remove the CD-ROM and then restart the computer.

14. Setup copies additional files and then restarts your machine and loads the Windows 2000 Setup Wizard.

▶   **To run the GUI mode and gathering
information phase of Windows 2000 Server Setup**

Note   This procedure begins the graphical portion of setup on your computer.

1. On the Welcome To The Windows 2000 Setup Wizard page, click Next to begin gathering information about your computer.

Setup configures NTFS folder and file permissions for the operating system files, detects the hardware devices in the computer, and then installs and configures device drivers to support the detected hardware. This process takes several minutes.

2. On the Regional Settings page, make sure that the system locale, user locale, and keyboard layout are correct for your language and location, then click Next.

Note   You can modify regional settings after you install Windows 2000 by using Regional Options in Control Panel.

Setup displays the Personalize Your Software page, prompting you for your name and organization name. Setup uses your organization name to generate the default computer name. Many applications that you install later will use this information for product registration and document identification.

3. In the Name field, type your name; in the Organization field, type the name of your organization; then click Next.

Note If the Your Product Key screen appears, enter the product key, located on the yellow sticker on the back of your Windows 2000 Server CD-ROM case.

Setup displays the Licensing Modes page, prompting you to select a licensing mode. By default, the Per Server licensing mode is selected. Setup prompts you to enter the number of licenses you have purchased for this server.

4. Select the Per Server Number Of Concurrent Connections button, type **5** for the number of concurrent connections, then click Next.

Important Per Server Number of concurrent connections and 5 concurrent connections are suggested values to be used to complete your self-study. You should use a legal number of concurrent connections based on the actual licenses that you own. You can also choose to use Per Seat instead of Per Server.

Setup displays the Computer Name And Administrator Password page. Notice that Setup uses your organization name to generate a suggested name for the computer.

5. In the Computer Name field, type **server1**.

Windows 2000 displays the computer name in all capital letters regardless of how it is entered.

Caution If your computer is on a network, check with the network administrator before assigning a name to your computer.

Throughout the rest of this self-paced training kit, the practices and exercises will refer to Server1. If you do not name your computer Server1, everywhere the materials reference Server1, you will have to substitute the name of your server.

6. In the Administrator Password field and the Confirm Password field, type **password** (all lowercase) and click Next. Passwords are case-sensitive, so make sure you type **password** in all lowercase letters.

For the labs in this self-paced training kit, you will use **password** for the Administrator account. In a production environment, you should always use a complex password for the Administrator account (one that others cannot easily guess). Microsoft recommends mixing uppercase and lowercase letters, numbers, and symbols (for example, Lp6*g9).

Setup displays the Windows 2000 Components page, indicating which Windows 2000 system components Setup will install.

7. On the Windows 2000 Components page, click Next.

You can install additional components after you install Windows 2000 by using Add/Remove Programs in Control Panel. Make sure to install only the components selected by default during setup. Later in your training, you will be installing additional components.

If a modem is detected in the computer during setup, Setup displays the Modem Dialing Information page.

8. If the Modem Dialing Information page appears, enter an area code or city code and click Next.

The Date And Time Settings page appears.

Important   Windows 2000 services perform many tasks, the successful completion of which depends on the computer's time and date settings. Be sure to select the correct time zone for your location to avoid problems in later labs.

---

9. Enter the correct Date And Time and Time Zone settings, then click Next.

The Network Settings page appears and Setup installs networking components.

▶ **To complete the installing Windows networking components phase of Windows 2000 Server Setup**

Networking is an integral part of Windows 2000 Server. There are many selections and configurations available. In this procedure, basic networking is configured. In a later exercise, you will install additional network components.

1. On the Networking Settings page, make sure that Typical Settings is selected, then click Next to begin installing Windows networking components.

This setting installs networking components that are used to gain access to and share resources on a network, and configures TCP/IP to automatically obtain an IP address from a DHCP server on the network.

Setup displays the Workgroup Or Computer Domain page, prompting you to join either a workgroup or a domain.

2. On the Workgroup Or Computer Domain page, make sure that the button No, This Computer Is Not On A Network or Is On A Network Without A Domain is selected, and that the workgroup name is WORKGROUP, then click Next.

Setup displays the Installing Components page, displaying the status as Setup installs and configures the remaining operating system components according to the options you specified. This will take several minutes.

Setup then displays the Performing Final Tasks page, which shows the status as Setup finishes copying files, making and saving configuration changes, and deleting temporary files. Computers that do not exceed the minimum hardware requirements might take 30 minutes or more to complete this phase of installation.

Setup then displays the Completing The Windows 2000 Setup Wizard page.

3. Remove the Windows 2000 Server CD-ROM from the CD-ROM drive, and then click Finish.

Important   If your computer supports booting from the CD-ROM drive and you did not remove the installation CD-ROM, and if you disable this feature in the BIOS, the computer will run Setup again soon after Setup restarts the computer. If this happens, remove the CD-ROM and then restart the computer.

Windows 2000 restarts and runs the newly installed version of Windows 2000 Server.

▶ **To complete the hardware installation phase of Windows 2000 Server Setup**

During this final phase of installation, any Plug and Play hardware not detected in the previous phases of Setup will be detected.

1. At the completion of the startup phase, log on by pressing Ctrl+Alt+Delete.

2. In the Enter Password dialog box, type **administrator** in the User Name field and type **password** in the Password field.

3. Click OK.

4. If Windows 2000 detects hardware that was not detected during Setup, the Found New Hardware Wizard screen displays, indicating that Windows 2000 is installing the appropriate drivers.

   If the Found New Hardware Wizard screen appears, verify that the Restart The Computer When I Click Finish check box is cleared, and click Finish to complete the Found New Hardware Wizard.

   Windows 2000 displays the Microsoft Windows 2000 Configure Your Server dialog box. From this dialog box, you can configure a variety of advanced options and services.

5. Select I Will Configure This Server Later, and then click Next.

6. From the next screen that appears, clear the Show This Screen At Startup check box.

7. Close the Configure Your Server screen.

   You have now completed the Windows 2000 Server installation and are logged on as Administrator.

Note   To properly shut down Windows NT Server, click Start, choose Shut Down, then follow the directions that appear.

For the exercises that require networked computers, you need to make sure the computers can communicate with each other. The first computer will be configured as a primary domain controller (PDC), and will be assigned the computer account name Server1 and the domain name Domain1. This computer will act as a domain controller in Domain1. The second computer will act as client or secondary server for most of the procedures in this course.

Caution   If your computers are part of a larger network, you must verify with your network administrator that the computer names, domain name, and other information used in setting up in this chapter do not conflict with network operations. If they do conflict, ask your network administrator to provide alternative values and use those values throughout all of the exercises in this book.

Running the Media Files

The Supplemental Course Materials CD-ROM contains a set of audiovisual demonstration files that you can view by running the files from the CD-ROM. You will find prompts within the book indicating when the demonstrations should be run.

▶   **To view the demonstrations**

1. Insert the Supplemental Course Materials CD-ROM into your CD-ROM drive.

2. Select Run from the Start menu on your desktop, and type **D:\Media*demonstration_filename*** (where D is the name of your CD-ROM disk drive).

   This will run the appropriate demonstration.

Installing the Online Book

The Supplemental Course Materials CD-ROM includes an online version of the book that you can view on-screen using Microsoft Internet Explorer 5 or later.

▶   **To use the online version of this book**

1. Insert the Supplemental Course Materials CD-ROM into your CD-ROM drive.

2. Select Run from the Start menu on your desktop, and type **D:\Ebook\Setup.exe** (where D is the name of your CD-ROM disk drive).

   This will install an icon for the online book in your Start menu.

3. Click OK to exit the Installation Wizard.

Note   You must have the Supplemental Course Materials CD-ROM inserted in your CD-ROM drive to run the online book.

The Microsoft Certified Professional Program

The Microsoft Certified Professional (MCP) program provides the best method to prove your command of current Microsoft products and technologies. Microsoft, an industry leader in certification, is on the forefront of testing methodology. Our exams and corresponding certifications are developed to validate your mastery of critical competencies as you design and develop, or implement and support, solutions with Microsoft products and technologies. Computer professionals who become Microsoft-certified are recognized as experts and are sought after industry-wide.

The Microsoft Certified Professional program offers eight certifications, based on specific areas of technical expertise:

- **Microsoft Certified Professional (MCP).**   Demonstrated in-depth knowledge of at least one Microsoft operating system. Candidates may pass additional Microsoft certification exams to further qualify their skills with Microsoft BackOffice products, development tools, or desktop programs.

- **Microsoft Certified Professional + Internet.**   MCPs with a specialty in the Internet are qualified to plan security, install and configure server products, manage server resources, extend servers to run scripts, monitor and analyze performance, and troubleshoot problems.

- **Microsoft Certified Professional + Site Building.**   These professionals have demonstrated what it takes to plan, build, maintain, and manage Web sites using Microsoft technologies and products.

- **Microsoft Certified Systems Engineer (MCSE).**   MCSEs are qualified to effectively plan, implement, maintain, and support information systems in a wide range of computing environments with Microsoft Windows NT Server and the Microsoft BackOffice integrated family of server software.

- **Microsoft Certified Systems Engineer + Internet.**   MCSEs with an advanced qualification to enhance, deploy, and manage sophisticated intranet and Internet solutions that include a browser, proxy server, host servers, database, and messaging and commerce components. In addition, an MCSE + Internet-certified professional is able to manage and analyze Web sites.

- **Microsoft Certified Database Administrator (MCDBA).**   These individuals derive physical database designs, develop logical data models, create physical databases, create data services by using Transact-SQL, manage and maintain databases, configure and manage security, monitor and optimize databases, and install and configure Microsoft SQL Server.

- **Microsoft Certified Solution Developer (MCSD).**   MCSDs are qualified to design and develop custom business solutions with Microsoft development tools, technologies, and platforms, including Microsoft Office and Microsoft BackOffice.

- **Microsoft Certified Trainer (MCT).**   MCTs are instructionally and technically qualified to deliver Microsoft Official Curriculum through a Microsoft Certified Technical Education Center (CTEC).

Microsoft Certification Benefits

Microsoft certification, one of the most comprehensive certification programs available for assessing and maintaining software-related skills, is a valuable measure of an individual's knowledge and expertise. Microsoft certification is awarded to individuals who have successfully demonstrated their ability to perform specific tasks and implement solutions with Microsoft products. Not only does this provide an objective measure for employers to consider, it also provides guidance for what an individual should know to be proficient. As with any skills-assessment and benchmarking measure, certification brings a variety of benefits to the individual, and to employers and organizations.

Microsoft Certification Benefits for Individuals

As an MCP, you receive many benefits:

- Industry recognition of your knowledge and proficiency with Microsoft products and technologies.

- Access to technical and product information directly from Microsoft through a secured area of the MCP Web site.

- MSDN Online Certified Membership that helps you tap into the best technical resources, connect to the MCP community, and gain access to valuable resources and services. (Some MSDN Online benefits may be available in English only or may not be available in all countries.) See the MSDN Web site for a growing list of certified member benefits.

- Logos that enable you to identify your Microsoft Certified Professional status to colleagues or clients.

- Invitations to Microsoft conferences, technical training sessions, and special events.

- A Microsoft Certified Professional certificate.

- Subscription to *Microsoft Certified Professional Magazine* (North America only), a career and professional development magazine.

Additional benefits, depending on your certification and geography, include:

- A complimentary one-year subscription to the Microsoft TechNet Technical Plus, providing valuable information on monthly CD-ROMs.

- A one-year subscription to the Microsoft Beta Evaluation program. This benefit provides you with up to 12 free monthly CD-ROMs containing beta software (English only) for many of Microsoft's newest software products.

Microsoft Certification Benefits for Employers and Organizations

Through certification, computer professionals can maximize the return on investment in Microsoft technology. Research shows that Microsoft certification provides organizations with:

- Excellent return on training and certification investments by providing a standard method of determining training needs and measuring results
- Increased customer satisfaction and decreased support costs through improved service, increased productivity, and greater technical self-sufficiency
- A reliable benchmark for hiring, promoting, and career planning
- Recognition and rewards for productive employees by validating their expertise
- Retraining options for existing employees so they can work effectively with new technologies
- Assurance of quality when outsourcing computer services

To learn more about how certification can help your company, see the back-grounders, white papers, and case studies available on *http:www.microsoft.com/mcp/mktg/bus_bene.htm:*

- Financial Benefits to Supporters of Microsoft Professional Certification, IDC white paper (1998WPIDC.DOC 1,608K)
- Prudential Case Study (PRUDENTL.EXE 70K self-extracting file)
- The Microsoft Certified Professional Program Corporate Backgrounder (MCPBACK.EXE 50K)
- A white paper (MCSDWP.DOC 158K) that evaluates the Microsoft Certified Solution Developer certification
- A white paper (MCSESTUD.DOC 161K) that evaluates the Microsoft Certified Systems Engineer certification
- Jackson Hole High School Case Study (JHHS.DOC 180K)
- Lyondel Case Study (LYONDEL.DOC 21K)
- Stellcom Case Study (STELLCOM.DOC 132K)

Requirements for Becoming a Microsoft Certified Professional

The certification requirements differ for each certification and are specific to the products and job functions addressed by the certification.

To become a Microsoft Certified Professional, you must pass rigorous certification exams that provide a valid and reliable measure of technical proficiency and expertise. These exams are designed to test your expertise and ability to perform a role or task with a product, and are developed with the input of professionals in the industry. Questions in the exams reflect how Microsoft products are used in actual organizations, giving them "real-world" relevance.

Microsoft Certified Product Specialists are required to pass one operating system exam. Candidates may pass additional Microsoft certification exams to further qualify their skills with Microsoft BackOffice products, development tools, or desktop applications.

Microsoft Certified Professional + Internet specialists are required to pass the prescribed Microsoft Windows NT Server 4.0, TCP/IP, and Microsoft Internet Information System exam series.

Microsoft Certified Professionals with a specialty in site building are required to pass two exams covering Microsoft FrontPage, Microsoft Site Server, and Microsoft Visual InterDev technologies to provide a valid and reliable measure of technical proficiency and expertise.

Microsoft Certified Systems Engineers are required to pass a series of core Microsoft Windows operating system and networking exams, and BackOffice technology elective exams.

Microsoft Certified Systems Engineer + Internet specialists are required to pass, all of which seven operating system exams and two elective exams that provide a valid and reliable measure of technical proficiency and expertise.

Microsoft Certified Database Administrators are required to pass three core exams and one elective exam, all of which provide a valid and reliable measure of technical proficiency and expertise.

Microsoft Certified Solution Developers are required to pass two core Microsoft Windows operating system technology exams and two BackOffice technology elective exams.

Microsoft Certified Trainers are required to meet instructional and technical requirements specific to each Microsoft Official Curriculum course they are certified to deliver. In the United States and Canada, call Microsoft at (800) 636-7544 for more information on becoming a Microsoft Certified Trainer or visit *http://www.microsoft.com/train_cert/mct/*. Outside the United States and Canada, contact your local Microsoft subsidiary.

Technical Training for Computer Professionals

Technical training is available in a variety of ways, with instructor-led classes, online instruction, or self-paced training available at thousands of locations worldwide.

Self-Paced Training

For motivated learners who are ready for the challenge, self-paced instruction is the most flexible, cost-effective way to increase your knowledge and skills.

A full line of self-paced print and computer-based training materials is available direct from the source—Microsoft Press. Microsoft Official Curriculum courseware kits from Microsoft Press are designed for advanced computer system professionals and are available from Microsoft Press and the Microsoft Developer Division. Self-paced training kits from Microsoft Press feature print-based instructional materials, along with CD-ROM-based product software, multimedia presentations, lab exercises, and practice files. The Mastering Series provides in-depth, interactive training on CD-ROM for experienced developers. They are both great ways to prepare for MCP exams.

Online Training

For a more flexible alternative to instructor-led classes, turn to online instruction. It is as near as the Internet and it is ready whenever you are. Learn at your own pace and on your own schedule in a virtual classroom, often with easy access to an online instructor. Without ever leaving your desk, you can gain the expertise you need. Online instruction covers a variety of Microsoft products and technologies. It includes options ranging from Microsoft Official Curriculum to choices available nowhere else. It is training on demand, with access to learning resources 24 hours a day. Online training is available through Microsoft Certified Technical Education Centers.

Microsoft Certified Technical Education Centers

Microsoft Certified Technical Education Centers (CTECs) are the best source for instructor-led training that can help you prepare to become a Microsoft Certified Professional. The Microsoft CTEC program is a worldwide network of qualified technical training organizations that provide authorized delivery of Microsoft Official Curriculum courses by Microsoft Certified Trainers to computer professionals.

For a listing of CTEC locations in the United States and Canada, visit *http:// www.microsoft.com/CTEC/default.htm*.

Technical Support

Every effort has been made to ensure the accuracy of this book and the contents of the companion disc. If you have comments, questions, or ideas regarding this book or the companion disc, please send them to Microsoft Press using either of the following methods:

E-mail
TKINPUT@MICROSOFT.COM

Postal Mail

Microsoft Press
Attn: *MCSE Training Kit—Microsoft Windows 2000
Network Infrastructure Administration* Editor
One Microsoft Way
Redmond, WA
98052-6399

Microsoft Press provides corrections for books through the World Wide Web at
the following address:

http://mspress.microsoft.com/support/

Please note that product support is not offered through the above mail addresses.
For further information regarding Microsoft software support options, please
connect to *http://www.microsoft.com/support/* or call Microsoft Support Network
Sales at (800) 936-3500.

CHAPTER 1

Designing a Windows 2000 Network

About This Chapter

In this chapter, you will learn how to plan a Windows 2000 network. In addition, you will learn about important considerations when developing an implementation plan. You will also learn about various network protocols used by Microsoft Windows 2000, and how they relate to network services.

Before You Begin

To complete this chapter, you must have

- There are no prerequisites for this chapter.

Lesson 1: Network Services Overview

Microsoft Windows 2000 provides many network features and services that can be used by your organization to meet your business objectives. Windows 2000 includes key technologies that add value to both new and existing networks. Some technologies must be implemented on your network in order to use certain services. For example, Transmission Control Protocol/Internet Protocol (TCP/IP) must be installed in order to implement the Windows 2000 Active Directory service.

This lesson introduces the following Windows 2000 network services:

- Domain Name System (DNS)
- Dynamic Host Configuration Protocol (DHCP)
- Windows Internet Name Service (WINS)

You will also learn about remote networking with the Routing and Remote Access feature of Windows 2000 service. This includes features such as network address translators (NATs). You will also learn how security is implemented using Microsoft Certificate Services.

After this lesson, you will be able to
- Explain the purpose of DNS, DHCP, and WINS
- Describe the Routing and Remote Access Service
- Describe the benefit of a network address translator (NAT)
- Identify the features of Microsoft Certificate Services

Estimated lesson time: 40 minutes

TCP/IP

There are many networking protocols supported in Windows 2000; however, TCP/IP is the core protocol used in Windows 2000, and is the default networking protocol installed by Windows 2000 Setup. Many networking services in Windows 2000 use TCP/IP, and some services, such as Internet Information Server (IIS) and Active Directory, require it to be installed. TCP/IP is a routable protocol used by many wide area networks (WANs) and the Internet. Other protocols, such as NetBEUI (NetBIOS Enhanced User Interface), are designed only for local area networks (LANs) and thus do not support Internet connectivity. This issue is important to consider when planning your network.

Domain Name System

Although TCP/IP uses Internet Protocol (IP) to locate and connect to hosts (computers and other TCP/IP network devices), users typically prefer to use friendly names. For example, users prefer the name ftp.microsoft.com, instead of its IP address, 172.16.23.55. Domain Name System (DNS) enables you to use hierarchical, friendly names to easily locate computers and other resources on an IP network.

DNS is used on the Internet to provide a standard naming convention for locating IP-based computers. Before the implementation of DNS, a Hosts file was used to locate resources on TCP/IP networks including the Internet. Network administrators entered names and IP addresses into the Hosts file, and computers used the file for name resolution.

Dynamic Host Configuration Protocol

Dynamic Host Configuration Protocol (DHCP) simplifies administrating and managing IP addresses on a TCP/IP network by automating address configuration for network clients. A DHCP server is defined as any computer running the DHCP service. Windows 2000 Server provides the DHCP Server service, which enables a computer to function as a DHCP server and configure DHCP-enabled client computers on your network. This architecture is illustrated in Figure 1.1.

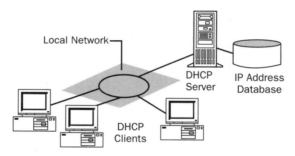

Figure 1.1   The basic DHCP model

The DHCP Server service for Windows 2000 also provides

- Integration with the Microsoft Active Directory directory service and DNS
- Enhanced monitoring and statistical reporting
- Vendor-specific options and user-class support
- Multicast address allocation
- Rogue DHCP server detection

Every computer on a TCP/IP-based network must have a unique IP address in order to access the network and its resources. Without DHCP, IP configuration must be done manually for new computers, computers moving from one subnet to another, and computers removed from the network. By deploying DHCP in a network, this entire process is automated and centrally managed.

The DHCP implementation is so closely linked to the Windows Internet Name Service (WINS) and DNS that network administrators will benefit from combining all three when planning deployment. If you use DHCP servers for Microsoft network clients, you must use a name resolution service. Windows 2000 networks use the DNS service to support Active Directory, in addition to general name resolution. Networks supporting Windows NT 4.0 and earlier clients must use WINS servers. Networks supporting a combination of Windows 2000 and Windows NT 4.0 clients should implement both WINS and DNS.

Windows Internet Name Service

Windows Internet Name Service (WINS) is the name resolution system used for Windows NT Server 4.0 and earlier operating systems. WINS provides a distributed database for registering and querying a computer name (which is the same as the NetBIOS name) to IP address mapping in a routed network environment. If you are administering a routed network, WINS is your best choice for NetBIOS name resolution. WINS reduces the use of local broadcasts for name resolution and allows users to easily locate systems on remote networks. In a dynamic DHCP environment, the IP addresses of the hosts can change frequently; WINS provides a way to dynamically register the changes for computer names-to-IP addresses mapping. This feature is necessary for the name-to-IP address resolution to work properly in a DHCP environment.

Name Resolution

Whether your network uses DNS or WINS, name resolution is an essential part of network administration. Although Windows 2000 primarily uses DNS to match host names to IP addresses, Windows 2000 still supports WINS for this purpose.

Name resolution allows you to search your network and connect to resources using names such as "printer1" or "fileserver1" rather than memorizing a host's IP address. Remembering IP addresses would be even more impractical when using DHCP for address assignment because the assignments can change over time. WINS is tightly integrated with DHCP services. Because of this integration, whenever the computer you named "fileserver1" is dynamically assigned a new IP address, the change is transparent. When you connect to fileserver1 from another node, you can use the name fileserver1 rather than the new IP address because WINS keeps track of the changing IP addresses associated with that name.

Remote Access Overview

With the Windows 2000 Routing and Remote Access feature, remote clients are transparently connected to the remote server, known as point-to-point remote access connectivity. Clients can also be transparently connected to the network to which the routing and remote access server is attached. This is known as point-to-LAN remote access connectivity. This transparent connection allows clients to dial in from remote locations and access resources as if they were physically attached to the network. Windows 2000 remote access provides two different types of remote access connectivity:

- **Dial-up remote access.**   With dial-up remote access, a remote access client uses the telecommunications infrastructure to create a temporary physical circuit or a virtual circuit to a port on a remote access server. Once the physical or virtual circuit is created, the rest of the connection parameters can be negotiated.

- **Virtual private network remote access.**   With virtual private network (VPN) remote access, a VPN client uses an IP internetwork to create a virtual point-to-point connection with a remote access server acting as the VPN server. Once the virtual point-to-point connection is created, the rest of the connection parameters can be negotiated.

Elements of a Dial-Up Remote Access Connection

The Windows 2000 Routing and Remote Access Service accepts dial-up connections and forwards packets between remote access clients and the network to which the remote access server is attached. A remote connection consists of a remote access client, a WAN infrastructure, and a remote access server, as illustrated in Figure 1.2.

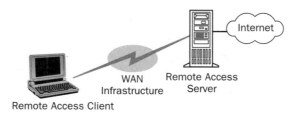

Figure 1.2   Elements of a dial-up remote access connection

Remote Access Protocols

Remote access protocols control the connection establishment and transmission of data over WAN links. The operating system and LAN protocols used on remote access clients and servers dictate which remote access protocol your clients can use.

There are three types of remote access protocols supported by Windows 2000 Routing and Remote Access:

1. Point-to-Point Protocol (PPP) is an industry-standard set of protocols providing the best security, multiprotocol support, and interoperability.
2. Serial Line Internet Protocol (SLIP) is used by legacy remote access servers.

3. Microsoft remote access service protocol, also known as Asynchronous NetBEUI (AsyBEUI), is a remote access protocol used by legacy remote access clients running Microsoft operating systems, such as Windows NT 3.1, Windows for Workgroups, MS-DOS, and LAN Manager.

LAN protocols are the protocols used by the remote access client to access resources on the network connected to the remote access server. Windows 2000 remote access supports TCP/IP, IPX, AppleTalk, and NetBEUI.

▶ **To configure a routing and remote access server**

1. Click Start, point to Programs, point to Administrative Tools, then click Routing And Remote Access.

   The Routing and Remote Access management tools appear in the Microsoft Management Console.

2. Right-click the server in the left pane, and then click Configure And Enable Routing And Remote Access, as illustrated in Figure 1.3.

   The Routing and Remote Access Server Setup Wizard appears allowing you to specify server configuration information.

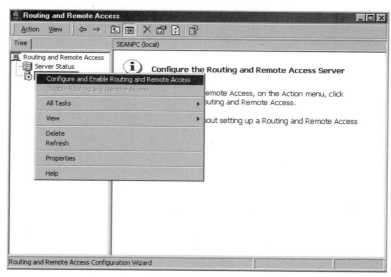

Figure 1.3   Creating a routing and remote access server

Network Address Translator

There are two types of IP addresses: public and private. Public addresses are assigned to you by the Internet service provider (ISP) you use to connect to the Internet. For the hosts within the organization that do not require direct access to the Internet, IP addresses that do not duplicate already assigned public addresses are required. To solve this addressing problem, designers of the Internet reserved a portion of the IP address space and named this space the private address space. An IP address in the private address space is never assigned as a public address. IP addresses within the private address space are known as private addresses. Using private IP addresses, you can provide protection from network hacking.

Because the IP addresses in the private address space will never be assigned by the Internet Network Information Center (InterNIC) as public addresses, routes in the Internet routers for private addresses will never exist. Private addresses are not reachable on the Internet. Therefore, when using private IP addresses, you need some type of proxy or server to convert the private IP address range(s) on your local network to a public IP address that can be routed. Another option is to have private addresses translated into valid public addresses by a network address translator (NAT) before it is sent on the Internet. Support for network address translation to translate private and public addresses to allow the connection of small office or home office networks to the Internet is illustrated in Figure 1.4.

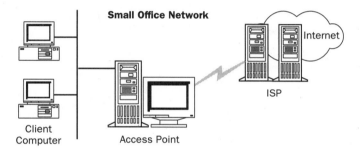

Figure 1.4   Connecting a small office network to the Internet

An NAT hides internally managed IP addresses from external networks by translating the private internal address to a public external address. This reduces IP address registration costs by letting customers use unregistered IP addresses internally, with translation to a small number of registered IP addresses externally. It also hides the internal network structure, reducing risks of denial of service attacks against internal systems.

Certificate Services

Designing an appropriate security system to protect your organization's confidential and proprietary information requires developing a set of appropriate solutions for specific risk scenarios. Windows 2000 provides a range of technologies from which to choose in developing your security plan. One of these technologies is Microsoft Certificate Services. You can deploy Microsoft Certificate Services to create and manage Certificate Authorities (CAs) that issue digital certificates.

Digital certificates are electronic credentials that certify the online identities of individuals, organizations, and computers. Certificates function similarly to identification cards, such as passports and driver's licenses. When an identification card is presented to others, they can verify the identify of its owner because the card provides the following security benefits:

- It contains personal information to help identify and trace the owner.
- It contains the signature of the rightful owner to enable positive identification.
- It contains the information that is required to identify and contact the issuing authority.
- It is designed to be tamper resistant and difficult to counterfeit.
- It is issued by an authority that can revoke the identification card at any time (for example, if the card is misused or stolen).
- It can be checked for revocation by contacting the issuing authority.

Digital certificates can be used in the same way to provide a variety of security functions. Some common security functions of digital certificates include the following:

- Secure e-mail
- Secure communications between Web clients and servers
- Code signing for executable code for distribution on public networks
- Local network and remote access logon authentication
- IPSec authentication

Certificate Services provides a means for an enterprise to easily establish CAs in support of their business needs. Certificate Services includes a default policy module suitable for issuing certificates to enterprise entities such as users, machines, or services.

Lesson Summary

Windows 2000 includes key technologies that add value to both new and existing TCP/IP-based networks. Although TCP/IP uses IP to locate and connect to hosts, users typically prefer to use friendly names. DNS enables you to use hierarchical, friendly names to easily locate computers and other resources on an IP network. DHCP simplifies administrating and managing IP addresses on a TCP/IP network by automating address configuration for network clients. WINS provides a distributed database for registering and querying a computer name (which is the same as the NetBIOS name) to IP address mapping in a routed network environment. With Windows 2000 Routing and Remote Access Service, clients are transparently connected to the remote access server. Clients can also be transparently connected to the network to which the routing and remote access server is attached.

Lesson 2: Developing a Network Implementation Plan

Implementing new technologies in an enterprise network environment requires research, planning, approval, and funding. To obtain the greatest benefit from Windows 2000, you need to plan your deployment carefully. As you begin your Windows 2000 operating system deployment planning, you should understand its features so you can utilize them to your advantage. This will help people in your organization to increase productivity and will reduce total cost of ownership (TCO). In this lesson, you will learn how to plan your Windows 2000 network implementation.

After this lesson, you will be able to

- Describe the various Windows 2000 operating systems
- Describe the phases of a network deployment project life cycle
- Identify hardware and software considerations when designing a network
- Identify network protocol and legacy system integration issues on a network

Estimated lesson time: 40 minutes

Operating System Considerations

When planning your Windows 2000 network, you should consider operating systems based on the needs of your users and business requirements. For example, if your network servers run demanding memory- and processor-intensive applications, implementing a Windows 2000 Advanced Server is your best choice. You should review specific Windows 2000 technology features to determine which technologies are most important for your organization, while considering your organization's short-term, mid-term, and long-term objectives. The following sections describe the different Windows 2000 operating systems.

Windows 2000 Professional

Windows 2000 Professional is a desktop operating system that provides advanced features of Windows NT, including security and fault tolerance, with the easy-to-use features of Windows 98, including plug and play and device support. Windows 2000 Professional can be upgraded from Windows NT Workstation 3.51 and greater, or Windows 98. The minimum system requirements for running Windows 2000 Professional include:

- **133 MHz or higher Pentium-compatible CPU.**   Windows 2000 Professional supports single and dual CPU systems.
- **64 megabytes (MB) of RAM.**   More memory generally improves responsiveness.
- **2 GB hard disk.**   Your hard disk must have a minimum of 650 MB of free space to install Windows 2000 Professional.

Windows 2000 Server

Windows 2000 Server builds on the powerful features of the Windows NT Server 4.0 operating system. Windows 2000 Server integrates standards-based directory, Web, application, communications, file, and print services with high reliability, efficient management, and support for the latest advances in networking hardware to provide the best foundation for integrating your business with the Internet. These features include:

- Information Services 5.0 (IIS)
- Active Server Pages (ASP) programming environment
- XML parser
- Windows DNA 2000
- Component Object Model + (COM+)
- Multimedia platform
- Directory-enabled applications
- Web folders
- Internet printing

Windows 2000 minimum hardware requirements are

- **133 MHz or higher Pentium-compatible CPU.** Windows 2000 Server supports up to four CPUs on one computer.
- **128 MB of RAM.** 256 MB of RAM is recommended. More memory generally improves responsiveness, and Windows 2000 Server supports a maximum 4 gigabytes (GB) of RAM.
- **2 GB hard disk.** You must have a minimum of 1 GB free disk space to install Windows 2000 Server. Additional free hard disk space is required if you are installing over a network.

Windows 2000 Advanced Server

Windows 2000 Advanced Server is the new version of Windows NT Server 4.0, Enterprise Edition. Windows 2000 Advanced Server is ideal for line-of-business and e-commerce applications, where scalability and high availability demands are most critical. While the hardware requirements for Windows 2000 Advanced Server are the same, Advanced Server includes

- All Windows 2000 Server features
- Network (TCP/IP) Load Balancing
- Up to 8 GB main memory on Intel Page Address Extension (PAE) systems
- Support of up to eight processors

Note Be sure to schedule enough time to install a Windows 2000 server, as it can take several hours.

Windows 2000 Datacenter Server

Another Windows 2000 operating system that builds upon the features of Windows 2000 Advanced Server is the Windows 2000 Datacenter Server, which supports 32 processors and more RAM than the other Windows 2000 Server operating systems. Physical memory support includes

- 64 GB of RAM on Intel-based computers

Consider installing Windows 2000 Datacenter Server if you must support intensive online transaction processing (OLTP), large data warehouses, and large Internet and application service providers (ISPs and ASPs).

Phases of Deployment

The purpose of your Windows 2000 network planning process is to ensure that your network performs the required activities. When planning your Windows 2000 network deployment, you should follow a process, or life cycle. The phases of this project life cycle should include the following:

1. **Analysis.** During the analysis phase, determine IT goals and objectives. This will help you to design a network to support bandwidth, meet security needs, measure cost versus benefits, and provide deliverables appropriate to your organization.

2. **Design.** During the design phase, evaluate the Windows 2000 Infrastructure design. This includes features such as DNS, WINS, DHCP, and network protocols. Your design will be based on your analysis, interoperability issues, and desired features.

3. **Testing.** During the testing phase, conduct a pilot project to test the Windows 2000 network you designed in a production environment with a low number of users. You might have to adjust your designs based upon pilot-testing results to achieve a completely functional and stable network environment.

4. **Production.** The production phase is the final phase of Windows 2000 deployment. The network has been tested using the pilot program based on your designs, and you are ready to deploy Windows 2000 throughout your enterprise. During this phase, create a disaster recovery plan and provide training material for user and helpdesk personnel.

Hardware Considerations

Compatibility issues with devices and programs can compromise reliability and quality. You can check hardware and software compatibility with Windows 2000 at *http://www.microsoft.com/windows2000/default.asp*.

Before deploying Windows 2000, you should record hardware and software inventories of all servers and client computers in use on your network, and include basic input/output system (BIOS) settings. You should also record the configuration of peripheral devices, driver versions, service packs, and other software and firmware information. In addition, establish standard configurations for your clients and servers. This includes guidelines for minimum and recommended values for CPU, RAM, hard disks, and accessories such as CD-ROM drives and uninterruptible power supplies.

Make sure that network devices, such as hubs and cabling, are fast enough for your needs. If your organization transfers voice and video over your network, the cabling and switches must be capable of handling the bandwidth demand of those services. Some remote users do not generate much network traffic. For example, a remote user who works with Microsoft Word or Microsoft Excel files does not generate as much network traffic to a routing and remote access server as databases and accounting systems. Therefore, a Category 3 10-Mbps cable matched with the same speed hubs might be acceptable for some situations, whereas Category 5 100-Mbps devices and cabling might be required for applications generating considerably more network traffic. Try to record available bandwidth during the course of low, normal, and high network utilization.

Interaction with Legacy Systems

Many networks are heterogeneous, which means that there are a mix of operating systems and network protocols. For example, your Windows 2000 computers might interact with mainframe hosts, UNIX systems, or other network operating systems. You should concentrate on the interoperability issues that are most important to your organization during planning.

In addition, Windows 2000 Server offers gateway services to other operating systems allowing you to access network resources. Gateway Service for NetWare, for example, allows your Windows 2000 network clients to navigate Novell Directory Services (NDS) hierarchies, use Novell version 4.2 or later logon scripts, and authenticate with a Novell server.

Network Protocol Considerations

Some networks use a variety of protocols based on their needs. For example, a small Ethernet network could use NetBEUI as the LAN protocol, while using TCP/IP for Internet connectivity. In addition, networks that include both Novell NetWare and Windows NT servers might use both IPX/SPX and TCP/IP. Always identify the protocols in use on your current network, and consider whether any of these protocols can be replaced or eliminated by Windows 2000. For example, if you upgrade clients that use IPX/SPX with Windows 2000 Professional, it's possible to eliminate the use of IPX/SPX on your network.

Windows 2000 contains a TCP/IP protocol suite with more functionality than previous versions of Windows. You must use TCP/IP to use Active Directory and to utilize advanced features of Windows 2000; therefore, you should consider simplifying your network by using only TCP/IP.

You can obtain network settings and protocol information in Windows NT by right-clicking on the My Network Places icon on your desktop and choosing Properties.

Lesson Summary

You should plan your deployment carefully to obtain the greatest benefit from Windows 2000, and be aware of the different Windows 2000 operating systems. An enterprise network deployment consists of different phases of a project life cycle: analysis, design, testing, and production. Before deploying Windows 2000, record hardware and software inventories of all servers and client computers in use on your network. Additionally, consider interoperability issues and decide which protocols best meet your needs.

Lesson 3: Common Protocols Supported by Windows 2000

When planning your network, consider the connectivity requirements of your users. Network protocols are similar to languages in the sense that languages haves different words, word patterns, and punctuation. A network protocol serves a similar role for computers attempting to communicate. The network protocol used on a network determines how packets (units of data) are configured and sent over the network cable. Consider the following questions:

- **Do network users connect to Novell NetWare servers?**   Clients that connect to NetWare servers must use the NWLink protocol. Even if the NetWare servers are configured to use TCP/IP, Windows-based clients must use NWLink to communicate with them.

- **Is your network connected by routers?**   NetBEUI is not routable. For computers across routers to communicate, they must use a routable network protocol such as TCP/IP or NWLink.

- **Are you connected to the Internet?**   For clients to connect to the Internet, they must use the TCP/IP protocol.

Additionally, some features require that particular protocols be installed. If you want to implement Active Directory, use IIS, or provide clients with access to the Internet, you will need to install TCP/IP. This lesson describes the TCP/IP protocol and other protocols that you can use with Windows 2000.

After this lesson, you will be able to
- Identify different network architectures
- Identify various network protocols used in Windows 2000

Estimated lesson time: 30 minutes

Transmission Control Protocol/Internet Protocol

Transmission Control Protocol/Internet Protocol (TCP/IP) is an industry-standard suite of protocols designed for large networks. TCP/IP is routable, which means that data packets can be switched (routed to a different subnet) by use of the packet's destination address. TCP/IP's ability to be routed provides fault tolerance, which is the ability of a computer or an operating system to respond to a catastrophic event or fault, such as a power outage or a hardware failure, to ensure that data is not lost or corrupted. If a network failure occurs, TCP/IP packets are transported on a different route.

Although the original purpose of TCP/IP was to provide connection between disparate networks, TCP/IP now provides high-speed communication network links between networks. Microsoft has implemented TCP/IP as a standard network transport for Windows 2000. You will learn more about the architecture, installation, and configuration of TCP/IP in Chapter 2, "Implementing TCP/IP."

Benefits of Implementing TCP/IP

TCP/IP in Windows 2000 includes many performance improvements for high-bandwidth networks. These features are described in the following sections.

Large Window Support

The window size in TCP-based communication is the maximum number of packets that can be sent before the first packet must be acknowledged. Window size is typically fixed and established at the beginning of a session between sending and receiving hosts. With large window support, window size is dynamically recalculated and increased if a large number of packets is exchanged during a lengthy session. This increases bandwidth and allows more data packets to be in transit on the network at one time.

Selective Acknowledgments

With selective acknowledgments, the receiver can notify and request specific packets that were missing or corrupted during delivery from the sender. This allows networks to recover quickly from a state of temporary congestion or interference, because only corrupted packets are re-sent. In previous TCP/IP implementations, if a receiving host failed to receive a single TCP packet, the sender was forced to retransmit all packets transmitted following the negatively acknowledged packet. Using selective acknowledgments, fewer packets are re-sent, providing better network utilization and performance.

Round Trip Time Estimation

Round Trip Time (RTT) is the amount of time it takes for a round-trip communication between a sender and receiver on a TCP-based connection. RTT estimation is a technique of estimating packet transit times and adjusting for the optimum retransmission time for packets. Because performance depends on knowing how long to wait for a missing packet, improving the accuracy of RTT estimation results in better time-out values being set on each host, so that a host cannot request a packet to be retransmitted until the requisite time interval expires. Better timing improves performance over long round-trip network links, such as WANs, that span large distances (for example, continent-to-continent) or use either wireless or satellite links.

IP Security (IPSec) Support

IPSec provides the ideal platform for safeguarding intranet and Internet communications. IPSec can secure paths between two computers, two security gateways, or a host and a security gateway. Windows 2000 Server tightly integrates IPSec with system policy management to enforce encryption between systems. Customers can have encryption-secured communications managed by group policy—a safeguard that protects information sent over networks. Because IPSec is integrated into the operating system, it is easier to configure and manage than add-on solutions.

The services available and required for traffic are configured using IPSec policy. IPSec policy can be configured locally on a computer, or can be assigned through Windows 2000 Group Policy mechanisms using the Active Directory directory service, as illustrated in Figure 1.5. When using Active Directory, hosts detect policy assignment at startup, retrieve the policy, and periodically check for policy updates. The IPSec policy specifies the trust relationship among computers. The easiest trust relationship to use is the Windows 2000 domain trust based on the Kerberos version 5 protocol. Predefined IPSec policies are configured to trust computers in the same or other trusted Windows 2000 domains.

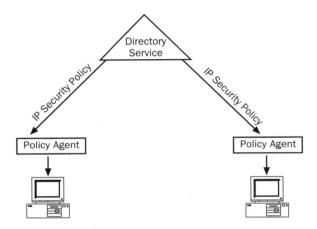

Figure 1.5   Windows 2000 Group Policy using Active Directory

At the IP (network) layer, each incoming or outgoing packet is referred to as a datagram. Each IP datagram bears the source IP address of the sender and the destination IP address of the intended recipient. Each IP datagram processed at the IP layer is compared against a set of filters that are provided by the security policy, which is maintained by an administrator for a computer, user, group, or an entire domain. The IP layer can perform one of the following actions with a datagram:

- Provide IPSec services to the datagram
- Allow the datagram to pass unmodified
- Discard the datagram

Because IPSec typically encrypts the entire IP packet, capturing an IPSec datagram sent after the security association (SA) is established reveals very little of what is actually in the datagram. The only parts of the packet that can be parsed or read by a network sniffer such as Network Monitor are the Ethernet and IP headers. This lends greater security to IP transactions. IPSec is covered in more detail in Chapter 5, "Implementing IPSec."

Generic Quality of Service

Generic Quality of Service (GQoS) is a method by which a TCP/IP network can offer Quality of Service guarantees for multimedia applications. Generic Quality of Service allocates different bandwidths for each connection on an as-needed basis.

Quality of Service (QoS) allows network administrators to use their existing resources efficiently and to guarantee that critical applications receive high-quality service without having to expand as quickly or upgrade their networks. Deploying QoS means that network administrators can have better control over their networks, reduce costs, and improve customer satisfaction. The suite of QoS components included in Windows 2000 works with the different QoS mechanisms that can exist in network elements such as routers and switches. These host mechanisms give administrators an idea of which applications are in use and what their resource requirements are without having to calculate the mappings between actual users, network ports, and addresses. When the host and the network operate cooperatively, resources can be utilized easily and more knowledgeably.

The following QoS components are currently included with the Windows 2000 operating system:

- **The Generic Quality of Service (GQoS) application programming interface (API).**   The GQoS API is a subset of the WinSock 2 API that allows applications to invoke QoS services from the operating system without needing to understand the underlying mechanisms.

- **The QoS service provider.**   This responds to requests from the GQoS API. It provides Resource Reservation Protocol (RSVP) signaling and QoS policy support with Kerberos. It also invokes the traffic control mechanisms.

- **The Admission Control Service (ACS) service and Subnet Bandwidth Manager (SBM) protocol.**   This provides management of shared network resources over a standardized signaling protocol.

- **A traffic control infrastructure.**   This infrastructure includes a packet scheduler and marker for providing traffic control over drivers and network cards that have no packet scheduling features of their own. It also marks packets for diffserv and 802.1p. Windows 2000 traffic control also includes additional mechanisms such as Integrated Services over Slow Links (ISSLOW) and Asynchronous Transfer Mode (ATM).

Microsoft is working closely with Cisco on the delivery of qualitative QoS services, and is working along with Cisco, Extreme Networks, Intel, Sun, 3Com, and others on the continuing development of the Internet Engineering Task Force (IETF) RSVP standard.

NWLink

NWLink is a Microsoft-compatible IPX/SPX protocol for Windows 2000. NWLink is useful if there are Novell NetWare client/server programs running that use WinSock or NetBIOS over IPX/SPX protocols. WinSock is an API that allows Windows-based applications to access the transport protocols. NWLink can be run on a computer running Windows 2000 Server or Windows 2000 Professional to access a NetWare server.

NWLink alone does not allow a computer running Windows 2000 to access files or printers shared on a NetWare server, or to act as a file or print server to a NetWare client. To access files or printers on a NetWare server, a redirector must be used, such as Client Service for NetWare on Windows 2000 Professional, or Gateway Service for NetWare on Microsoft Windows 2000 Server. NWLink is included with both Windows 2000 Server and Windows 2000 Professional, and installs automatically during Client Service for NetWare or Gateway Service for NetWare installation. Both Client Service for NetWare and Gateway Service for NetWare depend on the NWLink protocol. NWLink is covered in more detail in Chapter 3, "Implementing NWLink."

Gateway Service for NetWare

Gateway Service for NetWare works with NWLink to provide access to NetWare file, print, and directory services by acting as a gateway through which multiple clients can access NetWare resources. With Gateway Service for NetWare, you can connect a computer running Windows 2000 Server to NetWare bindery-based servers and Novell NDS servers. Multiple Windows-based clients can then use Gateway Service for NetWare as a common gateway to access NetWare file, print, and directory services, without requiring special client software.

Gateway Service for NetWare supports direct access to NetWare services from the computer running Windows 2000 Server in the same way that Client Service for NetWare supports direct access from the client computer. Additionally, Gateway Service for NetWare supports NetWare login scripts.

Note   Gateway Service for NetWare is included only with Windows 2000 Server and Windows 2000 Advanced Server.

Client Service for NetWare

Similar to Gateway Service for NetWare, Client Service for NetWare works with NWLink to provide access to NetWare file, print, and directory services. However, rather than acting as a gateway for clients, Client Service for NetWare enables clients to connect directly to file and print services on NetWare bindery-based servers and NetWare servers running NDS. Client Service for NetWare also supports NetWare login scripts. Client Service for NetWare is included only with Windows 2000 Professional.

NetBEUI

NetBIOS Enhanced User Interface (NetBEUI) was originally developed as a protocol for small departmental LANs of 20 to 200 computers. NetBEUI is not routable because it does not have a network layer. NetBEUI is included with Windows 2000 Server and Windows 2000 Professional, and is primarily a legacy protocol to support existing workstations that have not been upgraded to Windows 2000.

AppleTalk

AppleTalk is a protocol suite developed by Apple Computer, Inc. for communication between Apple Macintosh computers. Windows 2000 includes support for AppleTalk, which allows Windows 2000 to function as a router and a dial-up server. Support is natively provided as a service for file sharing and printer sharing.

Windows 2000 supports an AppleTalk protocol stack and AppleTalk routing software so that the Windows 2000 server can connect to and provide routing for AppleTalk-based Macintosh networks.

Data Link Control

Data Link Control (DLC) was originally developed for IBM mainframe communications. The protocol was not designed to be a primary protocol for network use between personal computers. The other use of DLC is to print to Hewlett-Packard printers connected directly to networks. Network-attached printers use the DLC protocol because the received frames are easy to disassemble and DLC functionality can easily be coded into read-only memory (ROM). DLC's usefulness is limited because it does not directly interface with the Transport Driver Interface layer. DLC needs to be installed only on those network computers that perform these two tasks, such as a print server sending data to a network Hewlett-Packard printer. Clients sending print jobs to a network printer do not need the DLC protocol installed on their computers. Only the print server communicating directly with the printer needs the DLC protocol installed.

Infrared Data Association

Infrared Data Association (IrDA) has defined a group of short-range, high-speed, bidirectional wireless infrared protocols, generically referred to as IrDA. IrDA allows a variety of devices to communicate with each other. Cameras, printers, portable computers, desktop computers, and personal digital assistants (PDAs) can communicate with compatible devices using this technology.

Lesson Summary

TCP/IP is an industry-standard suite of protocols designed for large networks. TCP/IP is routable, which means that data packets can be switched by use of the packet's destination address. TCP/IP's ability to be routed provides fault tolerance. Other protocols supported by Windows 2000 include

- NWLink
- NetBEUI
- AppleTalk
- Data Link Control
- Infrared Data Association

Review

Answering the following questions will reinforce key information presented in this chapter. Answers to the questions can be found in Appendix A, "Questions and Answers."

1. You are currently configuring TCP/IP manually for new computers and computers moving from one subnet to another. You want to simplify management of TCP/IP addresses and assign them automatically. Which Windows 2000 network service should you use?

2. You have an Intel-compatible server with 8 GB of RAM and 8 CPUs. You want to provide file services to over 400 people in your company. Which Windows 2000 operating system would be most appropriate to deploy, and why?

3. You want a Windows 2000 server to connect to and provide routing for AppleTalk-based Macintosh networks. What protocol should you install?

CHAPTER 2

Implementing TCP/IP

About This Chapter

This chapter gives you an overview of Transmission Control Protocol/Internet Protocol (TCP/IP). The lessons provide a brief history of TCP/IP, discuss the Internet standards process, and review TCP/IP utilities. You will learn how to assign Internet Protocol (IP) addresses to multiple TCP/IP networks with a single network identifier (ID). The lessons provide fundamental concepts and procedures for implementing subnetting and supernetting. During the lessons, you learn when subnetting is necessary, how and when to use a default subnet mask, how to define a custom subnet mask, and how to create a range of valid IP addresses for each subnet.

Before You Begin

To complete this chapter, you must have

- Installed Microsoft Windows 2000 Server

Lesson 1: TCP/IP Overview

Transmission Control Protocol/Internet Protocol (TCP/IP) is an industry-standard suite of protocols designed for wide area networks (WANs). Microsoft Windows 2000 has extensive support for TCP/IP both as a protocol suite and a set of services for connectivity and management of IP networks. This lesson includes an overview of TCP/IP concepts, terminology, and how the Internet standards are created. You will also learn how Windows 2000 integrates with TCP/IP.

After this lesson, you will be able to

- Define TCP/IP and describe its advantages on Windows 2000
- Describe how the TCP/IP protocol suite maps to a four-layer model
- Describe how Transmission Control Protocol (TCP) and User Datagram Protocol (UDP) transmit data

Estimated lesson time: 45 minutes

Benefits of TCP/IP

All modern operating systems offer TCP/IP support, and most large networks rely on TCP/IP for much of their network traffic. TCP/IP is also the protocol standard for the Internet. In addition, many standard connectivity utilities are available to access and transfer data between dissimilar systems. Several of these standard utilities, such as File Transfer Protocol (FTP) and Telnet, are included with Windows 2000 Server. TCP/IP networks can be easily integrated with the Internet. Because of its popularity, TCP/IP is well developed and offers many utilities that improve usability, performance, and security. Networks that are based on other transport protocols, such as ATM or AppleTalk, can interface with TCP/IP networks through a device known as a gateway. Adding TCP/IP to a Windows 2000 configuration offers the following advantages:

- It offers a technology for connecting dissimilar systems. TCP/IP is routable and can be connected to different networks through gateways.
- It allows for a robust, scalable, cross-platform client/server framework. Microsoft TCP/IP offers the WinSock interface, which is ideal for developing client/server applications that can run on WinSock-compliant stacks from other vendors.
- It provides a method of gaining access to the Internet. By connecting to the Internet, a virtual private network (VPN) or extranet can be established, allowing for inexpensive remote access.

In addition, Macintosh clients can now use the TCP/IP protocol to access shares on a Windows 2000 server that is running File Services for Macintosh (AFP [AppleShare File Server] over IP), making it easier to network with Macintosh computers.

Windows 2000 TCP/IP Communication Protocols

A significant feature of Windows 2000 is the ability to connect to the Internet and to dissimilar systems. Windows 2000 also includes advanced security features that can be implemented when connecting to a system across a network. In order to support all of these features, Windows 2000 TCP/IP has new and enhanced capabilities. These include:

- **IP Security.**   IP Security (IPSec) is a technology used to encrypt TCP/IP network traffic. IPSec enables secure data transfer between remote clients and private enterprise servers through a virtual private network (VPN).

- **Point-to-Point Tunneling Protocol.**   The Point-to-Point Tunneling Protocol (PPTP) provides VPN functionality similar to that which IPSec provides. PPTP also supports multiple network protocols such as IP, Internetwork Packet Exchange (IPX), and NetBIOS Enhanced User Interface (NetBEUI).

- **Layer Two Tunneling Protocol.**   The Layer Two Tunneling Protocol (L2TP) is a combination of Point-to-Point Tunneling Protocol (PPTP) and Layer 2 Forwarding (L2F). L2F is a transmission protocol that allows dial-up access servers to frame dial-up traffic in Point to Point Protocol (PPP) and transmit it over WAN links to an L2F server (a router).

Finally, Microsoft continues to support legacy systems and protocols to preserve the past investments of its customers and reduce the risk, pressure, and financial burden of managing heterogeneous environments. For this reason Windows 2000 supports

- AppleTalk
- Internetwork Packet Exchange/Sequenced Packet Exchange (IPX/SPX)
- NetBEUI

These protocols assist in the maintenance of heterogeneous environments and facilitate the migration to a richer, more flexible Windows 2000-based TCP/IP transport protocol platform.

TCP/IP Stack Enhancements

Windows 2000 includes several TCP/IP stack enhancements, including:

- Large window support that improves performance when many packets are in transit for long periods of time.
- Selective acknowledgments that allow a system to recover from congestion quickly. The sender needs to retransmit only the packets that were not received.
- The ability to better estimate round-trip time.
- The ability to better prioritize traffic for demanding applications.

TCP/IP Utilities

TCP/IP utilities in Windows 2000 include:

- **Data transfer utilities.** Windows 2000 provides support for several different IP-based data transfer protocols. These include File Transfer Protocol (FTP), HyperText Transfer Protocol (HTTP), and the Common Internet File System (CIFS).

- **Telnet.** UNIX hosts have traditionally been managed using Telnet—a text interface similar to a command prompt that can be accessed across an IP network. Windows 2000 provides both a Telnet client and server.

- **Printing utilities.** Windows 2000 can print directly to IP-based printers. Additionally, two TCP/IP utilities provide the ability to print and obtain print status on a TCP/IP printer. Line Printer Remote (LPR) prints a file to a host running the Line Printing Daemon (LPD) service. Line Printer Queue (LPQ) obtains the status of a print queue on a host running the LPD service.

- **Diagnostics utilities.** Windows 2000 provides several utilities for diagnosing TCP/IP-related problems including PING, Ipconfig, Nslookup, and Tracert.

Architectural Overview of the TCP/IP Protocol Suite

TCP/IP protocols provide networking support to connect all hosts and sites, and follow a set of standards for how computers communicate and how networks are interconnected. TCP/IP protocols follow a four-layer conceptual model known as the Department of Defense (DOD) model: Application, Transport, Internet, and Network Interface, as illustrated in Figure 2.1.

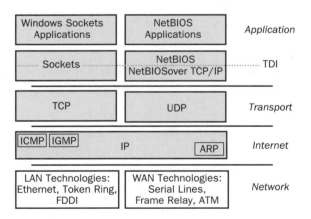

Figure 2.1 Four-layer conceptual model

Application Layer

The Application layer is at the top of the four-layer conceptual TCP/IP model, and is where software programs gain access to the network. This layer corresponds roughly to the Session, Presentation, and Application Layers of the OSI model. Some TCP/IP utilities and services run at the Application Layer. These utilities and services include:

- **HyperText Transfer Protocol (HTTP).**   HTTP is the protocol used for the majority of World Wide Web communications. Windows 2000 includes Internet Explorer as an HTTP client, and Internet Information Server (IIS) as an HTTP server.

- **File Transfer Protocol (FTP).**   FTP is an Internet service that transfers files from one computer to another. Internet Explorer and the command-line utility FTP both act as FTP clients. IIS includes an FTP server.

- **Simple Mail Transfer Protocol (SMTP).**   SMTP is a protocol that mail servers use to transfer e-mail. IIS can send messages using the SMTP protocol.

- **Telnet.**   Telnet is a terminal emulation protocol that can be used to log on to remote network hosts. Telnet offers users the capability of running programs remotely and facilitates remote administration. Telnet is available for practically all operating systems and eases integration in heterogeneous networking environments. Windows 2000 includes both a Telnet client and server.

- **Domain Name System (DNS).**   DNS is a set of protocols and services on a TCP/IP network that allows users of the network to utilize hierarchical user-friendly names when locating hosts instead of having to remember and use their IP addresses. DNS is used extensively on the Internet and in many private enterprises today. When you use a Web browser, Telnet application, FTP utility, or other similar TCP/IP utilities on the Internet, then you are probably using a DNS server. Windows 2000 also includes a DNS server.

- **Simple Network Management Protocol (SNMP).**   SNMP allows you to manage network nodes such as servers, workstations, routers, bridges, and hubs from a central host. SNMP can also be used to configure remote devices, monitor network performance, detect network faults or inappropriate access, and audit network usage.

Network Application APIs

Microsoft TCP/IP provides two interfaces for network applications to use the services of the TCP/IP protocol stack:

- **WinSock.**   The Windows 2000 implementation of the widely used Sockets application programming interface (API). The Sockets API is the standard mechanism for accessing datagram and session services over TCP/IP.

- **NetBIOS.**   A standard API used as an inter-process communication (IPC) mechanism in the Windows environment. Although NetBIOS can be used to provide a standard connection to protocols that support the NetBIOS naming and messaging services, such as TCP/IP and NetBEUI, it is included with Windows 2000 mainly to support legacy applications.

Transport Layer

Transport protocols provide communication sessions between computers and define the type of transport service as either connection-oriented (TCP) or connectionless datagram-oriented (UDP). TCP provides connection-oriented, reliable communications for applications that typically transfer large amounts of data at one time. It is also used for applications that require an acknowledgment for data received. UDP, however, provides connectionless communications and does not guarantee to deliver packets. Applications that use UDP typically transfer small amounts of data at one time. Reliable delivery of data is the responsibility of the application. The Transport Layer in the DOD model corresponds roughly to the Transport Layer in the OSI model.

Internet Layer

Internet protocols encapsulate packets into Internet datagrams and run all of the necessary routing algorithms. The routing functions that the Internet layer performs is necessary to allow hosts to interoperate with other networks. The Internet Layer corresponds roughly to the Network Layer in the OSI model. Five protocols are implemented at this layer:

- Address Resolution Protocol (ARP), which determines the hardware address of the hosts.

- Reverse Address Resolution Protocol (RARP), which provides reverse address resolution at the receiving host. (Although Microsoft does not implement the RARP protocol, it is found on other vendors' systems, and is mentioned here for completeness.)

- Internet Control Message Protocol (ICMP), which sends error messages to IP when problems crop up.

- Internet Group Management Protocol (IGMP), which informs routers of the availability of members of multicast groups.

- Internet Protocol (IP), which addresses and routes packets.

Network Interface Layer

At the base of the model is the Network Interface Layer. Each of the local area network (LAN), metropolitan area network (MAN), WAN, and dial-up types, such as Ethernet, Token Ring, Fiber Distributed Data Interface (FDDI), and ARCnet, have different requirements for cables, signaling, and data encoding. The Network Interface Layer specifies the requirements equivalent to the Data Link and Physical Layers of the OSI model. The Network Interface Layer is responsible for sending and receiving frames, which are packets of information transmitted on a network as a single unit. The Network Interface Layer puts frames on the network, and pulls frames off the network.

TCP/IP WAN Technologies

There are two major categories of WAN technologies supported by TCP/IP:

1. Serial lines, which include dial-up analog, digital lines, and leased lines.

   TCP/IP is typically transported across a serial line using either the Serial Line Internet Protocol (SLIP) or the Point-to-Point Protocol (PPP). Windows 2000 Server supports both protocols with the Routing and Remote Access Service. Because PPP provides greater security, configuration handling, and error detection than SLIP, it is the recommended protocol for serial line communication.

2. Packet-switched networks, which include X.25, frame relay, and asynchronous transfer mode (ATM).

Note Windows 2000 supports only SLIP client functionality, not SLIP server functionality. The Windows 2000 Routing and Remote Access Service does not accept SLIP client connections.

Transmission Control Protocol

Transmission Control Protocol (TCP) is a reliable, connection-oriented delivery service. TCP data is transmitted in segments, and a session must be established before hosts can exchange data. TCP uses byte-stream communications, which means that the data is treated as a sequence of bytes.

TCP achieves reliability by assigning a sequence number to each segment transmitted. If a segment is broken into smaller pieces, the receiving host knows whether all pieces have been received. An acknowledgment verifies that the other host received the data. For each segment sent, the receiving host must return an acknowledgment (ACK) within a specified period. If the sender does not receive an ACK, then the data is retransmitted. If the segment is received damaged, the receiving host discards it. Because in this case an ACK is not sent, the sender retransmits the segment.

Internet Protocol (IP)

Although TCP separates data into discrete packets and is responsible for guaranteeing their delivery, IP does the actual delivery. At the IP Layer, each incoming or outgoing packet is referred to as a datagram. The IP datagram fields in the following table are added to the header when a packet is passed up from the Network Interface Layer.

Field	Function
Source IP Address	Identifies the sender of the datagram by the IP address.
Destination IP Address	Identifies the destination of the datagram by the IP address.
Protocol	Informs IP at the destination host whether to pass the packet up to TCP or UDP.
Checksum	A simple mathematical computation that is used to verify that the packet arrived intact.
Time to Live (TTL)	Designates the number of seconds a datagram is allowed to spend in transport before it's discarded. This prevents packets from endlessly looping around an internetwork. Each router that forwards the packet decrements the TTL by one. The default TTL in Windows 2000 is 128 seconds.

User Datagram Protocol

UDP offers a connectionless datagram service that guarantees neither delivery nor correct sequencing of delivered packets. UDP data checksums are optional, providing a way to exchange data over highly reliable networks without unnecessarily consuming network resources or processing time. UDP is used by applications that do not require an acknowledgment of data receipt. These applications typically transmit small amounts of data at one time. Broadcast packets must use UDP. Examples of services and applications that use UDP are DNS, RIP, and SNMP.

Lesson Summary

TCP/IP is an industry-standard suite of protocols designed for WANs. Adding TCP/IP to a Windows 2000 configuration offers several advantages, including high interoperability, reliability, scalability, and security. Windows 2000 supplies a number of utilities that can help you connect to other TCP/IP-based hosts or help you troubleshoot TCP/IP connection problems.

TCP/IP protocols use a four-layer conceptual model: Application, Transport, Internet, and Network Interface. IP works at the Internet level and supports virtually all LAN and WAN interface technologies, such as Ethernet, Token Ring, Frame Relay, and ATM. IP is a connectionless protocol that addresses and routes packets between hosts. IP is unreliable because delivery is not guaranteed.

At the Transport Layer, TCP provides IP with reliable, connection-oriented delivery. Once a session is established, TCP delivers data through unique port numbers to applications. UDP, an alternative transport protocol to TCP, is a connectionless datagram service that does not guarantee delivery of packets. It is used by applications that do not require an acknowledgment of data receipt.

Lesson 2: Internet Protocol Addressing

A unique IP address is required for each host and network component that communicates using TCP/IP. TCP/IP networks are usually categorized into three main classes that have predefined sizes. Each network can be divided into smaller subnetworks by system administrators by using a subnet mask to divide an IP address into two parts. One part identifies the host (computer), the other part identifies the network to which it belongs. Each TCP/IP host is identified by a logical IP address. The IP address is a network layer address and has no dependence on the data-link layer address (such as a media access control address of a network interface card). In this lesson, you will learn how IP addressing works in a TCP/IP network.

After this lesson, you will be able to

- Describe the purpose of an IP address
- Convert IP addresses from binary to decimal
- Identify different classes of IP addresses

Estimated lesson time: 30 minutes

The IP Address

An IP address is a 32-bit number that uniquely identifies a host (computer or other device, such as a printer or router) on a TCP/IP network. IP addresses are normally expressed in dotted-decimal format, with four numbers separated by periods, such as 192.168.123.132.

For a TCP/IP WAN to work efficiently as a collection of networks, the routers that pass packets of data between networks do not need to know the exact location of a host for which a packet of information is destined. Routers only know what network the host is a member of and use information stored in their route table to determine how to get the packet to the destination host's network. After the packet is delivered to the destination's network, the packet is delivered to the appropriate host. For this process to work, an IP address has two parts: a network ID and a host ID.

The Network ID

The network ID identifies the TCP/IP hosts that are located on the same physical network. All hosts on the same physical network must be assigned the same network ID to communicate with each other. If routers connect your networks, as illustrated in Figure 2.2, a unique network ID is required for each wide area connection. For example, in the following illustration:

- Networks 1 and 2 represent two routed networks.
- Network 3 represents the WAN connection between the routers.

- Network 3 requires a network ID so that the interfaces between the two routers can be assigned unique host IDs.

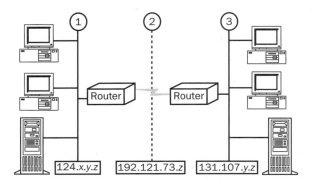

Figure 2.2   Routers connecting networks

Note   If you plan to connect your network to the Internet, you must obtain the network ID portion of the IP address. This will guarantee IP network ID uniqueness. For domain name registration and IP network number assignment, contact your Internet service provider.

The Host ID

The host ID identifies a host within a network. The host ID must be unique to the network designated by the network ID. An IP address identifies a system's location on the network in the same way a street address identifies a house on a city block, as illustrated in Figure 2.3.

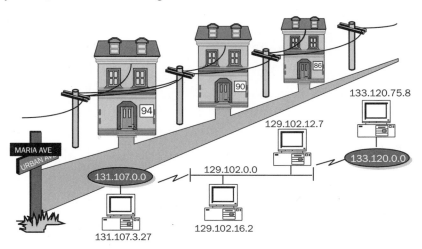

Figure 2.3   Hosts and network components communicating through TCP/IP

Dotted Decimal Notation

There are two formats for referencing an IP address—binary and dotted decimal notation. As illustrated in Figure 2.4, each IP address is 32 bits long and is composed of four 8-bit sections. These 8-bit sections are known as octets. The example IP address 192.168.123.132 becomes 11000000.10101000.01111011. 10000100 in binary format. The decimal numbers separated by periods in the dotted decimal notation are the octets converted from binary to decimal notation. The octets represent a decimal number ranging from zero to 255, and the entire 32 bits of the IP address are allocated to the network and host IDs as illustrated in Figure 2.4.

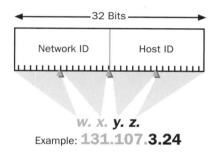

Figure 2.4   How an IP address is composed

Note   The network ID cannot be 127. This ID is reserved for loopback and diagnostic functions.

IP Address Conversion from Binary to Decimal

To administer TCP/IP on your network, you should be able to convert bit values in an octet from binary code to a decimal format. In binary format, each bit in an octet has an assigned decimal value. A bit that is set to 0 always has a zero value, and a bit that is set to 1 can be converted to a decimal value. The low-order bit represents a decimal value of one. The high-order bit represents a decimal value of 128. The highest decimal value of an octet is 255—that is, when all bits are set to 1, as illustrated in Figure 2.5.

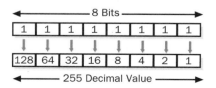

Figure 2.5   All bits set to 1 equating to a decimal value of 255

The following table shows how the bits in one octet are converted from binary code to a decimal value.

Binary Code	Bit Values	Decimal Value
00000000	0	0
00000001	1	1
00000011	1+2	3
00000111	1+2+4	7
00001111	1+2+4+8	15
00011111	1+2+4+8+16	31
00111111	1+2+4+8+16+32	63
01111111	1+2+4+8+16+32+64	127
11111111	1+2+4+8+16+32+64+128	255

Address Classes

Internet addresses are allocated by the InterNIC (*http://www.internic.net*), the organization that administers the Internet. These IP addresses are divided into classes. The most common of these are Classes A, B, and C. Classes D and E exist, but are not generally used by end users. Each of the address classes has a different default subnet mask. You can identify the class of an IP address by looking at its first octet. Following are the ranges of Class A, B, and C Internet addresses, each with an example address:

- Class A addresses are assigned to networks with a very large number of hosts. Class A networks use a default subnet mask of 255.0.0.0 and have 0-126 as their first octet. The address 10.52.36.11 is a Class A address. Its first octet is 10, which is between 1 and 126, inclusive.

- Class B addresses are assigned to medium-sized to large-sized networks. Class B networks use a default subnet mask of 255.255.0.0 and have 128-191 as their first octet. The address 172.16.52.63 is a Class B address. Its first octet is 172, which is between 128 and 191, inclusive.

- Class C addresses are used for small LANs. Class C networks use a default subnet mask of 255.255.255.0 and have 192-223 as their first octet. The address 192.168.123.132 is a Class C address. Its first octet is 192, which is between 192 and 223, inclusive.

The class of address defines which bits are used for the network ID and which bits are used for the host ID, as illustrated in Figure 2.6. The class also defines the possible number of networks and the number of hosts per network.

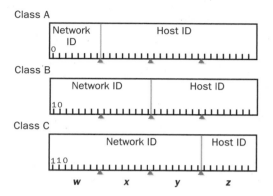

Figure 2.6   How bits are set up for each IP address class

The differences between Class A, B, and C addresses are illustrated in Figure 2.7.

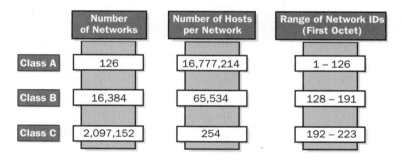

Class	Number of Networks	Number of Hosts per Network	Range of Network IDs (First Octet)
Class A	126	16,777,214	1 – 126
Class B	16,384	65,534	128 – 191
Class C	2,097,152	254	192 – 223

Figure 2.7   How address classes affect a network

IP Address Guidelines

Although there are no rules for how to assign IP addresses, be sure to assign valid network IDs and host IDs. There are several general guidelines you should follow when assigning network IDs and host IDs:

- The network ID cannot be 127. This ID is reserved for loopback and diagnostic functions.

- The network ID and host ID bits cannot all be "1"s. If all bits are set to 1, the address is interpreted as a broadcast rather than a host ID.

- The network ID and host ID bits cannot all be "0"s. If all bits are set to 0, the address is interpreted to mean "this network only."

- The host ID must be unique to the local network ID.

■ A unique network ID is required for each network and wide area connection. If you are connecting to the public Internet, you are required to obtain a network ID.

■ All TCP/IP hosts, including interfaces to routers, require unique host IDs. The host ID of the router is the IP address configured as a workstation's default gateway.

■ Each host on a TCP/IP network requires a subnet mask—either a default subnet mask, which is used when a network is not divided into subnets, or a custom subnet mask, which is used when a network is divided into subnets. A subnet mask is a 32-bit address used to block or "mask" a portion of the IP address to distinguish the network ID from the host ID. This is necessary so that TCP/IP can determine whether an IP address is located on a local or remote network. The default subnet mask you use depends on the address class, as illustrated in Figure 2.8.

Address Class	Bits Used for Subnet Mask				Dotted Decimal Notation
Class A	11111111	00000000	00000000	00000000	255.0.0.0
Class B	11111111	11111111	00000000	00000000	255.255.0.0
Class C	11111111	11111111	11111111	00000000	255.255.255.0

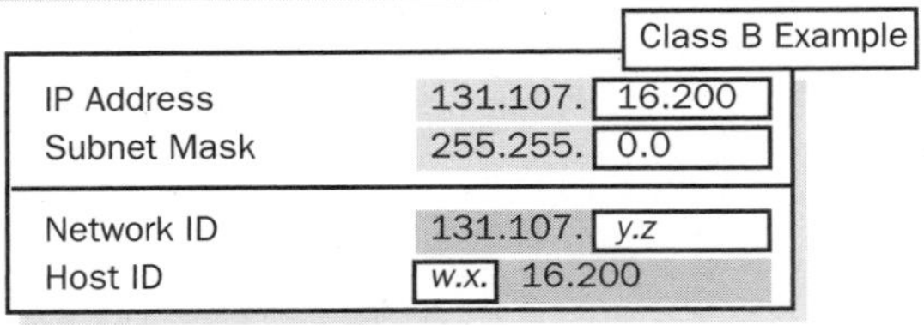

Class B Example

IP Address	131.107. 16.200
Subnet Mask	255.255. 0.0
Network ID	131.107. y.z
Host ID	w.x. 16.200

Figure 2.8   Example of a subnet mask used for a Class B IP address

Lesson Summary

Each TCP/IP host is identified by a logical IP address, and a unique IP address is required for each host and network component that communicates using TCP/IP. Each IP address defines the network ID and host ID. An IP address is 32 bits long and is composed of four 8-bit fields, called octets. There are five address classes. Microsoft supports Class A, B, and C addresses assigned to hosts. Each address class can accommodate networks of different sizes.

There are several guidelines you should follow to make sure you assign valid IP addresses. All hosts on a given network must have the same network ID to communicate with each other. All TCP/IP hosts, including interfaces to routers, require unique host IDs.

Lesson 3: Microsoft TCP/IP Installation and Configuration

This lesson describes the procedure for installing and configuring Microsoft TCP/IP. Follow this procedure if you have not previously installed the TCP/IP network protocol on the computer(s) you are using to perform the practice procedures during this course.

After this lesson, you will be able to

- Set TCP/IP configuration parameters
- Identify some common TCP/IP utilities
- Describe packet filtering

Estimated lesson time: 15 minutes

Installing TCP/IP

TCP/IP can be used in network environments ranging from small LANs to the global Internet. When you run Windows 2000 Setup, TCP/IP is installed as the default network protocol if a network adapter is detected. Therefore, you only need to install the TCP/IP protocol if the TCP/IP default protocol selection was overridden during setup, or you have deleted it from a connection in Network and Dial-Up Connections.

Practice: Installing the TCP/IP Protocol

In this practice, you will install TCP/IP on your Local Area Network Connection in Network and Dial-Up Connections. You must be logged on as an administrator or a member of the Administrators group in order to complete this practice.

Before you continue with the lesson, run the Ch02.exe demonstration file located in the Media folder on the Supplemental Course Materials CD-ROM that accompanies this book. The file provides an overview of installing the TCP/IP protocol.

▶ **To install TCP/IP on your local area network connection**

1. Click Start, point to Settings, and then click Network And Dial-Up Connections.

   The Network And Dial-Up Connections dialog box appears.

2. Right-click Local Area Connection and then click Properties.

   The Local Area Connection Properties dialog box appears.

3. Click Install.

   The Select Network Component Type dialog box appears.

4. Click Protocol and then click Add.

   The Select Network Protocol dialog box appears.

5. Click Internet Protocol (TCP/IP) as illustrated in Figure 2.9, and then click OK.

   The TCP/IP protocol is installed and added to the Components list in the Local Area Connection Properties dialog box.

6. Click Close.

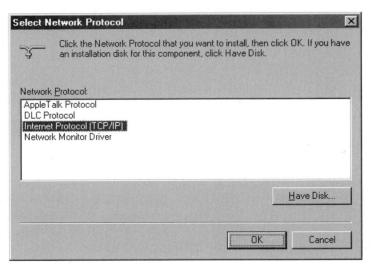

Figure 2.9   Selecting the Internet Protocol (TCP/IP)

Configuring TCP/IP

If you are implementing TCP/IP for the first time on your network, you should construct a detailed plan for IP addressing on your network. Your TCP/IP network addressing scheme can include either public or private addresses. You can use either public or private addresses if your network is not connected to the Internet. However, you will most likely implement some public IP addresses for Internet interconnectivity support. This is because devices connected directly to the Internet require a public IP address. InterNIC assigns public addresses to Internet service providers (ISPs). ISPs, in turn, assign IP addresses to organizations when network connectivity is purchased. IP addresses assigned this way are guaranteed to be unique and are programmed into Internet routers in order for traffic to reach the destination host.

Furthermore, you can implement a private addressing scheme to shield your internal addresses from the rest of the Internet by configuring private addresses on all the computers on your private network (or intranet). Private addresses are not reachable on the Internet because they are separate from public addresses, and they do not overlap.

You can assign IP addresses in Windows 2000 dynamically using Dynamic Host Configuration Protocol (DHCP), and you can address assignment using Automatic Private IP Addressing. You can also configure TCP/IP manually. You configure TCP/IP on a computer based on its function. For example, servers in a client/ server relationship within an organization should be assigned an IP address manually. However, you can configure TCP/IP dynamically through a DHCP server for the majority of clients on a network.

Dynamic Configuration

Windows 2000 computers will attempt to obtain the TCP/IP configuration from a DHCP server on your network by default, as illustrated in Figure 2.10. If a static TCP/IP configuration is currently implemented on a computer, you can implement a dynamic TCP/IP configuration.

▶ **To implement a dynamic TCP/IP configuration**

1. Click Start, point to Settings, and then click Network And Dial-Up Connections.

2. Right-click the Local Area Connection, and then click Properties.

3. On the General tab, click Internet Protocol (TCP/IP), and then click Properties.

   For other types of connections, click the Networking tab.

4. Click Obtain An IP Address Automatically, and then click OK.

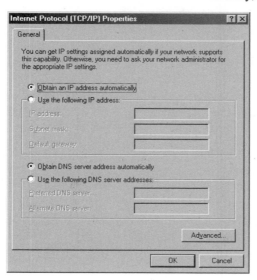

Figure 2.10   Configuring your computer to obtain TCP/IP settings automatically

Manual Configuration

Some servers, such as DHCP, DNS, and WINS servers, should be assigned an IP address manually. If you do not have a DHCP server on your network, you must configure TCP/IP computers manually to use a static IP address.

▶ **To configure a TCP/IP computer to use static addressing**

1. Click Start, point to Settings, and then click Network And Dial-Up Connections.

2. Right-click Local Area Connection, and then click Properties.

3. On the General tab, click Internet Protocol (TCP/IP), and then click Properties.

4. Select Use The Following IP Address.

You will then have to type in an IP, subnet mask, and default gateway address. If your network has a DNS server, you can set up your computer to use DNS.

▶ **To set up your computer to use DNS**

1. Select Use The Following DNS Server Addresses.

2. In Preferred DNS Server and Alternate DNS Server, type the primary and secondary DNS server addresses, as illustrated in Figure 2.11.

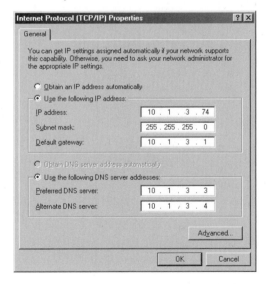

Figure 2.11   Manually configuring TCP/IP settings on your computer

You can also configure additional IP addresses and default gateways by performing the following procedure.

▶ **To configure additional IP addresses and default gateways**

1. In the Internet Protocol (TCP/IP) Properties dialog box, click Advanced.

2. On the IP Settings tab, in IP Addresses, click Add.

3. In IP Address And Subnet Mask, type an IP address and subnet mask, and then click Add.

4. Repeat steps 2 and 3 for each IP address you want to add, then click OK.

5. On the IP Settings tab, in Default Gateways, click Add.

6. In Gateway And Metric, type the IP address of the default gateway and the metric, and then click Add.

   You can also type a metric value in Interface Metric to configure a custom metric for this connection.

7. Repeat steps 5 and 6 for each IP address you want to add, and then click OK.

Note You will learn how to configure a client to use a WINS server in Chapter 9, "Implementing Windows Internet Naming Service (WINS)."

Automatic Private IP Address Assignment

Another TCP/IP address configuration option is to use Automatic Private IP Addressing when DHCP is not available. In previous versions of Windows, IP address configuration could be performed either manually or dynamically through DHCP. If a client was not able to obtain an IP address from a DHCP server, network services for the client were unavailable. The Automatic Private IP Addressing feature of Windows 2000 automates the process of assigning an unused IP address in the event that DHCP is not available.

The Automatic Private IP Addressing address is selected from the Microsoft-reserved address block 169.254.0.0, with the subnet mask 255.255.0.0. When the Automatic Private IP Addressing feature of Windows 2000 is used, an address in the Microsoft-reserved IP addressing range from 169.254.0.1 through 169.254.255.254 is assigned to the client. The assigned IP address is used until a DHCP server is located. The subnet mask 255.255.0.0 is automatically used.

Testing TCP/IP with Ipconfig and PING

You should always verify and test your TCP/IP configuration to make sure your computer can connect to other TCP/IP hosts and networks. You can perform basic TCP/IP configuration testing using Ipconfig and PING utilities.

With Ipconfig, you verify the TCP/IP configuration parameters on a host, including the IP address, subnet mask, and default gateway, from a command prompt. This is useful in determining whether the configuration is initialized, or if a duplicate IP address is configured.

▶   **To use Ipconfig from a command prompt**

1. Open a command prompt.

2. When the command prompt is displayed, type **Ipconfig** and then press Enter.

   TCP/IP configuration information is displayed, as illustrated in Figure 2.12.

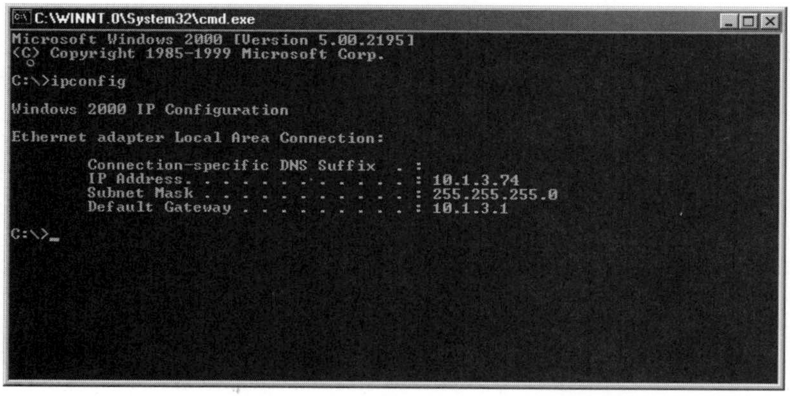

Figure 2.12   Using Ipconfig to display TCP/IP configuration information

After you verify the configuration with the Ipconfig utility, you can use the PING utility to test connectivity. The PING utility is a diagnostic tool that tests TCP/IP configurations and diagnoses connection failures. PING uses the Internet Control Message Protocol (ICMP) Echo Request and Echo Reply messages to determine whether a particular TCP/IP host is available and functional. Like the Ipconfig utility, the PING utility is executed at the command prompt. The command syntax is:

```
Ping IP_Address
```

If PING is successful, a message similar to the illustration in Figure 2.13 appears.

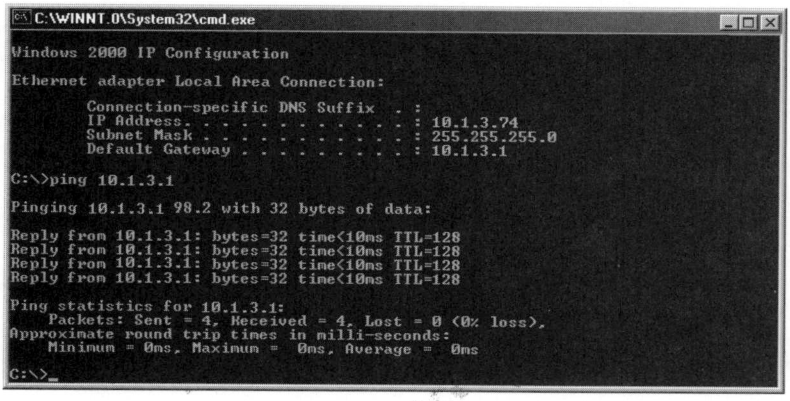

Figure 2.13   Reply messages displayed by the PING utility

Configuring Packet Filters

You can use IP packet filtering to trigger security negotiations for a communication based on the source, destination, and type of IP traffic. This allows you to define which specific IP and IPX traffic triggers will be secured, blocked, or allowed to pass through unfiltered.

For example, you can limit the type of access allowed to and from the network to restrict traffic to desired systems. You should make sure that you do not configure packet filters that are too restrictive, impairing the functionality of useful protocols on the computer. For example, if a computer running Windows 2000 is also running Internet Information Services (IIS) as a Web server, and packet filters are defined so that only Web-based traffic is allowed, you cannot use PING (which uses ICMP Echo Requests and Echo Replies) to perform basic IP troubleshooting.

You can configure the TCP/IP protocol to filter IP packets based on:

- The TCP port number
- The UDP port number
- The IP protocol number

Practice: Implementing IP Packet Filters

In this practice, you will implement TCP/IP packet filtering on a Windows 2000 Server computer for a LAN connection.

▶ **To implement TCP/IP packet filtering**

1. Click Start, point to Settings, and then click Network And Dial-Up Connections.
2. Right-click Local Area Connection and then click Properties.
   The Local Area Connection Properties dialog box appears.
3. Select Internet Protocol (TCP/IP), then click Properties.
   The Internet Protocol (TCP/IP) Properties dialog box appears.
4. Click Advanced.
   The Advanced TCP/IP Settings dialog box appears.
5. Click the Options tab, select TCP/IP Filtering, and then click Properties.
   The TCP/IP Filtering dialog box appears, as illustrated in Figure 2.14.
6. Click Enable TCP/IP Filtering (All Adapters).

   You can now add TCP, UDP, and IP protocol filtering by clicking the Permit Only option and then clicking Add below the TCP, UDP, or IP Protocols list.

   Some TCP/IP filtering implementations you can use include:

   - Enabling only TCP port 23, which filters all traffic except Telnet traffic
   - Enabling only TCP port 80 on a dedicated Web server to process only Web-based TCP traffic

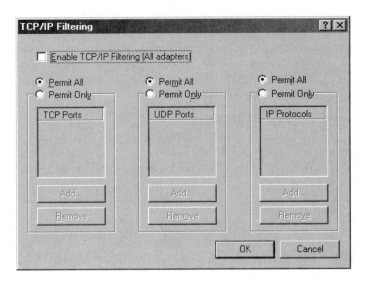

Figure 2.14   Setting TCP/IP packet filters in the TCP/IP Filtering dialog box

Caution   By enabling only TCP port 80, all network communications outside of port 80 will be disabled.

7. Click OK repeatedly to close all open dialog boxes.

Lesson Summary

By default, Windows 2000 installs the TCP/IP protocol if Setup detects a network adapter. You can also manually install TCP/IP. After you install TCP/IP on a computer, you can either configure it to obtain an IP address automatically, or set configuration properties manually. You can also implement packet filters to limit the type of access allowed to and from the network to restrict traffic to desired systems.

Lesson 4: Basic Concepts of IP Routing

Routing is the process of choosing a path over which to send packets, which is a primary function of IP. A router (commonly referred to as a gateway) is a device that forwards the packets from one physical network to another. When a router receives a packet, the network adapter forwards the datagrams to the IP Layer. IP examines the destination address on the datagram and then compares it to an IP routing table. A decision is then made as to where the packet is to be forwarded. This lesson explains basic IP routing concepts.

After this lesson, you will be able to

- Update a Windows 2000-based routing table by means of static routes
- Manage and monitor internal routing
- Manage and monitor border routing

Estimated lesson time: 40 minutes

Overview of Routing

A router helps LANs and WANs achieve interoperability and connectivity, and can link LANs that have different network topologies, such as Ethernet and Token Ring. Each packet sent over a LAN has a packet header that contains source and destination address fields. Routers match packet headers to a LAN segment and choose the best path for the packet, optimizing network performance. For example, if a packet is sent from Computer A to Computer C, as illustrated in Figure 2.15, the best route uses only one hop. If Router 1 is the default router for Computer A, the packet will be rerouted through Router 2. Computer A will be notified of the better route by which to send packets to Computer C. As each route is found, the packet is sent to the next router, called a *hop*, until finally delivered to the destination host. If a route is not found, an error message is sent to the source host.

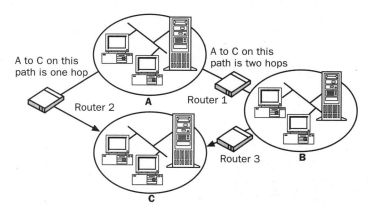

Figure 2.15   Packet routed from Computer A to Computer C

To make routing decisions, the IP Layer consults a routing table that is stored in memory, as illustrated in Figure 2.16.

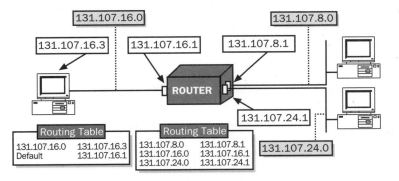

Figure 2.16   IP layer consulting a routing table

A routing table contains entries with the IP addresses of router interfaces to other networks that it can communicate with. A routing table is a series of entries, called *routes*, that contain information on where the network IDs of the internetwork are located. A routing table in a computer that is running Windows 2000 is built automatically, based on its TCP/IP configuration. You can view a routing table by typing **route print** at a command prompt, as illustrated in Figure 2.17.

```
C:\WINNT.0\System32\cmd.exe                                    _ □ ×
(C) Copyright 1985-1999 Microsoft Corp.

C:\>route print
===========================================================================
Interface List
0x1 .......................... MS TCP Loopback interface
0x1000003 ...00 50 04 94 ec 1d ...... FE575 Ethernet Adapter
0x2000004 ...00 53 45 00 00 00 ...... WAN (PPP/SLIP) Interface
===========================================================================
===========================================================================
Active Routes:
Network Destination        Netmask          Gateway       Interface  Metric
          0.0.0.0          0.0.0.0    10.33.238.171   10.33.238.171     1
        127.0.0.0        255.0.0.0        127.0.0.1       127.0.0.1     1
     10.33.224.19  255.255.255.255    10.33.238.171   10.33.238.171     1
    10.33.238.171  255.255.255.255        127.0.0.1       127.0.0.1     1
   10.33.255.255  255.255.255.255    10.33.238.171   10.33.238.171     1
        224.0.0.0        224.0.0.0    10.33.238.171   10.33.238.171     1
  255.255.255.255  255.255.255.255    10.33.238.171         1000003     1
Default Gateway:      10.33.238.171
===========================================================================
Persistent Routes:
  None

C:\>_
```

Figure 2.17   Displaying a routing table at a command prompt

Note   The routing table is not exclusive to a router. Hosts also have a routing table that is used to determine the optimal route.

Static and Dynamic IP Routing

The process that routers use to obtain routing information is different based on whether the router performs static or dynamic IP routing. Static routing is a function of IP that limits you to fixed routing tables. Static routers require that routing tables are built and updated manually. You use the ROUTE command to add static entries to the routing table.

To add or modify a static route	Function
route add [*network*] **mask** [*netmask*] [*gateway*]	Adds a route
route -p add [*network*] **mask** [*netmask*] [*gateway*]	Adds a persistent route
route delete [*network*] [*gateway*]	Deletes a route
route change [*network*] [*gateway*]	Modifies a route
route print	Displays the routing table
route -f	Clears all routes

Practice: Updating a Windows 2000-Based Routing Table

In this practice, you will update a Windows 2000-based routing table by means of static routes.

▶ **To update a routing table**

1. Open a command prompt.

2. At the command prompt, type **route add** *IP_ address* **mask** *subnet_mask gateway* to add a route to enable communications with a network from a host on another network.

   For example, to add a route to enable communications with network 10.107.24.0 from a host on network 10.107.16.0, you would type **route add 10.107.24.0 mask 255.255.255.0 10.107.16.2**, as illustrated in Figure 2.18.

```
C:\WINNT.0\System32\cmd.exe                                    _ □ ×
Microsoft Windows 2000 [Version 5.00.2195]
(C) Copyright 1985-1999 Microsoft Corp.

C:\>route add 10.107.24.0 mask 255.255.255.0 10.107.16.2
```

Figure 2.18   Adding a static route to a routing table

Using Dynamic Routing

If a route changes, static routers do not inform each other of the change, nor do static routers exchange routes with dynamic routers. In contrast, dynamic routing automatically updates the routing tables, reducing administrative overhead. However, dynamic routing increases traffic in large networks.

Routing Protocols

Dynamic routing is a function of routing protocols, such as the Routing Information Protocol (RIP) and Open Shortest Path First (OSPF). Routing protocols periodically exchange routes to known networks among dynamic routers. If a route changes, other routers are automatically informed of the change. You must have multiple network adapters (one per network) on a Windows 2000 Server or Windows 2000 Advanced Server. In addition, you must install and configure Routing and Remote Access because dynamic routing protocols are not installed by default when you install Windows 2000. You will learn how to implement IP routing for remote users in Chapter 11, "Providing Your Clients Remote Access Service (RAS)."

Windows 2000 offers two primary IP routing protocols that you can choose, depending on factors such as network size and topology. These routing protocols are explained in the next two sections.

Routing Information Protocol (RIP)

RIP is a distance-vector routing protocol provided for backwards-compatibility with existing RIP networks. RIP allows a router to exchange routing information with other RIP routers to make them aware of any change in the internetwork layout. RIP broadcasts the information to neighboring routers, and sends periodic RIP broadcast packets containing all routing information known to the router. These broadcasts keep all internetwork routers synchronized.

Open Shortest Path First (OSPF)

OSPF is a link-state routing protocol that enables routers to exchange routing information and create a map of the network that calculates the best possible path to each network. Upon receiving changes to the link state database, the routing table is recalculated. As the size of the link state database increases, memory requirements and route computation times increase. To address this scaling problem, OSPF divides the internetwork into collections of contiguous networks called areas. Areas are connected to each other through a backbone area. A backbone router in OSPF is a router that is connected to the backbone area. Backbone routers include routers that are connected to more than one area. However, backbone routers do not have to be area border routers. Routers that have all networks connected to the backbone are internal routers.

Each router only keeps a link state database for those areas that are connected to the router. Area Border Routers (ABRs) connect the backbone area to other areas, as illustrated in Figure 2.19.

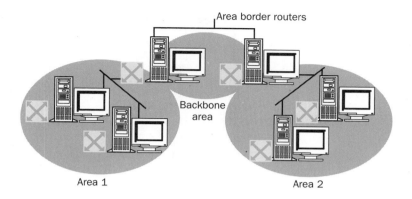

Figure 2.19 A basic OSPF area design

An OSPF-routed environment is best suited to a large-to-very-large, multipath, dynamic IP internetwork such as a corporate or institutional campus, or worldwide corporate or institutional internetwork. To manage your internal and border routers:

- Ensure that the ABRs for the area are configured with the proper pairs (Destination, Network Mask) that summarize that area's routes.

- Ensure that the source and route filtering configured on the ABR is not too restrictive, preventing proper routes from being propagated to the OSPF autonomous system. External source and route filtering is configured on the External Routing tab in the OSPF Routing Protocol Properties dialog box.

- Ensure that all ABRs are either physically connected to the backbone or logically connected to the backbone by using a virtual link. There should not be backdoor routers, which are routers that connect two areas without going through the backbone.

▶ **To administer a router**

1. Click Start, point to Programs, point to Administrative Tools, and then click Routing And Remote Access.

2. In the console tree, right-click Server Status, then click Add Server.

3. In the Add Server dialog box, do one of the following:

   ▪ Click The Following Computer, and type the computer name or IP address of the server.

   ▪ Click All Routing And Remote Access Servers In The Domain, and then type the domain containing the server you want to administer. Click OK, and then select the server.

- Click Browse The Active Directory, click Next, and in the Find Routers Or Remote Access Servers dialog box, select the check boxes next to the types of servers that you want to search for. Click OK, and then select the server.

4. You can administer a remote server once it appears as an item in the console tree.

Lesson Summary

Routers forward packets from one physical network to another. The IP layer consults a routing table that is stored in memory. A routing table contains entries with the IP addresses of router interfaces to other networks. Static routers require that routing tables are built and updated manually. With dynamic routing, if a route changes, other routers are automatically informed of the change.

Review

Answering the following questions will reinforce key information presented in this chapter. If you are unable to answer a question, review the appropriate lesson and then try the question again. Answers to the questions can be found in Appendix A, "Questions and Answers."

1. What is TCP/IP?

2. Which TCP/IP utilities are used to verify and test a TCP/IP configuration?

3. What is the purpose of a subnet mask?

4. What is the minimum number of areas in an OSPF internetwork?

5. What is an internal router?

6. What is a border router?

7. What Windows 2000 administrative tool can you use to manage internal and border routers?

C H A P T E R 3

Implementing NWLink

About This Chapter

This chapter gives an overview of internetworking with Microsoft Windows 2000 and Novell NetWare. This includes installing and configuring the NWLink protocol.

Before You Begin

To complete the lessons in this chapter, you must have

- Completed the Setup procedures located in "About This Book"

Lesson 1: Introducing NWLink

If some of your computer resources are on a Novell NetWare network, your Windows 2000-based network will have to communicate and share resources with the NetWare network. Novell uses the Internetwork Packet Exchange/ Sequenced Packet Exchange (IPX/SPX) protocol as its primary network protocol. NWLink is an IPX/SPX-compatible protocol developed by Microsoft to allow Windows 2000 computers to communicate with the NetWare services. This lesson provides an overview of the NWLink protocol.

After this lesson, you will be able to

- Explain the purpose of the NWLink protocol
- List some of the components used for internetworking Windows 2000 with Novell NetWare
- Identify the architecture of NWLink

Estimated lesson time: 25 minutes

Interoperability with NetWare

Windows 2000 provides protocols and services that allow you to integrate Windows 2000-based networks with Novell NetWare networks, including the IPX/SPX/NetBIOS Compatible Transport Protocol (NWLink), Windows 2000 Gateway Service for NetWare, and Windows 2000 Client Service for NetWare. These features allow you to create a network environment composed of both Windows 2000-based and NetWare servers. You can also migrate user accounts, groups, files, and permissions from NetWare to Windows 2000 using the Directory Services Migration Tool for NetWare provided with Windows 2000.

The following list describes services for Windows 2000 Server that enable computers running Windows 2000 to coexist and interoperate with Novell NetWare networks and servers. Some of these services are included in Windows 2000 Server and others are available as separate products.

- **IPX/SPX/NetBIOS Compatible Transport Protocol (NWLink).** NWLINK, an IPX/SPX-compatible protocol, is the fundamental building block for the NetWare-compatible services on the Windows 2000 platform. NWLink is included with all varieties of Windows 2000 Server and Windows 2000 Professional.

- **Gateway Service for NetWare.** Gateway Service for NetWare is included with all varieties of Windows 2000 Server. It enables a computer running Windows 2000 Server to communicate at the application layer to computers running NetWare 3.2 or later server software. Logon script support is also included. In addition, you can use Gateway Service for NetWare to create gateways to NetWare resources, enabling computers running only Microsoft client software to gain access to NetWare resources through the gateway. Gateway Service for NetWare is discussed in more detail in Lesson 2.

- **Directory Service Migration Tool.**   The Directory Service Migration Tool enables you to migrate user accounts, groups, files, and permissions from a NetWare server to Windows 2000 Active Directory. Windows 2000 replaces the old NetWare Convert Tool with the Directory Service Migration Tool. The Directory Service Migration Tool nondestructively migrates both NetWare binderies and Novell Directory Services into an offline database and permits administrators to model the account information before committing it to Active Directory, as illustrated in Figure 3.1.

NDS/Bindery   Off-Line Model   Windows 2000
                                            Active Directory

Directory Service
Migration Tool

Figure 3.1   Migration from Novell Directory Services to Windows 2000 Active Directory

- **File and Print Services for NetWare.**   File and Print Services for NetWare allows NetWare clients using the IPX/SPX-compatible transport to send print jobs over the network to Windows 2000 print servers. File and Print Services for NetWare is a separate product from Windows 2000 that does not require any changes to be made to NetWare clients.

Integrating NetWare 5.0 and Windows 2000 Servers

Like Windows 2000, NetWare 5.0 uses Transmission Control Protocol/Internet Protocol (TCP/IP) as the native protocol, and IPX is not installed by default. Neither Client Service for NetWare nor Gateway Service for NetWare supports connecting to NetWare resources over IP. Therefore, when you use NWLink to connect to NetWare 5.0 servers you must enable IPX on NetWare 5.0 servers.

NWLink and Windows 2000

NWLink provides the network and transport protocols to support communications with NetWare file servers, and must be installed if you want to use Gateway Service for NetWare or Client Service for NetWare to connect to NetWare servers. To log on to a NetWare network from a Windows 2000 Professional-based computer, you must use Client Service for NetWare or a third-party NetWare client such as Novell Client for Windows 2000. Alternately, you could use a gateway-based solution by installing Gateway Service for NetWare on a Windows 2000 server. Client Service for NetWare and Gateway Service for NetWare are discussed later in this chapter.

Because NWLink is Network Driver Interface Specification (NDIS)-compliant, the Windows 2000-based computer can simultaneously run other protocol stacks, such as TCP/IP. NWLink can bind to multiple network adapters with multiple frame types. NWLink requires little or no initial client configuration on small, nonrouted networks.

NetBIOS and Windows Sockets

NWLink supports two networking application programming interfaces (APIs): NetBIOS and Windows Sockets (WinSock). These APIs allow Windows 2000-based computers to communicate with NetWare clients and servers and any Windows-based computer that uses NWLink. Because NWLink supports NetBIOS, it allows communications with all NetBIOS-based applications, including Microsoft Systems Management Server, SNA Server, SQL Server, and Exchange Server. The WinSock interface to NWLink allows Windows-based client computers that only have NWLink installed to use sockets-based applications such as Microsoft Internet Explorer.

NWLink Architecture

NWLink provides a comprehensive set of transport and network layer protocols that allow for integration with the NetWare environment. Table 3.1 lists the subprotocols and components, and shows their function and associated drivers.

Table 3.1   NWLink Subprotocols

Protocol	Function	Driver
IPX	A peer-to-peer networking protocol that provides connectionless datagram transfer services and controls addressing and routing of packets of data within and between networks	NWLNKIPX.SYS
SPX and SPXII	Provide connection-oriented transfer services	NWLNKSPX.SYS
Router Information Protocol (RIP)	Provides route and router discovery services	NWLNKIPX.SYS
Service Advising Protocol (SAP)	Collects and distributes service names and addresses	NWLNKIPX.SYS
NetBIOS	Provides compatible support with NetBIOS for IPX/SPX	NWLNKNB.SYS
Forwarder	Provides IPX router support	NWLNKFWD.SYS

Figure 3.2 shows NWLink in the Windows 2000 architecture and the files in which each protocol is implemented.

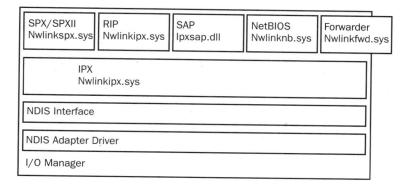

Figure 3.2   NWLink in the Windows 2000 architecture

IPX

IPX is a peer-to-peer networking protocol that provides connectionless datagram transfer services and controls addressing and routing packets of data within and between networks. With connectionless transmission, a session does not need to be set up each time packets are transmitted; packets are simply sent out on the wire. This requires less overhead than connection-oriented transmission, in which a session must be established each time packets are transmitted. Therefore, connectionless transmission is best when data is generated in intermittent, short bursts.

Because IPX is a connectionless protocol, it does not provide for flow control or acknowledgment that the receiving station has received the datagram packet. Instead, individual datagram packets travel independently to their destination, and IPX assumes that they arrive intact without guarantee that they arrive at their destination or that they arrive in sequence. However, because transmission on local area networks (LANs) is relatively error-free, IPX is efficient in delivering short-burst data on LANs.

NWLink enables application programming for WinSock and remote procedure calls (RPCs) over WinSock. IPX supports WinSock identifications for use by WinSock applications. IPX enables NetBIOS, Named Pipes, Mailslots, Network Dynamic Data Exchange (NetDDE) service, RPC over NetBIOS, and RPC over Named Pipes programming over NetBIOS over IPX (NBIPX). NWLink also supports other applications that use IPX through direct hosting. Direct hosting is a feature that allows computers to communicate over IPX, bypassing the NetBIOS layer. Direct hosting can lower overhead and increase throughput.

SPX

SPX is a transport protocol that offers connection-oriented services over IPX. Although connection-oriented service requires overhead for session setup, once a session is established, this service requires no more overhead for data transmission than connectionless service. Therefore, it works best for utilities that require a continuous connection. SPX provides reliable delivery through sequencing and acknowledgments and verifies successful packet delivery to any network destination by requesting verification from the destination on receipt of the data. The SPX verification must include a value that matches the value calculated from the data before transmission. By comparing these values, SPX ensures not only that the data packet made it to the destination, but that it arrived intact. SPX can track data transmissions consisting of a series of separate packets. If an acknowledgment request brings no response within a specified time, SPX retransmits the request as many as eight times. If no response is received, SPX assumes the connection has failed.

SPX also provides a packet burst mechanism. Packet burst, also known as burst mode, allows the transfer of multiple data packets without requiring that each packet be sequenced and acknowledged individually. By allowing multiple packets to be acknowledged once, burst mode can reduce network traffic on most IPX networks. Additionally, the packet burst mechanism monitors dropped packets and retransmits only the missing packets. In Windows 2000, burst mode is enabled by default.

SPXII

SPXII improves on SPX by allowing it to perform better on high-bandwidth networks. SPXII improves on SPX in the following ways:

- **SPXII allows for more outstanding unacknowledged packets than SPX.**   In SPX, there cannot be more than one outstanding unacknowledged packet at any time, whereas in SPXII, there can be as many outstanding packets as negotiated by the networked peers at connection setup time.
- **SPXII allows for larger packets.**   SPX has a maximum packet size of 576 bytes, whereas SPXII can use the maximum packet size of the underlying LAN. For example, on an Ethernet network, SPXII can use 1518 bytes.

Router Information Protocol

NWLink uses Router Information Protocol (RIP) over IPX (RIPX) to implement route and router discovery services used by SPX and NBIPX. RIP sends and receives IPX traffic and maintains a routing table. RIP runs on a layer equivalent to the Open Systems Interconnection (OSI) application layer. The RIP code is implemented within the NWLNKIPX.SYS file.

NWLink includes the RIP protocol for Windows-based clients and for computers running Windows 2000 Server that do not have Routing and Remote Access

Service installed. These computers do not forward packets as routers do, but they use an RIP table to determine where to send packets. RIP clients, such as workstations, can locate the optimal route to an IPX network number by broadcasting an RIP GetLocalTarget route request. Each router that can reach the destination responds to the GetLocalTarget route request with a single route. Based on the RIP responses from the local routers, the sending station chooses the best router through which to forward the IPX packet.

Service Advertising Protocol

Service Advertising Protocol (SAP) is the mechanism by which IPX clients collect and distribute the names and addresses of services running on IPX nodes. SAP clients use SAP broadcasts only when bindery-based or Novell Directory Services queries fail. SAP clients send the following types of messages:

- SAP clients request the name and address of the nearest server of a specific type by broadcasting an SAP GetNearestServer request.

- SAP clients request the names and addresses of all services, or of all services of a specific type, by broadcasting an SAP general service request.

NWLink includes a subset of the SAP protocol for Windows-based clients and for computers running Windows 2000 Server that do not have an IPX router installed.

NetBIOS over IPX

To facilitate the operation of NetBIOS-based applications on an IPX internetwork, NetBIOS over IPX (NWLNKNB.SYS) provides standard NetBIOS services such as the following:

- **NetBIOS Datagram Services.**   Applications use NetBIOS Datagram Services for fast, connectionless communications. Mailslots and user authentication make use of this service.

- **NetBIOS Session Services.**   NetBIOS Session Services provide connection-oriented, reliable communication between applications. File and print sharing rely on this service.

- **NetBIOS Name Service.**   Name management includes registering, querying, and releasing NetBIOS names.

Forwarder

The Forwarder is a kernel mode component that is installed with NWLink. However, the Forwarder is used only when the Windows 2000-based server is used as an IPX router running Routing and Remote Access Service.

When the IPX router software is activated, the Forwarder component works with the IPX Router Manager and the filtering component to forward packets. The Forwarder component obtains configuration information from the IPX Router Manager and stores a table of the best routes. When the Forwarder component receives an incoming packet, it passes it to the filtering driver to check for input filters. When it receives an outgoing packet, it first passes it to the filtering driver. Assuming no outgoing filters prevent the packet from being transmitted, the filtering component passes the packet back, and the Forwarder component forwards the packet over the appropriate interface.

Lesson Summary

NWLink is the Microsoft 32-bit implementation of IPX/SPX. IPX is a peer-to-peer networking protocol that provides connectionless datagram transfer services and controls addressing and routing of packets. SPX is a transport protocol that offers connection-oriented services over IPX. A Forwarder component works with the IPX Router Manager and the filtering component to forward packets on the best route.

Lesson 2: Using Gateway Service for NetWare

Gateway Service for NetWare allows a Microsoft networking client (LAN Manager, MS-DOS, Windows for Workgroups, Windows 95, Windows 98, Windows NT, or Windows 2000) to access NetWare server services through the Windows 2000 Server-based computer. In this lesson, you will learn how to install and utilize Gateway Service for NetWare.

After this lesson, you will be able to

- Install Gateway Service for NetWare
- Enable and activate gateways in Windows 2000

Estimated lesson time: 30 minutes

Gateway Service for NetWare Overview

With Gateway Service for NetWare, you can create a gateway through which Microsoft client computers without Novell NetWare client software can access NetWare file and print resources. You can make gateways for resources located on Novell NDS trees as well as for resources on servers with bindery security. These resources include volumes, directories, directory map objects, printers, and print queues. A user who works locally at a computer running Windows 2000 Server can use Gateway Service for NetWare to gain direct access to NetWare file and print resources, both on Novell NDS trees and on servers with bindery security. Gateway Service for NetWare depends on and works with NWLink.

Understanding Gateway Service for NetWare and Gateways

Gateway Service for NetWare acts as a bridge between the NetBIOS protocol used by the network using Windows and the NetWare Core Protocol used by the NetWare network. When a gateway is enabled, network clients running Microsoft client software can access NetWare files and printers without having to run NetWare client software locally. Figure 3.3 shows an example of a file gateway configuration.

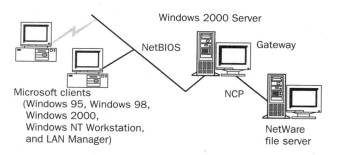

Figure 3.3   File gateway configuration

For file access, the gateway server redirects one of its own drives to the NetWare volume and then shares that drive with other Microsoft clients. The file gateway uses a NetWare account on the computer running Windows 2000 Server to create a validated connection to the NetWare server. This connection appears on the computer running Windows 2000 Server as a redirected drive. When you share the redirected drive, it becomes like any other shared resource on the computer running Windows 2000 Server.

For example, suppose you want to create a gateway from the computer AIREDALE (running Gateway Service for NetWare) to the Novell NDS folder \\NW4\Server1\Org_Unit.Org\Data volume on the NetWare server Nw4. When activating the gateway, you specify \\NW4\Server1\Org_Unit.Org\Data as the NetWare resource, and then you specify a share name for Microsoft clients, such as Nw_Data. Microsoft clients would then refer to this resource as \\AIREDALE\Nw_Data.

After the gateway connection is established, it is disconnected only if the computer running Windows 2000 Server is turned off, if the administrator disconnects the shared resource or disables the gateway, or if a network problem prevents access to the NetWare server. Logging off the computer running Windows 2000 Server does not, by itself, disconnect the gateway.

Note Because requests from Microsoft networking clients are processed through the gateway, access is slower than direct access from the client to the NetWare network. Clients who require frequent access to NetWare resources should run the NetWare client software to achieve better performance.

Installing Gateway Service for NetWare

You have the option to install Gateway Service for NetWare when you install Windows 2000 Server, or you can install GSNW later. You must be logged on as a member of the Administrators group to install and configure Gateway Service for NetWare. If you want to install Gateway Service for NetWare after you have already installed Windows 2000 Server, perform the following steps.

▶ **To install Gateway Service for NetWare**

1. Open the Network and Dial-Up Connections Control Panel applet.
2. Right-click a local area connection, then click Properties.
3. In the General tab, click Install.
4. In the Select Network Component Type dialog box, click Client, then click Add.
5. In the Select Network Client dialog box, click Gateway (And Client) Service For NetWare, then click OK.

During installation of Gateway Service for NetWare, NWLink is installed if it is not already on the server. Also during installation of Gateway Service for NetWare, Client Service for NetWare is installed and the Gateway Service for

NetWare icon is added to Control Panel. By default, the NetWare network is placed first in the network search order.

Important   Before you install Gateway Service for NetWare on a computer, remove any existing client software that is compatible with NetWare Core Protocol, including NetWare client software, from the computer.

Configuring Gateway Service for NetWare

When you first log on after Gateway Service for NetWare is installed, you are prompted to set your default tree and context or your preferred server. The tree and context define the position of the user object for the user name you use to log on to a Novell NDS tree. A preferred server is the NetWare server to which you are automatically connected when you log on if your network does not use Novell NDS. You should set a default tree and context only in a Novell NDS environment; otherwise, you can set a preferred server. The Gateway Service for NetWare dialog box is illustrated in Figure 3.4.

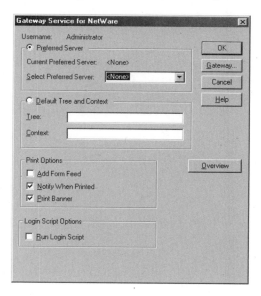

Figure 3.4   Gateway Service for NetWare dialog box

▶   **To set a preferred server**

1. Click Start, point to Settings, click Control Panel, then choose Gateway Service For NetWare.

2. Click Preferred Server and, in Select Preferred Server, enter the preferred server.

   If you do not want to set a preferred server, click None. You are then logged on to the nearest available NetWare server, and your interaction with the

NetWare network is through that server. If you do not set a preferred server, you are prompted to set one each time you log on.

You can have either a default tree and context or a preferred server, but not both. (In Novell NDS environments, you set a default tree and context.) If you select a default tree and context, you can still access NetWare servers that use bindery security.

▶ **To set a default tree and context**

1. Click Start, point to Settings, click Control Panel, then choose Gateway Service For NetWare.

2. Click Default Tree And Context and, in Tree And Context, type your tree and context.

Creating a Gateway

Before you can create a gateway to NetWare resources, the NetWare server must have a group named NTGATEWAY and a user account with the necessary rights for the resources that you want to access. The NetWare user account you use must be a member of the NTGATEWAY group.

The NetWare user account you use to enable gateways can be either a Novell NDS account or a bindery account. If the server will have gateways to both Novell NDS resources and resources on servers running bindery security, the user account must be a bindery account. (This account can connect to Novell NDS resources through bindery emulation.) If you create gateways only to Novell NDS resources, the account can be a Novell NDS account.

Enabling Gateways in Windows 2000

Creating a gateway is a two-step process. First, you enable gateways on the server running Windows 2000 Server. When you enable a gateway, you must type the name and password of the user account that has access to the NetWare server and is a member of the NTGATEWAY group on that NetWare server. You need to do this only once for each server that will act as a gateway.

▶ **To enable a gateway on the server**

1. Click Start, point to Settings, click Control Panel, then choose Gateway Service For NetWare.

2. Click Gateway, then select the Enable Gateway check box.

3. In Gateway Account, type the name of your gateway account.

4. In Password and Confirm Password, type the password for the gateway account.

   You can now share NetWare file and printing resources over a Windows-based network.

Activating Gateways

The second step is to activate a gateway for each volume or printer to which you want to create a gateway. When you activate a gateway, you specify the NetWare resource and a share name that Windows client users will use to connect to the resource. To activate a gateway for a volume, use the Gateway Service for NetWare Control Panel applet. To activate a gateway for a printer, use the Add Printer Wizard. If you are activating a gateway to a Novell NDS resource and the gateway user account is a bindery user account, specify the resource that uses the bindery context name. If you are using a Novell NDS user account and you do not plan on also creating gateways to bindery resources, specify the Novell NDS resource name.

▶ **To activate a gateway to a NetWare file resource**

1. Click Start, point to Settings, click Control Panel, then choose Gateway Service For NetWare.

2. Click Gateway, then select the Enable Gateway check box.

3. Click Add, and in Share Name, type a share name that Microsoft clients will use to access the NetWare resource.

4. In Network Path, type the network path of the NetWare volume or directory you want to share.

5. In Use Drive, enter the default drive you want to use, if necessary.

6. Click Unlimited, then click OK.

   You can also click Allow, enter a maximum number of concurrent users, then click OK.

▶ **To activate a gateway to a NetWare printer**

1. Click Start, point to Settings, then click Printers.

2. Click Add Printer, then click Next.

3. Click Network Printer, then click Next.

4. In Name, type the name of a printer in the following format: \\servername\sharename

   To find the NetWare printer in Shared Printers, click Next. If necessary, double-click Novell NDS tree names and NetWare server names until you find the printer you want.

Follow the remaining instructions in the Add Printer Wizard to finish connecting to the NetWare printer:

1. The icon for that printer appears in the Printers folder.

2. Click the printer you just created and, on the File menu, click Properties.

3. In the Sharing tab, click Shared and, in the Shared As dialog box, type a name for the printer.

Security for Gateway Resources

Security for gateway resources is provided on two levels:

- On the computer running Windows 2000 Server and acting as a gateway, you can set share-level permissions for each resource made available through the gateway.
- On the NetWare file server, the NetWare administrator can assign trustee rights to the user account that is used for the gateway or to the NTGATEWAY group. These rights are enforced for all Microsoft client users who access the resource through the gateway. There is no auditing of gateway access.

Connecting Directly to NetWare Resources

In addition to providing gateway technology, Gateway Service for NetWare enables users working locally at a computer running Windows 2000 Server to access NetWare resources directly, just as Client Service for NetWare provides this service to Windows 2000 Professional users. The information in this section applies to users working locally at a computer running Windows 2000 Server who access NetWare resources directly—not to Microsoft clients who access resources through a gateway. (This information does apply to users of Client Service for NetWare on computers running Windows 2000 Professional.)

Novell NDS trees (as well as NetWare servers running bindery security) appear in the NetWare or Compatible Network list in Windows Explorer. You can double-click a tree name to expand it, and then double-click any container object to expand its contents and structure. You can connect to and assign a local drive to any volume, folder, or directory map object anywhere in the tree hierarchy (for which you have credentials). To connect to a Novell NDS printer, you can use the Add Printer Wizard, just as you would to connect to any network printer.

If you have a default tree and context, once you have logged on, you do not need to log on again or supply another password to access any volume in your default tree. If you access another tree, you are prompted to supply a full context (including user name) for that tree.

Lesson Summary

Gateway Service for NetWare allows a Microsoft networking client (LAN Manager, MS-DOS, Windows for Workgroups, Windows 95, Windows 98, Windows NT, or Windows 2000) to access NetWare server services through the Windows 2000 server.

Lesson 3: Using Client Service for NetWare

Microsoft network clients can access the NetWare server through the Windows 2000 server running Gateway Service for NetWare. A Windows 2000-based computer can access resources on the NetWare server as a client through the integrated Client Service for NetWare component. In this lesson, you will learn how to install and use the Client Service for NetWare.

After this lesson, you will be able to

- Install Client Service for NetWare
- List advantages and disadvantages of using Client Service for Netware

Estimated lesson time: 15 minutes

NetWare Connectivity

Client Service for NetWare provides client-based NetWare connectivity, and Gateway Service for NetWare acts as a gateway through which multiple clients can access NetWare resources. Both depend on and work with the NWLink protocol, which is automatically installed with the redirector. Client Service for NetWare uses a subset of Gateway Service for NetWare code.

When a drive is mapped to a NetWare volume, the computer running Windows 2000 Professional uses a NetWare account to create a validated connection to the NetWare server. For example, it would be used to create a connection from computer A (running Client Service) to the Novell NDS volume \\T\Volname.Orgunit.Org\Folder, where T is the name of the Novell NDS tree, Volname.Orgunit.Org is the path to the volume name in the Novell NDS tree, and Folder is a subfolder on the Volname volume. In Windows Explorer, select Tools, then click Map Network Drive. You can also use the net use command line utility and specify the path \\B\Volname.Orgunit.Org\Folder for the NetWare resource. When using the net use command, after the mapped connection is established, it is disconnected only if the computer running Windows 2000 Professional is shut down, if the drive is manually disconnected, or if a network problem prevents access to the NetWare server. The mapped drive is then reestablished when the user logs on to the network.

Choosing Between Client Service for NetWare and Gateway Service for NetWare

If you intend to create or indefinitely maintain a heterogeneous environment containing both servers running Windows 2000 and servers running NetWare, consider using Client Service for NetWare. If you intend to migrate gradually from NetWare to Windows 2000 or if you want to reduce administration, consider using Gateway Service for NetWare.

Advantages of Client Service for NetWare

Client Service provides the following advantages over Gateway Service:

- **Client Service allows for user-level security rather than share-level security.** With Client Service for NetWare, you can allow users access to individual user home directories (directories where individual user data resides) that are stored on NetWare volumes. Users can then map to their home directories and any additional volumes to which they have been granted user-level security. To allow users access to individual home directories with Gateway Service, you need to give each user a separate drive letter.

- **Client Service performs better than Gateway Service.** Client Service communicates directly with NetWare servers, avoiding latency caused by requests moving through a Gateway Service for NetWare server.

Disadvantages of Client Service for NetWare

Client Service has the following disadvantages:

- **Client Service requires you to manage multiple user accounts for each user.** For each user, you must create and manage separate user accounts for both Windows 2000 and NetWare. However, you do not need to do so if you are using an additional product, such as Novell Client for Windows 2000. In Windows NT 4.0, Directory Service Manager eliminates the need to create separate user accounts on bindery-based servers.

- **Client Service requires more installation and management overhead.** With Client Service, you must install and maintain additional Client Service software on each computer running Windows 2000 Professional.

- **Client Service requires you to add IPX to your entire network.** Servers running Windows 2000 and servers running NetWare 5.0 use TCP/IP as the native protocol. However, Client Service requires you to use IPX (through NWLink), and may require enabling IPX routing throughout the entire network.

Configuring Client Service for NetWare

When you install Client Service for NetWare on Windows 2000 Professional, the NWLink IPX/SPX/NetBIOS Compatible Transport Protocol is automatically installed. To install Client Service for NetWare, you need Administrator rights to the computer running Windows 2000 Professional. Microsoft Unattended Setup Mode can be used for large deployments of Windows 2000 Professional and Client Service for NetWare. Refer to the Custom and Automated Installations in this book for more information.

▶ **To install Client Service for NetWare**

1. Open the Network and Dial-Up Connections Control Panel applet.

2. Right-click the local area connection for which you want to install Client Service for NetWare, then click Properties.

3. In the General tab, click Install.

4. In the Select Network Component Type dialog box, click Client, then click Add.

5. In the Select Network Client dialog box, click Client Service For NetWare, then click OK.

Lesson Summary

Windows 2000 includes client software to support connections to servers running NetWare. With the Client Service for NetWare in Windows 2000 and the Gateway Service for NetWare in Windows 2000 Server, users can use file and print resources on servers running NetWare.

Lesson 4: Installing and Configuring NWLink

In this lesson, you will learn how to install NWLink, which is included in all varieties of Windows 2000 to support connectivity to computers running NetWare and other compatible systems.

After this lesson, you will be able to

- Install the NWLink protocol in Windows 2000
- Configure the NWLink protocol in Windows 2000
- Identify the purpose of a frame type and network number

Estimated lesson time: 30 minutes

Windows 2000 Professional and NetWare Connectivity

Windows 2000 Professional uses Client Service for NetWare and NWLink protocol to provide connectivity between Windows 2000 Professional and servers running Novell NDS or NetWare bindery-based servers. NWLink is the Windows component that includes the IPX/SPX protocol.

With Windows 2000 Professional, you can leave the Novell Client 32 on the operating system while upgrading from Windows 95, Windows 98, or Windows NT 4.0 Workstation. Windows 2000 Professional upgrades computers running versions of Novell Client 32 earlier than 4.7. During the upgrade to Windows 2000 Professional, Novell Client 32 version 4.51 is installed. This process allows for a seamless upgrade of Novell Client 32 with no loss in functionality. To obtain a full version of Novell Client for Windows 2000, you can contact Novell directly.

Configuring Client Service for NetWare

When you install Client Service for NetWare on Windows 2000 Professional, the NWLink IPX/SPX/NetBIOS Compatible Transport Protocol is automatically installed.

▶ **To install Client Service for NetWare**

1. Open the Network and Dial-Up Connections Control Panel applet.
2. Right-click the local area connection for which you want to install Client Service for NetWare, then click Properties.
3. In the General tab, click Install.
4. In the Select Network Component Type dialog box, click Client, then click Add.
5. In the Select Network Client dialog box, click Client Service For NetWare, then click OK.

Note To install Client Service for NetWare, you need Administrator rights to the computer running Windows 2000 Professional.

Installing NWLink IPX/SPX/NetBIOS Compatible Transport Protocol

The NWLink protocol is not installed by default during Windows 2000 Setup, as is TCP/IP. However, you have the option of installing NWLink during Setup, along with other protocols, or you can install it later.

▶ **To install NWLink**

1. Open the Network and Dial-Up Connections Control Panel applet.
2. Right-click a local area connection, then click Properties.
3. In the General tab, click Install.
4. In the Select Network Component Type dialog box, click Protocol, then click Add.
5. In the Select Network Protocol dialog box, click NWLink IPX/SPX/NetBIOS Compatible Transport Protocol, then click OK.

   To confirm that NWLink is working properly, at a command prompt, type **ipxroute config**. You will see a table with information about the bindings for which NWLink is configured, as illustrated in Figure 3.5.

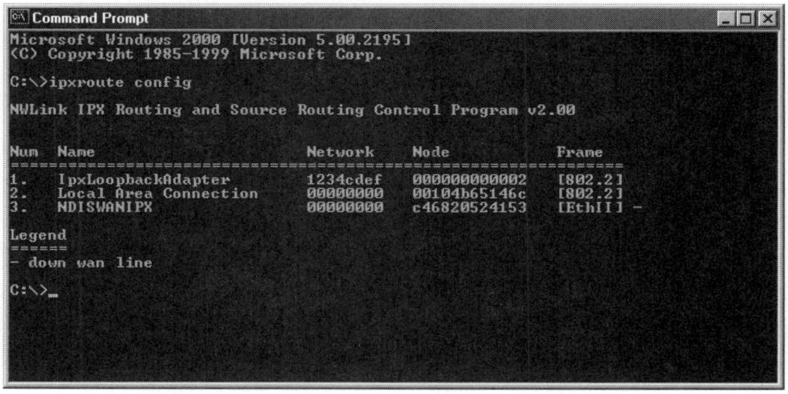

Figure 3.5   NWLink binding information

Internal Network Number

The internal network number is used for internal routing purposes when the computer running Windows 2000 is also hosting IPX services. When calculating the best possible route for transmitting packets to a specified computer, multiple routes with the same route metrics can present ambiguity to computer hosts. When you specify a unique internal network number, you create a virtual network inside the computer. This allows for a singular optimum path from the network to the services running on the computer.

▶ **To change the internal network number**

1. In Control Panel, double-click Network And Dial-Up Connections.

2. Right-click a local area connection, then click Properties.

3. In the General tab, click NWLink IPX/SPX/NetBIOS Compatible Transport Protocol, then click Properties.

4. Type a value in the Internal Network Number box, illustrated in Figure 3.6, then click OK.

Note   Generally, you do not need to change the internal network number.

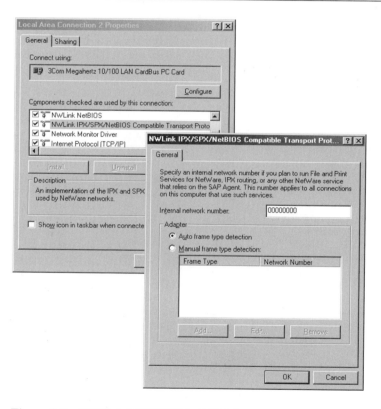

Figure 3.6   NWLink IPX/SPX/NetBIOS Compatible Transport Protocol dialog box

Frame Type and Network Number

The frame type defines the way in which the network adapter, in a computer running Windows 2000, formats data to be sent over a network. To communicate between a computer running Windows 2000 and NetWare servers, you need to configure the NWLink IPX/SPX/NetBIOS Compatible Transport Protocol

(NWLink) on the computer running Windows 2000 with the same frame type as the one used by the NetWare servers. Table 3.2 lists the topologies and frame types supported by NWLink.

Table 3.2 NWLink Frame Types

Network Type	Supported Frame Types
Ethernet	Ethernet II, 802.2, 802.3, 802.2 Subnetwork Access Protocol (SNAP)
Token Ring	802.5 and 802.5 SNAP
Fiber Distributed Data Interface	802.2 and SNAP

Frame types define frame header and footer formats used by the different data-link layer protocols.

During the Auto Detect process, NWLink tries each available frame type in the list for the associated medium access type. For example, on an Ethernet network, Ethernet 802.2, Ethernet 802.3, Ethernet II, and Ethernet Subnetwork Access Protocol (SNAP) are tested to see which frame types NWLink can communicate with. When NWLink receives a response from a NetWare server with one of the frame types, it also receives the network number associated with the frame type for the network segment where the client resides. NWLink then rebinds using the frame type(s) from which it received responses.

The external network number is a unique number that represents a specific network segment and associated frame type. All computers on the same network segment that use a given frame type must have the same external network number, which must be unique for each network segment.

The IPX frame type and network number are set during the initial NetWare server configuration. The Windows 2000 NWLink Auto Detect feature then detects the frame type and network number that were configured on the NetWare server(s). NWLink Auto Detect is the recommended option for configuring both the network number and the frame type.

Occasionally, Auto Detect selects an inappropriate network number and frame type combination for the adapter. Because Auto Detect uses the responses it receives from computers on the same network segment, Auto Detect might select an incorrect frame type and network number if computers responded with incorrect values. This is usually caused by an incorrect manual setting on another computer in the network. If the Auto Detect feature selects an inappropriate frame type and network number for a particular adapter, you can manually reset an NWLink frame type or network number for that given adapter. The frame type and network number on Windows 2000 Professional need to match the frame type and network number configured on the NetWare server. You can specify a frame type and network number of 00000000 to have the network number of the network segment automatically detected.

▶ **To change the network number and frame type**

1. Open the Network and Dial-Up Connections Control Panel applet.

2. Right-click a local area connection, and click Properties.

3. In the General tab, click NWLink IPX/SPX/NetBIOS Compatible Transport Protocol, then click Properties.

4. In the Frame Type drop-down list box, select a frame type.

5. In the Network Number text box, type a network number, then click OK.

Caution   In most cases, you should not need to change the network number and frame type, because Auto Detect should correctly detect the frame type and network number. If you choose an incorrect setting, the client cannot connect to NetWare servers.

Configuring NWLink

To configure NWLink, you must first install the NWLink IPX/SPX/NetBIOS Compatible Transport Protocol and be a member of the Administrators group. You can use the following procedure if you want to bind NWLink to a different network adapter or to manually change the frame type.

▶ **To configure NWLink**

1. Open the Network and Dial-Up Connections Control Panel applet.

2. Right-click a local area connection, then click Properties.

3. In the General tab, click NWLink IPX/SPX/NetBIOS Compatible Transport Protocol, then click Properties.

4. In the General tab, type a value for Internal Network Number or leave this setting at the default value of 00000000.

5. If you want Windows 2000 to automatically select the frame type, click Auto Frame Type Detection, and then click OK. Skip Steps 6 through 10.

   By default, NWLink automatically detects the frame type used by the network adapter to which it is bound. If NWLink detects no network traffic or if multiple frame types are detected in addition to the 802.2 frame type, NWLink sets the frame type to 802.2.

6. To manually set the frame type, click Manual Frame Type Detection.

7. Click Add.

8. In the Manual Frame Detection dialog box, in Frame Type, click a frame type.

   You can determine which external network number, frame type, and internal network number your routers are using by typing **ipxroute config** at a command prompt.

9. In Network Number, type a network number, then click Add.

10. Repeat these steps for each frame type you want to include, then click OK.

Practice: Installing and Configuring NWLink

In this practice, you will install and configure the NWLink IPX/SPX/NetBIOS Compatible Transport Protocol. You will also change the binding order of the NWLink protocol.

▶ **To install and configure NWLink**

1. Open the Network and Dial-Up Connections Control Panel applet.

2. Right-click a local area connection, then click Properties.

   The Local Area Connection Properties dialog box appears.

3. Click Add.

   The Select Network Component Type dialog box appears.

4. Click Protocol, then click ·Add.

5. Select NWLink IPX/SPX/NetBIOS Compatible Transport Protocol, then click OK.

   The Local Area Connection Properties dialog box appears.

6. Select NWLink IPX/SPX/NetBIOS Compatible Transport Protocol, then click Properties. At this point, you can select either auto or manual frame detection.

▶ **To modify the NWLink protocol bindings order**

1. Open the Network and Dial-Up Connections Control Panel applet.

2. Click the connection you want to modify and, on the Advanced menu, click Advanced Settings.

3. In the Adapters And Bindings tab, in Bindings For Adapter Name, click the NWLink protocol and move it down in the list by clicking the Down button, as illustrated in Figure 3.7.

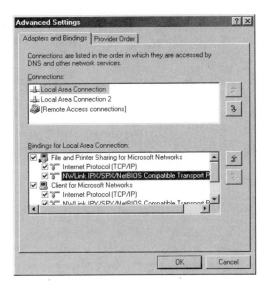

Figure 3.7   The Advanced Settings dialog box

Lesson Summary

IPX/SPX is a protocol stack that is used in Novell networks. The NWLink IPX/SPX/NetBIOS Compatible Transport Protocol allows Windows 2000-based computers to communicate with Novell networks. When you install Client Service for NetWare on Windows 2000, the NWLink IPX/SPX/NetBIOS Compatible Transport Protocol is automatically installed.

To configure NWLink, you must first install the NWLink IPX/SPX/NetBIOS Compatible Transport Protocol and be a member of the Administrators group. The internal network number is used for internal routing purposes when the computer running Windows 2000 is also hosting IPX services. The frame type defines the way in which the network adapter, in a computer running Windows 2000, formats data to be sent over a network. The external network number is a unique number that represents a specific network segment and associated frame type. All computers on the same network segment that use a given frame type must have the same external network number, which must be unique for each network segment.

Review

Answering the following questions will reinforce key information presented in this chapter. If you are unable to answer a question, review the appropriate lesson and then try the question again. Answers to the questions can be found in Appendix A, "Questions and Answers."

1. What is NWLink and how does it relate to Windows 2000?

2. What is SPX?

3. What is Gateway Service for NetWare?

4. When choosing between using Client Service for NetWare and Gateway Service for NetWare, what should you consider?

5. What is the NWLink Auto Detect feature?

C H A P T E R   4

Monitoring Network Activity

About This Chapter

Communication across a network is increasingly important in the work environment. Similar to processors or disks on your system, the behavior of the network has an impact on the operation of your computer. In this chapter, you will learn how to optimize your system's performance by analyzing network performance such as monitoring network traffic and resource utilization. Microsoft Windows 2000 provides two primary utilities for monitoring network performance: System Monitor and Network Monitor. System Monitor, installed with both Windows 2000 Professional and Windows 2000 Server, tracks resource utilization and network throughput. Network Monitor, an optional component for Windows 2000 Server, tracks network throughput in terms of captured network traffic. This chapter focuses on using Network Monitor to examine local traffic.

Before You Begin

To complete this chapter, you must have

- Installed Windows 2000 Server

Lesson 1: Introducing Network Monitor

You can use Microsoft Windows 2000 Network Monitor to view and detect problems on local area networks (LANs). For example, you can use Network Monitor to diagnose hardware and software problems when two or more computers cannot communicate. You can also copy a log of network activity into a file and then send the file to a professional network analyst or support organization. In addition, network application developers can use Network Monitor to monitor and debug network applications as they are developed.

After this lesson, you will be able to
- Install Network Monitor
- Describe the benefits of using Network Monitor

Estimated lesson time: 15 minutes

Understanding Network Monitor

You can use Network Monitor to collect data sent to and from computers and then view and analyze that data. Network Monitor captures frames and packets on the data-link layer through the application layer and presents it graphically. Frames and packets are composed of many different pieces of information including

- Source and destination addresses
- Sequencing information
- Checksums

Network Monitor decodes this information allowing you to analyze network traffic and troubleshoot network problems. In addition to data-link layer data, Network Monitor can also interpret some application layer data, such as Hypertext Transfer Protocol (HTTP) and File Transfer Protocol (FTP). This data can help you troubleshoot browser and Web server interactions.

Practice: Installing Network Monitor

In order for you to capture, display, and analyze network frames, you must install Network Monitor in Windows 2000 and a network protocol called the Network Monitor driver. In this practice, you will install Network Monitor in Windows 2000 Server.

▶ **To install Network Monitor**

1. Click Start, point to Settings, click Control Panel, then select Add/Remove Programs.

2. In Add/Remove Programs, click Add/Remove Windows Components.

3. In the Windows Components Wizard, highlight Management And Monitoring Tools, then click Details.

4. In the Management And Monitoring Tools window, select the Network Monitor Tools check box, as illustrated in Figure 4.1, then click OK.

5. Click Next in the Windows Components Wizard to continue. If you are prompted for additional files, insert your Windows 2000 Server disk or type a path to the location of the files on the network.

6. Click Finish to complete the setup process.

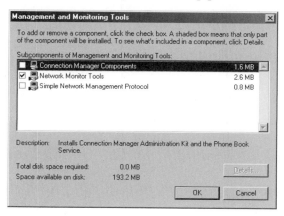

Figure 4.1   Selecting the Network Monitor Tools component

Note   Network Monitor is composed of a gathering agent that collects data, and an administrative utility that displays and analyzes the data. Installing the Network Monitor Tools component in Windows 2000 automatically installs both the Network Monitor utility and agent.

Network Monitor Driver

The Network Monitor driver gathers frames from a network adapter and passes the information to the Network Monitor utility for viewing and analysis. The driver can also forward frames to a remote administrator running the version of Network Monitor included with Microsoft Systems Management Server.

Note   When you install the Network Monitor driver, the Network Segment object is added for use in System Monitor.

Installing the driver alone does not install the Network Monitor administrative utility. If you want to view and analyze Network Monitor data on a system, you must install the Network Monitor Tools Windows component on a computer running Windows 2000 Server.

▶ **To install the Network Monitor driver**

1. Open the Network and Dial-Up Connections Control Panel applet.
2. Right-click the local area connection that you want to monitor, then click Properties.
3. In the Local Area Connection Properties dialog box, click Install.
4. In the Select Network Component Type dialog box, click Protocol, then click Add.
5. In the Select Network Protocol dialog box, click Network Monitor Driver, then click OK.

   If prompted for additional files, insert your Windows 2000 CD or type a path to the location of the files on a network.

Capturing Network Data

Network Monitor uses a process called capturing to examine network frames. You can capture all network traffic to and from the local network card, or capture a specific subset of frames. You can also set Network Monitor to respond to events on your network. You will learn how to capture and analyze network data in Lesson 2.

Lesson Summary

You can use Windows 2000 Network Monitor to view and analyze problems on your network. You can also store a log of network activity into a file and then send the file to a professional network analyst or support organization.

Lesson 2: Using Network Monitor

In this lesson, you will learn how to use Network Monitor to troubleshoot network problems. When using Network Monitor, you should remember two key points:

1. Run Network Monitor at low-usage times or for short periods of time. This decreases the effect on system performance caused by Network Monitor.

2. Capture only as many statistics as you need for evaluation. This prevents you from capturing too much information to make a reasonably quick diagnosis of the problem.

After this lesson, you will be able to
- Capture data using Network Monitor
- Examine frames using Network Monitor
- View data with Network Monitor

Estimated lesson time: 40 minutes

Examining Frames

Network Monitor can capture frames sent to and from a network adapter. Frames are made up of many different pieces of information, including:

- The protocol being used
- The source address of the computer that sent the message
- The destination address of the frame
- The length of the frame

▶ **To capture network frames**

1. Click Start, point to Programs, select Administrative Tools, then choose Network Monitor.

   If you are prompted for a default network on which to capture frames, select the local network from which you want to capture data by default.

2. On the Capture menu, click Start.

Viewing Data

After you have captured data, you can view it in the Network Monitor user interface as illustrated in Figure 4.2. Network Monitor performs some data analysis automatically because it translates raw capture data and organizes it into the structure of a logical frame. Network Monitor also displays overall network segment statistics, including:

- Broadcast frames

- Multicast frames
- Network utilization
- Total bytes received per second
- Total frames received per second

Note   For security reasons, Windows 2000 Network Monitor captures only those frames, including broadcast and multicast frames, sent to or from the local computer.

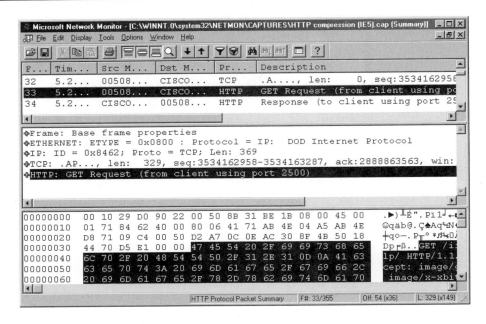

Figure 4.2   The Network Monitor user interface

Network Monitor acts as a Network Driver Interface Specification-Compliant (NDIS) driver to copy frames to the capture buffer, a resizable storage area in memory. The default size is 1 MB; you can adjust the size manually as needed. Make sure there is enough memory free to allow for this.

Note   Because Network Monitor uses the local-only mode of NDIS instead of promiscuous mode (in which the network adapter passes on all frames sent on the network), you can use Network Monitor even if your network adapter does not support promiscuous mode. Networking performance is not affected when you use an NDIS driver to capture frames. (Putting the network adapter in promiscuous mode can add 30 percent or more to the load on the CPU.)

Network Monitor displays session statistics from the first 100 unique network sessions it detects. To reset statistics and see information on the next 100 network sessions detected, on the Capture menu, click Clear Statistics. The Network Monitor Capture window includes the panes listed in Table 4.1.

Table 4.1   Statistics Displayed in the Capture Window

Pane	Displays
Graph	A graphical representation of the activity currently taking place on the network
Session Stats	Statistics about individual sessions currently taking place on the network
Station Stats	Statistics about the sessions participated in by the computer running Network Monitor
Total Stats	Summary statistics about the network activity detected since the capture process began

To capture only those frames that originate with specific computers, determine the addresses of the computers on your network and associate the address with its Domain Name System (DNS) or NetBIOS name. After these associations are made, you can save the names to an address database (.adr) file that can be used to design capture filters and display filters. A capture filter allows you to specify criteria for inclusion in or exclusion from the capture. Figure 4.3 shows the Capture Filter dialog box, accessed from the Capture menu or by pressing F8 in the Capture window.

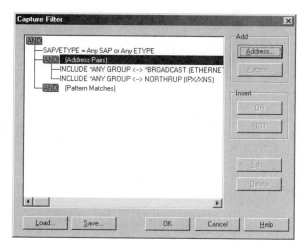

Figure 4.3   The Capture Filter dialog box

Note   Capture filters can significantly increase the processor's workload because each packet must be processed through the filter and either saved or discarded. In some cases, using complex filters might result in missed frames.

To design a capture filter, specify decision statements in the Capture Filter dialog box. By specifying a pattern match in a capture filter, you can

- Limit a capture to frames consisting of specific data types
- Capture frames sent using a specific protocol
- Use a capture trigger to initiate actions following the capture

Table 4.2 describes the trigger types you can use to specify the condition that starts the trigger.

Table 4.2   Descriptions of Capture Triggers

Trigger Type	Description
Nothing	No trigger is initiated. This is the default.
Pattern Match	Initiates the trigger when the specified pattern occurs in a captured frame.
Buffer Space	Initiates the trigger when a specified amount of the capture buffer is filled.
Pattern Match Then Buffer Space	Initiates the trigger when the pattern occurs, and is followed by a specified percentage of the capture buffer being filled.
Buffer Space Then Pattern Match	Initiates the trigger when the specified percentage of the capture buffer fills, and is followed by the occurrence of the pattern in a captured frame.
No Action	No action is taken when a trigger condition is met. This is the default. Even though you select **No Action**, the computer beeps when the trigger condition is met.
Stop Capture	Stops the capture process when the trigger condition is met.
Execute Command Line	Runs a program or batch file when a trigger condition is met. If you select this option, provide a command or the path to a program or batch file.

Note   If your computer uses multiple network adapters, either switch between the two adapters or run multiple instances of Network Monitor. To switch between adapters, on the Capture menu, click Networks, then select a different adapter.

After capturing data, you might want to save it. For example, it is useful to save captures before starting another capture (to prevent loss of the captured data) if you think you might need to analyze the data later or if you need to document network use or problems. When you save captured data, the data in the capture buffer is written to a capture (.cap) file.

Using Display Filters

Similar to a capture filter, you can use a display filter like a database query to specify which frames to display. Because a display filter operates on data that has already been captured, it does not affect the contents of the Network Monitor capture buffer. A frame can be filtered based on the following data:

- The frame's data-link layer or network layer source or destination address.
- The protocols used to send the frame or packet.
- The properties and values the frame contains. (A property is a data field within a protocol header. A protocol's properties, collectively, indicate the purpose of the protocol.)

To design a display filter, specify decision statements in the Display Filter dialog box. Information in the Display Filter dialog box is in the form of a decision tree, which is a graphical representation of a filter's logic. When you modify display filter specifications, the decision tree reflects these modifications. Table 4.3 lists various types of filter items you can use.

Table 4.3 Display Filter Types

Filter Item	Description
Protocol	Specifies the protocols or protocol properties
Address Filter (default is ANY <– –> ANY)	Specifies the computer addresses on which you want to capture data
Property	Specifies property instances that match your display criteria

With display filters, you use AND, OR, and NOT logic, and, unlike a capture filter, you can use more than four address filter expressions. When you display captured data, all available information about the captured frames appears in the Frame Viewer window. To display only those frames sent by a specific protocol, edit the Protocol line in the Display Filter dialog box. Protocol properties are made up of information extracted from the protocol's data. Because the purpose of protocols varies, properties differ from one protocol to another. Suppose, for example, that you have captured a large number of frames using the Server Message Block (SMB) protocol but want to examine only those frames in which the SMB protocol was used to create a directory on your computer. In this instance, you can examine only frames where the SMB command property is equal to make directory. Additionally, you can display only those frames originating from a specific computer, by editing the ANY <- -> ANY line in the Display Filter dialog box.

Reviewing Captured Data

Perform the steps in the following list as part of your routine for reviewing and analyzing captured data:

- Follow a session using source and destination IP address and port numbers.
- If you find a Reset, focus on the sequence numbers and acknowledgments that precede it.

- Use a calculator to see which acknowledgments are associated with the data sent.
- Try to understand the activity you are seeing:
  - Is the sender doing retries?

    If so, note the number of retries and the time elapsed. The default number of retries for Transmission Control Protocol/Internet Protocol (TCP/IP) is 5. This value might be different for other protocols.
  - Did the sender back up and re-send the previous packet?
  - Is the receiver asking for a missed frame by acknowledging a previous sequence number?

A reset can be caused by time-outs at the TCP layer or by time-outs of higher-layer protocols. Resets originating at the TCP layer should be easy to read from the trace. It might be more difficult to determine the cause of resets originating from higher-layer protocols such as the SMB.

For example, an SMB read might time out in 45 seconds and cause a reset of the session even though communications are slow but working at the TCP layer. The trace might only narrow down what component is at fault. From there you might need to use other troubleshooting methods to determine the cause.

To see TCP sequencing when higher-layer protocols are present, start Network Monitor and edit the Expression dialog box, using the steps in the following practice. Figure 4.4 shows the Expression dialog box.

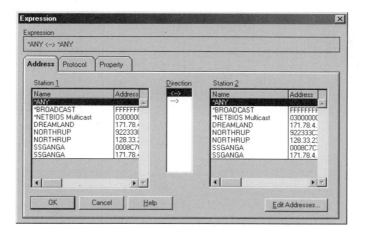

Figure 4.4   The Expression dialog box

Practice: Capturing Frames with Network Monitor

You can use Network Monitor to capture frames from your network data stream and copy those frames to a temporary capture file. In this practice, you will use Network Monitor to display statistics for the captured frames dynamically in the Capture window, and design a capture filter to copy only the frames that match your specific criteria.

▶ **To see TCP sequencing**

1. Start Network Monitor.
2. Display captured data.
3. On the Display menu, click Options.
4. Select Auto (based on protocols in the display filter), then click OK.
5. From the Display menu, click Filter.
6. Double-click Protocol=Any.
7. Click the Protocol tab, then click Disable All.
8. In the Disabled Protocols list box, select TCP.
9. Click the Enable button, then click OK.
10. On the Capture menu, click Start.

Network Monitor Performance Issues

Network Monitor creates a memory-mapped file for its capture buffer. For best results, make sure to create a capture buffer large enough to accommodate the traffic you need. In addition, although you cannot adjust the frame size, you can store only part of the frame, thus reducing the amount of wasted capture buffer space. For example, if you are interested only in the data in the frame header, set the frame size (in bytes) to the size of the header frame. Network Monitor discards the frame data as it stores frames in the capture buffer, thereby using less capture buffer space.

Detecting Network Monitor

To help protect your network from unauthorized use of Network Monitor installations, Network Monitor can detect other installations of Network Monitor that are running on the local segment of your network. When Network Monitor detects other Network Monitor installations running on the network, it displays the following information:

- The name of the computer
- The name of the user logged on at the computer
- The state of Network Monitor on the remote computer (running, capturing, or transmitting)

- The adapter address of the remote computer
- The version number of Network Monitor on the remote computer

In some instances, your network architecture might prevent one installation of Network Monitor from detecting another. For example, if an installation is separated from yours by a router that does not forward multicasts, your installation cannot detect that installation.

Lesson Summary

Network Monitor monitors the network data stream, which consists of all information transferred over a network at any given time. You can use a display filter to determine which frames to display. To design a capture filter, specify decision statements in the Capture Filter dialog box. After you have captured data, you can view it in the Network Monitor user interface. Make sure you specify a capture buffer large enough to accommodate the traffic you need.

Lesson 3: Windows 2000 Administration Tools

Windows 2000 has tools and technologies to simplify administration of computers in your network. Terminal Services provides access to Windows 2000 and the latest Windows-based applications for client computers. It also allows system administrators to remotely administer network resources. In addition, Windows 2000 provides the Simple Network Management Protocol (SNMP), which allows you to monitor and communicate status information from SNMP agents to network management software. In this lesson, you will learn how to use Terminal Services and SNMP to better manage and monitor your network.

After this lesson, you will be able to

- Configure Terminal Server for remote administration
- Install and configure the SNMP service
- Describe how the Windows 2000 SNMP service works

Estimated lesson time: 25 minutes

Windows 2000 Administration Capabilities

With Windows 2000, you can administer computers and services on your network either locally or remotely. Remote administration is using one computer to connect to another computer on a network for management purposes. Windows 2000 allows you to perform administration tasks for all computers on a network centrally, rather than at each computer's physical location. You can either use third-party management systems, or use some of the tools and methods that Windows 2000 provides for remote administration.

Terminal Services

When you enable Terminal Services on a Windows 2000 Server, you either select Remote Administration or Application Server mode, as illustrated in Figure 4.5.

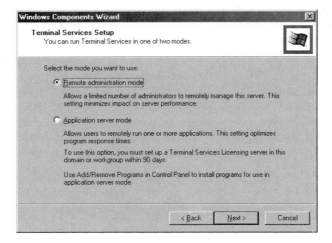

Figure 4.5   Selecting a mode for Terminal Services

Application Server mode allows you to deploy and manage applications from a central location. You can deploy a Windows 2000 interface as well as applications to computers that cannot run Windows 2000. Because Terminal Services is integrated into the Windows 2000 server products, you can run your applications on the server, and provide the user interface to clients that cannot run Windows 2000, such as Windows 3.11 or Windows CE computers connected to a terminal server.

Terminal Services also offers a remote administration mode that allows you to access, manage, and troubleshoot clients. Remote Administration mode allows you to remotely administer Windows 2000 servers over any TCP/IP connection, including remote access, Ethernet, the Internet, wireless, wide area network (WAN), or a virtual private network (VPN). You can install Terminal Services from the Windows Components dialog box of the Add/Remove Programs applet in Control Panel, as illustrated in Figure 4.6.

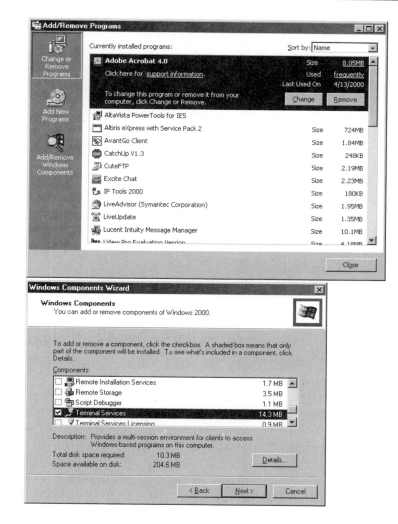

Figure 4.6   Terminal Services option

Using Terminal Server

Although a Remote Desktop Protocol (RDP) connection is configured automatically when Terminal Services is installed, you can use the following general steps to make a new connection. Only one RDP connection can be configured for each network adapter in a Terminal server; however, you can configure additional connections using RDP if you install a network adapter for each connection on your computer.

► **To install a network adapter**

1. Click Start, point to Programs, point to Administrative Tools, and then click Terminal Services Configuration.

2. Right-click the Connections tab, then click Create New Connection.

   The Terminal Services Connection Wizard appears.

3. In the first dialog of the wizard, you select a connection type, such as Microsoft RDP 5.0.

4. In the second dialog of the wizard, you set the encryption level to either Low, Medium, or High. You can also select standard Windows authentication.

5. In the third dialog of the wizard, you can set remote control options and set the level of control.

6. In the fourth dialog of the wizard, you select the connection name, transport type, and an optional comment.

7. In the fifth dialog of the wizard, you can select one or all network adapters for the transport type, and set the number of connections.

8. Click Finish to close the wizard.

Terminal Services allows a maximum of two concurrent Remote Administration connections that do not require licenses. A negligible amount of disk space, memory, and configuration for Terminal Services clients is required.

► **To allow a Terminal Server client computer
to log on to a Windows 2000 Terminal Server**

1. Click Start, point to Programs, point to Administrative Tools, and then click Computer Management.

2. To expand the branches, click the plus symbol (+) next to System Tools, click the plus symbol (+) next to Local Users And Groups, and then click the plus symbol (+) next to Users.

3. Double-click the user that you would like to enable to log on as a Windows NT Terminal Server client.

4. On the Terminal Services Profile tab, click the Allow Logon To Terminal Server check box, as illustrated in Figure 4.7, and then click OK.

5. Close Computer Management.

6. Click Start, point to Programs, point to Administrative Tools, and then click Terminal Services Configuration.

7. Open the Connections folder, and then click Rdp-Tcp.

8. On the Actions menu, click Properties.

9. On the Permissions tab, add the users or groups that you want to have permissions to this Windows NT Terminal Server.

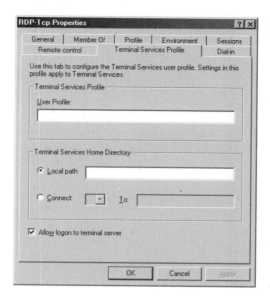

Figure 4.7   Allowing logon to the terminal server

10. Click OK to close the connection's Properties dialog box.

11. Close Terminal Services Configuration.

Simple Network Management Protocol (SNMP)

SNMP is a network-management protocol frequently used in TCP/IP networks to monitor and manage computers and other devices (such as printers) connected to the network. SNMP can be installed and used on any computer running Windows 2000 and TCP/IP or IPX/SPX.

▶   **To install the SNMP service**

1. Click Start, point to Settings, click Control Panel, double-click Add/Remove Programs, and then click Add/Remove Windows Components.

   The Windows Component Wizard appears.

2. In Components, click Management And Monitoring Tools, and then click Details.

   The Management And Monitoring Tools dialog box appears.

3. Select the Simple Network Management Protocol check box, and click OK.

4. In the Windows Component Wizard, click Next.

   The Windows Component Wizard installs SNMP.

5. Click Finish to close the Windows Component Wizard.

Management Systems and Agents

SNMP is comprised of management systems and agents. A management system is any computer running SNMP management software. Although Windows 2000 does not include a management system, many third-party products such as Sun Net Manager or HP Open View are available. A management system requests information from an agent.

As illustrated in Figure 4.8, an agent is any computer running SNMP agent software, such as a Windows 2000-based computer, router, or hub. The Microsoft SNMP service is SNMP agent software. The primary function of an agent is to perform operations that a management system calls for.

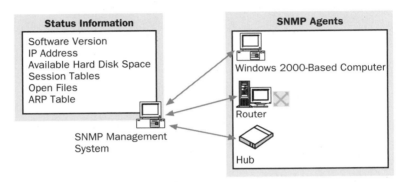

Figure 4.8   SNMP agents

The SNMP agent component also allows a Windows 2000 computer to be administered remotely. The only operation initiated by an agent is called a *trap*. A trap is a message sent by an agent to a management system indicating that an event has occurred on the host running the agent. As illustrated in Figure 4.9, the SNMP management software application does not have to run on the same computer as the SNMP agents.

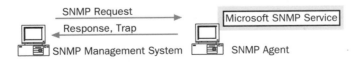

Figure 4.9   SNMP management system and agent

Benefits of SNMP

If you have installed a DHCP server, Internet Information Server, or WINS server software on a Windows 2000-based computer on the network, you can monitor these services by using an SNMP manager program. In addition, you can use Performance Monitor to examine TCP/IP-related performance counters. When you install the SNMP service, TCP/IP performance counters become available in Performance Monitor. The TCP/IP objects that are added include ICMP, TCP, IP, UDP, DHCP, WINS, FTP, Network Interface, and Internet Information Server. As illustrated in Figure 4.10, Performance Monitor is counting

- Active TCP connections
- UDP datagrams received per second
- ICMP messages per second
- Total network interface bytes per second

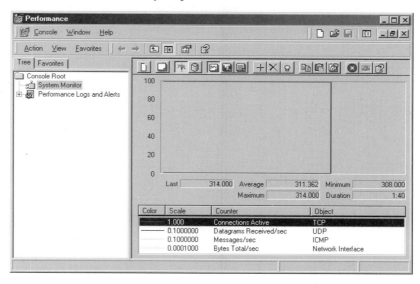

Figure 4.10 SNMP management system and agent

Lesson Summary

SNMP is a network-management protocol widely used in TCP/IP networks. It can be used to communicate between a management program run by an administrator and the network-management agent running on a host or gateway. You can also use SNMP to monitor and control remote hosts and gateways on an internetwork. The Windows 2000 SNMP service allows a Windows 2000 computer to be monitored remotely. The SNMP service can handle requests from one or more hosts, and it can also report network-management information to one or more hosts, in discrete blocks of data called traps. When you install the SNMP service, TCP/IP performance counters become available in Performance Monitor.

Review

Answering the following questions will reinforce key information presented in this chapter. If you are unable to answer a question, review the appropriate lesson and then try the question again. Answers to the questions can be found in Appendix A, "Questions and Answers."

1. What is the purpose of analyzing frames with Network Monitor?

2. What kind of data does a frame contain?

3. What is a capture filter, and what is it used for?

C H A P T E R   5

Implementing IPSec

About This Chapter

To keep network data confidential, you can use Internet Protocol Security (IPSec) to encrypt network traffic among some or all of your systems. IPSec provides the ability to set up authenticated and encrypted network connections between two computers. In this chapter, you will learn how to enable, configure, and monitor IPSec. You will also learn how to customize IPSec policies and rules.

Before You Begin

To complete this chapter, you must have

- Two computers running Microsoft Windows 2000 Server with Network Monitor version 2.0 installed

Lesson 1: Introducing and Enabling IPSec

IPSec is the long-term direction for secure networking. It provides a key line of defense against private network and Internet attacks, balancing ease of use with security. This lesson discusses the technologies collectively referred to as Internet Protocol Security (IPSec).

After this lesson, you will be able to

- Explain the benefits of IPSec
- Describe the architecture of IPSec

Estimated lesson time: 50 minutes

Internet Protocol Security

As the Internet has evolved, along with intranets, the need for security has increased. The main areas of concern are that network traffic is safe from

- Data modification while en route
- Interception, viewing, or copying when intercepted
- Being accessed by unauthenticated parties

IPSec is a framework of open standards for ensuring private, secure communications over IP networks through the use of cryptographic security services. The Microsoft Windows 2000 implementation of IPSec is based on standards developed by the Internet Engineering Task Force (IETF) IPSec working group. IPSec has two goals:

1. To protect IP packets
2. To provide a defense against network attacks

Both goals are met through the use of cryptography-based protection services, security protocols, and dynamic key management. This foundation provides both the strength and flexibility to protect communications among computers on a private network and in remote sites connected by the Internet, and dial-up clients. It can even be used to filter data packets on a network.

IPSec is based on an end-to-end security model, meaning that the only computers that must know about IPSec are the sending and receiving computers. Each handles security at its respective end, with the assumption that the medium over which the communication takes place is not secure. Routers that forward packets between the source and destination are not required to support IPSec. This model allows IPSec to be successfully deployed for your existing enterprise scenarios:

- Local area network (LAN): client/server, peer to peer
- Wide area network (WAN): router to router
- Remote access: dial-up clients and Internet access from private networks

In-Depth Defense

Data must be protected from interception, modification, or access by unauthorized parties. Network attacks can result in system downtime and public exposure of sensitive information.

Network protection strategies generally focus only on preventing attacks from outside the private network by using firewalls, secure routers (security gateways), and user authentication of dial-up access. This is referred to as perimeter security, and it does not protect against attacks from within the network.

User-access control security methods (smart cards, Kerberos version 5 authentication) are not adequate to protect against most network-level attacks, because they rely solely on user names and passwords. Many computers are shared by multiple users. As a result, the computer is often left in a logged-on state, making it unsecured. If a user name and password have been hijacked, user-access control security cannot stop the attacker's access to network resources.

Physical-level protection strategies protect the actual network wires from being accessed and the network access points from being used. However, these strategies cannot guarantee protection when the data crosses multiple networks, as it must on the Internet. Instead, the best method of protecting data is provided with IPSec's end-to-end model: The sending computer encrypts the data prior to transmission (before it ever reaches the network wires) and the receiving computer decrypts the data only after it has been received. For this reason, IPSec should be one of the components in a layered enterprise security plan. It protects your private data in a public environment by providing a strong, cryptography-based defense against attacks. Used in combination with strong user-access control, perimeter, and physical-level security, IPSec ensures an in-depth defense for your data.

Benefits of IPSec

Windows 2000 IPSec is implemented transparently to the user. Users do not have to be in the same domain to communicate with IPSec protection. They can each be in any trusted domain in the enterprise. IPSec Management allows administration to be centralized. Security policies are created by a domain administrator for the most common communication scenarios. These policies are stored in the directory service and assigned to domain policies.

When each computer logs on to the domain, it automatically downloads its security policy, avoiding the need to configure each computer individually. Windows 2000 IPSec provides the following advantages to help achieve a high level of secure communications with a low cost of use:

- Centralized security policy administration, which reduces administrative overhead costs.
- Transparency of IPSec to users and applications.
- Flexibility in configuring security policies that meet the needs of a diverse enterprise.
- Confidentiality services, which prevent unauthorized access to sensitive data as it passes between communicating parties.
- Strong authentication services verify the identity of both the sender and receiver to prevent security compromises caused by using falsely claimed identities.
- Each packet is encrypted using time-specific information to prevent data from being captured and later replayed.
- Long key lengths and dynamic rekeying during ongoing communications help protect against attacks.
- Secure links end to end for private network users within the same domain or across any trusted domain in the enterprise.
- Secure links end to end based on IP address between remote users and users in any domain in the enterprise.

Simplified Deployment

To achieve secure communications with a low cost of ownership, Windows 2000 simplifies the deployment of IPSec with the following features:

Integration with the Windows 2000 Security Framework

IPSec uses the Windows 2000 secure domain as a trust model. By default, IPSec policies use the Windows 2000 default authentication (Kerberos V5 authentication) method to identify and trust communicating computers. Computers that are members of a Windows 2000 domain or trusted domain can easily establish IPSec secured communications.

Centralized IPSec Policy Administration at the Active Directory Level

IPSec policies can be assigned through the Group Policy features of Active Directory. This allows the IPSec policy to be assigned at the domain or organizational unit level, which eliminates the administrative overhead of configuring each computer individually.

Transparency of IPSec to Users and Applications

IPSec's high level of protection comes from its implementation at the IP transport level (network Layer 3). Implementing security at Layer 3 (see Figure 5.1) provides protection for upper-layer protocols in the Transmission Control Protocol/ Internet Protocol (TCP/IP) protocol suite, such as TCP, User Datagram Protocol (UDP), Hypertext Transfer Protocol (HTTP), and even custom protocols that send traffic at the IP layer. The primary benefit of securing information at this low level is that all applications and services using IP for transport of data can be protected with IPSec. This is an improvement over other security mechanisms that operate above Layer 3, such as Secure Sockets Layer (SSL), which only protects applications that use SSL. If protection were required for all applications, then modifications to each application would be necessary.

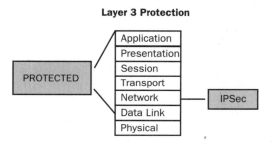

Figure 5.1   Layer 3 protection

Flexible Security Configuration
The security services within each policy can be customized to meet the majority of security requirements for the network and data traffic.

Automatic Key Management
IPSec services dynamically exchange and manage cryptography-based keys between communicating computers.

Automatic Security Negotiation
IPSec services dynamically negotiate a mutual set of security requirements between communicating computers, eliminating the need for both computers to have identical policies.

Public Key Infrastructure Support
Using public key certificates for authentication is supported to allow authentication and secure communication with computers that do not belong to a Windows 2000 trusted domain.

Preshared Key Support
If authentication using the Kerberos V5 protocol or public key certificates is not possible, a preshared key (a shared, secret password) can be configured to enable authentication and trust between the communicating computers.

IP Security Process

This is an overview of the IP Security process, as illustrated in Figure 5.2:

■ An IP packet matches an IP filter that is part of an IPSec policy.

■ The IPSec policy can have several optional security methods. The IPSec driver needs to know which method to use to secure the packet. The IPSec driver requests that Internet Security Association and Key Management Protocol (ISAKMP) negotiate a security method and security key.

■ ISAKMP negotiates a security method and sends it plus a security key to the IPSec driver.

■ The method and key become the IPSec security association (SA). The IPSec driver stores this SA in its database.

■ Both communicating hosts need to encrypt or decrypt IP traffic, so both need to know and store the SA.

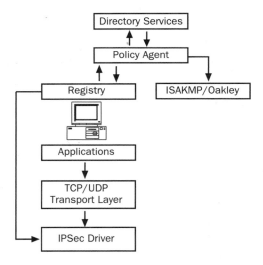

Figure 5.2   IP Security process overview

IPSec Architecture

IPSec is implemented in Windows 2000 using the following components:

■ IPSec policy agent

■ ISAKMP/Oakley Key Management Service

■ IPSec driver

■ IPSec model

IPSec Policy Agent Service

The policy agent is an IPSec mechanism residing on each Windows 2000 computer. The policy agent starts automatically when the computer is started. The policy agent performs the following tasks at the interval specified in the IPSec policy, as illustrated in Figure 5.3:

1. Retrieves the computer's assigned IPSec policy from Windows 2000 Active Directory.

2. If there are no IPSec policies in the directory service or if the policy agent cannot connect to the directory service, it attempts to read the policy from the computer's registry. The policy agent service stops if there are no IPSec policies in the directory service or registry.

3. If there are policies in the directory service, the data transfer of policy information from the directory service to the computer is protected with data integrity and encryption services.

4. Sends the policy information to the IPSec driver, the ISAKMP/Oakley service, and the computer's registry.

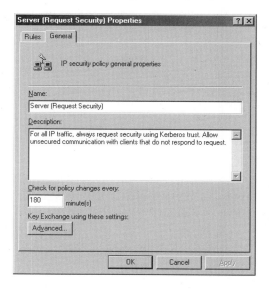

Figure 5.3   Tasks performed by the policy agent

ISAKMP/Oakley Key Management Service

This service is an IPSec mechanism residing on each computer running Windows 2000. Before IP datagrams can be transmitted from one computer to another, a security association must be established between the two computers. A security association is a set of parameters that defines the common security services and mechanisms used to protect the communication, such as keys and security properties.

The ISAKMP centralizes security association management, reducing connection time. The Oakley protocol generates the actual keys that will be used to encrypt and decrypt the transferred data. ISAKMP/Oakley performs a two-phase operation:

1. Establishes a secure channel between the two computers for the communication. To achieve this, it authenticates computer identities, and exchanges keying data to establish the shared, secret key the computers will use to encrypt and decrypt the data.

2. Establishes a security association between the two computers, which is passed to the IPSec driver, along with the shared key, on both the sending and receiving computers.

The policy agent automatically starts the ISAKMP/Oakley service. This service will not start automatically or manually unless the policy agent service is running. If a security association cannot be established, the IPSec policy can be configured to either block communication or accept unsecured communication.

IPSec Driver

The IPSec driver (IPSEC.SYS) resides on each computer running Windows 2000. The driver watches all IP datagrams for a match with a filter list in the computer's security policy. The filter list defines which computers and networks require secure communications. If a filter match is found, the IPSec driver on the sending computer uses the SA and shared key to encrypt the data and sends it to the receiving computer. The IPSec driver on the receiving computer decrypts the transferred data and passes it to the receiving application.

Note   The policy agent automatically starts the IPSec driver.

The IPSec Model

Figure 5.4 shows two users on intranet computers running Windows 2000 Server. Both Computer A and Computer B have an active IPSec policy.

1. Alice launches the File Transfer Protocol (FTP) application from Host A and sends data to Bob, who will receive it on Host B.

2. The IPSec driver on Host A notifies the ISAKMP/Oakley service that IPSec is needed for this communication by using the policies in the registry written by the policy agent.

3. The ISAKMP/Oakley services on Host A and Host B establish a shared key and SA.

4. The IPSec drivers on Host A and Host B each receive the key and SA.

5. The IPSec driver on Host A uses the key to encrypt the data and sends the data to Host B.

6. Host B's IPSec driver decrypts the data and passes it to the receiving application, where Bob retrieves the data.

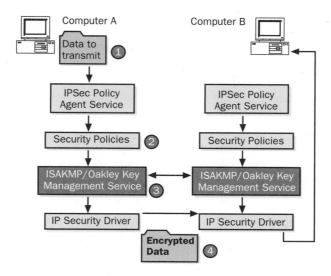

Figure 5.4   IPSec policy flow to encrypt data between two computers

---

Note   Any routers or switches that are in the path between the communicating computers should only participate in forwarding the encrypted IP datagrams to their destination. However, if a firewall or other security gateway is between the communicating computers, IP forwarding must be enabled or special filtering must be created to permit forwarding of encrypted IP datagrams.

Considerations for IPSec

IPSec provides encryption of outgoing packets, but at a cost in performance. IPSec implements symmetric encryption of network data that is very efficient. However, for servers supporting many simultaneous network connections, the additional cost of encryption is significant, so you need to plan to test IPSec using simulated network traffic before deploying it. Testing is also important if you are using a third-party hardware or software product to provide IP security. You can define IPSec policies for each domain. You can configure IPSec policies to

- Specify the types of authentication and the levels of confidentiality required between IPSec clients

- Specify the lowest security level at which communications are allowed to occur between IPSec-aware clients

- Allow or prevent communications with non-IPSec-aware clients

- Require all communications to be encrypted for confidentiality, or you can allow communications in plaintext

Consider using IPSec to provide security for the following applications:

- Peer-to-peer communications over your organization's intranet, such as legal-department or executive-committee communications.
- Client/server communications to protect sensitive (confidential) information stored on servers.
- Remote access (dial-up or virtual private network [VPN]) communications (For VPNs using IPSec with Layer Two Tunneling Protocol [L2TP], remember to set up Group Policy to permit auto enrollment for IPSec certificates. For detailed information about machine certificates for L2TP over IPSec VPN connections, see Windows 2000 Help.).
- Secure router-to-router WAN communications.

Consider the following strategies for IPSec in your network security deployment plan:

- Identify clients and servers to use IPSec communications.
- Identify whether client authentication is based on Kerberos trust or digital certificates.
- Describe each IPSec policy, including rules and filter lists.
- Describe certificate services needed to support client authentication by digital certificates.
- Describe enrollment processes and strategies to enroll users for IPSec certificates.

Lesson Summary

IPSec is a framework of open standards for ensuring private, secure communications over IP networks through the use of cryptographic security services. IPSec is transparent to the user and provides a high level of secure communications with a low cost of use.

The architecture of IPSec is comprised of four major components: IPSec policy agent, ISAKMP/Oakley Key Management Service, IPSec driver, and IPSec model.

Lesson 2: Configuring IPSec

The Microsoft Management Console (MMC) can be used to create and configure IPSec policies. It can be configured to centrally manage policy (for Active Directory), manage policy locally, or manage policy remotely for a computer. In this lesson you will explore various screens used to configure IPSec. Additionally, you will create a test IP Security policy.

After this lesson, you will be able to

- Describe how to implement IPSec
- Configure IPSec policies
- Describe the various property sheets of an IPSec policy, Authentication Method, IP Packet Filtering, Filter Actions, and additional IPSec tasks

Estimated lesson time: 30 minutes

Prerequisites for Implementing IPSec

The computers in your network need to have an IPSec policy defined that is appropriate for your network security strategy. Computers in the same domain might be organized into groups with IPSec policy applied to the groups. Computers in different domains might have complementary IPSec policies to support secure network communications.

How to Implement IPSec

You can view the default IP Security policies in the Group Policy snap-in to MMC. The policies are listed under IP Security Policies on Active Directory: Group Policy Object\Computer Configuration\Windows Settings\Security Settings\IP Security Policies on Active Directory.

You can also view IPSec policies by using the IP Security Policy Management snap-in to MMC. Each IPSec policy is governed by rules that determine when and how the policy is applied. Right-click a policy and select Properties. The Rules tab lists the policy rules. Rules can be further subdivided into filter lists, filter actions, and additional properties. The default snap-in is started from the Administrative Tools menu; this allows configuration of the local computer only. To centrally manage policy for multiple computers, add the IP Security Management snap-in to an MMC.

Configuring IPSec Policies

The initial window displays three predefined policy entries: Client (Respond Only), Secure Server (Require Security), and Server (Request Security). By default, none of these policies is enabled. These policies are shown in Figure 5.5.

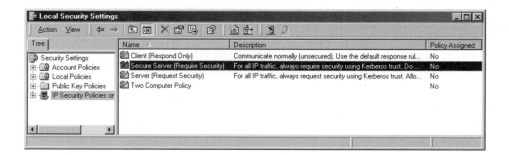

Figure 5.5   MMC of a Windows 2000 member server

These defaults are the same whether the IPSec policy is local or stored in Active Directory as part of a group policy. In this example, the policy is local to a member server.

- The Client (Respond Only) policy allows communications in plaintext but will respond to IPSec requests and attempt to negotiate security. This policy effectively allows clear-text communication but will attempt to negotiate security if a security request is made. Uses Kerberos V5 for authentication.

- The Server (Request Security) policy causes the server to attempt to initiate secure communications for every session. If a client who is not IPSec-aware initiates a session, it will be allowed.

- The Secure Server (Require Security) policy requires Kerberos trust for all IP packets sent from this computer, with the exception of broadcast, multicast, Resource Reservation Setup Protocol (RSVP), and ISAKMP packets. This policy does not allow unsecured communications with clients. Therefore, any clients who connect to a server with this policy must be IPSec-aware.

To edit policies, right-click on the policy and select Properties.

Note   Only one policy can be assigned at a time. If an IPSec policy is configured in several overlapping group policies, the normal group policy hierarchy applies.

Connection Types

The Connection Type tab can be chosen from the Edit Rule Properties dialog box (see Figure 5.6). It will also be displayed as part of the Rule Creation Wizard.

Note   All policy settings can be configured through wizards. Use of the wizards is turned on by default, but can be turned off by deselecting the Use Add Wizard check box.

Figure 5.6   Edit Rule Properties dialog box

Designating a connection type for each rule will determine which computer connections (network adapters or modems) will be affected by an IPSec policy. Each rule has a connection property that designates whether the rule applies to LAN connections, Remote Access connections, or all network connections.

Authentication Method

The authentication method defines how each user is going to be assured that the other computers or users really are who they say they are. As illustrated in Figure 5.7, each authentication method provides the necessary pieces to assure identity. Windows 2000 supports three authentication methods:

- **Kerberos.**   The Kerberos V5 security protocol is the default authentication technology. The Kerberos protocol issues tickets, or virtual proof-of-identity cards, when a computer logs on to a trusted domain. This method can be used for any clients running the Kerberos V5 protocol (whether or not they are Windows-based clients) who are members of a trusted domain.

- **Certificates.**   This requires that at least one trusted certificate authority (CA) has been configured. Windows 2000 supports X.509 Version 3 certificates, including CA certificates generated by commercial certifying authorities. A rule may specify multiple authentication methods. This ensures that a common method can be found when negotiating with a peer.

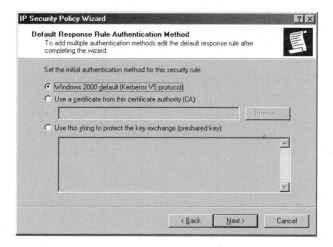

Figure 5.7   Default Response Rule Authentication Method dialog box

- **Preshared Key.**   This is a shared key that is secret and is previously agreed
  on by two users. It is quick to use and does not require the client to run the
  Kerberos protocol or have a public key certificate. Both parties must manually
  configure IPSec to use this preshared key. This is a simple method for authenticating non-Windows-based hosts and stand-alone hosts.

Note   The key derived from the authentication is for authentication *only*; it is *not*
the key used to encrypt or authenticate the data.

Each rule may be configured with one or more authentication methods. Each
configured authentication method appears in a list in the order of preference. If
the first method cannot be used, then the next will be attempted.

IP Packet Filtering

IP Security is applied to packets as they are sent and received. Packets are matched
against filters when being sent (outbound) to see if they should be secured,
blocked, or passed through in clear text. Packets are matched when received
(inbound) to also see if security should be negotiated, or if the packets should be
blocked or passed through and permitted into the system.

Individual filter specifications are grouped into a filter list to enable complex
patterns of traffic to be grouped and managed as one named filter list, such as
Building 7 File Servers, or All Blocked Traffic. Filter lists can be shared as
necessary between different IPSec rules in the same policy or in different IPSec
policies. Filter specifications should be set for incoming and outgoing traffic.

- Input filters, which apply to traffic received, allow the receiving computer to match the traffic with the IP filter list, respond to requests for secure communication, or match the traffic with an existing SA and decrypt the secured packets.

- Output filters, which apply to traffic leaving a computer toward a destination, trigger a security negotiation that must take place before traffic is sent.

Important   Although input and output filters are defined and used in the filter list, it is unclear in the user interface as to which filter is being created. The source and destination addresses determine whether the filter is inbound or outbound.

There must be a filter to cover any traffic scenarios to which the associated rule applies. A filter contains the following parameters:

1. The source and destination address of the IP packet. As illustrated in Figure 5.8, the following address options can be chosen when creating or editing the filter:

   - **My IP Address.**   The IP address of the local machine.

   - **Any IP Address.**   Unicast addresses only. IPSec does not support multicast or broadcast addresses.

   - **A Specific IP Address.**   This is a specific IP address on the local network or on the Internet.

   - **A Specific IP Subnet.**   This includes any IP address on a specified IP subnet.

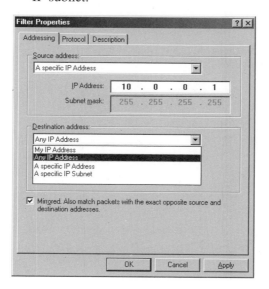

Figure 5.8   IP packet Filter Properties dialog box

Note   IPSec populates My IP Address with the first bound IP address only. If the machine is multihomed, IPSec will use only one of the IP addresses, not both. Routing and Remote Access clients are considered to be multihomed, and therefore IPSec may not populate the IP address properly.

2. The protocol over which the packet is being transferred. This automatically defaults to cover all IP client protocols in the TCP/IP suite.

   Table 5.1 provides a list of the protocol types available in the Protocol tab in the Filter Properties dialog box illustrated in Figure 5.9.

Table 5.1   Protocol Filtering

Protocol Type	Description
ANY	Any Protocol
EGP	Exterior Gateway Protocol
HMP	Host Monitoring Protocol
ICMP	Internet Control Message Protocol
Other	Unspecified protocol based on IP protocol number
RAW	Raw data on top of IP
RDP	Reliable Datagram Protocol
RVD	MIT Remote Virtual Disk
TCP	Transmission Control Protocol
UDP	User Datagram Protocol
XNS-IDP	Xerox NS IDP

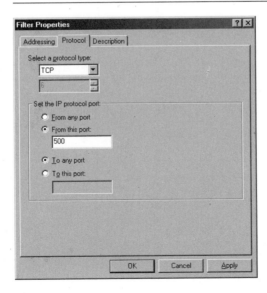

Figure 5.9   Filter Properties dialog box

3. The source and destination port of the protocol for TCP and UDP. This also defaults to cover all ports, but can be configured to apply only to packets sent or received on a specific port.

Select the filter properties when editing or creating a filter. Filters can be managed globally by right-clicking on the managed computer in the left pane. They can also be managed within each of the policies' Rule Properties pages. The Filter Creation Wizard allows these properties to be configured.

Mirroring

Mirroring allows a filter to match packets with the exact opposite source and destination addresses. An outbound filter specifying the IP address as the source address and the second computer as the destination address, for example, will automatically create an inbound filter specifying the second computer as the source address and the initiating computer's IP address as the destination.

Note   The mirrored filter does not actually show in the filter list. Instead, the Mirrored check box will be checked in the Filter Properties dialog box.

If Host A wants to always exchange data securely with Host B

- To send secured data to Host B, Host A's IPSec policy must have a filter specification for any outbound packets going to Host B.

- To receive secured data from Host A, Host B's IPSec policy must have a filter specification for any inbound packets from Host A, or must have a policy with the default-response rule set to active.

- Mirroring would allow each host to send or receive from the other host without creating another filter to do so.

Filter Actions

The filter action specifies what security action to take once a filter has been triggered. The action specifies whether to block the traffic, permit the traffic, or negotiate the security for the given connection. The negotiation consists of support for *only* authenticity and integrity using the authentication header (AH) protocol, or for integrity and confidentiality using the Encapsulating Security Payload (ESP) protocol. Each filter action can be customized, giving the administrator the option of choosing which protocols require authenticity and which protocols require confidentiality.

One or more negotiated filter actions may be specified. As illustrated in Figure 5.10, the filter actions appear as a list with the first method listed taking precedence. If that filter action cannot be negotiated, then the next filter action will be attempted.

Figure 5.10   Secure Initiator Negotiation policy properties

It is also possible to choose either high or medium security rather than specifying a custom method. High security both encrypts and provides data integrity. Medium security provides only for data integrity.

Additional IPSec Tasks

Several other tasks available to the administrator are accessed by right-clicking on the IP Security Policy icon in the left window. These tasks include:

- **Manage IP Filter Lists and Filter Actions.**   This allows the administrator to configure filters and filter actions separate from individual rules. Once a rule is created, the filters or filter actions may be activated, as illustrated in Figure 5.11.

- **Check Policy Integrity.**   Because Active Directory takes the last information saved as current, if multiple administrators are editing a policy, the links between policy components could be broken. For example:

Policy A uses Filter A.

Policy B uses Filter B.

This means that Filter A has a link to Policy A, and Filter B links to Policy B.

Suppose Bob edits Policy A, and adds a rule that uses Filter C.

At the same time, Alice edits Policy B from a different location, and adds a rule that also uses Filter C.

If both save the changes simultaneously, Filter C could link to both Policy A and Policy B; however, that timing is unlikely. Instead, if Policy A is saved last, it will overwrite the link from Filter C to Policy B. Filter C will link only to

Policy A. This will cause problems in the future when Filter C is modified, because Policy A users will pick up the new changes, but Policy B users will not.

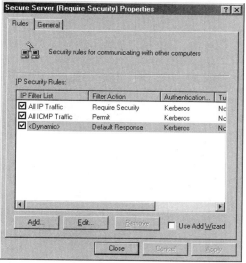

Figure 5.11   The Rules tab of the Main Policy properties dialog box

The policy integrity check eliminates this problem by verifying the links in all IPSec policies. It is a good idea to run the integrity check after modifications to a policy. Several other tasks available to the administrator are accessed by right-clicking on the IP Security Policy icon in the left window. These tasks are described in the following list:

- **Restore Default Policies.**   Restores the predefined policies to the original configuration.
- **Import Policies.**   Allows policies to be imported from another host on the network.
- **Export Policies.**   Allows a policy to be exported to another host on the network.

Practice: Testing IPSec

In this practice, you will activate a built-in IPSec policy to see that it does block communications if the traffic cannot be secured. If both computers running Windows 2000 Server are members of the same or trusted Windows 2000 Server secure domains, then the built-in IPSec policies can be used to easily establish secure communications. Otherwise, you will need to configure your own IPSec policy for testing on each computer with the steps provided in later sections.

Before you continue with the lesson, run the Ch05.exe demonstration file located in the Media folder on the Supplemental Course Materials CD-ROM that accompanies this book. The file provides an overview of testing IPSec.

▶ **To test communications with another computer**

1. Ping the other computer's IP address.

   You should receive four replies to the PING. This verifies that you can communicate with your partner.

▶ **To add IPSec to the MMC**

1. Using the Administrative Tools on the Start menu, run the Local Security Policy MMC plug-in.

2. Select IP Security Policies On Local Machine in the left pane.

3. In the right pane, right-click on Secure Server (Require Security), then click Properties.

4. In the Secure Server (Require Security) Properties dialog box, click Add. The Security Rule Wizard appears.

5. At the Welcome screen, click Next.

6. At the Tunnel Endpoint screen, click Next.

7. At the Network Type screen, click Next.

8. At the Authentication Method screen, click the Use This String To Protect The Key Exchange (Preshared Key) radio button. Type **MSPRESS** in the scroll box, then click Next.

9. Click All IP Traffic, then click Next at the IP Filter List screen.

10. Click Require Security, then click Next at the Filter Action screen.

11. Click Finish to close the wizard.

12. Now that you have added a restrictive filter list, deselect all default filter lists.

13. Close the Secure Server (Require Security) Properties dialog box.

14. Right-click on Secure Server (Require Security), and click Assign from the pop-up menu.

15. Ping your partner host.

    Notice that the PING was unsuccessful.

16. To let yourself communicate on the network again, unassign the Secure Server (Require Security) policy using the pop-up menu.

Lesson Summary

Three predefined policy entries—Client (Respond Only), Secure Server (Require Security), and Server (Request Security)—come with Windows 2000. These can be modified or removed at any time. Additionally, customized policies can be added. Using IPSec, Windows 2000 can support various host authentication methods and provide IP packet filtering, thus allowing computers to communicate or deny communication based on a wide variety of rules and filters.

Lesson 3: Customizing IPSec Policies and Rules

IPSec is easily customizable with policies and rules. In this lesson you will explore how to secure a network using these various methods, taking into consideration such things as proxies, network address translation (NAT), Simple Network Management Protocol (SNMP), Dynamic Host Configuration Protocol (DHCP), Domain Name System (DNS), Windows Internet Name Service (WINS), and domain controllers.

After this lesson, you will be able to

- Explain IPSec policies and rules
- Describe how to configure IPSec for use with firewalls, NAT, and proxies
- Describe how to use IPSec to secure a network with SNMP, DHCP, DNS, WINS, or domain controllers

Estimated lesson time: 40 minutes

Policy-Based Security

Strong, cryptographic security methods have become necessary to protect communications, but they can also increase administrative overhead. IPSec reduces this by providing policy-based administration. Your network security administrator can configure IPSec policies to meet the security requirements of a user, group, application, domain, site, or global enterprise. Windows 2000 provides an administrative interface, called IPSec Policy Management, to define IPSec policies for individual computers or groups of computers within Active Directory.

IPSec Policies

An IPSec policy is a named collection of rules and key exchange settings. The policy may be assigned as a domain security policy or an individual computer's security policy. A domain computer will automatically inherit the IPSec policy assigned to the domain security policy when it logs on to the domain. If a computer is not connected to a domain (for example, a roving laptop or a stand-alone server), IPSec policies are stored in and retrieved from the computer registry.

This allows great flexibility in configuring security policies for groups of similar computers or individual computers with special requirements. For example, one security policy can be created for all users on the same network or all users in a particular department. IPSec policies are created with the IPSec Management snap-in, as illustrated in Figure 5.12, for a Windows 2000 member server.

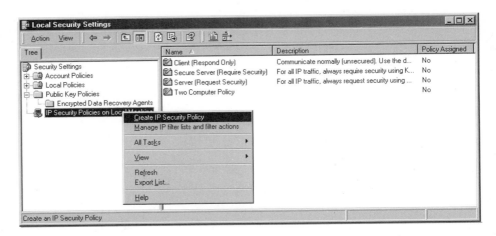

Figure 5.12   MMC of a Windows 2000 member server

Rules

Rules govern how and when IPSec is used. A rule contains a list of IP filters and specifies the security actions that will take place upon a filter match. A rule is a collection of

- IP filters
- Negotiation policies
- Authentication methods
- IP tunneling attributes
- Adapter types

Each security policy may contain multiple rules. This provides the flexibility of assigning one IPSec policy to multiple computers with different communication scenarios. For example, one policy may cover all users in a department or network, but multiple rules may be required: one for intranet communications and another for Internet communications that require tunneling.

IP Filters and Filter Specifications

All rules are based on packets matching an IP filter. Each rule may only have a single IP filter active. The IPSec driver watches each IP datagram for a match with the active IP filter. If a match occurs, the action specified in the associated rule is implemented for that communication.

Filter Specifications

IP datagrams are checked for a match against each filter specification. Filter specifications contain the following properties:

- The source and destination address of an IP datagram, based on IP address, DNS name, or by a specific subnet or network
- The protocol, TCP or UDP
- The specific source and destination protocol port numbers for either TCP or UDP

Security Methods and Negotiation Policies

The level of security used for a communication is determined by the security methods and the negotiation policy.

Security Methods

Each security method specifies a unique level of security to be used for the communication. Multiple security methods can be part of a single negotiation policy to increase the ability of two computers finding a common security method. The ISAKMP/Oakley service on each computer traverses the list of security methods in descending order until a common method is found. You can choose between preconfigured security methods or your own custom method:

- **High.**   The IP ESP provides confidentiality, integrity, authentication, and antireplay protection services.
- **Medium.**   The IP AH security protocol provides integrity, authentication, and antireplay protection services. Confidentiality is not a part of AH.
- **Custom.**   In addition to choosing between ESP and AH, expert users can specify the algorithms for authentication, integrity, and confidentiality.

Negotiation Policies

A negotiation policy is a named collection of security methods. Each rule can have a single negotiation policy specified as currently active. If a common security method cannot be established between two computers, the negotiation policy can be configured to refuse communication with that computer or send the data in the clear (without encryption).

Because IPSec does not disturb the original IP header, it is considered normal IP traffic and is routed as such. This is also true for both transport and tunnel modes.

ESP and Routers

ESP neither encrypts nor authenticates the IP header, leaving it undisturbed. Even in tunnel mode, where the original IP header is encrypted, routing does not pose a problem. The new tunnel IP header (left undisturbed) is used to route between the tunnel endpoints. Once the packet reaches the tunnel destination endpoint, it is authenticated and decrypted. The original IP packet is forwarded without IPSec authentication or encryption to the final destination.

AH and Routers

AH uses all fields in the IP header to create the Integrity Check Value (ICV). Because routers modify fields in the IP header as they forward packets, this could cause problems; however, the fields that may be modified are set to zero for ICV calculation. Therefore, routers can change the mutable fields (Time to Live [TTL], checksum, and so on) without affecting the ICV calculation. At the receiving end, IPSec once again sets the mutable fields to zero for ICV calculation.

The same is true for tunnel mode, where the new tunnel IP header would be used to calculate the ICV, but the mutable fields would be set to zero. At the tunnel destination endpoint, the hash is verified and the original IP packet forwarded without further authentication.

IPSec Through Firewalls

Any routers or switches in the data path between the communicating hosts will simply forward the encrypted and/or authenticated IP packets to their destination. However, if there is a firewall or filtering router, IP forwarding must be enabled for the following IP protocols and UDP port:

- **IP Protocol ID of 51.** Both inbound and outbound filters should be set to pass AH traffic.
- **IP Protocol ID of 50.** Both inbound and outbound filters should be set to pass ESP traffic.
- **UDP Port 500.** Both inbound and outbound filters should be set to pass ISAKMP traffic.

Be aware that these settings would be used to allow IPSec traffic to pass through the firewall only when using transport mode, or if the firewall is on the public side of the tunnel server. IPSec cannot be used in such a way that the firewall would implement IPSec on all incoming or outgoing packets. The router would have to create and maintain all the SAs associated with each connection.

Note   Traditional firewall filtering (filtering on TCP or UDP ports) cannot be done to ESP traffic, as the port numbers are encrypted.

IPSec Through NAT and Proxies

It is not possible to use IPSec through a NAT or application proxy. Even though the IP header is left intact, the encryption and authentication do not allow for other fields in the packet to be changed.

NAT

The following sections will discuss why IPSec does not work through NAT.

Inability to Distinguish Multiple IPSec Data Streams

The ESP header contains the Security Parameters Index (SPI). The SPI is used in conjunction with the destination IP address in the standard IP header and IPSec header to identify an IPSec SA.

For outbound traffic from the NAT gateway, the destination IP address is not changed, but the source IP address is. For inbound traffic to the NAT, the destination IP address must be mapped to a private IP address. For IPSec to work properly, the SPI would also have to be mapped. Although mapping the SPI could be done, it would require the SPI field to change. If the SPI field changes, the ICV calculation would not validate.

The same holds true for AH, where the SPI is part of the AH and is used in calculating the ICV.

Inability to Change TCP and UDP Checksums

The UDP and TCP headers contain a checksum that includes the source and destination IP address of the standard IP header. The addresses in the standard IP header cannot be changed without invalidating the checksum in the TCP and UDP headers. Therefore, NAT cannot update the UDP and TCP headers because they are within the encrypted portion of the ESP or have been used in the ICV calculation.

Application Proxies

Because application proxies operate at the application layer they would need to be IPSec-aware and have a security association for each IPSec client. This is obviously unreasonable and not provided by application proxies.

Other IPSec Considerations

In this section, you will learn about other IPSec configuration considerations. This includes secured communications with SNMP and running server services such as DNS and WINS.

Securing SNMP

All SNMP-enabled systems must be configured to use IPSec, or at a minimum, the IPSec policies must be configured to allow unsecured communications if all the SNMP-enabled hosts *cannot also* be IPSec-enabled. Otherwise, secured communication will fail and SNMP messages will not be exchanged.

IPSec does not automatically encrypt the SNMP protocol. The only exceptions are the predefined polices Secure Initiator and Lockdown, which have been configured to secure SNMP traffic as well. To secure SNMP, add two pairs of filter specifications to a new or existing policy on the SNMP-enabled host.

The first pair would be for typical SNMP traffic (SNMP messages) and would consist of one inbound and one outbound filter specification.

▶ **In the Addressing page of the IP Filter List dialog box**

1. Set the Source address to the IP address of the SNMP management system.
2. Set the Destination address to My IP Address, which will translate to the IP address of the host to which the policy is assigned (an SNMP agent).
3. Enable Mirrored to automatically create the outbound filter specification.

▶ **In the Protocol page of the IP Filter List dialog box**

1. Set the Protocol Type to TCP or UDP (if both are required, create an additional filter specification).
2. Set From This Port and To This Port to 161.

The second set of filter specifications would be for SNMP trap messages and would also consist of one inbound and one outbound filter specification.

▶ **In the Addressing page of the IP Filter List dialog box**

1. Set the Source address to the IP address of the SNMP management system.
2. Set the Destination address to My IP Address, which will translate to the IP address of the host to which the policy is assigned (an SNMP agent).
3. Enable Mirrored to automatically create the outbound filter specification.

▶ **In the Protocol page of the IP Filter List dialog box**

1. Set the Protocol Type to TCP or UDP (if both are required, create an additional filter specification).
2. Set From This Port and To This Port to 162.

The SNMP management system or console must also be IPSec-enabled. The SNMP service in Windows 2000 supports SNMP management software, but does not currently include SNMP management software. To secure SNMP traffic with IPSec, the third-party management software must be IPSec-capable.

DHCP, DNS, WINS Servers, or Domain Controllers

If enabling IPSec for any servers running these services, consider whether or not all their clients are IPSec-capable. Ensure that the policies, especially the authentication and negotiation settings, are compatible. Otherwise, secure negotiation might erroneously fail, and clients will not be able to access network resources.

When DNS Is Not IPSec-Enabled

To specify a host's DNS name in an IP Filter List specification (rather than the IP address) if DNS servers are not IPSec-enabled, a special policy setting is required. Otherwise, IPSec will not be able to successfully resolve the DNS host name to a valid IP address. The setting consists of a filter specification to exempt traffic between the host and the DNS server from requiring IPSec.

Add a filter specification to the applicable policy and rule.

▶ **In the Addressing page of the IP Filter List dialog box**

1. Set the Source address to My IP Address.

2. Set the Destination address to the IP address of the DNS server.

3. Enable Mirrored to automatically create the outbound filter specification.

▶ **In the Protocol page of the IP Filter List dialog box**

1. Set From This Port and To This Port to 53. (This is the common port used by most DNS servers for communication; set this to whatever port the DNS service has been configured to for traffic use.)

Additionally, the negotiation policy for this rule must be set to Do Not Allow Secure Communication: No security methods should be configured. This will ensure that DNS traffic is never secured with IPSec.

TCP/IP Properties

If a computer that is a member of a domain is disconnected from its domain, then a copy of the domain IPSec properties will be retrieved from the computer's registry. If the computer is not a member of a domain, a local IPSec policy will be stored in the registry. The TCP/IP properties allow the nondomain computer to always use IPSec, use IPSec only if possible, or never use IPSec.

Note If the computer is connected to a domain, these properties will not be configurable.

Practice: Building a Custom IPSec Policy

Several built-in policies have been defined to permit you to examine and investigate their behavior and configuration. However, most deployments of IPSec will require custom policies to be built. In this practice, you will build your own IPSec policy. You should perform this practice on both computers.

▶ **To build your own IPSec policy**

1. Using the Administrative Tools on the Start menu, run the Local Security Policy MMC plug-in.

2. In the left pane, right-click IP Security Policy On Local Machine.

3. From the pop-up menu, choose Create IP Security Policy.

4. When the wizard appears, click Next to continue.

5. Type the policy name **Two Computer Policy**, then click Next.

6. Accept the default for the Requests For Secure Connection screen by leaving the Default Response Rule check box checked, then click Next.

7. Accept the default response rule for Kerberos Authentication, then click Next.

8. Be sure to leave the Edit Properties check box checked.

9. Click Finish to complete the initial setup.

10. The Properties box appears. *Do not close it.*

At this point, you still have not configured your custom rule. Only the default response rule properties have been configured.

What is the purpose of the default response rule?

For the remainder of this practice, you will not use the Add wizards when configuring IPSec policies. Instead, you will configure policies manually by navigating through the dialog boxes and property tabs.

▶ To add a new rule

1. At the bottom of the Properties dialog box, deactivate the Use Add Wizard check box.

2. In the Rules tab of the Property screen, click Add.

3. The New Rule Properties screen appears.

You will be configuring filters between your computer and your second computer. You will need to configure an outbound filter specifying your IP address as the source address and your second computer's IP as the destination address. The mirror processing will then automatically configure an inbound filter specifying your second computer as the source address and your computer as the destination address.

▶ To add a new filter

1. Click the Add button.
   The IP Filter List appears.

2. In the Name box, name the filter **Host A–Host B Filter**.

3. Deactivate the Use Add Wizard check box.

4. Click the Add button in the IP Filter List tab.

5. The Filter Properties box appears.

6. Change Source Address to a specific IP address.

7. Add your IP (*w.x.y.z*) address.

8. Change Destination Address to a specific IP address.

9. Add your second computer's IP (*w.x.y.z*) address.

10. Click OK and verify that your filter has been added in the Filters box of the IP Filter List dialog box.

11. Click Close.

12. In the IP Filter List tab, activate your filter by clicking the radio button next to the filter list you just added.

In the preceding procedure, you configured input and output filters for matching communication packets. In this procedure, you will configure the actions to take on the filtered packets.

▶ **To specify a filter action**

1. Click the Filter Action tab and deactivate the Use Add Wizard check box.

2. Click the Add button to create a filter action.

3. In the Security Methods tab, ensure Negotiate Security is selected.

4. Verify that Allow Unsecured Communication With Non IPSEC Aware Computer is not selected.

5. Click Add to choose a security method.

6. Select Medium (AH) and click OK.

7. Click OK to close the New Filter Action Properties dialog box.

8. Click the radio button next to the filter you just created to activate it.

In this procedure, you will specify how the two computers will trust each other by specifying the authentication method to use when attempting to establish an SA. In this procedure, you will use a preshared key. This is a word or phrase that both computers must know to be trusted by one another. Both sides of the IPSec communication must know this value. It is not used to encrypt application data. Rather, it is used during negotiation to establish whether or not the two computers will trust one another.

▶ **To set authentication method**

1. Click the Authentication Methods tab.

2. Click Add.

3. Click the Pre-Shared Key radio button.

4. Type a preshared key or password in the text box and click OK.

5. Choose Pre-Shared Key in the list and click Move Up so it appears first in the list.

▶ **To verify tunnel settings**

1. Click the Tunnel Setting tab.

2. Verify that This Rule Does Not Specify An IPSEC Tunnel is selected.

▶ **To verify connection type settings**

1. Click the Connection Type tab.

2. Verify that All Network Connections is selected.

▶ **To complete rule creation**

1. Click Close to return to Policy Properties and complete the creation of this rule.

2. Verify that This New Rule is selected in the list box.

3. Close Policy Properties.

▶ **To activate the new policy**

1. In the right pane of the MMC, right-click the Two Computer Policy you just created.

2. Click Assign.

3. The Policy Assigned column value should now be Yes.

▶ **To test IPSec**

1. Enable the policy on your computer and your second computer.

2. PING your second computer.

3. The first PING after enabling the policy will usually fail due to the time it takes to negotiate policy.

4. With matching policies active on both computers, future PINGs will work.

5. Alternatively, enable and disable the policy on your computer and your second computer to see the effects of nonmatching policy settings.

Lesson Summary

IPSec is very easy to customize with policies and rules. In this lesson, we learned how to secure a network using these various methods and taking into consideration such things as proxies, NAT, SNMP, DHCP, DNS, WINS, and domain controllers.

Lesson 4: Monitoring IPSec

To view how your IPSec policies and rules are being used in your network, you may want to monitor IPSec. In this lesson, you will use several tools to do just that. You will focus on IPSec monitoring tools like IPSECMON.EXE, Event Viewer, Performance Monitor, and Network Monitor. These tools will help you maintain a secure, IPSec-rich network.

After this lesson, you will be able to

- Troubleshoot IPSec with IPSECMON.EXE
- Troubleshoot IPSec with Event Viewer
- Troubleshoot IPSec with Network Monitor
- Describe troubleshooting with an IPSECPA.LOG or OAKLEY.LOG file

Estimated lesson time: 30 minutes

IPSec Management and Troubleshooting Tools

Windows 2000 provides tools that you can use to manage and troubleshoot IPSec. This section provides an overview of these tools.

Management Tools

- The IP Security Policy Management snap-in creates and edits policies (the Group Policy Editor can also be used).
- The IP Security Management tool is also on the default Start/Programs/ Administrative Tools menu.

Monitoring and Troubleshooting Tools

IP Security Monitor (IPSECMON.EXE), illustrated in Figure 5.13, is started at a command prompt. This tool monitors IP SAs, rekeys, negotiation errors, and other IP Security statistics.

IPSec Statistics

The following IPSec statistics can be measured using IP Security Monitor:

- **Active Associations.**   Simply a counter of active SAs.
- **Confidential Bytes Sent/Received.**   Total of bytes sent and received using the ESP protocol.
- **Authenticated Bytes Sent/Received.**   Total of bytes sent and received using the AH protocol.

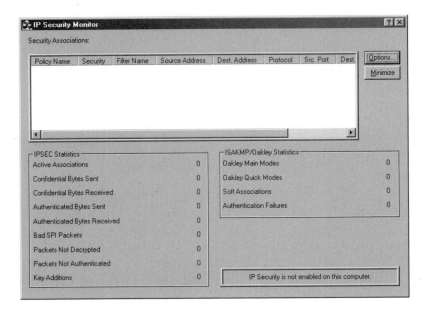

Figure 5.13   IP Security Monitor

- **Bad SPI Packets.**   Total number of packets for which the SPI was wrong. As discussed earlier in this module, the SPI is used to match inbound packets with SAs. If the SPI is bad, it may mean that the inbound SA has expired but that a packet using the old SPI has just arrived. This number is likely to increase if rekey intervals are short and there are a large number of SAs. Because SAs expire normally, a bad SPI packet does not necessarily indicate that IPSec is failing.

- **Packets Not Decrypted.**   Total number of packets that failed decryption. As with bad SPI packets, this failure may indicate that a packet arrived for which the SA had expired. If the SA expires, the session key used to decrypt the packet dies, too. This does not necessarily indicate that IPSec is failing.

- **Packets Not Authenticated.**   Similar to Bad SPI Packets and Packets Not Decrypted, this is the total number of packets containing data that could not be verified. The most likely cause is an expired SA.

- **Key Additions.**   The total number of keys that ISAKMP has sent to the IPSec driver. This indicates the total number of successful Phase 2 negotiations.

ISAKMP/Oakley Statistics

The following ISAKMP/Oakley statistics can be measured using IP Security Monitor:

- **Oakley Main Modes.**   Total number of successful ISAKMP SAs created during Phase 1 negotiations.

- **Oakley Quick Modes.** Total number of successful IPSec SAs created during Phase 2 negotiations. Because these SAs may expire at different rates, this number will not necessarily match the Main Modes number.

- **Soft Associations.** Total number of Phase 2 negotiations that resulted in agreements to send using clear text. This typically reflects the number of associations formed with non-IPSec-aware computers.

- **Authentication Failures.** Total number of identity authentication failures (Kerberos, user certificate, manually configured passwords). This is not the same statistic as Packets Not Authenticated (message authentication through hashing).

Note To reset the statistics in IP Security Monitor, restart the IP Security Policy Agent.

Performance Monitor includes IPSec objects and counters that can be examined. These related events can also be recorded and then later analyzed in Event Viewer:

- Policy agent and IPSec driver events in the system log
- Oakley events in the application log
- ISAKMP events (SA details) in the security log (if logon auditing is enabled)

Using Network Monitor

Network Monitor Version is a useful troubleshooting tool with IPSec. Both the limited version included with Windows 2000 Server and the full version included with Microsoft Systems Management Server version 2.0 feature parsers for ISAKMP, AH, and ESP. Network Monitor captures all information transferred over a network interface at any given time.

Network Monitor version 2.0 contains parsers for IPSec packets. If IPSec is encrypting the packets, then the contents will not be visible, but the packet itself will. If only authentication is being used, the entire packet, including its contents, will be visible. ESP will be displayed as IP protocol number 50 (decimal) and AH will be displayed as 51 (decimal). ISAKMP/Oakley will be displayed as UDP port number 500 (decimal).

Note The ESP data itself will not be readable because of the encryption.

Practice: Using Network Monitor to View Clear Text Traffic

Using this tool, you will capture and view the data being sent across the wire between your computer and your second computer. Network Monitor version 2.0 contains parsers for IPSec and ISAKMP packets. Network Monitor gets the packet after IPSec, so if IPSec encrypts the packet, then the contents will not be visible.

Note   Do the entire practice on both computers. This exercise will be done one computer at a time.

▶ **To view IPSec integrity packets (AH format)**

1. Start Network Monitor and set the capture network to the media access control address of the network card that connects to the second system.

Note   You can run ipconfig with the /all parameter to find the media access control address of your network interface card.

2. In the Local Security Settings MMC interface, assign the Two Computer Policy (from the practice in Lesson 3).
3. Start capturing packets with Network Monitor.
4. Run the ipsecmon utility.
5. PING your second computer's IP address.
6. You may have to repeat this step, as PING has a very short time-out, and there is some delay in establishing the IPSec association between the two computers.
7. Stop and view the Network Monitor trace.
8. View ipsecmon.
9. Double-click the first Internet Control Message Protocol (ICMP) packet.
10. Notice that you see lines indicating headers for frame, Ethernet, IP, and AH.
11. From the details pane, expand the IP entry.
12. Record the IP Protocol number.

    Scroll to the bottom of the IP details and click on IP Data: Number Of Data Bytes Remaining = 64 (0x0040). Notice the IP payload is in clear text. The data in a PING is abcdefghij...

IPSec has created an ICV from the IP, ICMP, and Data fields of the frame. By doing this, IPSec prevents someone from capturing the data, altering it, and re-sending the bad data. Looking at the Hex pane you can still see the 32 characters sent in the PING. By configuring AH security method, we ensure authentication but do not encrypt the data in the packet. AH just makes sure that the packet data, as well as most parts of the IP header, such as source and destination IP addresses, are not modified. Next we will look at packets using the ESP security method that will encrypt the data part of the IP packet.

Practice: Using Network Monitor to View Encrypted Traffic

In this practice, you will use Network Monitor to set ESP encryption and view encrypted packets.

▶ **To set ESP encryption**

1. Unassign the Two Computer Policy.

2. Edit the Two Computer Policy by right-clicking on it, then click Properties.

3. Click the Filter Action tab.

4. Edit the active New Filter Action.

5. Click Edit to modify the Security Method.

6. Change Medium to High (ESP).

7. Close all dialog boxes.

8. Assign the Two Computer Policy.

▶ **To view IPSec encrypted (ESP) packets**

1. Begin capturing packets with Network Monitor.

2. Run the ipsecmon utility.

3. PING the second computer's IP Address.

4. You may have to repeat this step as PING has a very short time-out and there is some delay in establishing the IPSec association between the two computers.

5. Stop and view the Netmon trace.

6. View ipsecmon.

7. Double-click the first ESP frame.

8. This time you will see four entries in the details pane: Frame, Ethernet, IP, and ESP. IPSec has created a hash of the ICMP and Data fields of the frame.

9. Expand the IP section and record the IP Protocol.

10. Scroll to the bottom of the IP details and double-click the IP: Data: Number Of Data Bytes Remaining = 76 (0x004C) line. Look at the Hex pane; you will see the data has been encrypted.

Practice: Using Diagnostic Aids

In this practice, you will use the IPSec Monitor diagnostic aid to verify that IPSec is active and to view the active SAs.

Using IPSec Monitor

Windows 2000 Server contains a monitoring tool for IPSec called IPSecmon. Run this tool to see active security associations, "soft" or "hard," on the local or remote machines. It does not show failed SAs or other filters.

Click Start, point to Run, then type **ipsecmon [machine name]**. For each soft or hard SA, you will see one line in the white box. The column on the left titled Policy Name is the name of the policy that had been assigned and enforced on the computer. The Negotiation Policy column is actually the specific security method that was agreed to during the negotiation. An attempt is made to resolve the IP addresses for source and destination to DNS names.

There are a number of global statistics to note that are accumulated since the computer was last started:

- Successful IPSec SAs will initially cause one ISAKMP/Oakley Main Mode and one Quick Mode. Key renewal operations are generally reflected as additional quick modes.

- The total number of confidential (ESP) or authenticated (ESP and AH) bytes sent or received for all "hard" SAs is shown on the left. Because ESP provides both confidentiality and authenticity, both counters are incremented. Because AH provides only authenticity and not confidentiality, only the authenticated-bytes-sent counter is incremented.

- The total number of soft associations is shown on the right.

▶ **To see if IPSec is active and to view the active SAs**

1. Open Network and Dial-Up Connections from Control Panel.
2. Right-click on Local Area Connection, then click Properties.
3. Select Internet Protocol (TCP/IP), then click Properties.
4. Click Advanced.
5. Click the Options tab, select IP Security, then click Properties.

   If the computer is using local policy, then the name of the local policy will be shown under Use This IP Security Policy. If you are using policy assigned through the Group Policy mechanisms in Active Directory, then the dialog will be grayed out and the name of the assigned policy will be shown in the same box.

Lesson Summary

We have seen how to view your IPSec policies and rules used in a network. In this lesson, you used several tools to do just that. You focused on IPSec monitoring tools like IPSECMON.EXE and Network Monitor. These tools will help you to monitor and troubleshoot IPSec communications on your network.

Review

Answering the following questions will reinforce key information presented in this chapter. If you are unable to answer a question, review the appropriate lesson and then try the question again. Answers to the questions can be found in Appendix A, "Questions and Answers."

1. IPSec is defined by what standards group?

2. Define the difference between secret and public key cryptography.

3. ISAKMP/Oakley provides what functionality?

4. What are rules comprised of?

5. When would a public key certificate be used?

6. What is an IP filter used for?

C H A P T E R   6

Resolving Network Host Names

About This Chapter

Both clients and servers on a network must resolve the user-friendly host names to the Internet Protocol (IP) addresses used in network communications. In this chapter, you will learn how the Transmission Control Protocol/Internet Protocol (TCP/IP) protocol resolves host names. This knowledge is important as you design your network and plan how names and IP addresses will be resolved. Advanced resolution capabilities, such as Domain Name System (DNS) and Windows Interface Name Service (WINS), are discussed in later chapters.

Before You Begin

To complete this chapter, you must have

- Completed Chapter 2, "Implementing TCP/IP"

Lesson 1: TCP/IP Naming Schemes

When computers connect and share data across a TCP/IP network, they use the specific, assigned IP address that is associated with their host. However, network users can remember text-based names easier than IP addresses. For example, it is much easier for users to remember *www.microsoft.com* than the specific IP address associated with this web site. Although TCP/IP hosts require an IP address to communicate, hosts can be referenced by a name rather than an IP address. Because text-based names can be used as aliases for IP addresses, a mechanism must exist for assigning those names to the appropriate IP node. This ensures the name's uniqueness and resolution to its IP address.

After this lesson, you will be able to

- Explain the different naming schemes used by hosts

Estimated lesson time: 10 minutes

Windows 2000 Naming Schemes

Windows 2000 provides several different types of name resolution, including DNS, WINS, broadcast name resolution, and name resolution using HOSTS or LMHOSTS files. Different naming schemes are used by Microsoft Windows 2000 and other hosts such as UNIX. A Windows 2000 host can be assigned a host name, but the host name is used only with TCP/IP applications. UNIX hosts require only an IP address. Using a host or domain name to communicate is optional.

Before communication can take place, an IP address is required on each TCP/IP host. However, the naming scheme affects the way a host is referenced; for example:

- To perform a NET USE command between two computers running Windows 2000, a user has several choices for how to specify the computer's name.
  Any of the following three methods can work:

  net use x: \\netbios_name\share

  net use x: \\10.1.3.74\share

  net use x: \\host.domain.com\share

  The NetBIOS name or the host name must be resolved to an IP address before Address Resolution Protocol (ARP) can resolve the IP address to a hardware address. If an IP address is used, no name resolution is required.

- To reference a UNIX host running TCP/IP, a user specifies either the IP address or the host name. If a host name is used, the name is resolved to an IP address. If the IP address is used, name resolution is not necessary and the IP address is resolved to a hardware address.

Lesson Summary

Windows 2000 and UNIX hosts can both be referenced by either an IP address or host name. Windows 2000 and other Microsoft network operating systems also allow naming using a NetBIOS name.

Lesson 2: Host Names

A host name simplifies the way a host is referenced because names are easier for people to remember than IP addresses. Host names are used in virtually all TCP/IP environments. This lesson describes how host name resolution works.

After this lesson, you will be able to

- Explain how the HOSTS file resolves a host name to an IP address
- Explain how a host name is resolved to an IP address using a DNS server and Microsoft-supported methods

Estimated lesson time: 20 minutes

Understanding Host Names

A host name is an alias assigned to an IP node to identify it as a TCP/IP host. The host name can be up to 255 characters long and can contain alphabetic and numeric characters and the "-" and "." characters. Multiple host names can be assigned to the same host. For computers running Windows 2000, the host name does not have to match the Windows 2000 computer name.

Windows Sockets (WinSock) applications, such as Microsoft Internet Explorer and the File Transfer Protocol (FTP) utility, can use one of two values for the destination to be connected: the IP address or a host name. When the IP address is specified, name resolution is not needed. When a host name is specified, the host name must be resolved to an IP address before IP-based communication with the desired resource can begin.

Host names can take various forms. The two most common forms are a nickname and a domain name. A nickname is an alias to an IP address that individual people can assign and use. A domain name is a structured name that follows Internet conventions.

Purpose of Host Names

A host name is an alias assigned to a computer by an administrator to identify a TCP/IP host. The host name does not have to match the NetBIOS computer name, and can be a 255-character alphanumeric value. Multiple host names can be assigned to the same host.

A host name simplifies the way a user references other TCP/IP hosts. Host names are easier to remember than IP addresses. In fact, a host name can be used in place of an IP address when using PING or other TCP/IP applications.

A host name always corresponds to an IP address that is stored in a HOSTS file or in a database on a DNS server. Windows clients can translate between host names and NetBIOS names in many cases, allowing a WINS server or the LMHOSTS file to perform resolution for a host name.

The hostname utility will display the host name assigned to your system. By default, the host name is the computer name of your computer running Windows 2000.

Host Name Resolution

Host name resolution is the process of mapping a host name to an IP address. Before the IP address can be resolved to a hardware address, the host name must be resolved to an IP address.

Windows 2000 can resolve host names using several methods including:

- **NetBIOS name resolution.**   NetBIOS defines a session-level interface and a session management/data transport protocol. NetBIOS uses name registration, name release, and name discovery for interacting with NetBIOS hosts. NetBIOS name resolution is the process of mapping a computer's NetBIOS name to an IP address. There are several methods available for resolving NetBIOS names, each depending on your network configuration. The methods are NetBIOS name cache, NetBIOS name server, local broadcast, LMHOSTS file, HOSTS file, and DNS.

- **Resolving names with a HOSTS file.**   The HOSTS file is a text file stored locally on a system that contains host names and associated IP addresses. The HOSTS file is discussed in more detail in the next lesson.

- **Resolving names with a DNS server.**   A DNS server is a centralized online database that is used in IP networks to resolve fully qualified domain names (FQDNs) and other host names to IP addresses. Windows 2000 can use a DNS server and provides DNS server service. DNS is explained in Chapter 7, "Implementing Domain Name System (DNS)."

Microsoft TCP/IP can use any of the methods shown in Tables 6.1 and 6.2 to resolve host names. The methods that Windows 2000 can use to resolve a host name are configurable.

Table 6.1   Standard Host Name Resolution Methods

Standard Methods of Resolution	Description
Local host name	The configured host name for the computer. This name is compared to the destination host name.
HOSTS file	A local text file in the same format as the 4.3 Berkeley Software Distribution UNIX\Etc\HOSTS file. This file maps host names to IP addresses. This file is typically used to resolve host names for TCP/IP applications.
DNS server	A server that maintains a database of IP address/ computer name (host name) mappings.

Table 6.2   Microsoft Host Name Resolution Methods

Microsoft Methods of Resolution	Description
NetBIOS Name Server	A server implemented under Requests for Comment (RFCs) 1001 and 1002 to provide name resolution of NetBIOS computer names. The Microsoft implementation of this is WINS.
Local broadcast	A broadcast on the local network for the IP address of the destination NetBIOS name.
LMHOSTS file	A local text file that maps IP addresses to the NetBIOS computer names of Windows hosts.

NetBIOS Name Resolution

A NetBIOS name is a unique, 16-byte address used to identify a NetBIOS resource on the network. The NetBIOS name resolution process converts a NetBIOS name to an IP address. An example of a process that uses a NetBIOS name is the File and Printer Sharing for Microsoft Networks service on a computer running Windows 2000. When your computer starts, File and Printer Sharing for Microsoft Networks registers a unique NetBIOS name based on the name of your computer. Computers running Microsoft TCP/IP can use local broadcast name resolution, which is a NetBIOS-over-TCP/IP mode of operation. This method relies on a computer making IP-level broadcasts to register its name by announcing it on the network. Each computer in the broadcast area is responsible for challenging attempts to register a duplicate name and for responding to name queries for its registered name.

Resolving Names with a HOSTS File

As shown in Figure 6.1, the process of resolving a host name using the Hosts file is as follows:

1. Name resolution begins when a user calls a WinSock-based application referencing a host name rather than an IP address.

2. Windows 2000 checks to see if the host name is the same as the local host name. If the two names are different, the HOSTS file is parsed. If the host name is found in the HOSTS file, it is resolved to an IP address.

   If the host name cannot be resolved and no other resolution methods—such as DNS, a NetBIOS name server, or the LMHOSTS file—are configured, the process stops and the user receives an error message.

3. After the host name is resolved to an IP address, an attempt is made to resolve the destination host's IP address to its hardware address.

   If the destination host is on the local network, ARP obtains its hardware address by consulting the ARP cache or by broadcasting the destination host's IP address.

If the destination host is on a remote network, ARP obtains the hardware address of a router and the request is routed to the destination host.

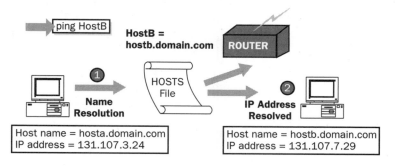

Figure 6.1   Resolving a destination host's IP address to its hardware address

Resolving Names with a DNS Server

A DNS server is a centralized online database that is used in IP networks to resolve host names to IP addresses. Windows 2000 can act as a DNS client and the Windows 2000 Server family provides DNS server services. Resolving a domain name using a DNS server is very similar to using a HOSTS file.

If Windows 2000 is configured to resolve host names using a DNS server, it uses two steps to resolve a host name, as shown in the following process and illustrated in Figure 6.2:

1. When a user types a command using an FQDN or a host name, the process for resolving the name using the HOSTS file is followed first. If the IP address cannot be resolved using the HOSTS file, a request is sent to the DNS server to look up the name in its database and resolve it to an IP address.

   If the DNS server does not respond to the request, additional attempts are made at intervals of 1, 2, 2, and 4 seconds. If the DNS server does not respond to these five attempts, and there are no other resolution methods configured such as a NetBIOS name server or LMHOSTS, the process stops and an error is reported.

2. After the host name is resolved, ARP obtains the hardware address. If the destination host is on the local network, ARP obtains its hardware address by consulting the ARP cache or by broadcasting the IP address. If the destination host is on a remote network, ARP obtains the hardware address of a router that can deliver the request.

   If the DNS server is on a remote network, ARP must obtain the hardware address of a router before the name can be resolved.

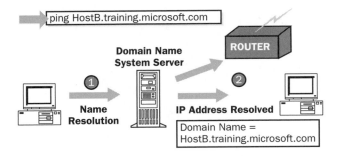

Figure 6.2   Resolving a host name with a DNS server

Microsoft Methods of Resolving Host Names

Windows 2000 can be configured to resolve host names using a NetBIOS name server, broadcast, and LMHOSTS in addition to the HOSTS file and DNS server. If one of these methods fails, the other methods provide a backup, as shown in the following example and illustrated in Figure 6.3. If WINS and LMHOSTS are configured, the order of resolution is as follows:

1. When a user types a command referencing a host name, Windows 2000 checks to see if the host name is the same as the local host name. If they are the same, the name is resolved and the command is carried out without generating network activity.

2. If the host name and local host name are not the same, the HOSTS file is parsed. If the host name is found in the HOSTS file, it is resolved to an IP address and address resolution occurs.

3. If the host name cannot be resolved using the HOSTS file, the source host sends a request to its configured domain name servers. If the host name is found by a DNS server, it is resolved to an IP address and address resolution occurs.

   If the DNS server does not respond to the request, additional attempts are made at intervals of 1, 2, 2, and 4 seconds.

4. If the DNS server cannot resolve the host name, the source host checks its local NetBIOS name cache before it makes three attempts to contact its configured NetBIOS name servers. If the host name is found in the NetBIOS name cache or by a NetBIOS name server, it is resolved to an IP address and address resolution occurs.

5. If the host name is not resolved by the NetBIOS name server, the source host generates three broadcast messages on the local network. If the host name is found on the local network, it is resolved to an IP address and address resolution occurs.

6. If the host name is not resolved using broadcasts, the local LMHOSTS file is parsed. If the host name is found in the LMHOSTS file, it is resolved to an IP address and address resolution occurs.

If none of these methods resolves the host name, the only way to communicate with the other host is to specify the IP address.

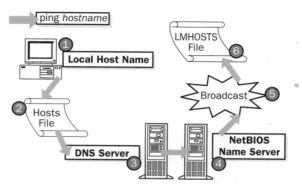

Figure 6.3   Backup methods for resolving host names

Lesson Summary

A host name is used to identify a TCP/IP host or default gateway. Host name resolution is the process of mapping a host name to an IP address. This is necessary before ARP can resolve the IP address to a hardware address.

Lesson 3: The HOSTS File

Now that you have learned the concepts of how host names are resolved using different methods, you will look at the HOSTS file. In this lesson, you modify the Hosts file so that host names are resolved correctly.

After this lesson, you will be able to

- Configure and use the HOSTS file

Estimated lesson time: 15 minutes

Understanding the HOSTS File

The HOSTS file is a static file used to map host names to IP addresses. This file provides compatibility with the UNIX HOSTS file. The HOSTS file is used by PING and other TCP/IP applications to resolve a host name to an IP address. The HOSTS file can be used to resolve NetBIOS names (Microsoft TCP/IP-32-specific).

A HOSTS file must reside on each computer. A single entry consists of an IP address corresponding to one or more host names. By default, the host name localhost is an entry in the HOSTS file. The HOSTS file is parsed whenever a host name is referenced. Names are read in a linear fashion. The most commonly used names should be near the beginning of the file.

Note   The HOSTS file can be edited with any text editor. It is located in the \systemroot\System32\Drivers\Etc directory. Each host entry is limited to 255 characters, and entries in the HOSTS file are not case-sensitive.

Figure 6.4 shows an example of the contents of the HOSTS file.

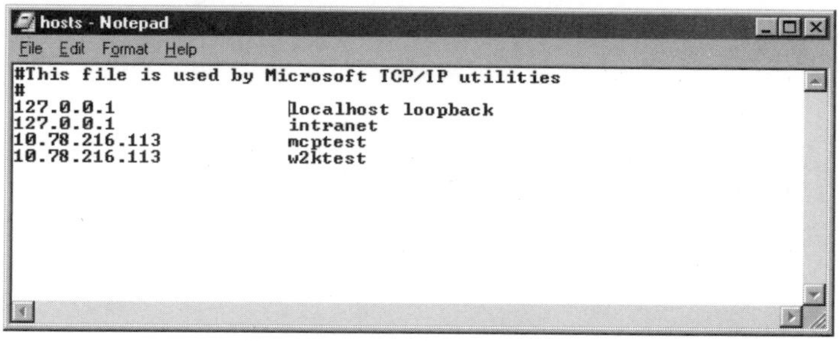

Figure 6.4   A HOSTS file

Within the HOSTS file

- Multiple host names can be assigned to the same IP address. Note that the server at the IP address 172.16.94.97 can be referred to by its fully qualified domain name (rhino.microsoft.com) or a nickname (rhino). This allows the user at this computer to refer to this server using the nickname rhino rather than typing the entire FQDN.

- Entries can be case-sensitive depending on the platform. Entries in the HOSTS file for some UNIX operating systems are case-sensitive. Entries in the HOSTS file for Windows 2000 and Windows 2000-based computers are not case-sensitive.

Advantage of Using a HOSTS File

The advantage of using a HOSTS file is that it is customizable for the user. Each user can create whatever entries he or she wants, including easy-to-remember nicknames for frequently accessed resources. However, the individual maintenance of the HOSTS file does not scale well to storing large numbers of FQDN mappings.

Practice: Working with the HOSTS File and DNS

In this procedure, you configure and use the HOSTS file, configure Windows 2000 to use DNS, and identify problems associated with host name and domain name resolution. In the first part of the procedure, you add host name/IP address mappings to your HOSTS file and then use the file to resolve host names.

In this procedure, you determine the local host used for TCP/IP applications, such as PING.

► **To determine the local host name**

1. Open a command prompt.
2. Type **hostname** and then press the Enter key.

   The local host name is displayed.

In this procedure, you PING the name of the local host to verify that your system can resolve local host names without entries in the HOSTS file.

► **To ping your local host name**

1. Type **ping Server1** (where Server1 is the name of your computer) and then press the Enter key.

   What was the response?

Perform the following procedure from Server1 to attempt to ping a local computer name.

▶ **To ping a local computer name**

1. Type **ping computertwo** and then press the Enter key.

   What was the response?

▶ **To add an entry to the HOSTS file on Server1**

1. Change to the following directory by typing:

   cd %systemroot%\system32\drivers\etc

2. Use a text editor to modify a file called HOSTS by typing:

   notepad hosts

3. Add an entry in the HOSTS file for computertwo. This will be the IP address, followed by a space, and then the host name.

4. Save the file, then exit Edit.

▶ **To use the Hosts file for name resolution**

1. Type **ping computertwo** and then press the Enter key.

   What was the response?

Lesson Summary

The HOSTS file is a text file that you can edit with any text editor (such as Notepad). The HOSTS file maps host names to IP addresses and provides compatibility with the UNIX HOSTS file. If your network uses HOSTS files for host name resolution and you cannot connect to the other computer using its host name, there may be an invalid entry in your HOSTS file. Search your HOSTS file for the host name of the other computer, verify that there is only one entry per host name, and then verify that the entry for the host name of the other computer is valid. For more information on the HOSTS file, see the sample HOSTS file in the %SystemRoot%\System32\Drivers\Etc folder.

Review

Answering the following questions will reinforce key information presented in this chapter. If you are unable to answer a question, review the appropriate lesson and then try the question again. Answers to the questions can be found in Appendix A, "Questions and Answers."

1. What is a host name?

2. What is the purpose of a host name?

3. What does a HOSTS file entry consist of?

4. During the name resolution process, what occurs first: ARP resolution or host name resolution?

CHAPTER 7

Implementing Domain Name System (DNS)

About This Chapter

In this chapter, you will learn how Domain Name System (DNS) is used to resolve host names on your local area network (LAN) and across the public Internet. Microsoft Windows 2000 includes an enhanced version of DNS. For more information about how Windows 2000 uses DNS, see the next chapter, "Using Windows 2000 Domain Name Service." This chapter is designed to provide you with an overview of DNS and how to implement the service on Windows 2000. By the end of this chapter, you will be able to identify the primary components of DNS, install and configure DNS, and troubleshoot the Domain Name Service on Windows 2000.

Before You Begin

To complete this chapter, you must have

- Installed Microsoft Windows 2000 Server with Transmission Control Protocol/Internet Protocol (TCP/IP)

Lesson 1: Introducing DNS

DNS is similar to a telephone book. Each computer on the Internet has both a host name and an Internet Protocol (IP) address. Typically, when you want to connect to another computer, you must enter a host name. Your computer then contacts a DNS server that cross-references the host name you provided to the actual IP address. This IP address is then used to connect to the remote computer. This lesson describes the architecture and structure of DNS.

After this lesson, you will be able to

- Describe the structure, architecture, and components of DNS
- Explain how DNS is used to resolve names and IP addresses

Estimated lesson time: 25 minutes

DNS Origins

Before the implementation of DNS, the creation of user-friendly computer names was done using HOSTS files that contained a list of names and associated IP addresses. On the Internet, this file was centrally administered and each location would periodically download a new copy. As the number of computers on the Internet grew, this became an unmanageable solution. As a result, DNS was designed to replace the singularly administered HOSTS file with a distributed database that would allow for a hierarchical name space, distribution of administration, extensible data types, virtually unlimited database size, and better performance. DNS is the name service for Internet addresses that translates friendly domain names to numeric IP addresses. For example, *www.microsoft.com* translates to 207.46.130.149. DNS is analogous to a telephone book. The user looks up the name of the person or organization that he or she wants to contact and cross-references the name to a telephone number. Similarly, a host computer queries the name of a computer and a domain name server cross-references the name to an IP address.

The Microsoft implementation of DNS Server became a part of the operating system in Windows NT Server 4.0 and has continued to be included in Windows 2000.

DNS and Windows 2000

In addition to providing traditional Internet name resolution, DNS is the primary name service of Windows 2000. It is, by design, a highly reliable, hierarchical, distributed, and scalable database. Windows 2000 clients use DNS for name resolution and service location, including locating domain controllers for logon. DNS in Windows 2000 provides a unique DNS Server implementation that is fully interoperable with other standards-based implementations of DNS Server. For more information about the version of DNS included in Windows 2000, please see the next chapter, "Using Windows 2000 Domain Name Service."

How DNS Works

The purpose of the DNS database is to translate computer names into IP addresses, as illustrated in Figure 7.1. In the DNS, the clients are called resolvers and the servers are called name servers. DNS works using three main components: resolvers, name servers, and the domain name space. With basic DNS communication, a resolver sends queries to a name server. The name server returns the requested information, a pointer to another name server, or a failure message, if the request cannot be satisfied.

DNS maps to the application layer and uses User Datagram Protocol (UDP) and Transmission Control Protocol (TCP) as the underlying protocols. For performance reasons, resolvers send UDP queries to servers first, then resort to TCP if truncation of the returned data occurs.

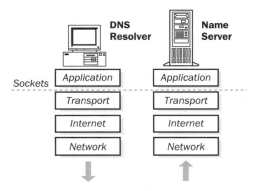

Figure 7.1   Resolvers and name servers

Resolvers

A resolver provides clients with address information about other computers on the network. The function of the resolvers is to pass name requests between applications and name servers. The name request contains a query, such as the IP address of a Web site. The resolver is often built into the application or is running on the host computer as a library routine. Resolvers first send UDP queries to servers for increased performance and resort to TCP only if truncation of the returned data occurs.

Name Servers

A name server contains address information about other computers on the network. This information can be given to client computers that make a request to the name server. If the name server is not able to resolve the request, it can forward the request to a different name server. The name servers are grouped into different levels that are called domains. A domain is a logical group of computers in a large network. Access to each computer in a given group is controlled by the same server.

The Structure of DNS

The domain name space is a hierarchical grouping of names, as illustrated in Figure 7.2.

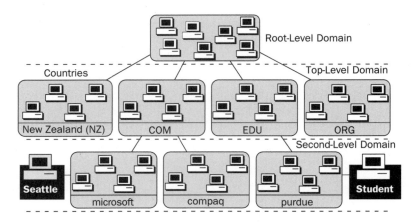

Figure 7.2   Domain name space separated into levels

Root-Level Domains

Domains define different levels of authority in a hierarchical structure. The top of the hierarchy is called the root domain. References to the root domain are expressed by a period (.).

Top-Level Domains

The following are the present top-level domains:

- **com**   Commercial organizations
- **edu**   Educational institutions and universities
- **org**   Not-for-profit organizations
- **net**   Networks (the backbone of the Internet)
- **gov**   Nonmilitary government organizations
- **mil**   Military government organizations
- **num**   Phone numbers
- **arpa**   Reverse DNS
- *xx*   Two-letter country code

Top-level domains can contain second-level domains and hosts.

Note   An Internet Society committee is planning several additional top-level domains such as firm and web.

Second-Level Domains

Second-level domains can contain both hosts and other domains, called subdomains. For example, the Microsoft domain, microsoft.com, can contain computers such as ftp.microsoft.com and subdomains such as dev.microsoft.com. The subdomain dev.microsoft.com can contain hosts such as ntserver.dev.microsoft.com.

Host Names

The domain name is used with the host name to create a fully qualified domain name (FQDN) for the computer. The FQDN is the host name followed by a period (.), followed by the domain name. For example, this could be fileserver1.microsoft.com, where fileserver1 is the host name and microsoft.com is the domain name.

Zones

The administrative unit for DNS is the zone. A zone is a subtree of the DNS database that is administered as a single, separate entity. It can consist of a single domain or a domain with subdomains. The lower-level subdomains of a zone can also be split into separate zones.

Zones of Authority

A zone of authority is the portion of the domain name space for which a particular name server is responsible. The name server stores all address mappings for the domain name space within the zone and answers client queries for those names. The name server's zone of authority encompasses at least one domain. This domain is referred to as the zone's root domain. You can also have a secondary DNS server that can copy domain information across the network from the primary DNS server that has authority over at least one zone. This is called a zone transfer.

As illustrated in Figure 7.3, microsoft.com is a domain, but the entire domain is not controlled by one zone file. Part of the domain is located in a separate zone file for DEV.MICROSOFT.COM. Breaking up domains across multiple zone files may be necessary for distributing management of the domain to different groups or for data replication efficiency.

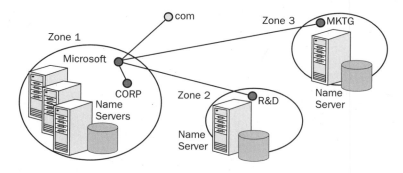

Figure 7.3 Domains across multiple zones

Name Server Roles

DNS name servers can be configured in different roles, affecting how they store and maintain their database of names. A Microsoft DNS server can be either a primary or secondary DNS server to another Microsoft DNS server, or to a DNS server running under another operating system such as UNIX. The minimum number of DNS servers you need in order to serve each zone is two—a primary and a secondary. Both a primary and a secondary server are required to provide database redundancy and a degree of fault tolerance.

Primary Name Servers

A primary name server is a DNS server that gets the data for its zones from the local DNS database files. When a change is made to the zone data, such as delegating a portion of the zone to another DNS server or adding hosts in the zone, the change must be made on the primary DNS server so that the new information is entered in the local zone file.

Secondary Name Servers

A secondary name server gets its zone data file from the primary DNS server that is authoritative for that zone. The primary DNS server sends a copy of the zone file to the secondary DNS server in a process referred to as a zone transfer.

There are three reasons to have secondary name servers:

- **Redundancy.**   You need at least one primary and one secondary name server for each zone. The computers should be as independent as possible. Generally, plan to install the primary and secondary servers on different subnets to provide continual support for DNS name queries if one subnet should go down.

- **Faster access for remote locations.**   If you have a number of clients in remote locations, having secondary name servers (or other primary name servers for subdomains) prevents these clients from communicating across slow links for name resolution.

- **Reduction of load.**   Secondary name servers reduce the load on the primary server.

Because information for each zone is stored in separate files, this primary or secondary designation is defined at a zone level. This means that a particular name server may be a primary name server for certain zones and a secondary name server for other zones.

Master Name Servers

When you define a zone on a name server as a secondary zone, you must designate another name server from which to obtain the zone information. The source of zone information for a secondary name server in a DNS hierarchy is referred to as a master name server. A master name server can be either a primary or secondary name server for the requested zone. When a secondary name server starts up, it contacts its master name server and initiates a zone transfer with that server.

Caching-Only Servers

Although all DNS name servers cache queries that they have resolved, caching-only servers are DNS name servers that only perform queries, cache the answers, and return the results. In other words, they are not authoritative for any domains (no zone data is kept locally) and they only contain information that they have cached while resolving queries.

When trying to determine when to use such a server, keep in mind that when the server is initially started, it has no cached information and must build this information up over time as it services requests. Less traffic is generated between servers because the server is not doing a zone transfer. This is important if you have a slow connection between sites.

Lesson Summary

As an improvement to the original method of resolving host names to an IP address on the Internet, DNS was created. In DNS, a client (called a resolver) sends queries to a name server. Name servers then take name requests and resolve computer names to IP addresses. The domain name space is a hierarchical grouping of root-level domains, top-level domains, second-level domains, and host names. Specific servers are responsible for portions of the domain name space called zones of authority.

Lesson 2: Name Resolution and DNS Files

There are three types of queries that a client (resolver) can make to a DNS server: recursive, iterative, and inverse. These servers store their DNS information in four possible files: database, reverse lookup, cache, and boot files.

After this lesson, you will be able to

- Explain how recursive, iterative, and inverse queries work
- Explain how queries are placed in a cache for future requests

Estimated lesson time: 10 minutes

Recursive Queries

In a recursive query, the queried name server is petitioned to respond with the requested data, or with an error stating that data of the requested type does not exist or that the domain name specified does not exist. The name server cannot refer the request to a different name server.

Iterative Queries

In an iterative query, the queried name server gives the best answer it currently has back to the requester. This answer may be the resolved name or a referral to another name server that may be able to answer the client's original request.

Figure 7.4 shows an example of both recursive and iterative queries. In this example, a client within a corporation is querying its DNS server for the IP address for *www.microsoft.com*.

1. The resolver sends a recursive DNS query to its local DNS server asking for the IP address of *www.microsoft.com*. The local name server is responsible for resolving the name and cannot refer the resolver to another name server.

2. The local name server checks its zones and finds no zones corresponding to the requested domain name. It then sends an iterative query for *www.microsoft.com* to a root name server.

3. The root name server has authority for the root domain and will reply with the IP address of a name server for the com top-level domain.

4. The local name server sends an iterative query for *www.microsoft.com* to the com name server.

5. The com name server replies with the IP address of the name server servicing the *microsoft.com* domain.

6. The local name server sends an iterative query for *www.microsoft.com* to the *microsoft.com* name server.

7. The microsoft.com name server replies with the IP address corresponding to *www.microsoft.com*.

8. The local name server sends the IP address of *www.microsoft.com* back to the original resolver.

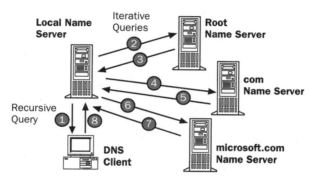

Figure 7.4 Recursive and iterative queries

Inverse Queries

In an inverse query, the resolver sends a request to a name server to resolve the host name associated with a known IP address. There is no correlation between host names and IP addresses in the DNS name space. Therefore, only a thorough search of all domains guarantees a correct answer.

To prevent an exhaustive search of all domains for an inverse query, a special domain called in-addr.arpa was created. Nodes in the in-addr.arpa domain are named after the numbers in the dotted-decimal representation of IP addresses. Because IP addresses get more specific from left to right and domain names get less specific from left to right, the order of IP address octets must be reversed when building the in-addr.arpa domain. With this arrangement, administration of lower limbs of the in-addr.arpa domain can be delegated to organizations as they are assigned their class A, B, or C IP addresses.

Once the in-addr.arpa domain is built, special resource records called pointer (PTR) records are added to associate the IP addresses and the corresponding host name. For example, to find a host name for the IP address 157.55.200.51, the resolver queries the DNS server for a PTR record for 51.200.55.157.in-addr.arpa. The PTR record found contains the host name and corresponding IP address 157.55.200.51. This information is sent back to the resolver. Part of the administration of a DNS name server is ensuring that PTR records are created for hosts.

Caching and Time to Live

When a name server is processing a recursive query, it may be required to send out several queries to find the answer. The name server caches all of the information that it receives during this process for a time that is specified in the returned data. This amount of time is referred to as the Time to Live (TTL). The name server administrator of the zone that contains the data decides on the TTL for the data. Smaller TTL values help ensure that data about the domain is more consistent across the network if this data changes often. However, this also increases the load on name servers.

Once data is cached by a DNS server, it must start decreasing the TTL from its original value so that it will know when to flush the data from its cache. If a query comes in that can be satisfied by this cached data, the TTL that is returned with the data is the current amount of time left before the data is flushed from the DNS server cache. Client resolvers also have data caches and honor the TTL value so that they know when to expire the data.

DNS Configuration Files

The DNS is a hierarchical, distributed database. The database itself consists of resource records, which primarily consist of a DNS name, a record type, and data values that are associated with that record type. For example, the most common records in the DNS database are address records, where the name of an address record is the name of a computer, and the data in the record is the TCP/IP address of that computer.

To resolve names, servers consult their zones (also called DNS database files, or simply, db files). The zones contain resource records (RRs) that make up the resource information associated with the DNS domain. For example, some RRs map friendly names to IP addresses, and others map IP addresses to friendly names.

Start of Authority Record

The first record in any database file must be the start of authority (SOA) record. The SOA defines the general parameters for the DNS zone. The following is an example of an SOA record:

```
@   IN  SOA     nameserver.example.microsoft.com.
postmaster.example.microsoft.com. (
                              1              ; serial number
                              3600           ; refresh   [1h]
                              600            ; retry     [10m]
                              86400          ; expire    [1d]
                              3600 )         ; min TTL   [1h]
```

The following rules apply to all SOA records:

- The at symbol (@) in a database file indicates "this server."
- IN indicates an Internet record.
- Any host name not terminated with a period (.) will be appended with the root domain.
- The @ symbol is replaced by a period (.) in the e-mail address of the administrator.
- Parentheses (()) must enclose line breaks that span more than one line.

Name Server Record

The name server (NS) record lists the additional name servers. A database file may contain more than one NS record. The following is an example of an NS record:

```
@ IN NS nameserver2.microsoft.com
```

Host Record

A host address resource record (A) statically associates a host name to its IP address. Host records will comprise most of the database file and will list all hosts within the zone. The following are examples of host records:

```
rhino        IN A 157.55.200.143
localhost    IN A 127.0.0.1
```

CNAME Record

A canonical name (CNAME) record enables you to associate more than one host name with an IP address. This is sometimes referred to as aliasing. The following is an example of a CNAME record:

```
FileServer1   CNAME rhino
www           CNAME rhino
ftp           CNAME rhino
```

The Reverse Lookup File

The reverse lookup file (z.y.x.w.in-addr.arpa) allows a resolver to provide an IP address and request a matching host name. A reverse lookup file is named like a zone file according to the in-addr.arpa zone for which it is providing reverse lookups. For example, to provide reverse lookups for the IP network 157.57.28.0, a reverse lookup file is created with a file name of 57.157.in-addr.arpa. This file contains SOA and NS records similar to other DNS database zone files, as well as PTR records.

This DNS reverse lookup capability is important because some applications provide the capabilities to implement security based on the connecting host names. For instance, if a browser sends a request to an Internet Information Server (IIS) Web server with this security arrangement, the Web server would contact the

DNS server and do a reverse name lookup on the client's IP address. If the host name returned by the DNS server is not in the access list for the Web site or if the host name was not found by DNS, then the request would be denied.

Note   Windows 2000 does not require reverse lookup zones to be configured. Reverse-lookup zones might be necessary for other applications or for administrative convenience.

The PTR Record

PTR records provide an address-to-name mapping within a reverse lookup zone. IP numbers are written in backward order and "in-addr.arpa" is appended to the end to create this PTR record. As an example, looking up the name for 157.55.200.51 requires a PTR query for the name 51.200.55.157.in-addr.arpa. An example might read

```
51.200.55.157.in-addr.arpa.  IN PTR mailserver1.microsoft.com.
```

The Cache File

The CACHE.DNS file contains the records of the root domain servers. The cache file is essentially the same on all name servers and must be present. When the name server receives a query outside its zone, it starts resolution with these root domain servers. An example entry might read

```
.                     3600000 IN    NS    A.ROOT-SERVERS.NET.
A.ROOT-SERVERS.NET.   3600000 A           198.41.0.4
```

The cache file contains host information that is needed to resolve names outside of authoritative domains, and also contains names and addresses of root name servers. The default file provided with the Windows 2000 DNS Server has the current records for all of the root servers on the Internet, and is stored in the %SystemRoot%\System32\Dns folder. For installations not connected to the Internet, the file should be replaced to contain the name server's authoritative domains for the root of the private network.

The Boot File

The boot file is the startup configuration file on the Berkeley Internet Name Daemon-specific implementation of DNS. This file contains host information needed to resolve names outside of authoritative domains. The file is not defined in a Request for Comments (RFC) and is not needed to be RFC-compliant. It is supported by Windows 2000 to improve compatibility with traditional, UNIX-based DNS services. The Berkeley Internet Name Daemon boot file controls the startup behavior of the DNS server. Commands must start at the beginning of a line and no spaces can precede commands. Table 7.1 shows descriptions of some of the boot file commands supported by Windows 2000.

Table 7.1   Windows 2000 Boot File Commands

Command	Description
Directory command	Specifies a directory where other files referred to in the boot file can be found.
Cache command	Specifies a file used to help the DNS service contact name servers for the root domain. This command and the file it refers to must be present. A cache file suitable for use on the Internet is provided with Windows 2000.
Primary command	Specifies a domain for which this name server is authoritative and a database file that contains the resource records for that domain (that is, the zone file). Multiple primary command records can exist in the boot file.
Secondary command	Specifies a domain for which this name server is authoritative and a list of master server IP addresses from which to attempt to download the zone information, rather than reading it from a file. It also defines the name of the local file for caching this zone. Multiple secondary command records could exist in the boot file.

Table 7.2 shows examples of the commands in a boot file.

Table 7.2   Examples of Boot File Commands

Syntax	Example
directory [*directory*]	directory c:\winnt\system32\dns
cache.[*file_name*]	cache.cache
primary [*domain*] [*file_name*]	primary microsoft.com.microsoft.dns primary dev.microsoft.com dev.dns
secondary [*domain*] [*hostlist*] [*local_file_name*]	secondary test.microsoft.com 157.55.200.100 test.dns

Lesson Summary

When clients need to resolve a host name or IP address, they can make one of three queries to DNS servers: recursive, iterative, or inverse. A DNS server will only return the information it has in cache, including the potential of an error, when a client makes a recursive request. A more typical query is an iterative query. When a client makes an iterative query, the DNS server will return the requested information or provide the client with an alternative DNS server that will provide the correct information. The third type of query, inverse, provides reverse-lookup information. If a DNS client needs a host name resolved from a known IP address, an inverse query is sent to the DNS server.

DNS servers store their name and configuration information in four files: database, reverse lookup, cache, and boot files. Windows 2000 and the included DNS Manager allow you to configure these files with a graphical user interface that is described in more detail in Chapter 8, "Using Windows 2000 Domain Name Service."

Lesson 3: Planning a DNS Implementation

The configuration of your DNS servers depends on factors such as the size of your organization, organization locations, and fault-tolerance requirements. This lesson gives you an idea of how to configure DNS for your site. It contains scenarios that measure your network planning knowledge prior to installing DNS.

After this lesson, you will be able to

- Register a DNS server with the parent domain
- Estimate the number of DNS name servers, domains, and zones needed for a network

Estimated lesson time: 40 minutes

DNS Considerations

Although Windows 2000 and its name resolution require a DNS server, the DNS server itself does not have to reside on a server running Windows 2000. In addition, it does not even have to be on your local network. As long as Windows 2000 can be configured to reference a valid DNS server that supports the necessary record types, such as one hosted by your Internet service provider (ISP), you can provide the required name resolution capabilities to Windows 2000. However, with the increased functionality implemented in the version of DNS provided with Windows 2000, you may decide it is worthwhile to install and configure your own DNS server. For purposes of this lesson, it is assumed you have decided to implement your own Windows 2000 DNS server.

If your organization, regardless of size, wants to use a second-level domain, the Internet Network Information Center (InterNIC) must be informed of the domain name of your organization and the IP addresses of at least two DNS servers that service the domain. You can also set up additional DNS servers within your organization that are independent of the Internet.

For reliability and redundancy, Microsoft recommends that at least two DNS servers be configured per domain—a primary and a secondary name server. The primary name server maintains the database of information, which is replicated to the secondary name server. This replication allows name queries to be serviced even if one of the name servers is unavailable. The replication schedule can be configured depending on how often names change in the domain. Replication should be frequent enough so that changes are known to both servers. However, excessive replication can increase network traffic and increase load on the name server.

Registering with the Parent Domain

Once you have your DNS server or servers configured and installed, you need to register with the DNS server that is above you in the hierarchical naming structure of DNS. Figure 7.5 provides an example of registering your DNS server with the domain level above it. The parent system needs the names and addresses of your name servers and may require other information, such as the date that the domain becomes available and the names and mailing addresses of contact people.

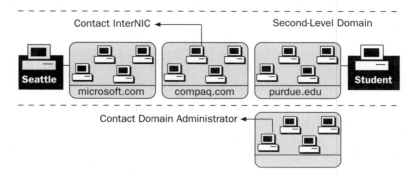

Figure 7.5 Registering your DNS server with the domain level above it

If you are registering with a parent below the second-level domain, check with the administrator of that system to determine the information you need to supply.

Practice: Implementing DNS

In this practice, you work through three DNS implementation scenarios. In each scenario, you estimate the number of DNS name servers, domains, and zones needed for a network. Each scenario describes a company that is migrating to Windows 2000 and wants to implement directory services. You will answer some questions involved in drafting a DNS network design for each company using unique criteria. The purpose of these practices is to measure your network planning knowledge prior to installing DNS. This will serve as a baseline to measure how much you have learned at the completion of this course and will help you start thinking about DNS network design.

Scenario 1: Designing DNS for a Small Network

The Northwind Company is in the process of replacing its older mid-range computer with a computer running Windows 2000. Most employees access the mid-range system through terminal devices. Some users have 486 computers and a few have Pentium computers; these computers are not networked. The company has already purchased the hardware for the migration.

The network will be used for basic file and print sharing and will also have one Windows 2000-based server running Microsoft SQL Server 7. The majority of users will need access to the computer running SQL Server 7. Desktop applications will be installed on the local computers, but data files will be saved on the servers.

The Northwind Company would like to be connected to the Internet so employees can receive e-mail.

Draft a network design using the criteria shown in Table 7.3.

Table 7.3   Network Design Criteria

Environmental Components	Detail
Users	100
Location(s)	Single office
Administration	One full-time administrator
Servers	3 computers: 2 Pentium 120s with 32 MB RAM, 3.2 GB hard disk; 1 Pentium 150 with 128 MB RAM dedicated to Exchange Server
Clients	All Pentium and 486 computers, running Windows 2000 Professional
Microsoft BackOffice applications	Exchange Server and DNS
Server usage	Basic file and print

The design will take into account

- Number of users
- Number of administrative units
- Number of sites

Based on these design objectives, answer the following questions:

1. How many DNS domains will you need to configure?
2. How many subdomains will you need to configure?
3. How many zones will you need to configure?
4. How many primary name servers will you need to configure?
5. How many secondary name servers will you need to configure?
6. How many DNS cache-only servers will you need to configure?

Scenario 2: Designing DNS for a Medium-Size Network

You are consulting for the Northwind Company, which has 8,795 users. There are 8,000 users located in four primary sites, with the remaining employees located in 10 branch offices in major U.S. cities. The company has decided to upgrade its existing LANs to Windows 2000 Server. The organization has also decided to centralize all user accounts in a single location at the corporate headquarters.

As illustrated in Figure 7.6, the four primary sites are connected by T1 lines. The branch offices are connected to the nearest primary site by 56 Kilobit per second (Kbps) lines.

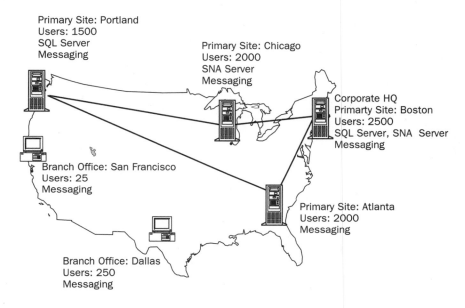

Figure 7.6   Connection of headquarters

Three of the four primary sites are independent business units and operate independently of the others. The fourth is corporate headquarters. Branch offices have between 25 and 250 users needing access to all four of the primary sites but seldom needing access to the other branch offices.

In addition to the 10 branch offices, you have discovered that the company has a temporary research location employing 10 people. The site has one server that connects to Boston using dial-on-demand routers. This site is expected to be shut down within six months. It is a stand-alone operation requiring connectivity for messaging only.

Primary sites will continue to maintain their own equipment and the equipment of the branch offices connected to them. Currently, bandwidth utilization is at 60 percent during peak times. Future network growth is expected to be minimal for the next 12 to 18 months.

Draft a network design using the criteria shown in Table 7.4.

Table 7.4   Network Design Criteria

Environmental Components	Detail
Users	8,795
Location(s)	Four primary sites, with 10 branch sites in major cities in the U.S. No plans for opening any international locations.
Administration	Full-time administrators at each of the four primary sites. Some of the smaller sites have part-time administrators.
Number of name servers	To be determined.
Number of cache servers	DNS cache servers are needed in each of the remote locations for the same zone.
Clients	386, 486, and Pentium computers running Windows 2000 Professional.
Server applications	SQL Server 7, Exchange Server, and DNS.

Other branch offices include: Los Angeles, 40 users; Salt Lake City, 25 users; Montreal, 30 users; New Orleans, 25 users; Kansas City, 25 users; Washington, DC, 100 users; Denver, 200 users; Miami, 75 users.

The design must take into account

- Number of users
- Number of administrative units
- Number of sites
- Speed and quality of links connecting sites
- Available bandwidth on links
- Expected changes to network
- Line of business applications

Based on these design objectives, answer the following questions:

1. How many DNS domains will you need to configure?
2. How many subdomains will you need to configure?
3. How many zones will you need to configure?
4. How many primary name servers will you need to configure?
5. How many secondary name servers will you need to configure?
6. How many DNS cache-only servers will you need to configure?
7. Use the following mileage chart to design a zone/branch office configuration based on the geographical proximity between each primary site and branch office. Branch offices should be in the same zone as the nearest primary site.

Zones for each branch office (based on geographical proximity):

Mileage Chart	Atlanta	Boston	Chicago	Portland, OR
Dallas	807	1817	934	2110
Denver	1400	1987	1014	1300
Kansas City	809	1454	497	1800
Los Angeles	2195	3050	2093	1143
Miami	665	1540	1358	3300
Montreal	1232	322	846	2695
New Orleans	494	1534	927	2508
Salt Lake City	1902	2403	1429	800
San Francisco	2525	3162	2187	700
Washington, DC	632	435	685	2700

Scenario 3: Designing DNS for a Large Network

The Northwind Company has 60,000 users located around the world. The corporate headquarters are in Geneva, Switzerland. Headquarters for North and South America are located in New York City. The Australia and Asian headquarters are located in Singapore. Each of the regional headquarters will maintain total control of users within their areas. Users require access to resources in the other regional headquarters. The three regional headquarters sites are connected by T1 lines.

Each of the three regional headquarters has lines of business applications that need to be available to all sites within their areas, as well as the other regional headquarters. The Malaysian and Australian subsidiaries have major manufacturing sites to which all regional subsidiaries need access.

These lines of business applications are all running on Windows 2000-based servers. These computers will be configured as servers within the domains. The links among Singapore, Australia, and Malaysia are typically operating at 90 percent utilization. The Asia and Australia region has 10 subsidiaries comprising Australia, China, Indonesia, Japan, Korea, Malaysia, New Zealand, Singapore, Taiwan, and Thailand.

Due to import restrictions with some of the subsidiaries, it has been decided to give control of the equipment to each subsidiary and to have a resource domain in each subsidiary. Lately, most of the computers the subsidiaries have purchased are running Windows 2000 Professional. The company has authorized redundant hardware where you can justify it.

To keep this scenario reasonable, the questions and answers deal only with the Asia and Australia region.

Draft a network design using the criteria in Table 7.5.

Table 7.5   Network Design Criteria

Environmental Components	Detail
Users in Asia and Australia domain	25,000 evenly distributed across all of the subsidiaries
Location(s)	Regional headquarters in Singapore; 10 subsidiaries in Australia, China, Indonesia, Japan, Korea, Malaysia, New Zealand, Singapore, Taiwan, and Thailand
Administration	Full-time administrators at the regional headquarters and each of the subsidiaries
Number of domains	To be determined
Clients	386, 486, and Pentium computers running Windows 2000 Professional
Server applications	SQL Server 7, SNA Server, Systems Management Server, Messaging, DNS
Number of cache servers	To be determined

The design for the Asia and Australia region must take into account

- Number of users
- Number of administrative units
- Number of sites
- Speed and quality of links connecting sites
- Available bandwidth on links
- Expected changes to network
- Line of business applications

Based on these design objectives, answer the following questions:

1. How many DNS domains will you need to configure?
2. How many subdomains will you need to configure?
3. How many zones will you need to configure?
4. How many primary name servers will you need to configure?
5. How many secondary name servers will you need to configure?
6. How many DNS cache-only servers will you need to configure?

Lesson Summary

Depending on the size of your organization and configuration, you may want to configure DNS for your site. Windows 2000 requires access to a DNS server to provide complete functionality. This DNS server can be on your local network or provided remotely by your ISP. However, the DNS implementation included in Windows 2000 has additional features beyond those of traditional DNS servers. For more information about these new features, please see Chapter 8, "Using Windows 2000 Domain Name Service."

Lesson 4: Installing DNS

Microsoft DNS is an RFC-compliant DNS server; as a result, it creates and uses standard DNS zone files and supports all standard resource record types. It is interoperable with other DNS servers and includes the DNS diagnostic utility NSLOOKUP. Microsoft DNS is tightly integrated with Windows Internet Name Service (WINS) and is administered through the graphical administration utility called DNS Manager. In this lesson, you will install the DNS service on Windows 2000.

After this lesson, you will be able to

- Install the Microsoft DNS Server service
- Troubleshoot DNS with NSLOOKUP

Estimated lesson time: 45 minutes

Before installing the Microsoft Windows 2000 DNS Server service, it is important that the Windows 2000 server's TCP/IP protocol be configured correctly. The DNS Server service obtains the default settings for the host name and domain name through the Microsoft TCP/IP Properties dialog box. The DNS Server service will create default SOA, host, and NS records based on the specified domain name and host name. If the host name and domain name are not specified, only the SOA record is created.

Practice: Installing the DNS Server Service

In this procedure, you install the Microsoft DNS Server service. You will configure DNS in a later lesson.

Before you continue with the lesson, run the Ch07a.exe demonstration file located in the Media folder on the Supplemental Course Materials CD-ROM that accompanies this book. The file provides an overview of installing the DNS server service.

Note   Complete this procedure from the computer you designate as the DNS server.

Before configuring DNS, verify that your DNS client settings are correct.

▶   **To verify DNS client settings**

1. Right-click My Network Places, then click Properties.

   The Network And Dial-Up Connections dialog box appears.

2. Right-click the connection (typically the Local Area Network properties) for which you want to configure the DNS server, then click Properties.

   The Connection Properties dialog box appears.

3. Click Internet Protocol (TCP/IP), then click Properties.

   The Internet Protocol (TCP/IP) Properties dialog box appears.

4. On the Internet Protocol (TCP/IP) Properties page, enter the IP address of the existing DNS server in the Preferred DNS Server field.

   You can also add the IP address of an alternate DNS server in the Alternate DNS Server field.

5. If you need to specify more than one alternate DNS server, click Advanced, click the DNS tab, then enter the servers in the DNS Server Addresses box.

6. Click OK to close the TCP/IP Properties dialog box.

7. Click OK to close the Connection Properties dialog box.

▶ **To install the DNS Server service**

1. In Control Panel, double-click Add/Remove Programs, then click Add/Remove Windows Components.

   The Windows Components Wizard appears.

2. Click Networking Services, then click Details.

   The Networking Services dialog box appears.

3. If it is not already selected, select the check box next to Domain Name System (DNS) as illustrated in Figure 7.7, then click OK.

4. Click Next.

   Windows 2000 installs DNS.

5. Click Finish.

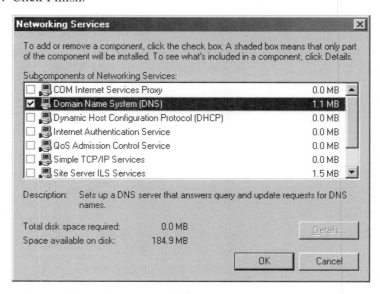

Figure 7.7   Domain Name System (DNS) check box in Networking Services

Troubleshooting DNS with NSLOOKUP

NSLOOKUP is a useful tool for troubleshooting DNS problems such as host name resolution. When you start NSLOOKUP, it shows the host name and IP address of the DNS server that is configured for the local system, and then displays a command prompt for further queries. If you type a question mark (?), NSLOOKUP shows all available commands. You can exit the program by typing exit. To look up a host's IP address using DNS, type the host name and press Enter. NSLOOKUP defaults to using the DNS server configured for the computer on which it is running, but you can focus it on a different DNS server by typing **server** *<name>* (where *<name>* is the host name of the server you want to use for future lookups). Once another server is specified, anything entered after that point is interpreted as a host name.

NSLOOKUP Modes

NSLOOKUP has two modes: interactive and noninteractive. If a single piece of data is needed, use noninteractive or command-line mode. If more than one piece of data is needed, interactive mode can be used.

NSLOOKUP Syntax

NSLOOKUP.EXE is a command line administrative tool for testing and trouble-shooting DNS servers. The following syntax is ued to run the NSLOOKUP utility:

nslookup [–option ...] [computer-to-find | – [server]]

Syntax	Description
–option ...	Specifies one or more NSLOOKUP commands. For a list of commands, use the help option inside NSLOOKUP.
computer-to-find	If *computer-to-find* is an IP address and the query type is host or PTR, the name of the computer is returned. If *computer-to-find* is a name and does not have a trailing period, the default DNS domain name is appended to the name. To look up a computer outside of the current DNS domain, append a period to the name. If a hyphen (–) is typed instead of *computer-to-find*, the command prompt changes to NSLOOKUP interactive mode.
server	Use this server as the DNS name server. If the server is omitted, the currently configured default DNS server is used.

▶ **To use NSLOOKUP in command mode**

1. At a command prompt, modify the properties so that the command prompt window has a screen buffer size of 50.

    As illustrated in Figure 7.8, use the Layout property page to do this. You should apply this change to all future instances of the command prompt window; it will be needed in later lessons.

2. Type the following command:

```
nslookup hostx
```

where hostx is a host in your domain.

3. NSLOOKUP will return the IP address of the computer hostx because the information is stored in the DNS database.

4. Exit the command prompt.

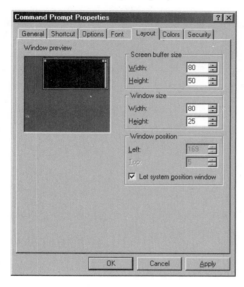

Figure 7.8   Command Prompt Properties dialog box

► **To use NSLOOKUP in interactive mode**

1. At a command prompt, type **nslookup** then press Enter.

   The > prompt appears.

2. Type **set all** at the > prompt.

   This command lists all of the current values of the NSLOOKUP options.

3. Use the following set commands to change the timeout value to 1 second and the number of retries to 7, as illustrated in Figure 7.9.

```
Set ti=1
Set ret=7
```

4. Use Set All to verify that the defaults were changed.

5. Type the names of the other computers, one at a time, at the > prompt. Press Enter after each name.

6. Exit the command prompt.

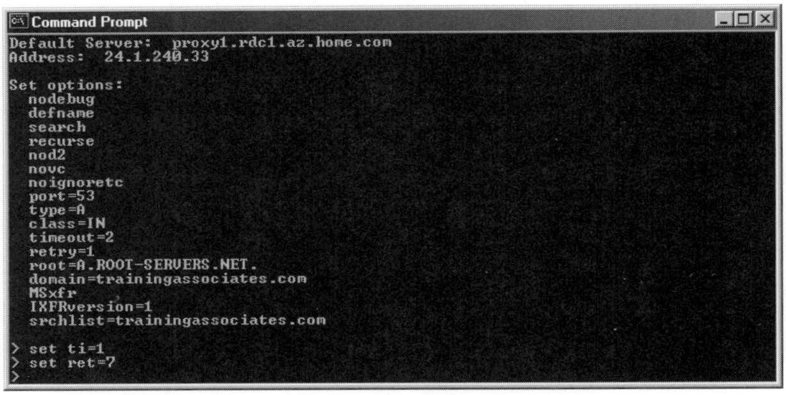

Figure 7.9   Setting the timeout and retry values in NSLOOKUP

Lesson Summary

Microsoft DNS is interoperable with other DNS servers. Before installing the DNS Server service, you should make sure that the Windows 2000 server's TCP/IP protocol is configured correctly.

The NSLOOKUP utility is the primary diagnostic tool for DNS. It lets you display resource records on DNS servers.

Lesson 5: Configuring DNS

There are two ways to administrate the Microsoft DNS server: use the DNS Manager or manually edit the DNS configuration files. This lesson reviews the tools used to administer a DNS server.

After this lesson, you will be able to

- Administer a DNS server
- Create a zone file and populate it with resource records

Estimated lesson time: 60 minutes

Configuring DNS Server Properties

The primary tool that you use to manage Windows 2000 DNS servers is the DNS console, illustrated in Figure 7.10. Because the DNS server has no initial information about a user's network, the DNS server installs as a caching-only name server for the Internet. This means that the DNS server contains only information on the Internet root servers. For most DNS server configurations, additional information must be supplied to obtain the preferred operation.

▶ **To open DNS**

1. Click Start, point to Programs, point to Administrative Tools, then click DNS.

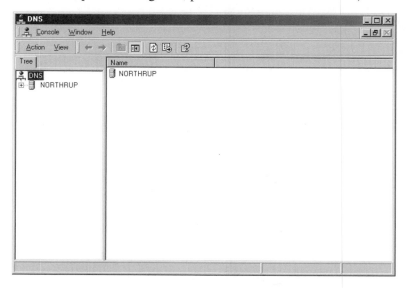

Figure 7.10   DNS settings in Microsoft Management Console (MMC)

▶ **To configure a new DNS server**

1. Click Start, point to Programs, point to Administrative Tools, then click DNS.

2. Highlight your server. On the Action menu, click Configure The Server.

3. Follow the instructions in the Configure DNS Server Wizard.

   In the Configure DNS Server Wizard, you can create one or more forward lookup zones. The type of zone you create can be

   ■ **Active Directory-integrated.**   Active Directory-integrated DNS enables Active Directory storage and replication of DNS zone databases. Zone data is stored as an Active Directory object and is replicated as part of domain replication.

   ■ **Standard primary.**   Standard primary zones are required to create and manage zones in your DNS name space if you are not using Active Directory.

   ■ **Standard secondary.**   Standard secondary zones help balance the processing load of primary servers and provide fault tolerance.

4. The next step in the New Zone Wizard is to create a forward or reverse lookup zone. If you select Forward lookup zone, you must provide a name for the new zone and then specify a zone file. If you select Reverse lookup zone, you must provide the network ID or zone name, and then specify a zone file.

5. Click Finish to close the wizard.

Manually Configuring DNS

The DNS server can be configured manually by editing files in the default installation path *system_root*\System32\Dns. Administration is identical to administration of traditional DNS. These files can be modified using a text editor, as illustrated in Figure 7.11. The DNS service must then be stopped and restarted.

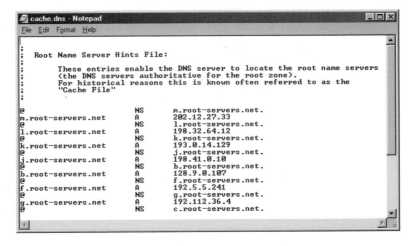

Figure 7.11   Editing the CACHE.DNS file

Adding DNS Domains and Zones

The first step in configuring the DNS server is to determine the hierarchy for your DNS domains and zones. Once the domain and zone information has been determined, this information must be entered into the DNS configuration using the DNS console.

Adding Primary or Secondary Zones

You add primary and secondary zones through the DNS console, as illustrated in Figure 7.12. After you enter your zone information, DNS Manager will construct a default zone file name. If the zone file already exists in the DNS directory, DNS console will automatically import these records.

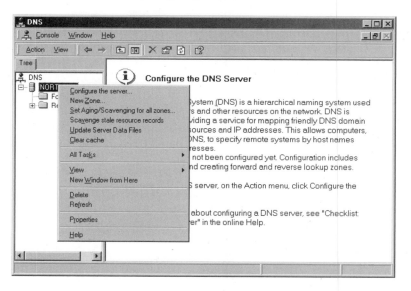

Figure 7.12   Creating a new zone with the DNS console

A primary zone stores name-to-address mappings locally. When you configure a primary zone, you need no information other than the zone name.

Secondary zones obtain name-to-address mappings from a master server by zone transfer. When you configure a secondary zone, you must supply the names for the zone and master name server.

Once all zones have been added to the server, subdomains under the zones can be added. If multiple levels of subdomains are needed, create each successive subdomain. There is a key written to the DNS registry entry for each zone for which the DNS will be authoritative. The keys are located under HKEY_LOCAL_MACHINE\SYSTEM\CurrentControlSet\Services\DNS\Zones.

Each zone has its own key that contains the name of the database file, which indicates whether the DNS server is a primary or secondary name server. For example, for the zone dev.volcano.com, there is the following registry entry: HKEY_LOCAL_MACHINE\SYSTEM\CurrentControlSet\Services\DNS\ Zones\dev.volcano.com.

Configuring Zone Properties

After you have successfully added a zone, you can configure and modify the zone properties (described in Table 7.6).

Table 7.6   Zone Properties

Property	Description
General	Configures the zone file in which the resource records are stored and specifies whether this is a primary or secondary name server.
SOA record	Configures zone transfer information and the name server administrator mailbox.
Notify	Specifies the secondary servers to be alerted when the primary server database changes. Also, additional security can be applied to the name server by specifying that only the listed secondary servers can contact this server.
WINS lookup	Enables the name server to query WINS to resolve names. A list of WINS servers can be configured in this dialog. The WINS servers can be set on a per-name-server basis by selecting the Settings Only Affect Local Server check box. If this is not selected, secondary servers will also use the configured WINS servers.

Practice: Configuring a DNS Server

In this procedure, you configure the DNS server by adding a primary zone. Complete this procedure from the DNS server computer.

Before you continue with the lesson, run the Ch07b.exe demonstration file located in the Media folder on the Supplemental Course Materials CD-ROM that accompanies this book. The file provides an overview of configuring the DNS server service.

▶   **To add a zone to a server**

1. Right-click your computer name, then click New Zone.
   The New Zone Wizard appears.
2. Click Next, select Standard Primary, then click Next.
3. Select Forward Lookup Zone, then click Next.
4. In the Name box, type **zone1.org** (where zone1.org is your zone name).
5. Click Create A New File With This File Name, then click Next.
   Zone1.org.dns will be the file name (where zone1.org is your zone name).
6. Click Finish to create the new zone.

The Forward Lookup Zones folder now contains your new zone, as illustrated in Figure 7.13.

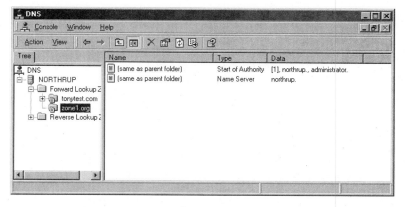

Figure 7.13   Zone added to the Forward Lookup Zones folder

Adding Resource Records

Once the zones and subdomains are configured, resource records can be added. To create a new host, right-click a zone or subdomain and then click New Host, as illustrated in Figure 7.14. Simply type the host name and click Add Host, and the host record will be created.

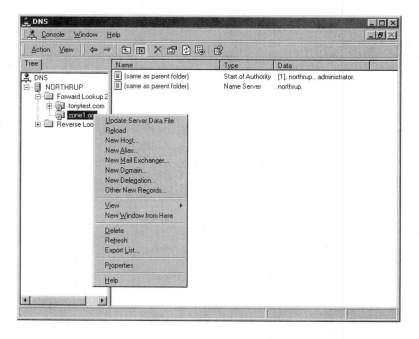

Figure 7.14   Adding a new host

To create a record of a different type, right-click a zone or subdomain and then click Other New Records. Next, select which resource record type to create. A dialog box displays various fields specific to record type, as illustrated in Figure 7.15.

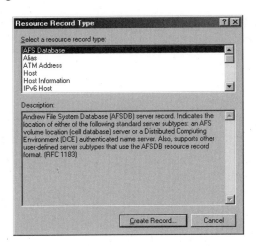

Figure 7.15   Selecting a type of record to create

Configuring Reverse Lookup

To find a host name, given the host's IP address, a reverse lookup zone must be created for each network on which hosts in the DNS database reside. Adding a reverse lookup zone is procedurally identical to adding any other type of zone, except for the zone name. For example, if a host has an address of 198.231.25.89, it would be represented in the in-addr.arpa domain as 89.25.231.198.in-addr.arpa. Furthermore, to enable this host to appear to a client who has its IP address, a zone would need to be added to the DNS for 25.231.198.in-addr.arpa. All PTR records for the network 198.231.25.0 would be added to this reverse lookup zone.

Lesson Summary

The first step in configuring Windows 2000 DNS server is to determine the hierarchy for your DNS domains and zones. Once the zones and subdomains are configured, resource records can be added. To find a host name, given the host's IP address, a reverse lookup zone must be created for each network on which hosts in the DNS database reside.

Review

Answering the following questions will reinforce key information presented in this chapter. If you are unable to answer a question, review the appropriate lesson and then try the question again. Answers to the questions can be found in Appendix A, "Questions and Answers."

1. Name the three components of the DNS.

2. Describe the difference between primary, secondary, and master name servers.

3. List three reasons to have a secondary name server.

4. Describe the difference between a domain and a zone.

5. Describe the difference between recursive and iterative queries.

6. List the files required for a Windows 2000 DNS implementation.

7. Describe the purpose of the boot file.

C H A P T E R   8

Using Windows 2000 Domain Name Service

About This Chapter

In this chapter, you will learn how to work with Domain Name System (DNS) zones. This includes implementing a delegated zone and configuring zones for dynamic updates. You will also learn how to configure a DNS server to work as a caching-only server and how to monitor DNS server performance.

Before You Begin

To complete this chapter, you must have

- Installed Microsoft Windows 2000 Server with Transmission Control Protocol/Internet Protocol (TCP/IP) and DNS services

Lesson 1: Working with Zones

Servers refer to their zones (also called DNS database files) to resolve names. The zones contain resource records that comprise the resource information associated with the DNS domain. For example, some resource records map friendly names to Internet Protocol (IP) addresses, and others map IP addresses to friendly names. Some resource records not only include information about servers in the DNS domain, but also serve to define the domain by specifying which servers are authoritative for which zones. In this lesson, you will learn how to configure DNS zones in Windows 2000.

After this lesson, you will be able to

- Implement a delegated zone for DNS
- Configure zones for dynamic updates

Estimated lesson time: 20 minutes

Delegating Zones

A DNS database can be partitioned into multiple zones. A zone is a portion of the DNS database that contains the resource records with the owner names that belong to the contiguous portion of the DNS name space. Zone files are maintained on DNS servers. A single DNS server can be configured to host zero, one, or multiple zones. Each zone is anchored at a specific domain name referred to as the zone's root domain. A zone contains information about all names that end with the zone's root domain name. A DNS server is considered authoritative for a name if it loads the zone containing that name. The first record in any zone file is a start of authority (SOA) resource record. The SOA resource record identifies a primary DNS name server for the zone as the best source of information for the data within that zone and as an entity processing the updates for the zone.

Names within a zone can also be delegated to other zone(s). Delegation is a process of assigning responsibility for a portion of a DNS name space to a separate entity. This separate entity could be another organization, department, or workgroup within your company. In technical terms, delegating means assigning authority over portions of your DNS name space to other zones. The name server record that specifies the delegated zone and the DNS name of the server authoritative for that zone represents such delegation. Delegating across multiple zones was part of the original design goal of DNS. The following are the main reasons for the delegation of a DNS name space:

- A need to delegate management of a DNS domain to a number of organizations or departments within an organization

- A need to distribute the load of maintaining one large DNS database among multiple name servers to improve the name resolution performance as well as create a DNS fault-tolerant environment

- A need to allow for hosts' organizational affiliations by including them in appropriate domains

The name server's resource records facilitate delegation by identifying DNS servers for each zone. They appear in all forward and reverse lookup zones. Whenever a DNS server needs to cross a delegation, it will refer to the name server's resource records for DNS servers in the target zone. In Figure 8.1, the management of the microsoft.com domain is delegated across two zones, microsoft.com and mydomain.microsoft.com.

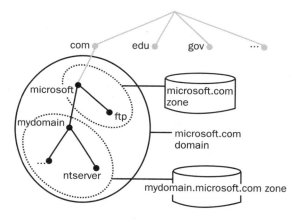

Figure 8.1 The microsoft.com domain delegated across two zones

---

Note If multiple name server records exist for a delegated zone identifying multiple DNS servers available for querying, the Windows 2000 DNS server will be able to select the closest DNS server based on the round-trip intervals measured over time for every DNS server.

Understanding DNS Zones and Domains

Domain name servers store information about part of the domain name space called a zone. The name server is authoritative for a particular zone. A single name server can be authoritative for many zones. Understanding the difference between a zone and a domain is sometimes confusing.

A zone is simply a portion of a domain. For example, the domain microsoft.com may contain all of the data for microsoft.com, marketing.microsoft.com, and development.microsoft.com. However, the zone microsoft.com contains only information for microsoft.com and references to the authoritative name servers for the subdomains. The zone microsoft.com can contain the data for subdomains of microsoft.com if they have not been delegated to another server. For example, marketing.microsoft.com may manage its own delegated zone. The parent, microsoft.com, may manage development.microsoft.com. If there are no subdomains, then the zone and domain are essentially the same. In this case the zone contains all data for the domain.

Note   All domains (or subdomains) that appear as part of the applicable zone delegation must be created in the current zone prior to performing delegation as described here. As necessary, use the DNS console to first add domains to the zone before completing this procedure.

▶   **To create a zone delegation**

1. Click Start, point to Programs, point to Administrative Tools, then click DNS.

2. In the console tree, right-click your subdomain and then click New Delegation, as illustrated in Figure 8.2.

    The New Delegation Wizard appears.

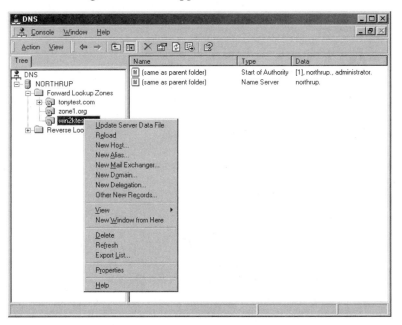

Figure 8.2   Adding a new delegation server

3. Click Next.

4. In the Delegated Domain Name dialog box, type a delegated domain name, then click Next.

5. In the Name Servers dialog box, click Add to specify names and IP addresses of DNS servers you want to have host the delegated zone.

   The New Resource Record dialog box will appear, allowing you to specify DNS servers.

6. Type the DNS server name, click Add, then click OK.

7. In the Name Servers dialog box, click Next.

8. Click Finish to close the New Delegation Wizard.

Configuring Zones for Dynamic Update

Originally, DNS was designed to support only static changes to a zone database. Because of the design limitations of static DNS, the ability to add, remove, or modify resource records could only be performed manually by a DNS system administrator. For example, a DNS system administrator would edit records on a zone's primary server and the revised zone database would then be propagated to secondary servers during zone transfer. This design is workable when the number of changes is small and updates occur infrequently, but can otherwise become unmanageable.

Windows 2000 provides client and server support for the use of dynamic updates. Dynamic updates enable DNS client computers to register and dynamically update their resource records with a DNS server whenever changes occur. This reduces the need for manual administration of zone records, especially for clients that frequently move or change locations and use DHCP to obtain an IP address.

By default, computers that run Windows 2000 and are statically configured for TCP/IP attempt to dynamically register host and pointer resource records for IP addresses configured and used by their installed network connections. Dynamic updates can be sent for any of the following reasons or events:

- An IP address is added, removed, or modified in the TCP/IP properties configuration for any one of the installed network connections

- An IP address lease changes or renews with the DHCP server any one of the installed network connections; for example, when the computer is started or if the ipconfig/renew command is used

- The ipconfig/registerdns command is used to manually force a refresh of the client name registration in DNS

- When the computer is turned on

Dynamic Update Requirements

For DNS servers, the DNS service allows dynamic update to be enabled or disabled on a per-zone basis at each server configured to load either a standard primary or directory-integrated zone. By default, client computers running under any version of Windows 2000 dynamically update their host resource records in DNS when configured for TCP/IP. When DNS zones are stored in Active Directory, DNS is configured by default to accept dynamic updates.

Note   Windows 2000 DNS servers support dynamic updates. The DNS server provided with Windows NT Server 4.0 does not.

For a request for a dynamic update to be performed, several prerequisite conditions can be configured. Each prerequisite must be satisfied for an update to occur. After all prerequisites are met, the zone's primary server can then proceed with an update of its local zones. Some examples of prerequisites that can be set are:

- A required resource record or resource record set already exists or is in use prior to an update.
- A required resource record or resource record set does not exist or is not in use prior to an update.
- A requester is permitted to initiate an update of a specified resource record or resource record set.

For client computers to be registered and updated dynamically with a DNS server, either:

- Install or upgrade client computers to Windows 2000.
- Install and use a Windows 2000 DHCP server on your network to lease client computers.

Practice: Enabling Dynamic Updates

In this practice, you will allow for DNS client computers to register and dynamically update their resource records with a DNS server whenever changes occur by enabling dynamic updates for a DNS zone.

▶ **To allow dynamic updates**

1. Click Start, point to Programs, point to Administrative Tools, then click DNS.

   The DNS administrative console appears.

2. In the console tree, right-click your zone, then click Properties.

   The Zone Properties dialog box appears, as illustrated in Figure 8.3.

3. In the Allow Dynamic Updates list box, click Yes.

4. Click OK to close the Zone Properties dialog box.

5. Close the DNS administrative console.

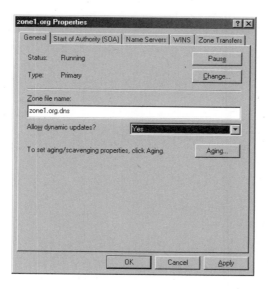

Figure 8.3 Zone Properties dialog box

Lesson Summary

Delegation is a process of assigning responsibility for a portion of a DNS name space to a separate entity. The names server's resource records facilitate delegation by identifying DNS servers for each zone. They appear in all forward and reverse lookup zones. Windows 2000 provides client and server support for the use of dynamic updates. Dynamic updates enable DNS client computers to register and dynamically update their resource records with a DNS server whenever changes occur.

Lesson 2: Working with Servers

Because DNS servers are of critical importance in most environments, it is important to continually monitor them. In this lesson, you will learn how to manage and monitor your DNS servers. In addition, you will learn how to implement a caching-only server.

After this lesson, you will be able to
- Configure a caching-only server
- Manage and monitor DNS servers

Estimated lesson time: 15 minutes

Overview of DNS Servers and Caching

As DNS servers process client queries using recursion or iteration, they discover and acquire a significant store of information about the DNS name space. The server then caches this information. Caching provides a way to speed the performance of DNS resolution for subsequent queries of popular names while substantially reducing DNS-related query traffic on the network.

As DNS servers make recursive queries on behalf of clients, they temporarily cache resource records. Cached resource records contain information obtained from DNS servers that are authoritative for DNS domain names learned while making iterative queries to search and fully answer a recursive query performed on behalf of a client. Later, when other clients place new queries that request resource record information matching cached resource records, the DNS server can use the cached resource record information to answer them.

When information is cached, a Time to Live (TTL) value applies to all cached resource records. As long as the TTL for a cached resource record does not expire, a DNS server can continue to cache and use the resource record again when answering queries by its clients that match these resource records. Caching TTL values used by resource records in most zone configurations are assigned the minimum (default) TTL, which is set in the zone's SOA resource record. By default, the minimum TTL is 3600 seconds (1 hour), but can be adjusted or, if needed, individual caching TTLs can be set at each resource record.

Implementing a Caching-Only Server

Although all DNS name servers cache queries that they have resolved, caching-only servers are DNS name servers that only perform queries, cache the answers, and return the results. They are not authoritative for any domains and the information that they contain is limited to what has been cached while resolving queries. The benefit provided by caching-only servers is that they do not generate zone transfer network traffic because they do not contain any zones. However, there is one disadvantage: When the server is initially started, it has no cached information and must build up this information over time as it services requests.

▶ **To install a caching-only DNS server**

1. Install the DNS Server service on the computer.

   It is strongly recommended that, when operating the computer as a DNS server, you manually configure TCP/IP and use a static IP address.

2. Do not configure the DNS server to load any zones.

   A caching-only DNS server can be valuable at a site where DNS functionality is needed locally but it is not administratively desirable to create a separate domain or zone for that location. Caching-only DNS servers do not host any zones and are not authoritative for a particular domain. They are DNS servers that build a local server cache of names learned while performing recursive queries on behalf of their clients. This information is then available from its cache when answering subsequent client queries.

3. Verify that server root hints are configured or updated correctly.

When a DNS server starts, it needs a list of root server "hints." These hints are name server (NS) and address (A) records for the root servers, which have historically been called the cache file.

You can configure root hints by clicking the Root Hints tab in the Properties dialog box for the DNS server in the DNS administrative console. The Root Hints tab is illustrated in Figure 8.4.

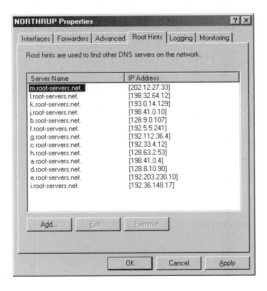

Figure 8.4   Root Hints tab on the DNS server's Properties dialog box

Monitoring DNS Server Performance

Because DNS servers are of critical importance in most environments, monitoring their performance can provide a useful benchmark for predicting, estimating, and optimizing DNS server performance. In addition, you can quickly identify degraded server performance either over time or during periods of peak activity. Windows 2000 Server provides a set of DNS server performance counters that can be used with System Monitor to measure and monitor various aspects of server activity.

Practice: Testing a Simple Query on a DNS Server

In this practice, you will use the DNS administrative console to test a query on your DNS server.

▶ **To test a query on your DNS server**

1. Click Start, point to Programs, point to Administrative Tools, then click DNS.

2. In the console tree, right-click the DNS server, then click Properties.

3. Click the Monitoring tab, illustrated in Figure 8.5.

4. Select the A Simple Query Against This DNS Server check box.

5. Click Test Now.

   Results of the query test appear in Test Results.

6. Click OK to close the DNS server's Properties dialog box.

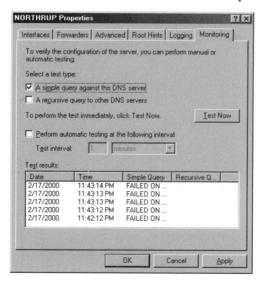

Figure 8.5　The Monitoring tab in the DNS server's Properties dialog box

DNS Server Performance Counters

Windows 2000 Server provides a set of DNS server performance counters that can be used to measure and monitor various aspects of server activity, such as the following:

- Overall DNS server performance statistics, such as the number of overall queries and responses processed by a DNS server

- User Datagram Protocol (UDP) or Transmission Control Protocol (TCP) counters, for measuring DNS queries and responses that are processed using either of these transport protocols, respectively

- Dynamic update and secure dynamic update counters, for measuring registration and update activity generated by dynamic clients

- Memory usage counters, for measuring system memory usage and memory allocation patterns created by operating the server computer as a Windows 2000 DNS server

- Recursive lookup counters, for measuring queries and responses when the DNS Server service uses recursion to look up and fully resolve DNS names on behalf of requesting clients

- Windows Internet Name Service (WINS) lookup counters, for measuring queries and responses made to WINS servers when the WINS lookup integration features of the DNS Server service are used

- Zone transfer counters, including specific counters for measuring all-zone transfer (AXFR), incremental zone transfer (IXFR), and DNS zone update notification activity.

Managing DNS Servers Remotely

DNS is an Internet and TCP/IP standard name service that enables a server running the DNS service to enable client computers on your network to register and resolve DNS domain names. These names can be used to find and access resources offered by other computers on the Internet. With Windows 2000 Administration Tools, included on the Windows 2000 Server and Windows 2000 Advanced Server compact disc sets, you can manage a server remotely from any computer that is running Windows 2000.

Windows 2000 Administration Tools contains Microsoft Management Console (MMC) snap-ins and other administrative tools that are used to manage computers running Windows 2000 Server and that are not provided with Windows 2000 Professional. Once Windows 2000 Administration Tools is installed on a computer, an administrator can open the server administrative tools and begin managing a remote server from that computer.

Lesson Summary

Although all DNS name servers cache queries that they have resolved, caching-only servers are DNS name servers that only perform queries, cache the answers, and return the results. The benefit provided by caching-only servers is that they do not generate zone transfer network traffic because they do not contain any zones. Windows 2000 Server provides a set of DNS server performance counters that can be used with System Monitor to measure and monitor various aspects of server activity. You can use the Monitoring tab in the DNS server's Properties dialog box in the DNS administrative console to perform tests on the DNS server. You can also use the Windows 2000 Administration Tools to manage a server remotely from any computer that is running Windows 2000.

Review

Answering the following questions will reinforce key information presented in this chapter. If you are unable to answer a question, review the appropriate lesson and then try the question again. Answers to the questions can be found in Appendix A, "Questions and Answers."

1. How many zones can a single DNS server host?

2. What benefits do DNS clients obtain from the dynamic update feature of Windows 2000?

3. Name one benefit and one disadvantage of a caching-only server.

4. List and describe three DNS performance counters.

C H A P T E R   9

Implementing Windows Internet Name Service (WINS)

About This Chapter

Although Microsoft Windows Internet Name Service (WINS) servers are not needed in a network consisting entirely of Microsoft Windows 2000-based computers, they are crucial in most Transmission Control Protocol/Internet Protocol (TCP/IP) networks containing computers based on the older architectures of Windows NT 4.0, Windows 98, or Windows 95. In this chapter, you will learn how to implement WINS on your network.

Before You Begin

To complete this chapter, you must have

- Installed Windows 2000 Server with TCP/IP

Lesson 1: Introduction to WINS

WINS provides a distributed database for registering and querying dynamic mappings of NetBIOS names for computers and groups used on your network. WINS maps NetBIOS names to IP addresses and was designed to solve the problems arising from NetBIOS name resolution in routed environments. WINS is the best choice for NetBIOS name resolution in routed networks that use NetBIOS over TCP/IP.

After this lesson, you will be able to

- Describe the relationship between NetBIOS and TCP/IP
- Describe the advantage of using WINS
- Describe a new Windows 2000 feature relating to NetBIOS

Estimated lesson time: 15 minutes

Name Resolution with NetBIOS

This section explains NetBIOS name resolution concepts and methods to help you better understand WINS functionality. This is because previous versions of Windows, such as Windows NT 4.0, and some Windows-based applications use NetBIOS names to identify network resources.

Overview of NetBIOS

NetBIOS was developed for IBM in 1983 by Sytek Corporation to allow applications to communicate over a network. As illustrated in Figure 9.1, NetBIOS defines two entities:

- A session-level interface
- A session management/data transport protocol

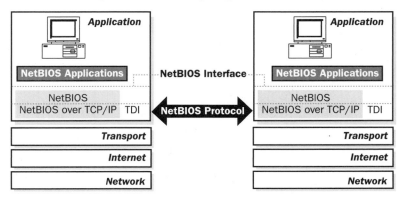

Figure 9.1   NetBIOS communication over TCP/IP

The NetBIOS interface is a presentation-layer application programming interface (API) for user applications to submit network input/output (I/O) and control directives to underlying network protocols. An application program that uses the NetBIOS interface API for network communication can be run on any protocol that supports the NetBIOS interface. This is implemented by the session layer software, such as NetBIOS Frame Protocol (NBFP) or NetBIOS over TCP/IP (NetBT), to perform the network I/O required to accommodate the NetBIOS interface command set.

NetBIOS provides commands and support for the following services:

- Network name registration and verification
- Session establishment and termination
- Reliable connection-oriented session data transfer
- Unreliable connectionless datagram data transfer
- Support protocol (driver) and adapter monitoring and management

NetBIOS Names

A NetBIOS name is a unique 16-byte address used to identify a NetBIOS resource on the network. This name is either a unique (exclusive) or group (nonexclusive) name. Unique names are typically used to send network communication to a specific process on a computer. Group names are used to send information to multiple computers at one time. An example of a process that uses a NetBIOS name is the File and Printer Sharing for Microsoft Networks service on a computer running Windows 2000. When your computer starts up, this service registers a unique NetBIOS name based on the name of your computer. The exact name used by the service is the 15-character computer name plus a 16th character of 0x20. If the computer name is not 15 characters long, it is padded with spaces up to 15 characters.

NetBIOS name resolution is the process of mapping a computer's NetBIOS name to an IP address. A computer's NetBIOS name must be resolved to an IP address before the IP address can be resolved to a hardware address. Microsoft TCP/IP uses several methods to resolve NetBIOS names; however, the exact mechanism by which NetBIOS names are resolved to IP addresses depends on the NetBIOS node type that is configured for the node. Request for Comments (RFC) 1001, "Protocol Standard for a NetBIOS Service on a TCP/UDP Transport: Concepts and Methods," defines the NetBIOS node types, as listed in Table 9.1.

Table 9.1   NetBIOS Node Types

Node Type	Description
B-node (broadcast)	B-node uses broadcast NetBIOS name queries for name registration and resolution. B-node has two major problems: (1) Broadcasts disturb every node on the network. (2) Routers typically do not forward broadcasts, so only NetBIOS names on the local network can be resolved.
P-node (peer–peer)	P-node uses a NetBIOS name server, such as a WINS server, to resolve NetBIOS names. P-node does not use broadcasts; instead, it queries the name server directly.
M-node (mixed)	M-node is a combination of B-node and P-node. By default, an M-node functions as a B-node. If an M-node is unable to resolve a name by broadcast, it queries a NetBIOS name server using P-node.
H-node (hybrid)	H-node is a combination of P-node and B-node. By default, an H-node functions as a P-node. If an H-node is unable to resolve a name through the NetBIOS name server, it uses a broadcast to resolve the name.

Computers running Windows 2000 are B-node by default and become H-node when they are configured with a WINS server. Windows 2000 can also use a local database file called LMHOSTS to resolve remote NetBIOS names. The LMHOSTS file is stored in the %systemroot%\System32\Drivers\Etc folder. A sample LMHOSTS file (LMHOSTS.SAM) is included in this directory.

The LMHOSTS File

The LMHOSTS file is a static ASCII file used to resolve NetBIOS names to IP addresses of remote computers running Windows NT and other NetBIOS-based hosts.

Figure 9.2 shows an example of the LMHOSTS file.

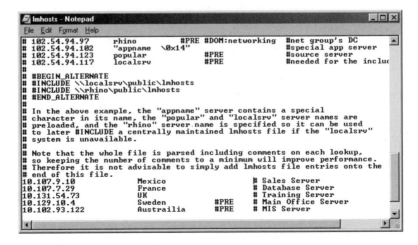

Figure 9.2   The LMHOSTS file

Predefined Keywords

An LMHOSTS file also contains predefined keywords that are prefixed with a #. If you use this LMHOSTS file on an older NetBT system such as LAN Manager, these directives are ignored as comments because they begin with a number sign (#). Table 9.2 lists the possible LMHOSTS keywords.

Table 9.2   LMHOSTS Keywords

Predefined Keyword	Description
#PRE	Defines which entries should be initially preloaded as permanent entries in the name cache. Preloaded entries reduce network broadcasts, because names are resolved from cache rather than from broadcast or by parsing the LMHOSTS file. Entries with a #PRE tag are loaded automatically at initialization or manually by typing **nbtstat –R** at a command prompt.
#DOM:[domain_name]	Facilitates domain activity, such as logon validation over a router, account synchronization, and browsing.
#NOFNR	Avoids using NetBIOS-directed name queries for older LAN Manager UNIX systems.
#BEGIN_ALTERNATE #END_ALTERNATE	Defines a redundant list of alternate locations for LMHOSTS files. The recommended way to #INCLUDE remote files is using a Universal Naming Convention (UNC) path, to ensure access to the file. Of course, the UNC names must exist in the LMHOSTS file with a proper IP address to NetBIOS name translation.
#INCLUDE	Loads and searches NetBIOS entries in a separate file from the default LMHOSTS file. Typically, an #INCLUDE file is a centrally located shared LMHOST file.
#MH	Adds multiple entries for a multihomed computer.

WINS Overview

WINS eliminates the need for broadcasts to resolve computer names to IP addresses and provides a dynamic database that maintains mappings of computer names to IP addresses. WINS is an enhanced NetBIOS name server (NBNS) designed by Microsoft to eliminate broadcast traffic associated with the B-node implementation of NetBT. It is used to register NetBIOS computer names and resolve them to IP addresses for both local and remote hosts.

There are several advantages of using WINS. The primary advantage is that client requests for computer name resolution are sent directly to a WINS server. If the WINS server can resolve the name, it sends the IP address directly to the client. As a result, a broadcast is not needed and network traffic is reduced. However, if the WINS server is unavailable, the WINS client can still use a broadcast in an attempt to resolve the name. Another advantage of using WINS is that the WINS database is updated dynamically, so it is always current. This eliminates the need for an LMHOSTS file. In addition, WINS provides network and interdomain browsing capabilities.

Before two NetBIOS-based hosts can communicate, the destination NetBIOS name must be resolved to an IP address. This is necessary because TCP/IP requires an IP address rather than a NetBIOS computer name to communicate. As illustrated in Figure 9.3, resolution uses the following process:

1. In a WINS environment, each time a WINS client starts, it registers its NetBIOS name/IP address mapping with a configured WINS server.

2. When a WINS client initiates a command to communicate with another host, the name query request is sent directly to the WINS server instead of being broadcast on the local network.

3. If the WINS server finds a NetBIOS name/IP address mapping for the destination host in this database, it returns the destination host's IP address to the WINS client. Because the WINS database obtains NetBIOS name/IP address mappings dynamically, it is always current.

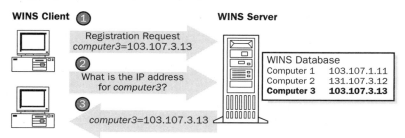

Figure 9.3   Name resolution with WINS

WINS and Windows 2000

Prior to Windows 2000, all MS-DOS and Windows-based operating systems required the NetBIOS naming interface to support network capabilities. With the release of Windows 2000, support for the NetBIOS naming interface is no longer required for networking computers because you can disable NetBT for each network connection. This feature is intended for computers that only use Domain Name System (DNS) name registration and resolution techniques, and communicate by using the Client for Microsoft Networks and the File and Print Sharing for Microsoft Networks components with other computers where NetBT is disabled. Examples of disabling NetBT include computers in specialized or secured roles for your network, such as an edge proxy server or bastion host in a firewall environment, where NetBT support is not required or desired.

Another example is an environment consisting of host computers and programs that support the use of the DNS that could be built to run using Windows 2000 and other operating systems not requiring NetBIOS names, such as some versions of UNIX. However, most networks still need to integrate legacy operating systems that require NetBIOS network names with computers running Windows 2000. For this reason, Microsoft has continued to provide default support for NetBIOS names with Windows 2000 to ease interoperability with legacy operating systems that require their use. This support is provided mainly in two ways:

- By default, all computers running Windows 2000 that use TCP/IP are enabled to provide client-side support for registering and resolving NetBIOS names.

  This support is provided through NetBT and can, if desired, be manually disabled.

- Windows 2000 Server continues to provide server-side support through WINS. WINS can be used to effectively manage NetBT-based networks.

Lesson Summary

Some applications and previous versions of Windows use NetBIOS names to identify network resources. WINS is an enhanced NBNS designed by Microsoft to eliminate broadcast traffic associated with the B-node implementation of NetBT. There are several advantages to using WINS. The primary advantage is that broadcast traffic is reduced because requests for name resolution are sent directly to the WINS server.

Lesson 2: The WINS Resolution Process

WINS uses standard methods of name registration, name renewal, and name release. This lesson introduces the different phases used to resolve a NetBIOS name to an IP address using WINS.

After this lesson, you will be able to

- Describe WINS name registration, renewal, release, query, and response.

Estimated lesson time: 25 minutes

Resolving NetBIOS Names with WINS

When a client needs to contact another host on the network, it first contacts the WINS server to resolve the IP address using mapping information from the database of the server. The relational database engine of the WINS server accesses an indexed sequential access method (ISAM) database. The ISAM database is a replicated database that contains NetBIOS computer names and IP address mappings. For a WINS client to log on to the network, it must register its computer name and IP address with the WINS server. This creates an entry in the WINS database for every NetBIOS service running on the client. Because these entries are updated each time a WINS-enabled client logs on to the network, information stored in the WINS server database remains accurate.

The process WINS uses to resolve and maintain NetBIOS names is similar to the B-node implementation. The method used to renew a name is unique to NetBIOS node types that use a NetBIOS name server. WINS is an extension of RFCs 1001 and 1002. Figure 9.4 shows the process of resolving a NetBIOS name.

Name Registration

Each WINS client is configured with the IP address of a primary WINS server and optionally, a secondary WINS server. When a client starts, it registers its NetBIOS name and IP address with the configured WINS server. The WINS server stores the client's NetBIOS name/IP address mapping in its database.

Name Renewal

All NetBIOS names are registered on a temporary basis, which means that the same name can be used later by a different host if the original owner stops using it.

Name Release

Each WINS client is responsible for maintaining the lease on its registered name. When the name will no longer be used, such as when the computer is shut down, the WINS client sends a message to the WINS server to release it.

Name Query and Name Resolution

After a WINS client has registered its NetBIOS name and IP address with a WINS server, it can communicate with other hosts by obtaining the IP address of other NetBIOS-based computers from a WINS server. All WINS communications are done using directed datagrams over UDP port 137 (NBNS).

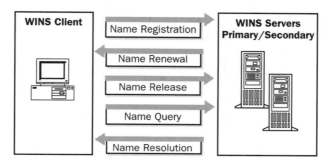

Figure 9.4   Name resolution between clients and a WINS server

Name Registration

Unlike the B-node implementation of NetBT, which broadcasts its name registration, WINS clients register their NetBIOS names with WINS servers.

When a WINS client initializes, it registers its NetBIOS name by sending a name registration request directly to the configured WINS server. NetBIOS names are registered when services or applications start, such as the Workstation, Server, and Messenger.

If the WINS server is available and the name is not already registered by another WINS client, a successful registration message is returned to the client. This message contains the amount of time the NetBIOS name is registered to the client, specified as the Time to Live (TTL). Figure 9.5 shows the name registration process.

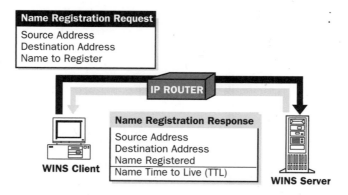

Figure 9.5   Name registration process

When a Duplicate Name Is Found

If there is a duplicate name registered in the WINS database, the WINS server sends a challenge to the currently registered owner of the name. The challenge is sent as a name query request. The WINS server sends the challenge three times at 500-millisecond intervals.

If the registered computer is a multihomed computer, the WINS server tries each IP address it has for the computer until it receives a response or until all of the IP addresses have been tried.

If the current registered owner responds successfully to the WINS server, the WINS server sends a negative name registration response to the WINS client that is attempting to register the name. If the current registered owner does not respond to the WINS server, the WINS server sends a successful name registration response to the WINS client that is attempting to register the name.

When the WINS Server Is Unavailable

A WINS client will make three attempts to find the primary WINS server. If it fails after the third attempt, the name registration request is sent to the secondary WINS server, if configured. If neither server is available, the WINS client may initiate a broadcast to register its name.

Name Renewal

To continue using the same NetBIOS name, a client must renew its lease before it expires. If a client does not renew the lease, the WINS server makes it available for another WINS client.

Name Refresh Request

WINS clients must renew their name registrations before the renewal interval expires. The renewal interval determines how long the server stores the name registration as an active record in the WINS database. When a WINS client renews its name registration, it sends a name refresh request to the WINS server. The name refresh request includes the IP address and the NetBIOS name that the client seeks to refresh. The WINS server responds to the name refresh request with a name refresh response that includes a new renewal interval for the name. When a WINS client refreshes its name, it performs the following steps:

1. When a client has consumed half of its renewal interval, it sends a name refresh request to the primary WINS server.

2. If its name is not refreshed by the primary WINS server, the WINS client tries to refresh again in 10 minutes and continues to try the primary WINS server repeatedly every 10 minutes for a total of 1 hour. The WINS client, after trying to refresh its name registration with the primary WINS server for 1 hour, stops trying and attempts to refresh its name with the secondary WINS server.

3. If it is not refreshed by the secondary WINS server, the WINS client tries to refresh its name again using the secondary WINS server in 10 minutes and continues to try every 10 minutes for a total of 1 hour. The WINS client, after trying to refresh on the secondary WINS server for 1 hour, stops trying and tries to refresh using the primary WINS server. This process of trying the primary WINS server and then the secondary WINS server continues until the renewal interval is consumed or the WINS client has its name refreshed.

4. If the WINS client succeeds in refreshing its name, the renewal interval is reset on the WINS server.

5. If the WINS client fails to register during the renewal interval on either the primary or secondary WINS server, the name is released.

Figure 9.6 shows how a WINS client renews its lease to use the same NetBIOS name.

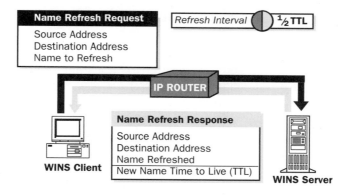

Figure 9.6   Renewing a lease using the same NetBIOS name

When a WINS server receives the name refresh request, it sends the client a name refresh response with a new TTL.

Name Release

When a WINS client is properly shut down, it sends a name release request directly to the WINS server for each registered name. The name release request includes the client's IP address and the NetBIOS name to be removed from the WINS database. This allows the name to be available for another client, as illustrated in Figure 9.7.

When the WINS server receives the name release request, it checks its database for the specified name. If the WINS server encounters a database error or if a different IP address maps the registered name, it sends a negative name release to the WINS client. Otherwise, the WINS server sends a positive name release and designates the specified name as inactive in its database. The name release response contains the released NetBIOS name and a TTL value of zero.

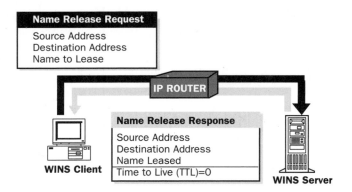

Figure 9.7   Name release request

Name Query and Name Response

A common method of resolving NetBIOS names to IP addresses is with an NBNS, such as WINS. When a WINS client is configured, by default, the H-node type of NetBT is used. The NBNS is always checked for a NetBIOS name/IP address mapping before initiating a broadcast. The following steps and illustration in Figure 9.8 demonstrate the process:

1. When a user initiates a Windows NT command, such as net use, the NetBIOS name cache is checked for the NetBIOS name/IP address mapping of the destination host.

2. If the name is not resolved from cache, a name query request is sent directly to the client's primary WINS server.

   If the primary WINS server is unavailable, the client resends the request two more times before switching to the secondary WINS server.

   When either WINS server resolves the name, a success message with the IP address for the requested NetBIOS name is sent to the source host.

3. If no WINS server can resolve the name, a name query response is sent back to the WINS client with the message "Requested name does not exist," and broadcast is implemented.

   If the name is not resolved from cache by a WINS server or broadcast, the name may still be resolved by parsing the LMHOSTS or Hosts file, or by using DNS.

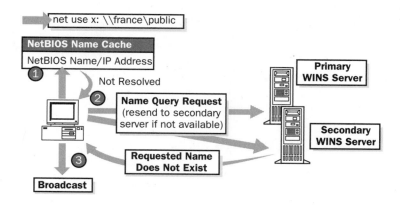

Figure 9.8   NetBIOS name server checked for NetBIOS name/IP address mapping

Lesson Summary

WINS uses standard name registration, name renewal, and name release methods. To continue using the same NetBIOS name, a client must renew its lease before it expires. When a WINS client is shut down, it notifies the WINS server that it no longer needs its NetBIOS name.

Lesson 3: Implementing WINS

For networks with servers running Windows 2000 Server and all other computers running Windows 2000 Professional, NetBIOS is no longer required for TCP/IP-based networking. Because of this change, WINS is needed for most networks but might not be required in some instances. In this lesson, you will learn how to implement WINS on your network.

After this lesson, you will be able to

- Install and configure a WINS server
- Install and configure a WINS client
- Troubleshoot WINS clients and servers
- Manage and monitor WINS

Estimated lesson time: 40 minutes

When to Use WINS

When deciding whether you need to use WINS, you should first consider the following questions:

- **Do I have any legacy computers or applications on my network that require the use of NetBIOS names?**   Remember that all networked computers that run under any previously released Microsoft operating system, such as versions of MS-DOS, Windows, or Windows NT, require NetBIOS name support. Windows 2000 is the first Microsoft operating system that no longer requires NetBIOS naming. Therefore, NetBIOS names can still be required on your network to provide basic file and print services and support for many legacy applications used.

- **Are all computers on my network configured and able to support the use of another type of network naming, such as DNS?**   Network naming is still a vital service for locating computers and resources throughout your network, even when NetBIOS names are not required. Before you decide to eliminate WINS or NetBIOS name support, be sure that all computers and programs on your network are able to function using another naming service, such as DNS.

- **Is my network a single subnet or routed with multiple subnets?**   If your entire network is a small local area network (LAN) that occupies one physical network segment and has less than 50 clients, you can probably do without a WINS server.

Considerations for WINS Servers

Before you implement WINS in an internetwork, consider the number of WINS servers you will need. Only one WINS server is required for an internetwork because requests for name resolution are directed datagrams that can be routed. Two WINS servers ensure a backup system for fault tolerance. If one server becomes unavailable, the second server can be used to resolve names. You should also consider the following WINS server recommendations:

- There is no built-in limit to the number of WINS requests that can be handled by a WINS server, but typically it can handle 1500 name registrations and about 4500 name queries per minute.

- A conservative recommendation is one WINS server and a backup server for every 10,000 WINS clients.

- Computers with multiple processors have demonstrated performance improvements of approximately 25 percent for each additional processor, as a separate WINS thread is started for each processor.

- If logging of database changes is turned off (through WINS Manager), name registrations are much faster, but if a crash occurs, there is a risk of losing the last few updates.

WINS Requirements

Before you install WINS, you should determine that your server and clients meet the configuration requirements. The WINS service must be configured on at least one computer within the TCP/IP internetwork running Windows NT Server or Windows 2000 Server (it does not have to be a domain controller). The server must have an IP address, subnet mask, default gateway, and other TCP/IP parameters. These parameters can be assigned by a DHCP server, but statically assigned parameters are recommended.

A WINS client can be a computer running any of the following supported operating systems:

- Windows 2000
- Windows NT 3.5 and later
- Windows 95 or Windows 98
- Windows for Workgroups 3.11 running Microsoft TCP/IP-32
- Microsoft Network Client 3.0 for MS-DOS
- LAN Manager 2.2c for MS-DOS

The client must have an IP address of a WINS server configured for a primary WINS server or for primary and secondary WINS servers.

▶ **To install WINS on a Windows 2000-based server**

1. In Control Panel, double-click Add/Remove Programs.

2. Click Add/Remove Windows Components.

    The Windows Component Wizard opens.

3. On the Windows Components page, under Components, click Networking Services, then click Details.

    The Networking Services dialog box appears.

4. Select the Windows Internet Name Service (WINS) check box, click OK, then click Next.

Using Static Mappings

Mapped name-to-address entries can be added to WINS in either of two ways:

- Dynamically, by WINS-enabled clients directly contacting a WINS server to register, release, or renew their NetBIOS names in the server database

- Manually, by an administrator using the WINS console or command-line tools to add or delete statically mapped entries in the server database

Static entries are only useful when you need to add a name-to-address mapping to the server database for a computer that does not directly use WINS. For example, in some networks, servers running other operating systems cannot register a NetBIOS name directly with a WINS server. Although these names might be added to and resolved from an LMHOSTS file or by querying a DNS server, you might consider using a static WINS mapping instead.

▶ **To configure a static mapping**

1. Click Start, point to Programs, point to Administrative Tools, then click WINS.

2. In the WINS console, click Active Registrations under your WINS server.

3. On the Action menu, click New Static Mapping.

    The New Static Mapping dialog box appears, as illustrated in Figure 9.9.

4. In Computer Name, type the NetBIOS name of the computer.

5. In NetBIOS Scope (optional), you can type a NetBIOS scope identifier, if one is used, for the computer. Otherwise, leave this field blank.

6. In Type, click one of the supported types to indicate whether this entry is a Unique, Group, Domain Name, Internet, or Multihomed type entry, as detailed in Table 9.3.

7. In IP Address, type the address for the computer.

8. Click Apply to add the static mapping entry to the database.

    You can aslo add additional static mapping entries. Click Apply each time you complete an entry, then click Cancel to close when you finish adding static mapping entries.

9. Click OK to close the Add Static Mapping dialog box.

Figure 9.9   The Add Static Mapping dialog box

Table 9.3   Static WINS Mapping Types

Type Option	Description
Unique	A unique name maps to a single IP address.
Group	Also referred to as a "Normal" group. When adding an entry to a group by using WINS Manager, you must enter the computer name and IP address. However, the IP addresses of individual members of a group are not stored in the WINS database. Because the member addresses are not stored, there is no limit to the number of members that can be added to a group. Broadcast name packets are used to communicate with group members.
Domain Name	A NetBIOS name-to-address mapping that has 0x1C as the 16th byte. A domain group stores up to a maximum of 25 addresses for members. For registrations after the 25th address, WINS overwrites a replica address or, if none is present, it overwrites the oldest registration.
Internet Group	Internet groups are user-defined groups that enable you to group resources, such as printers, for easy reference and browsing. An Internet group can store up to a maximum of 25 addresses for members. A dynamic member, however, does not replace a static member added by using WINS Manager or importing the LMHOSTS file.
Multihomed	A unique name that can have more than one address. This is used for multihomed computers. Each multihomed group name can contain a maximum of 25 addresses. For registrations after the 25th address, WINS overwrites a replica address or, if none is present, it overwrites the oldest registration.

Practice: Configuring a WINS Client

If a computer is a DHCP client, you can configure the DHCP server to provide DHCP clients with WINS configuration information. However, you can also manually configure WINS clients. If you manually configure WINS client computers with IP addresses of one or more WINS servers, those values take precedence over the same parameters that a DHCP server provides.

▶ **To configure a WINS client with the IP address of one or more WINS servers**

1. Open Network And Dial-Up Connections.

2. Right-click Local Area Connection, then click Properties.

   The Local Area Connection Properties dialog box appears.

3. Select the Internet Protocol (TCP/IP) Properties entry in the list, then click Properties.

   The Internet Protocol (TCP/IP) Properties dialog box appears.

4. Click Advanced and select the WINS Address tab, as illustrated in Figure 9.10.

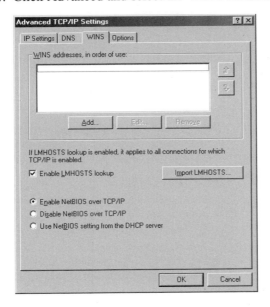

Figure 9.10   The WINS service on a Windows 2000 client

5. Click Add, type the IP address of your WINS server in the TCP/IP WINS Server dialog box, then click Add.

   The TCP/IP WINS Server dialog box will close and the WINS server you entered will be added to the list in the Advanced TCP/IP Settings dialog box.

6. Click OK to close the Advanced TCP/IP Settings dialog box.

7. Click OK to close the Internet Protocol (TCP/IP) Properties dialog box.

8. Click OK to close the Local Area Connection Properties dialog box.

Troubleshooting WINS

The following conditions can indicate basic problems with WINS:

- Administrator cannot connect to a WINS server using the WINS console

- TCP/IP NetBIOS Helper service on the WINS client is down and cannot be restarted

- WINS service is not running and cannot be restarted

The first action you should take to resolve WINS problems is to verify that the appropriate services are running. You can do this at both the WINS server and WINS client.

▶ **To verify running services**

1. Verify that the WINS service is running on the server.

2. Verify that the Workstation service, the Server service, and the TCP/IP NetBIOS Helper service are started on the clients.

If services do not start properly, you can use the Computer Management administrative tool to check the status column of the services, and then try to start them manually. If the service cannot be started, use Event Viewer to check the system event log and determine the cause of failure.

Note   For WINS clients, "Started" should appear in the status column for TCP/IP NetBIOS Helper service. For WINS servers, "Started" should appear in the status column for Windows Internet Name Service (WINS).

The most common WINS client problem is failed name resolution. When name resolution fails at a client, answer the following questions to identify the source of the problem:

- **Is the client computer able to use WINS, and is it correctly configured?**   First, check that the client is configured to use both TCP/IP and WINS. Client configuration of WINS-related settings can be done manually by an administrator setting the TCP/IP configuration of the client or it can be done dynamically by a DHCP server providing the client its TCP/IP configuration. In most cases, computers running earlier versions of Microsoft operating systems are already able to use WINS once TCP/IP is installed and configured at the client. For Windows 2000, administrators can optionally disable NetBT for each client. If you disable NetBT, WINS cannot be used at the client.

Note   If the WINS server does not respond to a direct ping, the source of the problem is likely to be a network connectivity problem between the client and the WINS server.

- **Was the name that failed to resolve a NetBIOS or DNS name?**   NetBIOS names are 15 characters or less and not structured like DNS names, which are generally longer and use periods to delimit each domain level within a name. For example, the short NetBIOS name PRINT-SRV1 and the longer DNS name print-srv1.example.microsoft.com might both refer to the same resource computer running Windows 2000 (a network print server) configured to use either name. If the short name was used at the client in the previous example, Windows 2000 would first involve NetBIOS name services, such as WINS or NetBT broadcasts, in its initial attempts to resolve the name. If a longer DNS name (or a name that uses periods) was involved in the failure, DNS is more likely the cause of the failed name resolution.

The most common WINS server problem is the inability to resolve names for clients. When a server fails to resolve a name for its clients, the failure most often is discovered by clients in one of two ways:

- The server sends a negative query response back to the client, such as an error message indicating "Name not found."

- The server sends a positive response back to the client, but the information contained in the response is incorrect.

If you determine that a WINS-related problem does not originate at the client, answer the following question to further troubleshoot the source of the problem at the WINS server of the client:

- **Is the WINS server able to service the client?**   At the WINS server for the client that cannot locate a name, use Event Viewer or the WINS management console to see if WINS is currently running. If WINS is running on the server, search for the name previously requested by the client to see if it is in the WINS server database.

If the WINS server is failing or registering database corruption errors, you can use WINS database recovery techniques to help restore WINS operations. You can back up the WINS database by using the WINS administrative console. First, you specify a backup directory for the database, and then WINS will execute database backups. The backup is performed every three hours by default. If your WINS database becomes corrupted, you can easily restore it. The easiest way to restore a local server database is to replicate data back from a replication partner. If the corruption is limited to a certain number of records, you can repair them by forcing replication of uncorrupted WINS records. This will remove the affected records from other WINS servers. If changes are replicated among WINS servers quickly, the best way to restore a local WINS server database is to use a replication partner, provided that the WINS data is mostly up to date on the replication partner.

Managing and Monitoring WINS

The WINS console is fully integrated with the Microsoft Management Console (MMC), a powerful and more user-friendly environment you can customize for your efficiency. Because all server administrative utilities included for your use in Windows 2000 Server are part of MMC, new MMC-based utilities are easier to use, as they operate more predictably and follow a common design. In addition, several useful WINS features from earlier versions of Windows NT Server that were only configurable through the registry are now more directly usable. These include the ability to block records by a specific owner or WINS replication partner (formerly known as Persona Non Grata) or the ability to allow override of static mappings (formerly known as Migrate On/Off). In this lesson, you will learn how to manage and monitor WINS through the WINS console.

Viewing WINS Server Statistics

You should view WINS server statistics periodically to monitor performance. By default, statistics automatically refresh every 10 minutes. As an option, you can also disable this feature by clearing the Automatically Update Statistics Every check box.

▶   **To open the WINS Server Statistics dialog box**

1. Click Start, point to Programs, point to Administrative Tools, then click WINS.

2. In the console tree, click the applicable WINS server.

3. On the Action menu, click Display Server Statistics.

4. To update the display while viewing WINS statistics, click Refresh.

Lesson Summary

To implement WINS, both the server and client require configuration. Configuring a static mapping for non-WINS clients allows WINS clients on remote networks to communicate with them. When troubleshooting WINS, the first action you should take is to verify that the appropriate services are running.

Lesson 4: Configuring WINS Replication

All WINS servers on an internetwork can be configured to fully replicate database entries with other WINS servers. This ensures that a name registered with one WINS server is eventually replicated to all other WINS servers. This lesson explains how WINS database entries are replicated to other WINS servers.

After this lesson, you will be able to
- Add a replication partner
- Perform WINS database replication

Estimated lesson time: 20 minutes

Replication Overview

Database replication occurs whenever the database changes, including when a name is released. Replicating databases enables a WINS server to resolve NetBIOS names of hosts registered with another WINS server. For example, if a host on Subnet 1 is registered with a WINS server on the same subnet but wants to communicate with a host on Subnet 2 and that host is registered with a different WINS server, the NetBIOS name cannot be resolved unless the two WINS servers have replicated their databases with each other.

To replicate database entries, each WINS server must be configured as either a pull or a push partner with at least one other WINS server. A push partner is a WINS server that sends a message to its pull partners notifying them when its WINS database has changed. When a WINS server's pull partners respond to the message with a replication request, the WINS server sends a copy of its new database entries (replicas) to its pull partners.

A pull partner is a WINS server that requests new database entries (replicas) from its push partners. This is done by requesting entries with a higher version number than the last entries it received during the last replication.

Note   WINS servers replicate only new entries in their database. The entire WINS database is not replicated each time replication occurs.

Configuring a WINS Server as a Push or Pull Partner

Determining whether to configure a WINS server as a pull partner or push partner depends on your network environment. Remember the following rules (depicted in Figure 9.11) when configuring WINS server replication:

- Configure a push partner when servers are connected by fast links, because push replication occurs when the configured number of updated WINS database entries is reached.

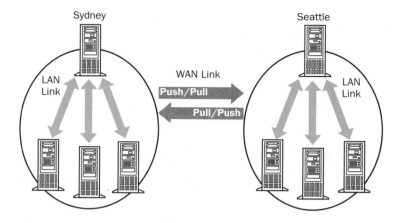

Figure 9.11   Push and pull partner configuration

- Configure a pull partner between sites, especially across slow links, because pull replication can be configured to occur at specific intervals.

- Configure each server to be both a push and pull partner to replicate database entries between them.

Note   You configure a WINS server as a push or pull partner with the WINS administration tool.

- In both Sydney and Seattle, all WINS servers at each site push their new database entries to a single server at their site.

- The servers that receive the push replication are configured for pull replication between each other because the network link between Sydney and Seattle is relatively slow. Replication should occur when the link is the least used, such as late at night.

Configuring Database Replication

Database replication requires that you configure at least one push partner and one pull partner. There are four methods of starting the replication of the WINS database:

1. At system startup. Once a replication partner is configured, by default, WINS automatically pulls database entries each time WINS is started. The WINS server can also be configured to push on system startup.

2. At a configured interval, such as every five hours.

3. When a WINS server has reached a configured threshold for the number of registrations and changes to the WINS database. When the threshold (the update count setting) is reached, the WINS server notifies all of its pull partners, which will then request the new entries.

4. By forcing replication in the WINS administrative console, as illustrated in Figure 9.12.

Figure 9.12   Forcing WINS database replication

Practice: Performing WINS Database Replication

In these procedures, you configure your WINS server to perform database replication with another WINS server.

Note   To complete this procedure you first need to configure your second computer (Server2) as a WINS server.

In this procedure, you configure your second computer (WINS server) as a replication partner.

▶ **To configure WINS replication partners**

1. Open the WINS administrative console.

2. Right-click the Replication Partners folder under your WINS server, then click New Replication Partner.

   The New Replication Partners dialog box appears.

3. In the WINS Server box, type an IP address of a partner WINS server, then click OK.

   The Replication Partners dialog box appears with your IP address added to the list of WINS servers, as illustrated in Figure 9.13.

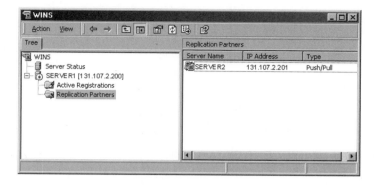

Figure 9.13 Replication partners listed in the WINS administrative console

4. Right-click the replication partner that you just added in the right pane, then click Properties.

   The Server Properties dialog box appears.

5. Click the Advanced tab.

6. In the Replication Partner Type drop-down list box, select Pull.

7. The replication interval is set for 30 minutes.

8. Click OK.

In this procedure, you force WINS to replicate the WINS database with the WINS server.

▶ **To force replication**

1. Right-click on the Replication Partners folder.

2. From the Context menu, click Replicate Now.

   A dialog box appears asking you if you are sure you want to start replication.

3. Click Yes.

   A message box appears indicating the replication request has been queued.

4. Click OK.

Planning How Many WINS Servers to Use

On a smaller network, a single WINS server can adequately service up to 10,000 clients for NetBIOS name resolution requests. To provide additional fault tolerance, you can configure a second computer running Windows 2000 Server as a backup WINS server for clients. If you use only two WINS servers, you can easily set them up as replication partners of each other. For simple replication between two servers, one server should be set as a pull partner and the other as a push partner. Replication can be either manual or automatic, which you can configure by selecting the Enable Automatic Partner Configuration check box in the Advanced tab of the Replication Partner Properties dialog box.

A larger network sometimes requires more WINS servers for several reasons including, most importantly, the number of client connections per server. The number of users that each WINS server can support varies with usage patterns, data storage, and the processing capabilities of the WINS server computer. Some enterprise network environments require more robust hardware to handle WINS activity, so you might benefit from upgrading the server computer. When planning your servers, remember that each WINS server can simultaneously handle hundreds of registrations and queries per second. Any number of WINS servers can be specified for fault tolerance purposes. However, you should avoid deploying large numbers of WINS servers unless they are definitely necessary. By limiting the number of WINS servers on your network, you minimize traffic that results from replication, provide more effective NetBIOS name resolution, and reduce administrative requirements.

WINS Automatic Replication Partners

If your network supports multicasting, the WINS server can be configured to automatically find other WINS servers on the network by multicasting to the IP address 224.0.1.24. This multicasting occurs by default every 40 minutes. Any WINS servers found on the network are automatically configured as push and pull replication partners, with pull replication set to occur every two hours. If network routers do not support multicasting, the WINS server will find only other WINS servers on its subnet. Automatic WINS server partnerships are turned off by default. To manually disable this feature, use the Registry Editor to set UseSelfFndPnrs to 0 and McastIntvl to a large value.

Backing Up the WINS Database

The WINS console provides backup tools so that you can back up and restore the WINS database. When WINS backs up the server database, it creates a \Wins_bak\New folder under the backup folder you have specified as the Default backup path in Server Properties. Actual backups of the WINS database (WINS.MDB) are stored in this folder. By default, the backup path is the root folder on your system partition, such as C:\. After you specify a backup folder for the database, WINS performs complete database backups every three hours using the specified folder. WINS can also be configured to back up the database automatically when the service is stopped or the server computer is shut down.

▶ **To back up the WINS database**

1. Click Start, point to Programs, point to Administrative Tools, then click WINS.

2. In the console tree, click the applicable WINS server.

3. On the Action menu, click Backup Database.

4. When prompted to confirm, click Yes.

5. After backup is completed, click OK.

Important Do not specify a network drive as the backup location. In addition, if you change the WINS backup or database path in server properties, perform new backups to ensure successful future restorations of the WINS database. This is the only way for the active WINS database to be backed up, because the database is locked open while the WINS server is running.

Lesson Summary

All of the WINS servers on a given network can be configured to communicate with each other so that a name registered with one WINS server will eventually be known by all WINS servers. A pull partner requests WINS new database entries. A push partner sends a message to its pull partners notifying them that its WINS database has changed.

Review

Answering the following questions will reinforce key information presented in this chapter. If you are unable to answer a question, review the appropriate lesson and then try the question again. Answers to the questions can be found in Appendix A, "Questions and Answers."

1. What are two benefits of WINS?

2. What two methods can be used to enable WINS on a client computer?

3. How many WINS servers are required in an intranet of 12 subnets?

4. What types of names are stored in the WINS database?

C H A P T E R   1 0

Implementing Dynamic Host Configuration Protocol (DHCP)

About This Chapter

In this chapter, you learn how to use the Dynamic Host Configuration Protocol (DHCP) to automatically configure Transmission Control Protocol/Internet Protocol (TCP/IP) and eliminate some common configuration problems. During the lessons, you install and configure a DHCP server, test the DHCP configuration, and then obtain an Internet Protocol (IP) address from a DHCP server.

Before You Begin

To complete the lessons in this chapter, you must have

- Installed Microsoft Windows 2000 Server with TCP/IP

Lesson 1: Introducing and Installing DHCP

DHCP automatically assigns IP addresses to computers. DHCP overcomes the limitations of configuring TCP/IP manually. This lesson gives you an overview of DHCP and how it works.

After this lesson, you will be able to

- Describe the difference between manual and automatic configuration of TCP/IP
- Identify TCP/IP configuration parameters that can be assigned by a DHCP server
- Describe IP Lease Requests and Offers
- Install DHCP in Windows 2000

Estimated lesson time: 20 minutes

DHCP Overview

DHCP is an extension of the Boot Protocol (BOOTP). BOOTP enables diskless clients to start up and automatically configure TCP/IP. DHCP centralizes and manages the allocation of TCP/IP configuration information by automatically assigning IP addresses to computers configured to use DHCP. Implementing DHCP eliminates some of the configuration problems associated with manually configuring TCP/IP.

As illustrated in Figure 10.1, each time a DHCP client starts, it requests IP addressing information from a DHCP server, including the IP address, the subnet mask, and optional values. The optional values may include a default gateway address, Domain Name System (DNS) address, and Windows Internet Name Service (WINS) server address.

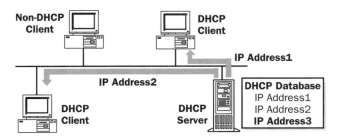

Figure 10.1   How a DHCP client interacts with a DHCP server

When a DHCP server receives a request, it selects IP addressing information from a pool of addresses defined in its database and offers it to the DHCP client. If the client accepts the offer, the IP addressing information is leased to the client for a specified period of time. If there is no available IP addressing information in the pool to lease to a client, the client cannot initialize TCP/IP.

Manual vs. Automatic Configuration

To understand why DHCP is beneficial in configuring TCP/IP on client computers, it is useful to contrast the manual method of configuring TCP/IP with the automatic method using DHCP.

Configuring TCP/IP Manually

Configuring TCP/IP manually means that users can easily pick a random IP address instead of getting a valid IP address from the network administrator. Using incorrect addresses can lead to network problems that can be very difficult to trace to the source.

In addition, typing the IP address, subnet mask, or default gateway can lead to problems ranging from trouble communicating if the default gateway or subnet mask is wrong to problems associated with a duplicate IP address.

Another limitation of configuring TCP/IP manually is the administrative overhead on internetworks where computers are frequently moved from one subnet to another. For example, when a workstation is moved to a different subnet, the IP address and default gateway address must be changed for the workstation to communicate from its new location.

Configuring TCP/IP Using DHCP

Using DHCP to automatically configure IP addressing information means that users no longer need to acquire IP addressing information from an administrator to configure TCP/IP. The DHCP server supplies all of the necessary configuration information to all of the DHCP clients. Many difficult-to-trace network problems are eliminated by using DHCP.

TCP/IP configuration parameters that can be assigned by the DHCP server include

- IP addresses for each network adapter in a client computer
- Subnet masks that are used to identify the IP network portion from the host portion of the IP address
- Default gateways (routers) that are used to connect a single network segment to others
- Additional configuration parameters that can optionally be assigned to DHCP clients (such as IP addresses for DNS or WINS servers a client may use)

How DHCP Works

DHCP uses a four-phase process to configure a DHCP client, as shown in Table 10.1. If a computer has multiple network adapters, the DHCP process occurs separately over each adapter. A unique IP address will be assigned to each adapter in the computer. All DHCP communication is done over User Datagram Protocol (UDP) ports 67 and 68.

Most DHCP messages are sent by broadcast. For DHCP clients to communicate with a DHCP server on a remote network, the IP routers must support forwarding DHCP broadcasts. DHCP configuration phases are shown in Table 10.1.

Table 10.1   Four Phases of DHCP Client Configuration

Phase	Description
IP lease discover	The client initializes a limited version of TCP/IP and broadcasts a request for the location of a DHCP server and IP addressing information.
IP lease offer	All DHCP servers that have valid IP addressing information available send an offer to the client.
IP lease request	The client selects the IP addressing information from the first offer it receives and broadcasts a message requesting to lease the IP addressing information in the offer.
IP lease acknowledgment	The DHCP server that made the offer responds to the message, and all other DHCP servers withdraw their offers. The IP addressing information is assigned to the client and an acknowledgment is sent. The client finishes initializing and binding the TCP/IP protocol. Once the automatic configuration process is complete, the client can use all TCP/IP services and utilities for normal network communications and connectivity to other IP hosts.

IP Lease Discover and Offer

As illustrated in Figure 10.2, in the first two phases, the client broadcasts for a DHCP server and a DHCP server offers an IP address to the client.

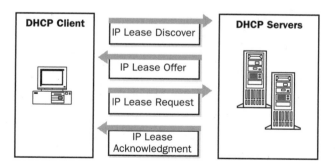

Figure 10.2   IP lease discover and offer

IP Lease Discover

During the boot process of a client, it requests to lease an IP address by broadcasting a request to all DHCP servers. Because the client does not have an IP address or know the IP address of a DHCP server, it uses 0.0.0.0 as the source address and 255.255.255.255 as the destination address.

The request for a lease is sent in a DHCPDISCOVER message. This message also contains the client's hardware address and computer name so that DHCP servers know which client sent the request.

The IP lease process is used when one of the following occurs:

- TCP/IP is initialized for the first time as a DHCP client
- The client requests a specific IP address and is denied, possibly because the DHCP server dropped the lease
- The client previously leased an IP address but released the lease and now requires a new lease

IP Lease Offer

All DHCP servers that receive the request and have a valid configuration for the client broadcast an offer with the following information:

- The client's hardware address
- An offered IP address
- Subnet mask
- Length of the lease
- A server identifier (the IP address of the offering DHCP server)

A broadcast is used because the client does not yet have an IP address. As illustrated in Figure 10.3, the offer is sent as a DHCPOFFER message. The DHCP server reserves the IP address so that it will not be offered to another DHCP client. The DHCP client selects the IP address from the first offer it receives.

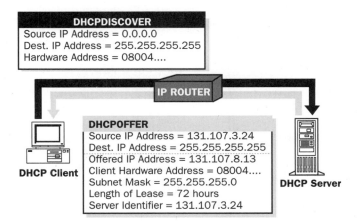

Figure 10.3   Sending a DHCPOFFER message

When No DHCP Servers Are Online

The DHCP client waits 1 second for an offer. If an offer is not received, the client will not be able to initialize and it will rebroadcast the request three times (at 9-, 13-, and 16-second intervals, plus a random length of time between 0 and 1000 milliseconds). If an offer is not received after four requests, the client will retry every 5 minutes.

Windows 2000-based clients can automatically configure an IP address and subnet mask if a DHCP server is unavailable at system start time. This is a new feature of Windows 2000 called Automatic Private IP Addressing (APIPA). This is useful for clients on small private networks, such as a small business office, a home office, or a remote access client. The Windows 2000 DHCP client service goes through the following process to autoconfigure the client:

1. The DHCP client attempts to locate a DHCP server and obtain an address and configuration.

2. If a DHCP server cannot be found or does not respond, the DHCP client autoconfigures its IP address and subnet mask using a selected address from the Microsoft-reserved Class B network, 169.254.0.0, with the subnet mask 255.255.0.0.

   The DHCP client tests for an address conflict to make sure that the IP address it has chosen is not already in use on the network. If a conflict is found, the client selects another IP address. The client will retry autoconfiguration for up to 10 addresses.

3. Once the DHCP client succeeds in self-selecting an address, it configures its network interface with the IP address. The client then continues, in the background, to check for a DHCP server every 5 minutes. If a DHCP server is found later, the client abandons its autoconfigured information. The DHCP client then uses an address offered by the DHCP server (and any other provided DHCP option information) to update its IP configuration settings.

IP Lease Request and Acknowledgment

In the last two phases, the client selects an offer and the DHCP server acknowledges the lease.

IP Lease Request

After the client receives an offer from at least one DHCP server, it broadcasts to all DHCP servers that it has made a selection by accepting an offer.

The broadcast is sent in a DHCPREQUEST message and includes the server identifier (IP address) of the server whose offer was accepted. All other DHCP servers then retract their offers so that their IP addresses are available for the next IP lease request.

IP Lease Acknowledgment (Successful)

The DHCP server with the accepted offer broadcasts a successful acknowledgment to the client in the form of a DHCPACK message. This message contains a valid lease for an IP address and possibly other configuration information. When the DHCP client receives the acknowledgment, TCP/IP is completely initialized and is considered a bound DHCP client. Once bound, the client can use TCP/IP to communicate on the internetwork.

IP Lease Acknowledgment (Unsuccessful)

An unsuccessful acknowledgment (DHCPNACK) is broadcast if the client is trying to lease its previous IP address and the IP address is no longer available. It is also broadcast if the IP address is invalid because the client has been physically moved to a different subnet. When the client receives an unsuccessful acknowledgment, it returns to the process of requesting an IP lease.

Installing a DHCP Server

Before you install a DHCP server, you should identify the following:

- The hardware and storage requirements for the DHCP server

- Which computers you can immediately configure as DHCP clients for dynamic TCP/IP configuration and which computers you should manually configure with static TCP/IP configuration parameters, including static IP addresses

- The DHCP option types and their values to be predefined for DHCP clients

Before you install DHCP, answer the following questions:

- **Will all of the computers become DHCP clients?**   If not, consider that non-DHCP clients have static IP addresses, and static IP addresses must be excluded from the DHCP server configuration. If a client requires a specific address, the IP address needs to be reserved.

- **Will a DHCP server supply IP addresses to multiple subnets?**   If so, consider that any routers connecting subnets act as DHCP relay agents. If your routers are not acting as DHCP relay agents, at least one DHCP server is required on each subnet that has DHCP clients. The DHCP server could be a DHCP relay agent or a router that has BOOTP enabled.

- **How many DHCP servers are required?**   Consider that a DHCP server does not share information with other DHCP servers. Therefore, it is necessary to create unique IP addresses for each server to assign to clients.

- **What IP addressing options will clients obtain from a DHCP server?**   The IP addressing options determine how to configure the DHCP server, and whether the options should be created for all of the clients in the internetwork, clients on a specific subnet, or individual clients. The IP addressing options might be:
  - Default gateway
  - DNS server
  - NetBIOS over TCP/IP name resolution
  - WINS server
  - NetBIOS scope ID

▶ **To install a DHCP server**

1. Open Windows Components Wizard by clicking Start, pointing to Settings, and clicking Control Panel.

   When Control Panel opens, double-click Add/Remove Programs, then click Add/Remove Windows Components.

2. Under Components, scroll to and click Networking Services.

3. Click Details.

4. Under Subcomponents Of Networking Services, select Dynamic Host Configuration Protocol (DHCP), click OK, then click Next.

   If prompted, type the full path to the Windows 2000 distribution files and click Continue. Required files will be copied to your hard disk.

5. Click Finish to close the Windows Components Wizard.

Note   It is strongly recommended that you manually configure the DHCP server computer to use a static IP address. The DHCP server cannot be a DHCP client. It must have a static IP address, subnet mask, and default gateway address.

Ipconfig

Ipconfig is a command-line tool that displays the current configuration of the installed IP stack on a networked computer. It can display a detailed configuration report for all interfaces, including any configured wide area network (WAN) miniports, such as those used for remote access or virtual private network (VPN) connections. A sample report is illustrated in Figure 10.4.

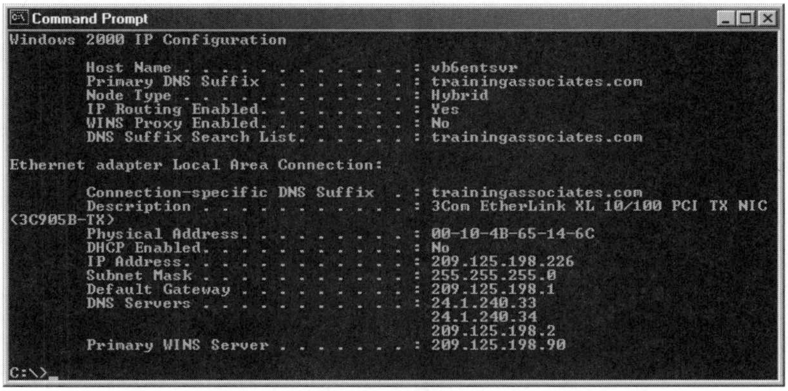

Figure 10.4   Report displayed for Ipconfig /all

Ipconfig Switches

The Ipconfig command is of particular use on systems running DHCP, allowing users to determine which TCP/IP configuration values have been configured by DHCP. Table 10.2 explains the switches used with the Ipconfig command.

Table 10.2   Ipconfig Command-Line Switches

Switch	Effect
/all	Produces a detailed configuration report for all interfaces
/flushdns	Removes all entries from the DNS name cache
/registerdns	The DNS domain name for client resolutions
/displaydns	Displays the contents of the DNS resolver cache
/release <adapter>	Releases the IP address for a specified interface
/renew <adapter>	Renews the IP address for a specified interface
/showclassid <adapter>	Displays all the DHCP class IDs allowed for the adapter specified
/setclassid <adapter> <classID to set>	Changes the DHCP class ID for the adapter specified
/?	Displays the items in this table

Note   Output can be redirected to a file and pasted into other documents.

▶ **To verify, release, or renew a client address lease**

1. At a DHCP-enabled client computer running Windows 2000, open a command prompt.

2. Use the Ipconfig command-line utility to verify, release, or renew the lease of the client with a DHCP server, as follows:

   To verify the current DHCP and TCP/IP configuration, type **ipconfig /all**.

   To release a DHCP client lease, type **ipconfig /release**.

   To renew a DHCP client lease, type **ipconfig /renew**.

The Ipconfig utility is also supported for use in Windows NT. For Windows 95 and Windows 98 clients, use Winipcfg, the Windows IP configuration program, to perform these same tasks. To run Winipcfg on supporting clients, type **winipcfg** at either an MS-DOS command prompt or in the Run command window. When using Winipcfg to release or renew leases, click Release or Renew to perform these respective tasks.

DHCP Relay Agent

A relay agent is a small program that relays DHCP/BOOTP messages between clients and servers on different subnets. The DHCP Relay Agent component provided with the Windows 2000 router is a BOOTP relay agent that relays DHCP messages between DHCP clients and DHCP servers on different IP networks. For each IP network segment that contains DHCP clients, either a DHCP server or a computer acting as a DHCP relay agent is required.

▶ **To add the DHCP Relay Agent**

1. Click Start, point to Programs, point to Administrative Tools, then click Routing And Remote Access.

2. In the console tree, click Server name\IP Routing\General.

3. Right-click General, then click New Routing Protocol.

4. In the Select Routing Protocol dialog box, click DHCP Relay Agent, then click OK.

Lesson Summary

DHCP was developed to solve configuration problems by centralizing IP configuration information for allocation to clients. DHCP uses a four-phase process to configure a DHCP client. The phases are, in order: lease discover, lease offer, lease request, and lease acknowledgment. In addition to verifying a computer's IP configuration, you can use the Ipconfig utility to renew options, lease time, and relinquish a lease.

Lesson 2: Configuring DHCP

In this lesson, you will learn how to configure DHCP on a Windows 2000-based server.

After this lesson, you will be able to
- Identify the benefits of using DHCP on a network
- Configure a DHCP server and clients

Estimated lesson time: 10 minutes

Using DHCP on a Network

Configuring DHCP servers for a network provides the following benefits:

- The administrator can assign and specify global and subnet-specific TCP/IP parameters centrally for use throughout the entire network.
- Client computers do not require manual TCP/IP configuration.

  When a client computer moves between subnets, its old IP address is freed for reuse. The client reconfigures its TCP/IP settings automatically when the computer is restarted in its new location.

- Most routers can forward DHCP and BOOTP configuration requests, so DHCP servers are not required on every subnet in the network.

How Clients Use DHCP Servers

A computer running Windows 2000 becomes a DHCP client if Obtain An IP Address is selected in its TCP/IP properties, as illustrated in Figure 10.5.

When a client computer is set to use DHCP, it accepts a lease offer and can receive from the server the following:

- Temporary use of an IP address known to be valid for the network it is joining
- Additional TCP/IP configuration parameters for the client to use in the form of options data

In addition, if conflict detection is configured, the DHCP server attempts to ping each available address in the scope prior to presenting the address in a lease offer to a client. This ensures that each IP address offered to clients is not already in use by another non-DHCP computer that uses manual TCP/IP configuration. Scopes are discussed in more detail later in this lesson.

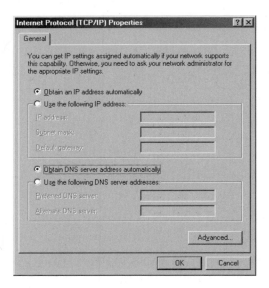

Figure 10.5   Setting a client to obtain an IP address from a DHCP server

How DHCP Servers Provide Optional Data

In addition to an IP address, DHCP servers can be configured to provide optional data to fully configure TCP/IP for clients. Some of the most common DHCP option types configured and distributed by the DHCP server during leases include

- Default gateways (routers), which are used to connect a network segment to other network segments

- Other optional configuration parameters to assign to DHCP clients, such as IP addresses for the DNS servers or WINS servers that the client can use in resolving network host names

Installing and Configuring a DHCP Server

The DHCP Server service must be running to communicate with DHCP clients. Once DHCP Server is installed and started, several options must be configured. The following are the general steps for installing and configuring DHCP:

- Install the Microsoft DHCP Server service.

- Authorize the DHCP server.

- A scope or pool of valid IP addresses must be configured before a DHCP server can lease IP addresses to DHCP clients.

- Global scope and client scope options can be configured for a particular DHCP client.

- The DHCP server can be configured to always assign the same IP address to the same DHCP client.

Authorizing a DHCP Server

When configured correctly and authorized for use on a network, DHCP servers provide a useful and intended administrative service. However, when a misconfigured or unauthorized DHCP server is introduced into a network, it can cause problems. For example, if an unauthorized DHCP server starts, it might begin either leasing incorrect IP addresses to clients or negatively acknowledging DHCP clients, attempting to renew current address leases. Either of these configurations can produce further problems for DHCP-enabled clients. For example, clients that obtain a configuration lease from the unauthorized server can fail to locate valid domain controllers, preventing clients from successfully logging on to the network.

To avoid these problems in Windows 2000, servers are verified as legal in the network before they can service clients. This avoids most of the accidental damage caused by running DHCP servers with incorrect configurations or correct configurations on the wrong network.

How DHCP Servers Are Authorized

The process of authorizing DHCP servers is useful or needed for DHCP servers running Windows 2000 Server. For the directory authorization process to work properly, it is assumed and necessary that the first DHCP server introduced onto your network participate in the Active Directory service. This requires that the server be installed as either a domain controller or a member server. When you are either planning for or actively deploying Active Directory services, it is important that you do not elect to install your first DHCP server computer as a stand-alone server. Windows 2000 Server provides some integrated security support for networks that use Active Directory. This avoids most of the accidental damage caused by running DHCP servers with wrong configurations or on the wrong networks.

The authorization process for DHCP server computers in Active Directory depends on the installed role of the server on your network. For Windows 2000 Server (as in earlier versions) there are three roles or server types for which each server computer can be installed:

1. **Domain controller.** The computer keeps and maintains a copy of the Active Directory service database and provides secure account management for domain member users and computers.

2. **Member server.** The computer is not operating as a domain controller but has joined a domain in which it has a membership account in the Active Directory service database.

3. **Stand-alone server.** The computer is not operating as a domain controller or a member server in a domain. Instead, the server computer is made known to the network through a specified workgroup name, which can be shared by other computers, but is used only for browsing purposes and not to provide secured logon access to shared domain resources.

If you deploy Active Directory, all computers operating as DHCP servers must be either domain controllers or domain member servers before they can be authorized in the directory service and provide DHCP service to clients.

▶ **To authorize a computer as a DHCP server in Active Directory**

1. Log on to the network using either an account that has enterprise administrative privileges or one that has been delegated authority to authorize DHCP servers for your enterprise.

   In most cases, it is simplest to log on to the network from the computer where you want to authorize the new DHCP server. This ensures that other TCP/IP configuration of the authorized computer has been set up correctly prior to authorization. Typically, you can use an account that has membership in the Enterprise Administrators group. The account you use must allow you to have Full control rights to the NetServices container object as it is stored in the enterprise root of the Active Directory service.

2. Install the DHCP service on this computer if necessary.

3. Click Start, point to Programs, point to Administrative Tools, then click DHCP.

4. On the Action menu, click Manage Authorized Servers, as illustrated in Figure 10.6.

   The Manage Authorized Servers dialog box appears.

5. Click Authorize.

6. When prompted, type the name or IP address of the DHCP server to be authorized, then click OK.

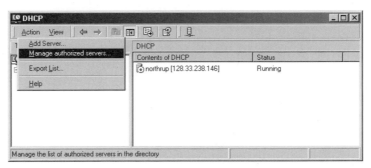

Figure 10.6   Authorizing a DHCP server

Protecting Against Unauthorized DHCP Servers

Active Directory is now used to store records of authorized DHCP servers. When a DHCP server comes up, the directory can now be used to verify the status of that server. If that server is unauthorized, no response is returned to DHCP requests. A network manager with the proper access rights has to respond. The domain administrator can assign access to the DHCP folder holding configuration data to allow only authorized personnel to add DHCP servers to the approved list.

The list of authorized servers can be created in Active Directory through the DHCP snap-in. When it first comes up, the DHCP server tries to find out if it is part of the directory domain. If it is, it tries to contact the directory to see if it is in the list of authorized servers. If it succeeds, it sends out DHCPINFORM to find out if there are other directory services running and makes sure that it is valid in others as well. If it cannot connect to the directory, it assumes that it is not authorized and does not respond to client requests. Likewise, if it does reach the directory but does not find itself in the authorized list, it does not respond to clients. If it does find itself in the authorized list, it starts to service client requests.

Creating a DHCP Scope

Before a DHCP server can lease an address to DHCP clients, you must create a scope. A scope is a pool of valid IP addresses available for lease to DHCP clients. After you have installed the DHCP service and it is running, the next step is to create a scope.

When creating a DHCP scope, consider the following points:

- You must create at least one scope for every DHCP server.
- You must exclude static IP addresses from the scope.
- You can create multiple scopes on a DHCP server to centralize administration and to assign IP addresses specific to a subnet. You can assign only one scope to a specific subnet.
- DHCP servers do not share scope information. As a result, when you create scopes on multiple DHCP servers, ensure that the same IP addresses do not exist in more than one scope to prevent duplicate IP addressing.
- Before you create a scope, determine starting and ending IP addresses to be used within it.

  Depending on the starting and ending IP addresses for your scope, the DHCP console suggests a default subnet mask useful for most networks. If you know a different subnet mask is required for your network, you can modify the value as needed.

▶ **To create a new scope**

1. Click Start, point to Programs, point to Administrative Tools, then click DHCP.
2. In the console tree, click the applicable DHCP server.
3. On the Action menu, click New Scope.
4. Follow the instructions in the New Scope Wizard.

   When you finish creating a new scope, you might need to complete additional tasks, such as activating the scope for use or assigning scope options.

After Scopes Are Added

After you define a scope, you can additionally configure the scope by performing the following tasks:

- **Set additional exclusion ranges.**   You can exclude any other IP addresses that must not be leased to DHCP clients. You should use exclusions for all devices that must be statically configured. The excluded ranges should include all IP addresses that you assigned manually to other DHCP servers, non-DHCP clients, diskless workstations, or Routing and Remote Access and Point-to-Point (PPP) clients.

- **Create reservations.**   You can choose to reserve some IP addresses for permanent lease assignment to specified computers or devices on your network. You should make reservations only for devices that are DHCP-enabled and that must be reserved for specific purposes on your network (such as print servers).

  If you are reserving an IP address for a new client or an address that is different from its current one, you should verify that the address has not already been leased by the DHCP server. Reserving an IP address in a scope does not auto-matically force a client currently using that address to stop using it. If the address is already in use, the client using the address must first release it by issuing a DHCP release message. To make this happen on a system running Windows 2000, at the command prompt type **ipconfig /release**. Reserving an IP address at the DHCP server also does not force the new client for which the reservation is made to immediately move to that address. In this case, too, the client must first issue a DHCP request message. To make this happen on a system running Windows 2000, at the command prompt type **ipconfig /renew**.

- **Adjust the length of lease durations.**   You can modify the lease duration to be used for assigning IP address leases. The default lease duration is eight days. For most local area networks (LANs), the default value is acceptable but can be further increased if computers seldom move or change locations. Infinite lease times can also be set, but should be used with caution. For information about circumstances under which modifying this setting is most useful, see Managing Leases.

- **Configure options and classes to be used with the scope.**   To provide full configuration for clients, DHCP options need to be configured and enabled for the scope. For more advanced discrete management of scope clients, you can add or enable user- or vendor-defined option classes.

Table 10.3 describes some of the available options in the Configure DHCP Options: Scope Properties dialog box and includes all of the options supported by Microsoft DHCP clients.

Table 10.3   DHCP Scope Configuration Options

Option	Description
003 Router	Specifies the IP address of a router, such as the default gateway address. If the client has a locally defined default gateway, that configuration takes precedence over the DHCP option.
006 DNS Servers	Specifies the IP address of a DNS server.
015 DNS Domain Name	The DNS domain name for client resolutions.
044 WINS/NBNS servers	The IP address of a WINS server available to clients. If a WINS server address is configured manually on a client, that configuration overrides the values configured for this option.
046 WINS/NBT node type	Specifies the type of NetBIOS over TCP/IP name resolution to be used by the client. Options are: 1 = B-node (broadcast); 2 = P-node (peer); 4 = M-node (mixed); 8 = H-node (hybrid)
044 WINS/NBNS servers	Specifies the IP address of a WINS server available to clients. If a WINS server address is manually configured on a client, that configuration overrides the values configured for this option.
047 NetBIOS Scope ID	Specifies the local NetBIOS scope ID. NetBIOS over TCP/IP will communicate only with other NetBIOS hosts using the same scope ID.

Implementing Multiple DHCP Servers

If your internetwork requires multiple DHCP servers, it is necessary to create a unique scope for each subnet. To ensure that clients can lease IP addresses in the event of a server failure, it is important to have multiple scopes for each subnet distributed among the DHCP servers in the internetwork. For example:

- Each DHCP server should have a scope containing approximately 75 percent of the available IP addresses for the local subnet.

- Each DHCP server should have a scope for each remote subnet containing approximately 25 percent of the available IP addresses for a subnet.

When a client's DHCP server is unavailable, the client can still receive an address lease from another DHCP server on a different subnet, assuming the router is a DHCP relay agent.

As illustrated in Figure 10.7, Server A has a scope for the local subnet with an IP address range of 131.107.4.20 through 131.107.4.150, and Server B has a scope with an IP address range of 131.107.3.20 through 131.107.3.150. Each server can lease IP addresses to clients on its own subnet.

Additionally, each server has a scope containing a small range of IP addresses for the remote subnet. For example, Server A has a scope for Subnet 2 with the IP address range of 131.107.3.151 through 131.107.3.200. Server B has a scope for Subnet 1 with the IP address range of 131.107.4.151 through 131.107.4.200. When a client on Subnet 1 is unable to lease an address from Server A, it can lease an address for its subnet from Server B, and vice versa.

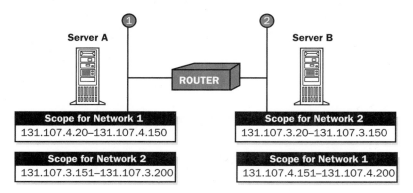

Figure 10.7   Scope and IP address ranges for Server A and Server B

Lesson Summary

A scope is a range of IP addresses that are available to be leased or assigned to clients. Multiple scopes and separate scopes for each subnet can be created to allow DHCP clients to obtain a valid IP address from any DHCP server. To implement DHCP, software is required on both the client and the server. Every DHCP server requires at least one scope.

Lesson 3: Integrating DHCP with Naming Services

With Windows 2000, a DHCP server can enable dynamic updates in the DNS name space for any of its clients that support these updates. Scope clients can then use DNS dynamic update protocol to update their host name-to-address mapping information (which is stored in zones on the DNS server) whenever changes occur to their DHCP-assigned address. In this lesson, you will learn how to integrate DHCP with DNS.

After this lesson, you will be able to

- Integrate DNS and DHCP
- Describe how Dynamic DNS updates work
- Identify how DHCP client updates are typically handled

Estimated lesson time: 25 minutes

DNS and DHCP

Although DHCP provides a powerful mechanism for automatically configuring client IP addresses, until recently DHCP did not notify the DNS service to update the DNS records on the client—specifically, updating the client name to an IP address, and IP address-to-name mappings maintained by a DNS server. Without a way for DHCP to interact with DNS, the information maintained by DNS for a DHCP client may be incorrect. For example, a client may acquire its IP address from a DHCP server, but the DNS records would not reflect the IP address acquired or provide a mapping from the new IP address to the computer name (fully qualified domain name [FQDN]).

Registering for Dynamic DNS Updates

In Windows 2000, DHCP servers and clients can register with DNS, if the server supports Dynamic DNS updates. The Windows 2000 DNS service supports dynamic updates. A Windows 2000 DHCP server can register with a DNS server and update pointer (PTR) and address (A) resource records (RRs) on behalf of its DHCP-enabled clients using the Dynamic DNS update protocol. The ability to register both A and PTR type records lets a DHCP server act as a proxy for clients using Windows 95 and Windows NT 4.0 for the purpose of DNS registration. DHCP servers can differentiate between Windows 2000 and other clients. An additional DHCP option code (Option Code 81) enables the return of a client's FQDN to the DHCP server. If implemented, the DHCP server can dynamically update DNS to modify an individual computer's RRs with a DNS server using the dynamic update protocol. This DHCP option permits the DHCP server the following possible interactions for processing DNS information on behalf of DHCP clients that include Option Code 81 in the DHCP request message they send to the server:

- The DHCP server always registers the DHCP client for both the forward (A-type records) and reverse lookups (PTR-type records) with DNS.

- The DHCP server never registers the name-to-address (A-type records) mapping information for DHCP clients.

- The DHCP server registers the DHCP client for both forward (A-type records) and reverse lookups (PTR-type records) only when requested to by the client.

DHCP and static DNS service are not compatible for keeping name-to-address mapping information synchronized. This might cause problems with using DHCP and DNS together on a network if you are using older, static DNS servers, which are incapable of interacting dynamically when DHCP client configurations change.

▶ **To avoid failed DNS lookups for DHCP-registered clients when static DNS service is in effect**

1. If WINS servers are used on the network, enable WINS lookup for DHCP clients that use NetBIOS.

2. Assign IP address reservations with an infinite lease duration for DHCP clients that use DNS only and do not support NetBIOS.

3. Wherever possible, upgrade or replace older, static-based DNS servers with DNS servers supporting updates. Dynamic updates are supported by the Microsoft DNS, included in Windows 2000.

Additional Recommendations

When using DNS and WINS together, consider the following options for interoperation:

- If a large percentage of clients use NetBIOS and you are using DNS, consider using WINS lookup on your DNS servers. If WINS lookup is enabled on the Microsoft DNS service, WINS is used for final resolution of any names that are not found using DNS resolution. The WINS forward lookup and WINS-R reverse lookup records are supported only by DNS. If you use servers on your network that do not support DNS, use DNS Manager to ensure that these WINS records are not propagated to DNS servers that do not support WINS lookup.

- If you have a large percentage of computers running Windows 2000 on your network, consider creating a pure DNS environment. This involves developing a migration plan to upgrade older WINS clients to Windows 2000. Support issues involving network name service are simplified by using a single naming and resource locator service (such as WINS and DNS) on your network.

Windows DHCP Clients and DNS Dynamic Update Protocol

In Windows 2000 Server, the DHCP Server service provides default support to register and update information for legacy DHCP clients in DNS zones. Legacy clients typically include other Microsoft TCP/IP client computers that were released prior to Windows 2000. The DNS/DHCP integration provided in Windows 2000 Server enables a DHCP client that is unable to dynamically update DNS RRs directly to have this information updated in DNS forward and reverse lookup zones by the DHCP server.

► **To allow dynamic updates for**
DHCP clients that do not support Dynamic DNS updates

1. Click Start, point to Programs, point to Administrative Tools, then click DNS.
2. In the console tree, click the applicable zone.
3. On the Action menu, click Properties.
4. In the DNS Property tab, select Enable Updates For DNS Clients That Do Not Support Dynamic Update.
5. Select Only Secure Updates If Your Zone Type Is Active Directory-Integrated.

DHCP clients running Windows 2000 and earlier versions of Windows interact differently when performing the DHCP/DNS interactions previously described. The following sections explain how this process varies in different cases.

DHCP/DNS Update Interaction for Windows 2000 DHCP Clients

Windows 2000 DHCP clients interact with DNS dynamic update protocol as follows:

1. The client initiates a DHCP request message (DHCPREQUEST) to the server.
2. The server returns a DHCP acknowledgment message (DHCPACK) to the client, granting an IP address lease.
3. By default, the client sends a DNS update request to the DNS server for its own forward lookup record, a host (A) RR.

   Alternately, the server can perform this update to the DNS server on behalf of the client if both the client and its configuration are modified accordingly.
4. The server sends updates for the DHCP client's reverse lookup record—a PTR RR—using the process defined by the DNS dynamic update protocol.

This process is illustrated in Figure 10.8.

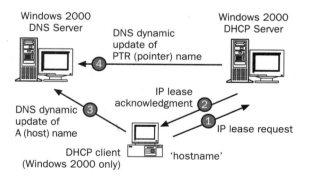

Figure 10.8   A DHCP client interacting with the DNS dynamic update protocol

DHCP/DNS Update Interaction for DHCP Clients Prior to Windows 2000

Earlier versions of Windows DHCP clients do not support the DNS dynamic update process directly and therefore cannot directly interact with the DNS server. For these DHCP clients, updates are typically handled as follows:

1. The client initiates a DHCP request message (DHCPREQUEST) to the server.

2. The server returns a DHCP acknowledgment message (DHCPACK) to the client, granting an IP address lease.

3. The server then sends updates to the DNS server for the client's forward lookup record, which is a host (A) RR.

4. The server also sends updates for the client's reverse lookup record, which is a PTR RR.

This process is illustrated in Figure 10.9.

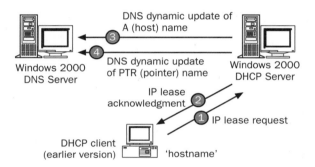

Figure 10.9   DHCP/DNS interaction with older Windows clients

Lesson Summary

With Windows 2000, a DHCP server can enable dynamic updates in the DNS name space for any of its clients that support these updates. With dynamic update, the primary server for a zone can also be configured to support updates that are initiated by another computer or device that supports dynamic update. For example, it can receive updates from workstations registering A and PTR RRs, or from DHCP servers.

Lesson 4: Using DHCP with Active Directory

Microsoft DHCP provides integration with the Active Directory service and DNS service, enhanced monitoring and statistical reporting for DHCP servers, vendor-specific options and user-class support, multicast address allocation, and rogue DHCP server detection.

After this lesson, you will be able to
- Describe how IP address and naming management is managed through DHCP and Active Directory integration
- Describe how DHCP servers are authorized

Estimated lesson time: 15 minutes

Windows 2000 Integrated IP Management

Windows 2000 Server naming and address services offer the flexibility to manage networks more easily and interoperate with other address and naming systems. As with Windows NT Server 4.0, Windows 2000 Server provides DHCP, DNS, and WINS services to continue to simplify address assignment and name resolution. New with Windows 2000 Server is support for Dynamic DNS, Active Directory integration of DHCP and DNS, and a DHCP relay agent.

Address Assignment and Naming Services

IP address and naming management is simplified through Active Directory integration. Customers can choose to use Active Directory to replicate and synchronize DNS naming throughout the corporate network. This eliminates the need to maintain a separate replication service for DNS. Integrated DHCP and Dynamic DNS services then utilize this directory-registered information to provide address assignment and naming services. As DHCP allocates addresses, DNS and Active Directory are dynamically updated. This lets administrators reassign IP addresses for end systems, and name resolution is updated automatically so they can be located easily.

Support for Legacy Servers

Interoperability with other DHCP and DNS services helps preserve investment in existing services. Customers have the option to use legacy IP address and naming management systems using the Windows 2000 Server DHCP, DHCP relay agent, and/or the DNS service. Standard zone transfer and referral support ensures that the Windows 2000 Server DNS interoperates with other DNS servers for enterprise and Internet address resolution. This lets customers use Active Directory integrated services for their network while maintaining interoperability with

Internet and other corporate DNS systems. For example, a company can deploy Active Directory-integrated DNS and DHCP in a core part of its network while interoperating with legacy DNS servers. Over time, the Active Directory-based IP management infrastructure can be expanded while interoperability with external DNS services is preserved.

Windows 2000 DHCP is also dynamically integrated with Windows 2000 DNS in support of Active Directory. Earlier versions of DNS do not offer this support, and you should consider upgrading if you plan to deploy Active Directory or want to use network load balancing.

Rogue DHCP Server Detection Feature

The Windows 2000 DHCP service provides a rogue DHCP server detection feature. This prevents rogue (unauthorized) DHCP servers from joining an existing DHCP network in which Windows 2000 Server and Active Directory are deployed. A DHCP server object is created in Active Directory, which lists the IP addresses of servers that are authorized to provide DHCP services to the network. When a DHCP server attempts to start on the network, Active Directory is queried and the server computer's IP address is compared to the list of authorized DHCP servers. If a match is found, the server computer is authorized as a DHCP server and is allowed to complete the system startup. If a match is not found, the server is identified as rogue, and the DHCP service is automatically shut down.

Lesson Summary

IP address and naming management is simplified through Active Directory integration. As DHCP allocates addresses, DNS and Active Directory are dynamically updated. Interoperability with other DHCP and DNS services helps preserve investment in existing services because you can use legacy IP address and naming management systems with Windows 2000 Server DHCP servers. The authorization process for DHCP server computers in Active Directory depends on whether the server is a domain controller, member server, or stand-alone server. In addition, Active Directory is now used to store records of authorized DHCP servers to protect against unauthorized DHCP servers. The list of authorized servers can be created in the Active Directory through the DHCP snap-in.

Lesson 5: Troubleshooting DHCP

The most common DHCP client problem is a failure to obtain an IP address or other configuration parameters from the DHCP server during startup. The most common DHCP server problems are the inability to start the server on the network in a Windows 2000 or Active Directory domain environment and the failure of clients to obtain configuration from a working server. In this lesson, you will learn how to troubleshoot DHCP clients and DHCP servers.

After this lesson, you will be able to

- Identify and solve DHCP client problems
- Identify and solve DHCP server problems

Estimated lesson time: 35 minutes

Preventing DHCP Problems

Many DHCP problems involve incorrect or missing configuration details. To help prevent the most common types of problems, you should do the following:

- **Use the 75/25 design rule for balancing scope distribution of addresses where multiple DHCP servers are deployed to service the same scope.**   Using more than one DHCP server on the same subnet provides increased fault tolerance for servicing DHCP clients located on it. With two DHCP servers, if one server is unavailable, the other server can take its place and continue to lease new addresses or renew existing clients.

- **Use superscopes for multiple DHCP servers on each subnet in a LAN environment.**   A superscope allows a DHCP server to provide leases from more than one scope to clients on a single physical network. When started, each DHCP client broadcasts a DHCP discover message (DHCPDISCOVER) to its local subnet to attempt to find a DHCP server. Because DHCP clients use broadcasts during their initial startup, you cannot predict which server will respond to a client's DHCP discover request if more than one DHCP server is active on the same subnet.

- **Deactivate scopes only when removing a scope permanently from service.**   Once you activate a scope, it should not be deactivated until you are ready to retire the scope and its included range of addresses from use on your network. Once a scope is deactivated, the DHCP server no longer accepts those scope addresses as valid addresses.

- **Use server-side conflict detection on DHCP servers only when it is needed.**   Conflict detection can be used by either DHCP servers or clients to determine whether an IP address is already in use on the network before leasing or using the address.

- **Reservations should be created on all DHCP servers that can potentially service the reserved client.**   You can use a client reservation to ensure that a DHCP client computer always receives lease of the same IP address at its startup. If you have more than one DHCP server reachable by a reserved client, add the reservation at each of your other DHCP servers.

- **For server performance, remember that DHCP is disk-intensive and purchase hardware with optimal disk performance characteristics.**   DHCP causes frequent and intensive activity on server hard disks. To provide the best performance, consider RAID 0 or RAID 5 solutions when purchasing hardware for your server computer.

- **Keep audit logging enabled for use in troubleshooting.**   By default, the DHCP service enables audit logging of service-related events. With Windows 2000 Server, audit logging provides for a long-term service monitoring tool that makes limited and safe use of server disk resources.

- **Integrate DHCP with other services, such as WINS and DNS.**   WINS and DNS can both be used for registering dynamic name-to-address mappings on your network. To provide name resolution services, you must plan for interoperability of DHCP with these services. Most network administrators implementing DHCP also plan a strategy for implementing DNS and WINS servers.

- **Use the appropriate number of DHCP servers for the number of DHCP-enabled clients on your network.**   In a small LAN (for example, one physical subnet not using routers), a single DHCP server can serve all DHCP-enabled clients. For routed networks, the number of servers needed increases, depending on several factors, including the number of DHCP-enabled clients, the transmission speed between network segments, the speed of network links, the IP address class of the network, and whether DHCP service is used throughout the enterprise network or only on selected physical networks.

Troubleshooting DHCP Clients

Most DHCP-related problems start as failed IP configuration at a client, so it is a good practice to start there. After you have determined that a DHCP-related problem does not originate at the client, check the system event log and DHCP server audit logs for possible clues. When the DHCP service does not start, these logs generally explain the source of the service failure or shutdown. Furthermore, you can use the Ipconfig TCP/IP utility at the command prompt to get information about the configured TCP/IP parameters on local or remote computers on the network.

The following sections describe common symptoms for DHCP client problems. When a client fails to obtain configuration, you can use this information to quickly identify the source of the problem.

Invalid IP Address Configuration

If a DHCP client does not have an IP address configured or has an IP address configured as 168.254.x.x, that means that the client was not able to contact a DHCP server and obtain an IP address lease. This is either because of a network hardware failure or because the DHCP server is unavailable. If this occurs, you should verify that the client computer has a valid, functioning network connection. First, check that related client hardware devices (cables and network adapters) are working properly at the client.

Autoconfiguration Problems on the Current Network

If a DHCP client has an autoconfigured IP address that is incorrect for its current network, this means that the Windows 2000 or Windows 98 DHCP client could not find a DHCP server and has used the APIPA feature to configure its IP address. In some larger networks, disabling this feature is desirable for network administration. APIPA generates an IP address in the form of 169.254.x.y (where x.y is a unique identifier on the network that the client generates) and a subnet mask of 255.255.0.0. Note that Microsoft has reserved IP addresses from 169.254.0.1 through 169.254.255.254 and uses this range to support APIPA.

▶   **To fix an invalid autoconfigured IP address for your network**

1. First, use the PING command to test connectivity from the client to the server. Next, verify or manually attempt to renew the client lease. Depending on your network requirements, it might be necessary to disable APIPA at the client.

2. If the client hardware appears to be functioning properly, check that the DHCP server is available on the network by pinging it from another computer on the same network as the affected DHCP client. Furthermore, you can try releasing or renewing the client's address lease, and check the TCP/IP configuration settings on automatic addressing.

Missing Configuration Details

If a DHCP client is missing configuration details, the client might be missing DHCP options in its leased configuration, either because the DHCP server is not configured to distribute them or the client does not support the options distributed by the server. If this occurs on Microsoft DHCP clients, verify that the most commonly used and supported options have been configured at either the server, scope, client, or class level of option assignment. Check the DHCP option settings.

Sometimes a client has the full and correct set of DHCP options assigned, but its network configuration does not appear to be working correctly. If the DHCP server is configured with an incorrect DHCP router option (Option Code 3) for the Windows 98 or earlier client's default gateway address, you can

1. Change the IP address list for the router (default gateway) option at the applicable DHCP scope and server.

2. Set the correct value in the Scope Options tab of the Scope Properties dialog box.

    In rare instances, you might have to configure the DHCP client to use a specialized list of routers different from other scope clients. In such cases, you can add a reservation and configure the router option list specifically for the reserved client.

Clients running Windows NT or Windows 2000 do not use the incorrect address because they support the dead gateway detection feature. This feature of the Windows 2000 TCP/IP protocol changes the default gateway to the next default gateway in the list of configured default gateways when a specific number of connections retransmits segments.

DHCP Servers Do Not Provide IP Addresses

If DHCP clients are unable to get IP addresses from the server, one of the following situations can cause this problem:

- **The IP address of the DHCP server was changed and now DHCP clients cannot get IP addresses.**   A DHCP server can only service requests for a scope that has a network ID that is the same as the network ID of its IP address. Make sure that the DHCP server IP address falls in the same network range as the scope it is servicing. For example, a server with an IP address in the 192.168.0.0 network cannot assign addresses from scope 10.0.0.0 unless superscopes are used.

- **The DHCP clients are located across a router from the subnet where the DHCP server resides, and are unable to receive an address from the server.**   A DHCP server can provide IP addresses to client computers on remote multiple subnets only if the router that separates them can act as a DHCP relay agent. Completing the following steps might correct this problem:

    1. Configure a BOOTP/DHCP relay agent on the client subnet (that is, the same physical network segment). The relay agent can be located on the router itself or on a Windows 2000 Server computer running the DHCP Relay service component.

    2. At the DHCP server, configure a scope to match the network address on the other side of the router where the affected clients are located.

    3. In the scope, make sure that the subnet mask is correct for the remote subnet.

    4. Do not include this scope (that is, the one for the remote subnet) in superscopes configured for use on the same local subnet or segment where the DHCP server resides.

- **Multiple DHCP servers exist on the same LAN.**   Make sure that you do not configure multiple DHCP servers on the same LAN with overlapping scopes. You might want to rule out the possibility that one of the DHCP servers in question is a Small Business Server (SBS) computer. By design, the DHCP service, when running under SBS, automatically stops when it detects another DHCP server on the LAN.

Troubleshooting DHCP Servers

When a server fails to provide leases to its clients, the failure most often is discovered by clients in one of three ways:

1. The client might be configured to use an IP address not provided by the server.
2. The server sends a negative response back to the client, and the client displays an error message or popup indicating that a DHCP server could not be found.
3. The server leases the client an address but the client appears to have other network configuration-based problems, such as the inability to register or resolve DNS or NetBIOS names, or to perceive computers beyond its subnet.

The first troubleshooting task is to make sure that the DHCP services are running. This can be verified by opening the DHCP service console to view service status, or by opening Services And Applications under Computer Manager. If the appropriate service is not started, start the service. In rare circumstances, a DHCP server cannot start, or a Stop error might occur. If the DHCP server is stopped, complete the following procedure to restart it:

▶ **To restart a DHCP server that is stopped**

1. Start Windows 2000 Server, and log on as an administrator.
2. At the command prompt, type **net start dhcpserver**, then press Enter.

Note Use Event Viewer in Administrative Tools to find the possible source of problems with DHCP services.

DHCP Relay Agent Service Is Installed But Not Working

The DHCP Relay Agent service is running on the same computer as the DHCP service. Because both services listen for and respond to BOOTP and DHCP messages sent using UDP ports 67 and 68, neither service works reliably if both are installed on the same computer. To solve this problem, install the DHCP service and the DHCP Relay Agent component on separate computers.

DHCP Console Incorrectly Reports Lease Expirations

When the DHCP console displays the lease expiration time for reserved clients for a scope, it indicates one of the following:

- If the scope lease time is set to an infinite lease time, the reserved client's lease is also shown as infinite.
- If the scope lease time is set to a finite length of time (such as eight days), the reserved client's lease uses this same lease time.

The lease term of a DHCP reserved client is determined by the lease assigned to the reservation. To create reserved clients with unlimited lease durations, create a scope with an unlimited lease duration and add reservations to that scope.

DHCP Server Uses Broadcast to Respond to All Client Messages

The DHCP server uses broadcast to respond to all client configuration request messages, regardless of how each DHCP client has set the broadcast bit flag. DHCP clients can set the broadcast flag (the first bit in the 16-bit flags field in the DHCP message header) when sending DHCPDISCOVER messages to indicate to the DHCP server that broadcast to the limited broadcast address (255.255.255.255) should be used when replying to the client with a DHCPOFFER response.

By default, the DHCP server in Windows NT Server 3.51 and earlier versions ignored the broadcast flag in DHCPDISCOVER messages and broadcasted only DHCPOFFER replies. This behavior is implemented on the server to avoid problems that can result from clients not being able to receive or process a unicast response prior to being configured for TCP/IP.

Starting with Windows NT Server 4.0, the DHCP service still attempts to send all DHCP responses as IP broadcasts to the limited broadcast address, unless support for unicast responses is enabled by setting the value of the IgnoreBroadcastFlag registry entry to 1. The entry is located in: HKEY_LOCAL_MACHINE\System\ CurrentControlSet\Services\DHCPServer\Parameters\IgnoreBroadcastFlag. When set to 1, the broadcast flag in client requests is ignored, and all DHCPOFFER responses are broadcast from the server. When it is set to 0, the server transmission behavior (whether to broadcast or not) is determined by the setting of the broadcast bit flag in the client DHCPDISCOVER request. If this flag is set in the request, the server broadcasts its response to the limited local broadcast address. If this flag is not set in the request, the server unicasts its response directly to the client.

DHCP Server Fails to Issue Address Leases for a New Scope

A new scope has been added at the DHCP server for the purpose of renumbering the existing network. However, DHCP clients do not obtain leases from the newly defined scope. This situation is most common when you are attempting to renumber an existing IP network. For example, you might have obtained a registered class of IP addresses for your network, or you might be changing the address class to accommodate more computers or networks. In these situations, you want clients to obtain leases in the new scope instead of using the old scope to obtain or renew their leases. Once all clients are actively obtaining leases in the new scope, you intend to remove the existing scope.

When superscopes are not available or used, only a single DHCP scope can be active on the network at one time. If more than one scope is defined and activated on the DHCP server, only one scope is used to provide leases to clients. The active scope used for distributing leases is determined by whether the scope range of addresses contains the first IP address that is bound and assigned to the DHCP server's network adapter hardware. When additional secondary IP addresses are configured on a server using the Advanced TCP/IP Properties tab, these addresses have no effect on the DHCP server in determining scope selection or responding to configuration requests from DHCP clients on the network.

This problem can be solved in the following ways:

- Configure the DHCP server to use a superscope that includes the old scope and the new scope.

- Change the primary IP address (the address assigned in the TCP/IP Properties tab) on the DHCP server's network adapter to an IP address that is part of the same network as the new scope.

  For Windows NT Server 3.51, support for superscopes is not available. In this case, you must change the first IP address configured for the DHCP server's network adapter to an address in the new scope range of addresses. If necessary, you can still maintain the prior address that was first assigned as an active IP address for the server computer by moving it to the list of multiple IP addresses maintained in the Advanced TCP/IP Properties tab.

Monitoring Server Performance

Because DHCP servers are of critical importance in most environments, monitoring the performance of servers can help in troubleshooting cases where server performance degradation occurs. For Windows 2000 Server, the DHCP service includes a set of performance counters that can be used to monitor various types of server activity. By default, these counters are available after the DHCP service is installed. To access these counters, you must use System Monitor (formerly Performance Monitor). The DHCP server counters can monitor

- All types of DHCP messages sent and received by the DHCP service

- The average amount of processing time spent by the DHCP server per message packet sent and received

- The number of message packets dropped because of internal delays on the DHCP server computer

Moving the DHCP Server Database

You may need to move a DHCP database to another computer. To do this, use the following procedure.

▶ **To move a DHCP database**

1. Stop the Microsoft DHCP service on the current computer.

2. Copy the \System32\Dhcp directory to the new computer that has been configured as a DHCP server.

   Make sure the new directory is under exactly the same drive letter and path as on the old computer. If you must copy the files to a different directory, copy DHCP.MDB, but do not copy the .log or .chk files.

3. Start the Microsoft DHCP service on the new computer. The service automatically starts using the .mdb and .log files copied from the old computer.

When you check DHCP Manager, the scope still exists because the registry holds the information on the address range of the scope, including a bitmap of the addresses in use. You need to reconcile the DHCP database to add database entries for the existing leases in the address bitmask. As clients renew, they are matched with these leases, and eventually the database is again complete.

▶ **To reconcile the DHCP database**

1. In DHCP Manager, on the Scope menu, click Active Leases.
2. In the Active Leases dialog box, click Reconcile.

Although it is not required, you can force DHCP clients to renew their leases in order to update the DHCP database as quickly as possible. To do so, type **ipconfig /renew** at the command prompt.

Lesson Summary

The most common DHCP client problem is a failure to obtain an IP address or other configuration parameters from the DHCP server during startup. The most common DHCP server problem is the inability to start the server on the network in a Windows 2000 or Active Directory domain environment. Most DHCP-related problems start as failed IP configuration at a client, so it is a good practice to start there.

Review

Answering the following questions will reinforce key information presented in this chapter. If you are unable to answer a question, review the appropriate lesson and then try the question again. Answers to the questions can be found in Appendix A, "Questions and Answers."

1. What is DHCP?

2. Describe the integration of DHCP with DNS.

3. What is a DHCP client?

4. What is IP autoconfiguration in Windows 2000?

5. Why is it important to plan an implementation of DHCP for a network?

6. What tool do you use to manage DHCP servers in Windows 2000?

7. What is the symptom of most DHCP-related problems?

C H A P T E R   1 1

Providing Your Clients Remote Access Service (RAS)

About This Chapter

In this chapter, you will learn how to implement remote access services to provide your clients the ability to access network resources from the road or their homes. You will also learn how to implement secure virtual private networks (VPNs).

Before You Begin

To complete this chapter, you must have

- Two Microsoft Windows 2000 servers with local area network (LAN) connectivity

Lesson 1: Introducing Remote Access Service

The remote access feature of Microsoft Windows 2000 Server enables remote or mobile workers who use dial-up communication links to access corporate networks as if they were directly connected. Remote access also provides VPN services so that users can access corporate networks over the Internet.

After this lesson, you will be able to

- Explain the features of remote access service
- Install remote access service
- Describe the difference between remote access service and remote control
- Explain the effect of an upgrade on Routing and Remote Access

Estimated lesson time: 25 minutes

Overview of Remote Access Service

Windows 2000 Server remote access, part of the integrated Routing and Remote Access service, connects remote or mobile workers to corporate networks. Remote users can work as if their computers were physically connected to the network. Users (or clients) run remote access software to initiate a connection to the remote access server. The remote access server, which is a computer running Windows 2000 Server with the Routing and Remote Access service enabled, authenticates users and services sessions until terminated. All services typically available to a LAN-connected user (including file and print sharing, Web server access, and messaging) are enabled by means of the remote access connection.

Remote access clients use standard tools to access network resources. For example, on a computer running Windows 2000, clients can use Windows Explorer to map network drives and connect to printers. Connections are persistent, so users do not need to reconnect to network resources during their remote sessions. Because drive letters and Universal Naming Convention (UNC) names are fully supported by remote access, most commercial and custom applications work without modification. A remote access server running Windows 2000 provides two different types of remote access connectivity:

- **Dial-up networking.**   Dial-up networking occurs when a remote access client makes a nonpermanent, dial-up connection to a physical port on a remote access server by using the service of a telecommunications provider such as analog phone, Integrated Services Digital Network (ISDN), or X.25. The best example of dial-up networking is that of a dial-up networking client who dials the phone number of one of the ports of a remote access server.

  Dial-up networking over an analog phone or ISDN is a direct physical connection between the dial-up networking client and the dial-up networking server. You can encrypt data sent over the connection, but it is not required.

- **Virtual private networking.**   Virtual private networking is the creation of secured, point-to-point connections across a private network or a public network such as the Internet. A virtual private networking client uses special Transmission Control Protocol/Internet Protocol (TCP/IP)-based protocols called tunneling protocols to make a call to a port on a VPN server. The most practical example of a VPN is a dial-up user connecting across the Internet to a server on the corporate network. The remote access server answers the virtual call, authenticates the caller, and transfers data between the virtual private networking client and the corporate network.

  In contrast to dial-up networking, virtual private networking is a logical (rather than physical) connection between the VPN client and server. To ensure privacy, you must encrypt data sent over the connection.

Routing and Remote Access Features

The Windows Routing and Remote Access feature set provides network address translation (NAT), multiprotocol routing, Layer Two Tunneling Protocol (L2TP), Internet Authentication Service (IAS), and Remote Access Policies (RAP). The lesson concludes with information about demand-dial filters, dial-out hours, dial-in user properties, remote access use of name servers and DHCP, Bandwidth Allocation Protocol (BAP), and monitoring remote access.

Router Discovery

Windows 2000 has a new feature called router discovery, specified in Request for Comments (RFC) 1256. Router discovery provides an improved method of configuring and detecting default gateways. When using DHCP or manual default gateway configuration, there is no way to adjust to network changes. Using router discovery, clients dynamically discover routers and can switch to backup routers if a network failure or administrative change is needed. Router discovery is made up of two types of packets:

1. **Router solicitations.**   When a host that supports RFC 1256 needs to be configured with a default gateway, it sends out a router solicitation using an Internet Control Message Protocol (ICMP) message. The router solicitation can be sent to the all-routers Internet Protocol (IP) multicast address of 224.0.0.2, the local IP broadcast address, or the limited broadcast address (255.255.255.255). In practice, hosts send router solicitation messages to the multicast address. Routers on the host's network that support RFC 1256 immediately respond with a router advertisement, and the host chooses the router with the highest preference level as its default gateway.

2. **Router advertisements.**   Router advertisements are explicit notifications to the hosts on the network that the router is still available. A router sends out a periodic router advertisement using an ICMP message. The router advertisement can be sent to the all-hosts local IP broadcast address or the limited broadcast address. Like router solicitations, the router advertisement is sent to the multicast address in practice.

Note   Windows 2000 supports router discovery as a host and router.

Network Address Translator

NAT is a standard defined in RFC 1631. A NAT is a router that translates IP addresses of an intranet or home LAN to valid Internet addresses. A NAT allows Internet connectivity for a private network with private addresses through a single Internet IP address. Windows 2000 Server includes a full-featured NAT implementation called Connection Sharing and a configuration-free version called Shared Access.

Multicast Routing

Windows 2000 Server implements a limited form of multicast routing using a multicast proxy. This proxy can be used to extend multicast support beyond a true multicast router. The multicast proxy is best used to provide multicast for remote access users or a single LAN network connected to the Internet. On one or more interfaces Windows 2000 acts like a multicast router, communicating with local clients about their multicast needs. On an interface that has direct access to a true multicast router, Windows acts as a multicast client, forwarding multicast traffic on behalf of the local clients.

Layer Two Tunneling Protocol

L2TP can be thought of as the next version of Point-to-Point Tunneling Protocol (PPTP). It works much like PPTP but is now a combined development effort with Cisco. L2TP combines Cisco's Layer 2 Forwarding (L2F) and PPTP technologies (created by Microsoft, Ascend, 3Com, U.S. Robotics, and ECI-Telematics). L2TP is currently an RFC draft, soon to be an industry standard. L2TP is an Open Systems Interconnection (OSI) layer 2 (Data-link layer) protocol used to create VPNs.

Internet Authentication Service

IAS is a Remote Authentication Dial-In User Service (RADIUS) server. RADIUS is a network protocol that enables remote authentication, authorization, and accounting of users who are connecting to a network access server (NAS). A network access server such as Windows Routing and Remote Access can be a RADIUS client or RADIUS server.

Note   Microsoft released a limited version of RADIUS server in the Windows NT 4.0 Option pack. A RADIUS server (IAS) is now available in Windows 2000.

Remote Access Policies

In Windows NT 3.5 and later versions, remote access was granted based on a simple Grant Dial-In Permission To User option in User Manager or the Remote Access Admin utility. Callback options were also granted on a per-user basis.

In Windows 2000, remote access connections are granted based on the dial-in properties of a user object and remote access policies. RAPs are a set of conditions and connection parameters that allow network administrators more flexibility in granting remote access permissions and usage. Some examples of conditions include time of day, group, and type of connection (VPN or Dial). Some examples of connection parameters may include authentication and encryption requirements, use of multilink, and length of session. One example of the benefit of this added control is requiring strong encryption on VPN connections and allowing no encryption on modem connections where it may not be needed.

RAPs are stored on the local computer and are shared between Windows 2000 Routing and Remote Access and Windows 2000 IAS. RAP is configured from the Internet Authentication Service Manager or from the Routing and Remote Access Manager.

Enabling Routing and Remote Access

Now that you have an understanding of Routing and Remote Access, you will enable the service. Before you enable this service, the Routing and Remote Access Manager will look like the illustration in Figure 11.1.

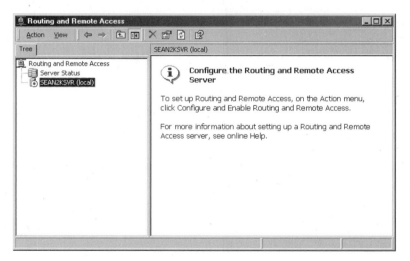

Figure 11.1 The Routing and Remote Access Manager before installation

Practice: Installing a Routing and Remote Access Server

In this procedure, you will install a Routing and Remote Access server using the Routing and Remote Access Manager.

Before you continue with the lesson, run the Ch11.exe demonstration file located in the Media folder on the Supplemental Course Materials CD-ROM that accompanies this book. The file provides an overview of installing a Routing and Remote Access server.

▶ **To install a Routing and Remote Access server**

1. Open the Routing and Remote Access Manager.

2. Right-click your machine name and choose Configure And Enable Routing And Remote Access.

3. In the Routing And Remote Access Server Setup Wizard, click Next.

4. On the Common Configurations page, select the Remote Access Server button, then click Next.

5. On the Remote Client Protocols page, under Protocols, make sure that TCP/IP is listed. Verify that Yes, All The Required Protocols Are On This List is selected, then click Next.

6. On the IP Address Assignment page, make sure From A Specified Range Of Addresses is selected, then click Next.

7. On the Address Range Assignment page, click New. Next to Starting Address type **10.0.0.10** (for computer 1, and 10.0.0.20 for computer 2). Under End Of IP Address type **10.0.0.19** (for computer 1, and 10.0.0.29 for computer 2). Under Number Of Addresses, verify that 10 is the number. Click OK to close the Edit Address Range window. Click Next.

8. On the Managing Multiple Remote Access Servers page, verify that No, I Don't Want To Set This Server Up To Use RADIUS Now is selected, then click Next.

9. Click Finish.

10. Click OK to any warning messages that pop up.

    The Routing and Remote Access Manager will look like the illustration in Figure 11.2.

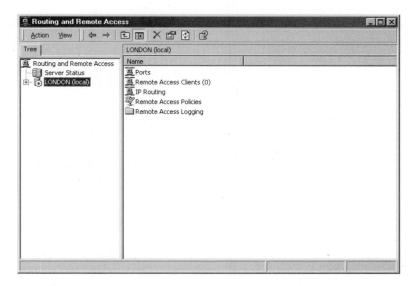

Figure 11.2 The Routing and Remote Access Manager after installation

▶ **To give dial-in permission to the Administrator account**

1. Open Directory Management (if in a domain) or Computer Management, System Tools, Local Computer Management (if in a workgroup).

2. Open the User Properties for Administrator and go to the Dial-In tab and select Allow Access.

Remote Access Versus Remote Control

The distinctions between remote access and remote control solutions are the following:

■ The remote access server is a software-based multiprotocol router; remote control solutions work by sharing screen, keyboard, and mouse over the remote link. In remote access, the applications are run on the remote access client computer.

■ In a remote control solution, users share a central processing unit (CPU) or multiple CPUs on the server. In remote control, the applications are run on the server. The remote access server's CPU is dedicated to facilitating communications between remote access clients and network resources, not to running applications.

The Effect of a Windows Upgrade on Routing and Remote Access

A system upgraded from Windows NT 4.0 Remote Access Service/Routing and Remote Access Service to Windows 2000 has one minor problem. Windows NT 4.0 uses the LocalSystem account. When any service logs on as LocalSystem, it logs on with NULL credentials, meaning that the service does not provide a user name or password.

Active Directory, by default, does not accept querying of object attributes through NULL sessions. Therefore, in a mixed environment, planning is necessary to allow Windows NT 4.0 Remote Access Service/Routing and Remote Access Service servers to retrieve user dial-in properties from Active Directory. The Remote Access Service/Routing and Remote Access Service servers require this access to determine whether the user has been granted dial-in permissions and whether any other dial-in settings, such as callback phone numbers, have been configured.

Note   Using NULL credentials prevents the account from being able to access network resources relying on Windows NT LAN Manager (NTLM) authentication (unless the remote computer specifically allows NULL sessions).

Remote Access Server Upgrade Considerations

For a Windows NT 4.0 Remote Access Service/Routing and Remote Access Service server to retrieve user properties from Active Directory, you must meet one of the following conditions:

- You have a domain in mixed mode and the Windows NT 4.0 Remote Access Service/Routing and Remote Access Service server is also a Windows NT 4.0 backup domain controller. Here, Remote Access Service/Routing and Remote Access Service has access to the local Security Accounts Manager (SAM) database.

- You have a domain in mixed mode and the Windows NT 4.0 Remote Access Service/Routing and Remote Access Service server contacts a Windows NT 4.0 backup domain controller to determine user dial-in properties. This also will allow access to the local SAM database.

- The domain is in mixed or native mode and Active Directory security has been loosened to grant the built-in user Everyone permissions to read any property on any user object. This is configured with the Active Directory Installation Wizard (DCPROMO.EXE) by selecting Permission Compatible With Pre-Windows 2000 Server.

Note Unless Active Directory security has been loosened, or the Remote Access Service/Routing and Remote Access Service server is installed on a backup domain controller, dial-in connectivity success could be intermittent. Even if your domain runs in mixed mode, it is impossible to configure the Remote Access Service/Routing and Remote Access Service server to contact a Windows NT 4.0 backup domain controller only for authentication. If a Windows 2000 domain controller authenticates the user, dial-in will fail.

The Permission Compatible With Pre-Windows 2000 Servers option places the Everyone group in the Pre-Windows 2000 Compatible Access Local Group. You can strengthen permissions by deleting the Everyone group from this group's membership list after all remote access servers have been upgraded to Windows 2000.

Note The Everyone group workaround should be used only after understanding its impact on Active Directory security. If it conflicts with your security require-ments, it is recommended that you upgrade the Windows NT 4.0 Remote Access Service/Routing and Remote Access Service server to Windows 2000 and make it a member of a Windows 2000 mixed or native domain. This will help prevent inconsistent dial-in access while the domain is in mixed mode.

If you would like to loosen security to allow Windows NT 4.0 Remote Access Service/Routing and Remote Access Service servers to function after running the Active Directory Installation Wizard, you can add the Everyone group to the Pre-Windows 2000 Pre-Compatible Access group by typing the command **net localgroup "Pre-Windows 2000 Compatible Access" Everyone /add**.

Lesson Summary

This lesson provided a basic summary of remote access features. This includes router discovery, NAT, multicast routing, L2TP, IAS, and RAPs. Installing and configuring Routing and Remote Access was also introduced.

Lesson 2: Configuring a Routing and Remote Access Server

Once Routing and Remote Access is installed, you can configure it for inbound connections, lock it down with RAPs, add remote access profiles for security, and control access with BAP. In this lesson, you will explore these configurable options.

After this lesson, you will be able to

- Explain how to allow inbound connections
- Create a RAP
- Describe how to configure a remote access profile
- Describe how to configure BAP

Estimated lesson time: 45 minutes

Allowing Inbound Connections

When Routing and Remote Access is started for the first time, Windows 2000 automatically creates five PPTP and five L2TP ports, as illustrated in Figure 11.3. The number of VPN ports that are available to any remote access server is not limited by the hardware and can be configured. You can configure VPN ports under Ports in the console tree of Routing and Remote Access.

You can also add a parallel port by configuring Ports. Serial communication ports will show up only after a modem is installed for the Routing and Remote Access machine. Both types of ports can be configured for inbound and outbound connections.

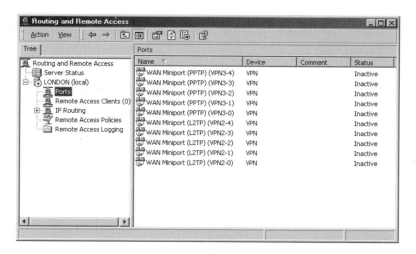

Figure 11.3   Routing and Remote Access Ports

Creating a Remote Access Policy (RAP)

RAPs are a named set of conditions, as illustrated in Figure 11.4, that are used to define who has remote access to the network and what the characteristics of that connection will be. Conditions for accepting or rejecting connections can be based on many different criteria, such as day and time, group membership, type of service, and so forth. Characteristics of the connection could be configured, for example, as an ISDN connection that can last only 30 minutes and that will not allow Hypertext Transfer Protocol (HTTP) packets.

Note RAPs are shared between Routing and Remote Access and IAS. They can be configured from either tool.

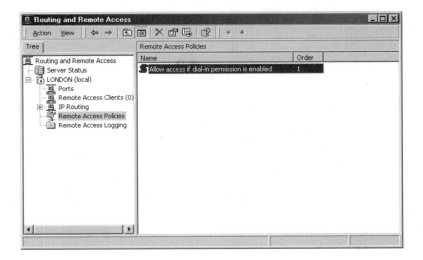

Figure 11.4 Routing and Remote Access Policies

From the IAS administration tool or the Routing and Remote Access Manager, RAPs can be created, deleted, renamed, and reordered. Note that there is no Save option, so it is not possible to save a copy to floppy disk. The order of policies is significant because the first matching policy will be used to accept or reject the connection.

Note Remote Access Policies are not stored in Active Directory; they are stored locally in the IAS.MDB file. Policies need to be created manually on each server. Remote Access Policies are applied to users in a mixed-mode domain, even though the user's dial-in permission can only be set to Allow Access or Deny Access, as illustrated in Figure 11.5 (Control Access Through Remote Access Policy is not available on mixed-mode domain controllers). If the user's permission is Allow Access, the user still must meet the conditions set forth in a policy before being allowed to connect.

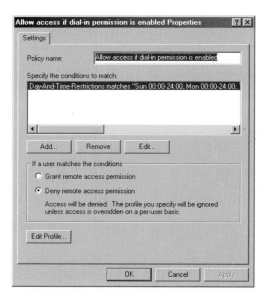

Figure 11.5   Configuring Remote Access Policies

Conditions

Conditions can be added to a RAP on what conditions must match in order for the system to grant or deny remote access permission. This works in conjunction with the remote access permission associated with the user to determine whether the user is given access. The flowchart in Figure 11.6 shows the logic used to decide whether the connection request is granted or denied.

Note   If no Remote Access Policy exists (if the default policy is deleted, for example), users will not be able to access the network, regardless of their individual Routing and Remote Access permission settings.

By using this flowchart, one can predict the outcome of a connection request for any given situation. For example, a user's dial-in property is set to Control Access Through Remote Access Policy and the RAP is the default Allow Access If Dial-In Permission Is Enabled (the policy is to deny access, and the condition is to permit any day, any time). By following the flowchart, the user connection attempt will be rejected.

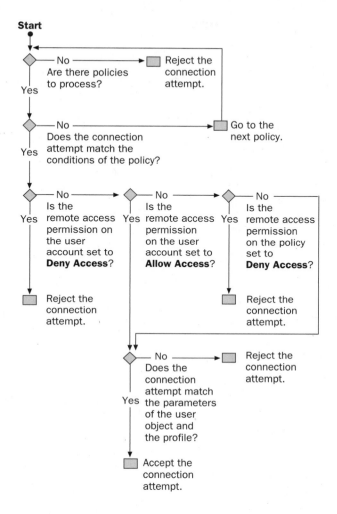

Figure 11.6 Flowchart of Remote Access Policy

However, if the user's dial-in property (illustrated in Figure 11.7) is set to Allow Access, then using the same default policy as above, the user connection attempt will be accepted.

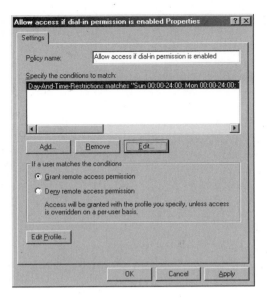

Figure 11.7   Setting dial-in properties to grant access

Grant or Deny Access

Policies can be configured to either grant or deny access. This works in conjunction with the user object's dial-in permission to decide whether or not a user is given access, by means of the logic shown in Figure 11.6.

Caller ID

Caller ID verifies that the caller is calling from the phone number specified. If caller ID is configured, support for the passing of caller ID information all the way from the caller to Routing and Remote Access is required, or the connection attempt will be denied.

Note   For backwards compatibility with previous versions of Windows NT, RAP, Caller ID, Apply Static Routes, and Assign A Static IP Address are not available in mixed mode.

Practice: Creating a New Remote Access Policy

In this procedure, a new policy will be created that allows remote access based on the user's group membership.

▶   **To create a new remote access policy**

1. Using the Routing and Remote Access administration tool, right-click Remote Access Policies and select New Remote Access Policy.

2. Add a friendly name of "Allow Domain Users," then click Next.

3. Click Add to add a condition.

4. Select Windows-groups, then click Add.

5. Click Add, select Domain Users, then click Add. Click OK.

6. Click OK to exit the Groups dialog.

7. Click Next, then select Grant Remote Access Permission.

8. Click next, then click Finish.

Configuring a Remote Access Profile

The profile specifies what kind of access the user will be given if the conditions match. There are six different tabs that can be used to configure a profile.

Dial-In Constraints

Constraints on the actual connection are configured in the Edit Dial-In Profile dialog box, on the Constraints tab, as shown in Figure 11.8. Possible settings include idle time disconnect, maximum session time, day and time, phone number, and media type (ISDN, tunnel, async, and so forth).

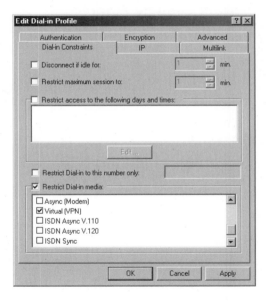

Figure 11.8   The Edit Dial-In Profile dialog box

IP

Configuration for client IP address assignment and IP packet filtering is found here. Packet filters can be set for either inbound or outbound and can be configured for protocol and port.

Multilink

Set multilink and BAP options here. A line can be dropped if bandwidth drops below a certain level for a given length of time.

Authentication

Authentication protocols such as Password Authentication Protocol (PAP), Challenge Handshake Authentication Protocol (CHAP), and Extensible Authentication Protocol (EAP) are set here.

Encryption

Encryption settings for Microsoft Routing and Remote Access servers are configured here. Options are to prohibit encryption, allow it, or require it.

Advanced

The Advanced tab allows for the configuration of additional network parameters that do not apply to Microsoft Routing and Remote Access servers. Included are standard RADIUS and Ascend attributes, which may apply to other manufacturers' NAS equipment.

Practice: Creating a Policy Filter

In this procedure, you will edit the profile of the Allow Access If Dial-In Permission Enabled policy so that users who gain access through that policy cannot ping the Routing and Remote Access server's network, whereas users who are granted access via the Allow Domain Users policy can ping the Routing and Remote Access server.

▶   **To create an ICMP Echo filter in the**
     Allow Access If Dial-In Permission Is Enabled policy

1. Right-click the Allow Access If Dial-In Permission Enabled policy and select Properties.
2. Click the Edit Profile button.
3. Select the IP tab.
4. Click the From Client IP Packet filter.
5. Click Add.
6. Click the destination network box.
7. For the IP address, type the network number and netmask of the Routing and Remote Access server.
8. For the protocol, select ICMP.
9. Enter **8** for ICMP type, and enter **0** for ICMP code. (ICMP type 8 designates an Echo request.)
10. Click OK to exit the Add/Edit IP filter, and OK to exit the IP Packet Filters Configuration dialog box. Click OK again to exit the dialog box.

Configuring Bandwidth Allocation Protocol (BAP)

BAP and Bandwidth Allocation Control Protocol (BACP) enhance multilink by dynamically adding or dropping links on demand. BAP and BACP are sometimes used interchangeably to refer to the same bandwidth-on-demand functionality. Both protocols are Point-to-Point (PPP) control protocols and work together to provide bandwidth on demand.

BAP functionality is implemented through a new Link Control Protocol (LCP) option, BACP, and BAP protocols, as described in the following list:

- **Link Discriminator.**   A new LCP option used as a unique identifier for each link of a multilink bundle.

- **BACP.**   BACP uses LCP negotiations to elect a "favored peer." The favored peer is used to determine which peer is favored if the peers simultaneously transmit the same BAP request.

- **BAP.**   BAP provides a mechanism for link and bandwidth management. Link management allows for the adding and dropping of links. This includes providing phone numbers as well as type of hardware (modem or ISDN) of the additional available links. Bandwidth management decides when to add and drop links based on link utilization.

BAP and BACP are encapsulated in PPP Data-Link layer frames with the following protocol field (in hex). This information may be useful when reading PPP logs. As illustrated in Figure 11.9, you can enable BAP and BACP bandwidth control using the PPP tab on the Connection Properties dialog box.

- C02D for BAP
- C02B for BACP

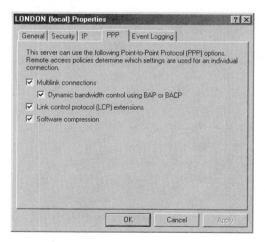

Figure 11.9   Setting PPP options for a remote access policy

▶ **To enable or disable BAP/BACP on a server-wide basis**

1. In Routing and Remote Access Manager, right-click the server on which you want to enable BAP/BACP, then click Properties.

2. In the PPP tab, select the Dynamic Bandwidth Control Using BAP Or BACP check box.

BAP policies are enforced through profile settings or Remote Access Policies. Remote Access Policies are accessed from Routing and Remote Access Manager or from IAS Manager.

BAP Additional Phone Numbers

The server can provide the client with additional phone numbers to dial if extra bandwidth is needed. Using this option, the client only needs to know one phone number but can still bring up extra lines as needed, as illustrated in Figure 11.10.

1. From the Routing and Remote Access Manager go to Ports, Properties, select a port, then click Configure.

2. Enter the phone number of other modems to be used for multilink.

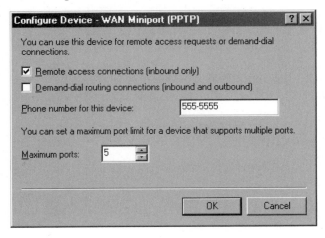

Figure 11.10 BAP additional phone numbers

Lesson Summary

With Routing and Remote Access already installed, we configured it for inbound connections, locked it down with RAPs, added remote access profiles for security, and controlled access with BAP.

Lesson 3: Implementing IP Routing on a Remote Access Server

In this lesson, you will learn how to turn your remote access server into an IP router, update its routing tables, and implement demand-dial routing.

After this lesson, you will be able to

- Install IP routing (Routing and Remote Access)
- Describe how to update routing tables
- Implement demand-dial routing

Estimated lesson time: 30 minutes

Installing IP Routing

Installing IP routing is very similar to installing remote access server. In fact, the same wizard is used for new installs, as the following practice shows. If you already have remote access installed, perform the following procedure to enable IP routing on your computer.

▶ **To enable IP Routing**

1. From the Routing and Remote Access Manager, right-click Properties, enable This Computer As A Router, then click OK.

2. Click Yes at the warning, You made changes to the router configuration that require the router to be restarted. Do you want to restart now?

If you have not previously installed remote access server, the following practice outlines the steps.

Practice: Enabling and Configuring a Routing and Remote Access Server

In this procedure, you will install a Routing and Remote Access server using the Routing and Remote Access Manager (see Figure 11.11).

▶ **To install a Routing and Remote Access server**

1. Open the Routing and Remote Access Manager.

2. Right-click your machine name and choose Configure And Enable Routing And Remote Access.

3. In the Routing And Remote Access Server Setup Wizard, click Next.

4. On the Common Configurations page, select the Network Router radio button, then click Next.

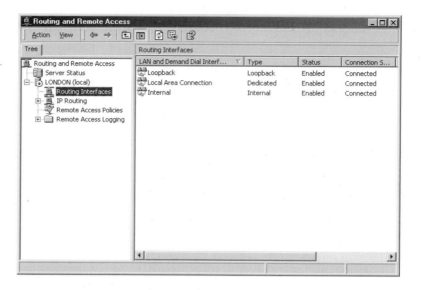

Figure 11.11   Managing a Routing and Remote Access server

5. On the Remote Client Protocols page, under Protocols, make sure that TCP/IP is listed, verify that Yes, All The Required Protocols Are On This List is selected, then click Next.

6. On the Demand Dial Connections page, make sure that No is specified from You Can Set Up Demand-Dial Routing Connections After This Wizard Finishes, then click Next.

7. Click Finish.

Updating the Routing Tables

The routing decision is aided by knowing which network addresses (or network IDs) are available in the internetwork. This knowledge is obtained from a database called the routing table. The routing table is a series of entries called routes that contain information on where the network IDs of the internetwork are located. The routing table is not exclusive to a router. Hosts (nonrouters) also have a routing table that is used to determine the optimal route.

Types of Routing Table Entries

Each entry in the routing table is considered a route and is one of the following types:

- **Network route.**   A network route provides a route to a specific network ID in the internetwork.

- **Host route.** A host route provides a route to an internetwork address (network ID and node ID). Host routes are typically used to create custom routes to specific hosts to control or optimize network traffic. A host route is equivalent to a network route with a netmask of 255.255.255.255.

- **Default route.** A default route is used when no other routes in the routing table are found. For example, if a router or host cannot find a network route or host route for the destination, the default route is used. The default route simplifies the configuration of hosts. Rather than configuring hosts with routes for all the network IDs in the internetwork, a single default route is used to forward all packets with a destination network or internetwork address that was not found in the routing table. A default route is equivalent to a network route with a netmask of 0.0.0.0.

Routing Table Structure

Figure 11.12 shows a routing table.

LONDON - IP Routing Table					
Destination	Network mask	Gateway	Interface	Metric	Protocol
10.0.0.0	255.0.0.0	10.45.45.45	Local Area C...	1	Local
10.45.45.45	255.255.255.255	127.0.0.1	Loopback	1	Local
127.0.0.0	255.0.0.0	127.0.0.1	Loopback	1	Local
127.0.0.1	255.255.255.255	127.0.0.1	Loopback	1	Local
224.0.0.0	240.0.0.0	10.45.45.45	Local Area C...	1	Local
255.255.255.255	255.255.255.255	10.45.45.45	Local Area C...	1	Local

Figure 11.12 Routing table

Each entry in the routing table consists of the following information fields:

- **Destination.** The network ID or an internetwork address for a host route. On IP routers, there is an additional subnet mask field that determines the IP network ID from a destination IP address.

- **Gateway.** The address to which the packet is forwarded. The forwarding address is a hardware address or an internetwork address. For networks to which the host or router is directly attached, the forwarding address field may be the address of the interface that is attached to the network.

- **Interface.** The network interface that is used when packets are forwarded to the network ID. This is a port number or other type of logical identifier.

- **Metric.** A measurement of the preference of a route. Typically, the lowest metric is the most preferred route. If multiple routes exist to a given destination network, the route with the lowest metric is used. Some routing algorithms only store a single route to any network ID in the routing table, even when multiple routes exist. In this case, the metric is used by the router to determine which route to store in the routing table.

Note   The preceding list is intended to be a representative list of fields in the routing tables used by routers. Actual fields in the routing tables for different routable protocols may vary.

Implementing Demand-Dial Routing

A demand-dial interface is a router interface that will be brought up on demand based on network traffic. The demand-dial link is only initiated if the routing table shows that this interface is needed to reach the IP destination address. The routing table does not provide any discretion on who or what protocol can bring up the demand-dial link. It is simply based on where the traffic needs to go.

Demand-dial filters control what traffic will initiate the demand-dial link. Filters can be set to permit or deny particular source or destination IP addresses, ports, or protocols. Further control is offered through the use of time-of-day restrictions. Even though the demand-dial filter requirements are met, if the time of day is restricted by the configuration of dial-out hours, the router will not dial.

The fields described in the following section for IP, TCP, and User Datagram Protocol (UDP) headers can be used to configure demand-dial filters. Routing and Remote Access allows filtering on the following fields:

IP Header

An IP datagram includes an IP header of 20 bytes. The following list describes the key fields in the IP header:

- **IP protocol.**   An identifier of the IP client protocol. For example, TCP uses a Protocol ID of 6, UDP uses a Protocol ID of 17, and ICMP uses a Protocol ID of 1. The Protocol field is used to demultiplex an IP packet to the upper layer protocol.

- **Source IP address.**   The source IP address stores the IP address of the originating host.

- **Destination IP address.**   The destination IP address stores the IP address of the destination host. The destination IP address can be configured with a subnet mask, allowing an entire range of IP addresses (corresponding with a network ID) to be specified with a single filter entry.

TCP Header

TCP uses byte-stream communications in which data contained by the TCP segment is considered as a sequence of bytes with no record or field boundaries. The following list describes the key fields in the TCP header:

- **TCP source port.**   The TCP source port is used to identify the source process that is sending the TCP segment.

- **TCP destination port.**   The TCP destination port is used to identify the destination process for this TCP segment.

UDP Header

UDP is used by applications that do not require an acknowledgment of receipt of data and that typically transmit small amounts of data at one time. The following list describes the key fields in the UDP header:

- **UDP source port.** The UDP source port is used to identify the source process that is sending the UDP message.

- **UDP destination port.** The UDP destination port is used to identify the destination process for the UDP message.

Note A list of well-known ports can be found in %winroot%\system32\drivers\ etc\services or RFC 1700.

ICMP

ICMP messages are encapsulated within IP datagrams so that they can be routed throughout an internetwork. The following list describes key fields in an ICMP packet:

- **ICMP type.** The ICMP type indicates the type of ICMP packet (Echo Request vs. Echo Reply, and so on).

- **ICMP code.** The ICMP code indicates one of possible multiple functions within a given type.

Configuring Demand-Dial Filters

Windows 2000 demand-dial routing allows the configuration of demand-dial filters and dial-out hours to prevent demand-dial connections from occurring.

▶ **To configure demand-dial filters**

1. Open the Routing and Remote Access Manager.

2. Click Routing Interfaces.

3. Right-click the demand-dial interface.

4. Choose Set Demand-Dial Filters.

5. In the Set Demand-Dial Filters dialog box, illustrated in Figure 11.13, click Add.

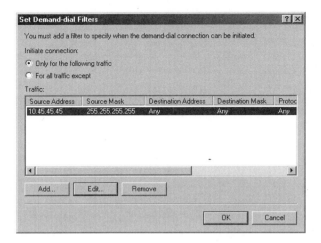

Figure 11.13   IP demand-dial filters configuration

Source and Destination IP Address

The source and destination IP address is configured with a subnet mask, allowing an entire range of IP addresses (corresponding to a network ID) to be specified with a single filter entry. For example, 10.45.45.45 mask 255.255.255.255 applies to only one address, whereas 10.0.0.0 mask 255.0.0.0 applies to the entire Class A network.

Protocol

For each filter, various protocols can be used:

- TCP, TCP-established, and UDP are configured with source and destination ports.
- ICMP is configured with ICMP type and ICMP code.
- ANY means any protocol.
- Other is used to specify an IP protocol ID. This can be entered as a protocol number or name. Protocol names are resolved to a protocol number using the PROTOCOL file in the %winroot%\system32\drivers\etc directory.

Action

The demand-dial filtering is based on exceptions. You can either configure Routing and Remote Access to initiate connection only for the traffic defined by the filters, or initiate connection for all traffic except those defined by filters.

Dial-Out Hours

Dial-out hours are used to specify when the demand-dial connection can be made. With dial-out hours, you can specify the time of day and day of week that a demand-dial connection is either allowed or denied.

▶ **To configure time-of-day restrictions**

1. Open the Routing and Remote Access Manager.
2. Click Routing Interfaces.
3. Right-click the demand-dial interface.
4. Choose Dial-Out Hours.
5. In the Dial-Out Hours dialog box, illustrated in Figure 11.14, select the desired hours to permit or deny.

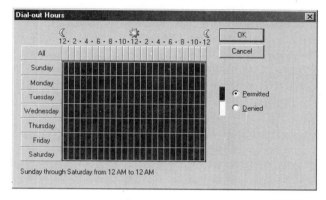

Figure 11.14   The Dial-Out Hours dialog box

Lesson Summary

In this lesson you learned how to turn your remote access server into an IP router or install Routing and Remote Access, update its routing tables, and implement demand-dial routing.

Lesson 4: Supporting Virtual Private Networks

A VPN is defined as the ability to send data between two computers across an internetwork in a manner that mimics the properties of a dedicated private network. In this lesson, you will learn about VPNs in a routed environment and with the Internet.

After this lesson, you will be able to

- Explain a VPN
- Describe a VPN in a routed environment
- Describe a VPN server with the Internet

Estimated lesson time: 20 minutes

Implementing a VPN

A VPN is defined as the ability to send data between two computers across an internetwork in a manner that mimics the properties of a dedicated private network (see Figure 11.15). VPNs allow users working at home or on the road to connect securely to a remote corporate server using the routing infrastructure provided by a public internetwork such as the Internet. From the user's perspective, the VPN is a point-to-point connection between the user's computer and a corporate server. The nature of the intermediate internetwork (hereafter referred to as the transit internetwork) is irrelevant because it appears as if the data is being sent over a dedicated private link.

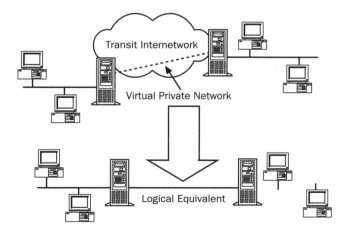

Figure 11.15   Virtual private network diagram

VPN technology also allows a corporation to connect with its branch offices or with other companies over a public internetwork (such as the Internet) while maintaining secure communications. The VPN connection across the Internet logically operates as a dedicated wide area network (WAN) link.

In both of these cases, the secure connection across the transit internetwork appears to the user as a virtual network interface providing private network communication over a public internetwork, hence the term virtual private network.

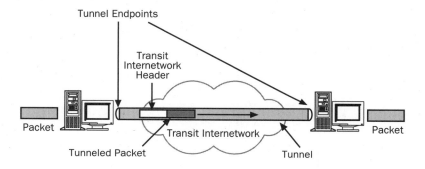

Figure 11.16   A VPN tunnel

Tunneling Basics

Tunneling, also known as encapsulation, is a method of using an internetwork infrastructure to transfer a payload (see Figure 11.16). The payload may be the frames (or packets) of another protocol. Instead of sending the frame as produced by the originating node, the frame is encapsulated with an additional header. The additional header provides routing information so that the encapsulated payload can traverse the intermediate internetwork. The encapsulated packets are then routed between tunnel endpoints over the transit internetwork. Once the encapsulated frames reach their destination on the transit internetwork, the frame is de-encapsulated and forwarded to its final destination.

This entire process (the encapsulation and transmission of packets) is known as tunneling. The logical path through which the encapsulated packets travel through the transit internetwork is called a tunnel.

Examples of Tunneling

Tunneling can be achieved in one of the following ways:

- **Point-to-Point Tunneling Protocol (PPTP).**   PPTP allows IP, Internetwork Packet Exchange (IPX), or NetBIOS Enhanced User Interface (NetBEUI) traffic to be encrypted and then encapsulated in an IP header to be sent across a corporate IP internetwork or public internetworks like the Internet.

- **Layer Two Tunneling Protocol (L2TP).**   L2TP allows IP traffic to be encrypted and then sent over any medium that supports point-to-point datagram delivery, such as IP, frame relay, or asynchronous transfer mode (ATM).

- **IP Security (IPSec) tunnel mode.**   IPSec tunnel mode allows IP payloads to be encrypted and then encapsulated in an IP header to be sent across a corporate IP internetwork or public internetworks like the Internet.

- **IP-in-IP tunneling.**   IP-in-IP tunneling encapsulates an existing IP datagram with an additional IP header. This allows a packet to traverse a network with disjointed capabilities or policies. A popular use of IP-in-IP tunneling is to forward multicast traffic through portions of the Internet that do not support multicast routing.

Integrating VPN in a Routed Environment

In some corporate internetworks (see Figure 11.17), the data of a department (such as the Human Resources department) is so sensitive that the department's LAN is physically disconnected from the rest of the corporate internetwork. Although this protects the department's data, it creates information accessibility problems for those users not physically connected to the separate LAN.

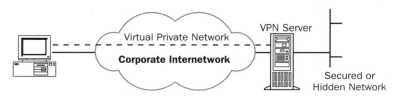

Figure 11.17   Corporate internetwork

VPNs allow the department's LAN to be physically connected to the corporate internetwork but separated by a VPN server. Note that the VPN server is not acting as a router between the corporate internetwork and the department LAN. Users on the corporate internetwork having the appropriate credentials (based on a need-to-know policy within the company) can establish a VPN with the VPN server and gain access to the protected resources of the department. Additionally, all communication across the VPN can be encrypted for data confidentiality. For those users not having proper credentials, the department LAN is essentially hidden from view.

Integrating VPN Servers with the Internet

Rather than having a remote user make a long distance call (or toll-free call) to a corporate or outsourced NAS, the user calls his or her local Internet service provider (ISP). Using the connection to the local ISP, a VPN is created between the dial-up user and the corporate VPN server across the Internet (see Figure 11.18).

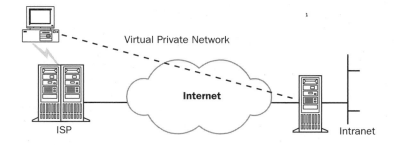

Figure 11.18   Remote Access over the Internet

To connect a network over the Internet (see Figure 11.19), you have two options:

- **Branch office using dedicated lines.**   Rather than using conventional methods such as frame relay, both the branch office and the corporate hub routers are connected to the Internet using a local dedicated circuit and local ISP. Utilizing the local ISP connections, a VPN is created between the branch office router and corporate hub router across the Internet.

- **Branch office using a dial-up line.**   Rather than having a router at the branch office make a long distance call (or toll-free call) to a corporate or outsourced NAS, the router at the branch office calls its local ISP. From the connection to the local ISP, a VPN is created between the branch office router and the corporate hub router across the Internet.

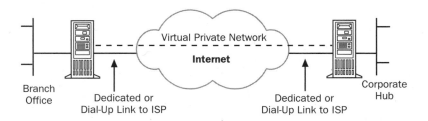

Figure 11.19   VPN over the Internet

Note   In both cases, the users are not charged based on the distance between the offices because only local physical links are being used.

For VPN connections to be reliably available, the corporate hub router acting as a VPN server must be connected to a local ISP using a dedicated line. The VPN server must be listening 24 hours a day for incoming VPN traffic. Although this is possible with a dial-up connection, it is less reliable because dynamically assigned IP addresses are commonly used and the connection may not be persistent.

Practice: Creating VPN Interfaces

In this procedure, you will create VPN interfaces on each router.

▶ **To create a router interface**

1. From the Routing and Remote Access Manager, right-click Routing Interfaces and choose New Demand-Dial Interface, then click Next.

2. Name the interface the name of the remote router you will be connecting to.

3. On the Connection Type page, select Connect Using Virtual Private Network (VPN), then click Next.

4. On the VPN Type page, select L2TP, then click Next.

5. Enter the IP address of the router you will be connecting to, then click Next.

6. On the Protocols And Security page, check Route IP Packet On This Interface, and Add A User Account So A Remote Router Can Dial In, then click Next.

   The Dial-In Credentials dialog box appears. This is the user name the remote router will be dialing in with. The name is grayed because it is the name of the interface you are creating.

7. Click Next.

8. Enter the local router name in the Dial-Out Credentials dialog box. This is the user name this router will use when connecting to the remote router. This user name will match the name of a demand-dial interface on the remote router. Leave Domain and Password blank, then click Next.

9. Click Finish.

10. Repeat Steps 1 to 9 on the other router.

Note   When creating a router-to-router tunnel over a public network, filters should be set on the external router interfaces to allow only the tunneled traffic.

▶ **To exchange routes using Auto Static update**

1. From the Routing and Remote Access Manager, go to IP Routing, General.

2. Right-click the demand-dial interface and choose Update Routes.

3. Repeat Steps 1 and 2 on the other router.

▶ **To see the routes received during the Auto Static update**

1. From the Routing and Remote Access Manager, go to IP Routing, Static Routes.

► **To test the tunnel**

1. From Router 1, ping the IP address of Router 2.

   The demand-dial tunnel should be initiated and the ping should succeed.

Lesson Summary

A VPN is defined as the ability to send data between two computers across an internetwork in a manner that mimics the properties of a dedicated private network. In this lesson, you learned about VPNs in a routed environment and with the Internet.

Lesson 5: Supporting Multilink Connections

Multilink was first introduced in Windows NT 4.0 Remote Access Service. It allows the combining of multiple physical links into one logical link. Typically, two or more ISDN lines or modem links are bundled together for greater bandwidth. In this lesson, we explain multilink.

After this lesson, you will be able to

- Explain Multilink connections

Estimated lesson time: 10 minutes

Point-to-Point Protocol

The PPP was designed to send data across dial-up or dedicated point-to-point connections. PPP encapsulates IP, IPX, and NetBEUI packets within PPP frames, and then transmits the PPP-encapsulated packets across a point-to-point link. PPP can be used between routers over dedicated links or by a Remote Access Service client and server over dial-up links. PPP is made up of the following three main functions or components:

- **Encapsulation.** This allows the multiplexing of multiple transport protocols over the same link.

- **LCP.** PPP defines an extensible LCP for establishing, configuring, and testing the data-link connection. LCP provides the handshake for encapsulation format, packet size, bringing up or dropping the link, and authentication. Some examples of authentication protocols include PAP, CHAP, and EAP.

- **Network Control Protocol.** Network Control Protocols (NCPs) provide specific configuration needs for their respective transport protocols. For example, IPCP is the IP Control Protocol.

Note More information can be found on PPP and Multilink in RFC 1661: The Point-to-Point Protocol, and RFC 1990: PPP Multilink.

Multilink PPP

Multilink was first introduced in Windows NT 4.0 Remote Access Service. It allows the combining of multiple physical links into one logical link. Typically, two or more ISDN lines or modem links are bundled together for greater bandwidth. Support for multilink was implemented through

- **A new LCP option.** The ability to support multilink is negotiated during PPP's LCP phase.

- **A new PPP network protocol.**   A new PPP network protocol was created called MP (Multilink PPP). MP appears to PPP as a normal PPP payload. MP will resequence and recombine packets before handing them off to the actual transport protocol such as TCP/IP.

MP is encapsulated in PPP Data-Link layer frames with the 003D hex protocol field. This information may be useful when reading PPP logs.

Lesson Summary

Multilink was first introduced in Windows NT 4.0 Remote Access Service. It allows the combining of multiple physical links into one logical link. Typically, two or more ISDN lines or modem links are bundled together for greater bandwidth.

Lesson 6: Using Routing and Remote Access with DHCP

When a Routing and Remote Access address pool is configured to use DHCP, no DHCP packets will go over the wire to the Routing and Remote Access clients. In this lesson, you will learn how Routing and Remote Access handles DHCP.

After this lesson, you will be able to

- Explain Routing and Remote Access and DHCP
- Describe how to implement the DHCP relay agent

Estimated lesson time: 10 minutes

Routing and Remote Access and DHCP

When a Routing and Remote Access address pool is configured to use DHCP, no DHCP packets will go over the wire to the Routing and Remote Access clients. Routing and Remote Access uses DHCP to lease addresses in blocks of 10, and stores them in the registry. The network information center (NIC) used to lease these DHCP addresses is configurable in the user interface if two or more NICs are in the server. In earlier versions of Windows, the Remote Access Service server would renew and maintain these DHCP addresses indefinitely. In Windows 2000, the DHCP leases are released when Routing and Remote Access is shut down.

The number of addresses that Routing and Remote Access will lease at a time is configurable in the registry under \System\CurrentControlSet\Services\ RemoteAccess\Parameters\Ip\InitialAddressPoolSize. The value in this key is the number of DHCP leases Routing and Remote Access will initially reserve. These addresses are stored in the registry and are given to Routing and Remote Access clients. When the initial pool is used up, another block of this size will be leased.

DHCP Relay Agent

The DHCP relay agent can now be used over Routing and Remote Access. The Routing and Remote Access client will receive an IP address from the Routing and Remote Access server, but may use DHCPINFORM packets to obtain Windows Internet Name Service (WINS) and Domain Name System (DNS) addresses, domain name, or other DHCP options. DHCPINFORM messages are used to obtain option information without getting an IP address.

Note   Sending the domain name using DHCPINFORM is of particular importance because PPP does configure this information.

DNS and WINS addresses received using DHCPINFORM will override addresses obtained from the Routing and Remote Access server.

Practice: Configuring the DHCP Relay Agent to Work over Routing and Remote Access

▶ **To configure a DHCP relay agent**

1. In the Routing and Remote Access Manager, right-click General under IP Routing, and select New Routing Protocol.

2. Choose DHCP Relay Agent, then click OK.

3. Highlight DHCP Relay Agent, and then right-click Properties.

   The DHCP Relay Agent Properties dialog box appears, allowing you to configure the IP addresses of any DHCP server.

4. Click OK to close the DHCP Relay Agent Properties dialog box.

5. Right-click the DHCP Relay Agent and choose New Interface.

6. Select Internal (Internal represents the virtual interface connected to all Routing and Remote Access clients), then click OK.

7. Click OK to close the DHCP Relay Agent Internal Properties dialog box.

Lesson Summary

When a Routing and Remote Access address pool is configured to use DHCP, no DHCP packets will go over the wire to the Routing and Remote Access clients. In this lesson, you learned how Routing and Remote Access handles DHCP and DHCP relay agents.

Lesson 7: Managing and Monitoring Remote Access

Managing and monitoring a remote access server can be done with several tools. In this lesson, you will learn about remote access logging, accounting, Netsh, Network Monitor, and various resource kit utilities.

After this lesson, you will be able to

- Explain remote access logging
- Describe accounting
- Explain Netsh
- Understand Network Monitor's role in remote access
- List several resource kit utilities to monitor remote access

Estimated lesson time: 30 minutes

Logging User Authentication and Accounting Requests

IAS can create log files based on the authentication and accounting requests received from the NASs, collecting these packets in a centralized location. Setting up and using such log files to track authentication information, such as each accept, reject, and automatic account lockout, can help simplify administration of your service. You can set up and use logs to track accounting information, such as logon and logoff records, to help maintain records for billing purposes (see Figure 11.20).

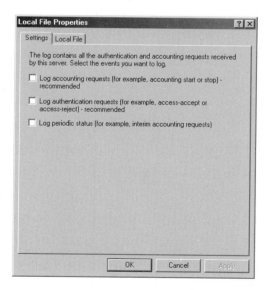

Figure 11.20   Remote Access logging

When you set up logging, you can specify

- The requests to be logged
- The file format for the logs
- The frequency with which new logs are started
- The location where the logs are to be maintained

You can also select the types of requests received by the IAS server that are to be logged:

- Accounting requests, including the following:
  - Accounting-on requests, which are sent by the NAS to indicate that the NAS is online and ready to accept connections
  - Accounting-off requests, which are sent by the NAS to indicate that the NAS is going offline
  - Accounting-start requests, which are sent by the NAS (after the user is accepted by the IAS server) to indicate the start of a user session
  - Accounting-stop requests, which are sent by the NAS to indicate the end of a user session
- Authentication requests, including the following:
  - Authentication requests, which are sent by the NAS on behalf of the connecting user. These entries in the log contain only incoming attributes.
  - Authentication accepts and rejects, which are sent by IAS to the NAS to indicate whether the user should be accepted or rejected. These entries contain only outgoing attributes.
  - Periodic status, to obtain interim accounting requests sent by some NASs during sessions.
  - Accounting-interim requests, which are sent periodically by the NAS during a user session (if the acct-interim-interval attribute is configured in the remote access profile on the IAS server to support periodic requests).

    Initially, it is recommended that you select the first two options and refine your logging methods after you determine which data best matches your needs.

When you set up your servers, specify whether new logs are started daily, weekly, monthly, or when the log reaches a specific size. You can also specify that a single log is maintained continually (regardless of file size), but this is not recommended. The file naming convention for logs is determined by the log period you select. Because changing this option can result in overwriting of existing logs, you should copy logs to a separate file before changing the log period. By default, the log files are located in the %systemroot%\system32\ LogFiles folder, but you have the option of specifying a different location.

Log File Records

Attributes are recorded in Unicode Translation Format-8 (UTF-8) encoding in a comma-delimited format. The format of the records in a log file depends on the file format.

- In IAS-formatted log files, each record starts with a fixed-format header, which consists of the NAS IP address, user name, record date, record time, service name, and computer name, followed by attribute-value pairs.

- In database-import log files, each record contains attribute values in a consistent sequence, starting with the computer name, service name, record date, and record time. An NAS may not use all of the attributes specified in the database-import log format, but the comma-delimited location for each of these predefined attributes is maintained, even for attributes that have no value specified in a record.

Accounting

Routing and Remote Access can be configured to log accounting information in the following locations:

- Locally stored log files when configured for Windows accounting. The information logged and where it is stored are configured from the properties of the Remote Access Logging folder in the Routing and Remote Access snap-in.

- At a RADIUS server when configured for RADIUS accounting. If the RADIUS server is an IAS server, the log files are stored on the IAS server. The information logged and where it is stored are configured from the properties of the Remote Access Logging folder in the Internet Authentication Service snap-in.

The configuration of the Routing and Remote Access accounting provider is done from the Security tab from the properties of a remote access router in the Routing and Remote Access snap-in, as in Figure 11.21, or by using the Netsh tool.

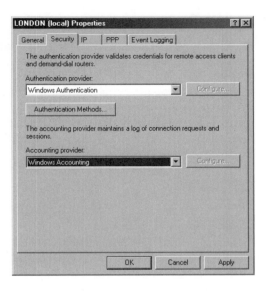

Figure 11.21   Remote Access accounting

Netsh Command-Line Tool

Netsh is a command-line and scripting tool for Windows 2000 networking components for local or remote computers. Netsh is supplied with Windows 2000. Netsh also provides the ability to save a configuration script in a text file for archival purposes or for configuring other servers.

Netsh is a shell that can support multiple Windows 2000 components through the addition of Netsh helper dynamic-link libraries (DLLs). A Netsh helper DLL extends Netsh functionality by providing additional commands to monitor or configure a specific Windows 2000 networking component. Each Netsh helper DLL provides a context (a group of commands for a specific networking component). Within each context, subcontexts can exist. For example, within the routing context, the subcontexts IP and IPX exist to group IP routing and IPX routing commands together.

For Routing and Remote Access, Netsh has the following contexts:

- **Ras.**   Use commands in the ras context to configure remote access configuration.

- **Aaaa.**   Use commands in the aaaa context to configure the AAAA component used by both Routing and Remote Access and IAS.

- **Routing.**   Use commands in the routing context to configure IP and IPX routing.

- **Interface.**   Use commands in the interface context to configure demand-dial interfaces.

Network Monitor

Network Monitor enables you to detect and troubleshoot problems on LANs and on WANs, including Routing and Remote Access links. With Network Monitor you can identify network traffic patterns and network problems. For example, you can locate client-to-server connection problems, find a computer that makes a disproportionate number of work requests, capture frames (packets) directly from the network, display and filter the captured frames, and identify unauthorized users on your network. For more information on Network Monitor, see Chapter 4, "Monitoring Network Activity."

Resource Kit Utilities

The following are Resource Kit Utilities that make the job of managing and monitoring Routing and Remote Access easier.

RASLIST.EXE

The RASLIST.EXE command-line tool displays Routing and Remote Access server announcements from a network. Raslist listens for Routing and Remote Access server announcements on all active network cards in the computer from which it is run. Its output shows which card received the announcement. Raslist is a monitoring tool. It may take a few seconds for the data to begin to appear; data will continue to appear until the tool is closed.

RASSRVMON.EXE

Using the RASSRVMON.EXE tool, you can monitor the remote access server activities on your server in greater detail than the standard Windows tools allow. Rassrvmon provides the following monitoring information:

- Server information such as the time of first call to server, time of most recent call to server, total calls, total bytes passed through server, peak connection count, total connect time, currently connected users, and their connection information.

- Per Port information, which is the time of first call to port, time of most recent call to port, total connections to this port since server started, total bytes passed on this port, total errors on this port, and current port status.

- Summary information such as statistics are kept for each unique user/computer combination since the start of the monitoring: total connect time, total bytes transmitted, connection count, average connect time, and total error count.

- Individual connection information, which includes per-connection statistics for each connection: user name/computer name, IP address, connection establishment time, duration, bytes transmitted, error count, and line speed.

To allow for more flexibility, the alerting is set up to run a program of your choosing. This gives you the flexibility to send mail, a page, a network popup, or any other action you can automate with an executable file name or a batch script.

RASUSERS.EXE

RASUSERS.EXE lets you list for a domain or a server all user accounts that have been granted permission to dial in to the network via Routing and Remote Access, a feature of Windows 2000 that implements remote access functionality.

TRACEENABLE.EXE

TRACEENABLE.EXE is a graphical user interface-based tool that enables tracing and displays current tracing options. Windows 2000 Routing and Remote Access has an extensive tracing capability that you can use to troubleshoot complex network problems. Tracing records internal component variables, function calls, and interactions. Separate Routing and Remote Access components can be independently enabled to log tracing information to files (file tracing). You must enable the tracing function by changing settings in the Windows 2000 registry using TRACEENABLE.EXE.

Using TRACEENABLE.EXE

As each tracing item is selected in the combo box, the values are displayed. Make your changes, then click Set. This will write your changes to the registry. To get console tracing, you must turn it on for the component, and turn it on with the master check box at the top of the Traceenable window. For example, to generate a log file for PPP:

1. Select PPP from the drop-down list.
2. Click Enable File Tracing.
3. Click Set.

   Tracing is now enabled for this component. In most cases the log file is created in %windir%\tracing.

Lesson Summary

Managing and monitoring a remote access server is done with several tools. In this lesson, you learned about remote access logging, accounting, Netsh, Network Monitor, and various resource kit utilities.

Review

Answering the following questions will reinforce key information presented in this chapter. If you are unable to answer a question, review the appropriate lesson and then try the question again. Answers to the questions can be found in Appendix A, "Questions and Answers."

1. What is a VPN?

2. Demand-dial filters can screen traffic based on what fields of a packet?

3. True or false: When setting dial-in user permissions (Allow Access, Deny Access) through the User Property page, RAPs are not used.

4. True or false: DHCP packets are never sent over Routing and Remote Access links.

5. What is the function of BAP?

CHAPTER 12

Supporting Network Address Translation (NAT)

About This Chapter

Network address translation (NAT) is a protocol that allows a network with private addresses to access information on the Internet through an Internet Protocol (IP) translation process. In this chapter, you will learn how to configure your home network or small office network to share a single connection to the Internet with NAT.

Before You Begin

To complete the lessons in this chapter, you must have

- Completed Chapter 10

Lesson 1: Introducing NAT

NAT enables private IP addresses to be translated into public IP addresses for traffic to and from the Internet. This keeps traffic from passing directly to the internal network, while saving the small office or home office user the time and expense of getting and maintaining a public address range. This lesson provides an overview of NAT.

After this lesson, you will be able to

- Describe the purpose of NAT
- Identify the components of NAT
- Describe how NAT works

Estimated lesson time: 45 minutes

Network Address Translation

Microsoft Windows 2000 Network Address Translation (NAT) allows computers on a small network, such as a small office or home office, to share a single Internet connection with only a single public IP address. The computer on which NAT is installed can act as a network address translator, a simplified DHCP server, a Domain Name System (DNS) proxy, and a Windows Internet Name Service (WINS) proxy. NAT allows host computers to share one or more publicly registered IP addresses, helping to conserve public address space.

Understanding Network Address Translation

With NAT in Windows 2000, you can configure your home network or small office network to share a single connection to the Internet. NAT consists of the following components:

- **Translation component.**   The Windows 2000 router on which NAT is enabled, hereafter called the NAT computer, acts as a network address translator, translating the IP addresses and Transmission Control Protocol/User Datagram Protocol (TCP/UDP) port numbers of packets that are forwarded between the private network and the Internet.

- **Addressing component.**   The NAT computer provides IP address configuration information to the other computers on the home network. The addressing component is a simplified DHCP server that allocates an IP address, a subnet mask, a default gateway, and the IP address of a DNS server. You must configure computers on the home network as DHCP clients to receive the IP configuration automatically. The default TCP/IP configuration for computers running Windows 2000, Windows NT, Windows 95, and Windows 98 is as a DHCP client.

- **Name resolution component.**   The NAT computer becomes the DNS server for the other computers on the home network. When name resolution requests are received by the NAT computer, it forwards the name resolution requests to the Internet-based DNS server for which it is configured, and returns the responses to the home network computer.

Routed and Translated Internet Connections

There are two types of connections to the Internet: routed and translated. When planning for a routed connection, you will need a range of IP addresses from your Internet service provider (ISP) to use on the internal portion of your network, and they will also give you the IP address of the DNS server you need to use. You can either statically configure the IP address configuration of each computer or use a DHCP server.

The Windows 2000 router needs to be configured with a network adapter for the internal network (10 or 100BaseT Ethernet, for example). It also needs to be configured with an Internet connection such as an analog or Integrated Services Digital Network (ISDN) modem, xDSL modem, cable modem, or a fractional T1 line.

The translated method, or NAT, gives you a more secure network because the addresses of your private network are completely hidden from the Internet. The connection shared computer, which uses NAT, does all of the translation of Internet addresses to your private network, and vice versa. However, be aware that the NAT computer does not have the ability to translate all payloads. This is because some applications use IP addresses in other fields besides the standard TCP/IP header fields.

The following protocols do not work with NAT:

- Kerberos
- IP Security Protocol (IPSec)

The DHCP allocator functionality in NAT enables all DHCP clients in the network to automatically obtain an IP address, subnet mask, default gateway, and DNS server address from the NAT computer. If you have any non-DHCP computers on the network, then statically configure their IP address configuration.

To keep resource costs to a minimum on a small network, only one server running Windows 2000 is needed. Depending on whether you are running a translated or routed connection, this single server can suffice for NAT, Automatic Private IP Addressing (APIPA), Routing and Remote Access, and DHCP.

Public and Private Addresses

If your intranet is not connected to the Internet, any IP addressing can be deployed. If direct (routed) or indirect (proxy or translator) connectivity to the Internet is desired, there are two types of addresses you can use: public addresses and private addresses.

Public Addresses

Public addresses are assigned by the Internet Network Information Center (InterNIC), and consist of class-based network IDs or blocks of Classless Inter-Domain Routing (CIDR)-based addresses (called CIDR blocks) that are guaranteed to be globally unique to the Internet. When the public addresses are assigned, routes are programmed into the routers of the Internet so that traffic to the assigned public addresses can reach its location. Traffic to destination public addresses is reachable on the Internet.

Private Addresses

Each IP node requires an IP address that is globally unique to the IP internetwork. In the case of the Internet, each IP node on a network connected to the Internet requires an IP address that is globally unique to the Internet. As the Internet grew, organizations connecting to the Internet required a public address for each node on their intranets. This requirement placed a huge demand on the pool of available public addresses.

When analyzing the addressing needs of organizations, the designers of the Internet noted that for many organizations, most of the hosts on the organization's intranet did not require direct connectivity to Internet hosts. Those hosts that did require a specific set of Internet services, such as World Wide Web access and e-mail, typically accessed the Internet services through application-layer gateways such as proxy servers and e-mail servers. The result was that most organizations only required a small amount of public addresses for those nodes (such as proxies, routers, firewalls, and translators) that were directly connected to the Internet.

For the hosts within the organization that do not require direct access to the Internet, IP addresses that do not duplicate already assigned public addresses are required. To solve this addressing problem, the Internet designers reserved a portion of the IP address space and named this space the private address space. Private IP addresses are never assigned as public addresses. Because the public and private address spaces do not overlap, private addresses never duplicate public addresses. The following private IP address ranges are specified by Internet Request for Comments (RFC) 1918:

- **10.0.0.0 through 10.255.255.255.**   The 10.0.0.0 private network is a class A network ID that allows the following range of valid IP addresses: 10.0.0.1 to 10.255.255.254. The 10.0.0.0 private network has 24 host bits that can be used for any subnetting scheme within the private organization.

- **172.16.0.0 through 172.31.255.255.**   The 172.16.0.0 private network can be interpreted either as a block of 16 class B network IDs or as a 20-bit assignable address space (20 host bits) that can be used for any subnetting scheme within the private organization. The 172.16.0.0 private network allows the following range of valid IP addresses: 172.16.0.1 to 172.31.255.254.

- **192.168.0.0 through 192.168.255.255.** The 192.168.0.0/16 private network can be interpreted either as a block of 256 class C network IDs or as a 16-bit assignable address space (16 host bits) that can be used for any subnetting scheme within the private organization. The 192.168.0.0 private network allows the following range of valid IP addresses: 192.168.0.1 to 192.168.255.254.

Private addresses are not reachable on the Internet. Therefore, Internet traffic from a host that has a private address must either send its requests to an application-layer gateway (such as a proxy server), which has a valid public address, or have its private address translated into a valid public address by a network address translator before it is sent on the Internet.

How NAT Works

A network address translator is an IP router defined in RFC 1631 that can translate IP addresses and TCP/UDP port numbers of packets as they are being forwarded. Consider a small business network with multiple computers connecting to the Internet. A small business would normally have to obtain an ISP-allocated public IP address for each computer on its network. With NAT, however, the small business can use private addressing (as described in RFC 1597) and have the NAT map its private addresses to a single or to multiple public IP addresses as allocated by its ISP. For example, if a small business is using the 10.0.0.0 private network for its intranet and has been granted the public IP address of 198.200.200.1 by its ISP, the NAT maps (using static or dynamic mappings) all private IP addresses being used on network 10.0.0.0 to the public IP address of 198.200.200.1.

Static and Dynamic Address Mapping

NAT can use either static or dynamic mapping. A static mapping is configured so that traffic is always mapped a specific way. You could map all traffic to and from a specific private network location to a specific Internet location. For instance, to set up a Web server on a computer on your private network, you create a static mapping that maps [Public IP Address, TCP Port 80] to [Private IP Address, TCP Port 80].

Dynamic mappings are created when users on the private network initiate traffic with Internet locations. The NAT service automatically adds these mappings to its mapping table and refreshes them with each use. Dynamic mappings that are not refreshed are removed from the NAT mapping table after a configurable amount of time. For TCP connections, the default time-out is 24 hours. For UDP traffic, the default time-out is 1 minute.

Proper Translation of Header Fields

By default, a NAT translates IP addresses and TCP/UDP ports. These modifications to the IP datagram require the modification and recalculation of the following fields in the IP, TCP, and UDP headers:

- Source IP address
- TCP, UDP, and IP checksum
- Source port

If the IP address and port information is only in the IP and TCP/UDP headers—for example, with Hypertext Transfer Protocol (HTTP) or World Wide Web traffic—the application protocol can be translated transparently. There are applications and protocols, however, that carry IP or port addressing information within their headers. File Transfer Protocol (FTP), for example, stores the dotted-decimal representation of IP addresses in the FTP header for the FTP port command. If the NAT does not properly translate the IP address, connectivity problems can occur. Additionally, in the case of FTP, because the IP address is stored in dotted-decimal format, the translated IP address in the FTP header can be a different size. Therefore, the NAT must also modify TCP sequence numbers to ensure that no data is lost.

NAT Editors

In the case where the NAT component must additionally translate and adjust the payload beyond the IP, TCP, and UDP headers, a NAT editor is required. A NAT editor is an installable component that can properly modify otherwise nontranslatable payloads so that they can be forwarded across a NAT. Windows 2000 includes built-in NAT editors for the following protocols:

- FTP
- Internet Control Message Protocol (ICMP)
- Point-to-Point Tunneling Protocol (PPTP)
- NetBIOS over TCP/IP

Additionally, the NAT routing protocol includes proxy software for the following protocols:

- H.323
- Direct Play
- Lightweight Directory Access Protocol (LDAP)-based Internet Locator Service (ILS) registration
- Remote procedure call

Note IPSec traffic is not translatable.

A NAT Example

If a small business is using the 192.168.0.0 private network ID for its intranet and has been granted the public address of w1.x1.y1.z1 by its ISP, then NAT maps all private addresses on 192.168.0.0 to the IP address of w1.x1.y1.z1. If multiple private addresses are mapped to a single public address, NAT uses dynamically chosen TCP and UDP ports to distinguish one intranet location from another. Figure 12.1 shows an example of using NAT to transparently connect an intranet to the Internet.

Note The use of w1.x1.y1.z1 and w2.x2.y2.z2 is intended to represent valid public IP addresses as allocated by InterNIC or an ISP.

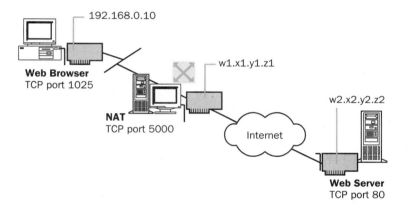

Figure 12.1 Using NAT to transparently connect an intranet to the Internet

NAT Processes in Windows 2000 Routing and Remote Access

For Windows 2000 Routing and Remote Access, the NAT component can be enabled by adding NAT as a routing protocol in the Routing and Remote Access snap-in.

Note NAT services are also available with the Internet connection sharing feature available from the Network and Dial-Up Connections folder, as explained in Lesson 2. Internet connection sharing performs the same function as the NAT routing protocol in Routing and Remote Access but it allows very little configuration flexibility. For information about configuring Internet connection sharing and why you would choose Internet connection sharing over the NAT routing protocol of Routing and Remote Access, see Windows 2000 Server Help.

Installed with the NAT routing protocol are a series of NAT editors. NAT consults the editors when the payload of the packet being translated matches one of the installed editors. The editors modify the payload and return the result to the NAT component. NAT interacts with the TCP/IP protocol in two important ways:

- To support dynamic port mappings, the NAT component requests unique TCP and UDP port numbers from the TCP/IP protocol stack when needed.
- With TCP/IP, so that packets being sent between the private network and the Internet are first passed to the NAT component for translation.

Figure 12.2 shows the NAT components and their relation to TCP/IP and other router components.

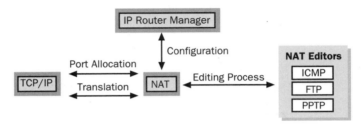

Figure 12.2   NAT components

Outbound Internet Traffic

For traffic from the private network that is outbound on the Internet interface, NAT first assesses whether or not an address/port mapping, whether static or dynamic, already exists for the packet. If not, a dynamic mapping is created. The NAT creates a mapping depending on whether there are single or multiple public IP addresses available.

- If a single public IP address is available, the NAT requests a new unique TCP or UDP port for the public IP address and uses that as the mapped port.
- If multiple public IP addresses are available, the NAT performs private-IP-address-to-public-IP-address mapping. For these mappings, the ports are not translated. When the last public IP address is needed, the NAT switches to performing address and port mapping, as it would in the case of the single public IP address.

After mapping, the NAT checks for editors and invokes one if necessary. After editing, the NAT modifies the IP and TCP or UDP headers and forwards the packet using the Internet interface. Figure 12.3 shows NAT processing for outbound Internet traffic.

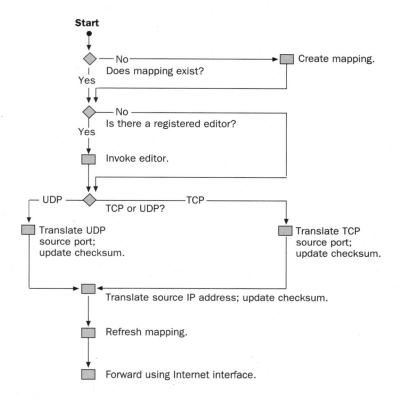

Figure 12.3   NAT processing of outbound Internet traffic

Inbound Internet Traffic

For traffic from the private network that is inbound on the Internet interface, the NAT first assesses whether an address/port mapping, whether static or dynamic, exists for the packet. If a mapping does not exist for the packet, it is silently discarded by the NAT.

This behavior protects the private network from malicious users on the Internet. The only way that Internet traffic is forwarded to the private network is either in response to traffic initiated by a private network user that created a dynamic mapping, or because a static mapping exists so that Internet users can access specific resources on the private network.

After mapping, the NAT checks for editors and invokes one if necessary. After editing, the NAT modifies the TCP, UDP, and IP headers and forwards the frame using the private network interface. Figure 12.4 shows NAT processing for inbound Internet traffic.

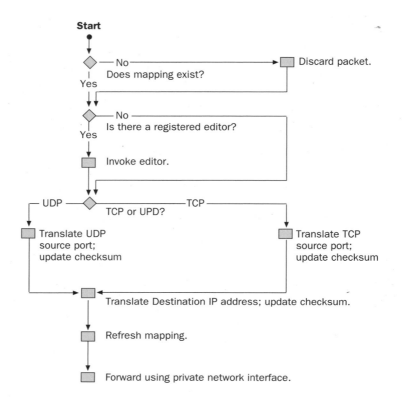

Figure 12.4 NAT processing of inbound Internet traffic

Additional NAT Routing Protocol Components

To help simplify the configuration of small networks connecting to the Internet, the NAT routing protocol for Windows 2000 also includes a DHCP allocator and a DNS proxy.

DHCP Allocator

The DHCP allocator component provides IP address configuration information to the other computers on the network. The DHCP allocator is a simplified DHCP server that allocates an IP address, a subnet mask, a default gateway, and the IP address of a DNS server. You must configure computers on the DHCP network as DHCP clients to receive the IP configuration automatically. The default TCP/IP configuration for Windows 2000, Windows NT, Windows 95, and Windows 98 computers is as a DHCP client.

Table 12.1 lists the DHCP options in the DHCPOFFER and DHCPACK messages issued by the DHCP allocator during the DHCP lease configuration process. You cannot modify these options or configure additional DHCP options.

Table 12.1   DHCP Lease Configuration Options

Option Number	Option Value	Description
1	255.255.0.0	Subnet mask
3	IP address of private interface	Router (default gateway)
6	IP address of private interface	DNS server (only issued if DNS proxy is enabled)
58 (0x3A)	5 minutes	Renewal time
59 (0x3B)	5 days	Rebinding time
51	7 days	IP address lease time
15 (0x0F)	Primary domain name of NAT computer	DNS domain

The DHCP allocator only supports a single scope of IP addresses as configured from the Address Assignment tab in the Properties Of The Network Address Translation (NAT) Routing Protocol dialog box in the Routing and Remote Access snap-in. The DHCP allocator does not support multiple scopes, superscopes, or multicast scopes. If you need this functionality, you should install a DHCP server and disable the DHCP allocator component of the NAT routing protocol.

DNS Proxy

The DNS proxy component acts as a DNS server to the computers on the network. DNS queries sent by a computer to the NAT server are forwarded to the DNS server. Responses to DNS queries computers receive via the NAT server are re-sent to the original small office or home office computer.

Lesson Summary

NAT enables private IP addresses to be translated into public IP addresses for traffic to and from the Internet. This keeps the internal network secure from the Internet, while saving the user the time and expense of acquiring and maintaining a public address range. A small business would normally have to obtain an ISP-allocated public IP address for each computer on its network. With the NAT, however, the small business can use private addressing and have the NAT map its private addresses to a single or to multiple public IP addresses as allocated by its ISP.

Lesson 2: Installing Internet Connection Sharing

Internet Connection Sharing (ICS) is a feature of Network and Dial-Up Connections that allows you to use Windows 2000 to connect your home network or small office network to the Internet. For example, you might have a home network that connects to the Internet by using a dial-up connection. In this lesson, you will learn how to install ICS in Windows 2000.

After this lesson, you will be able to

- Enable the ICS feature of Windows 2000
- Configure Internet options for ICS

Estimated lesson time: 35 minutes

Internet Connection Sharing

Internet Connection Sharing (ICS) is a simple package consisting of DHCP, NAT, and DNS. You can use ICS to easily connect your entire network to the Internet. Because ICS provides a translated connection, all of the computers on the network can access Internet resources such as e-mail, Web sites, and FTP sites. ICS provides the following:

- Ease of configuration
- Single public IP address
- Fixed address range for hosts
- DNS proxy for name resolution
- Automatic IP addressing

ICS provides many more features than just address translation. Microsoft has added many features to make the configuration of Internet connections as simple as possible. ICS can be fully configured and administered from the Routing and Remote Access Manager. For a simple home network, a Connection Sharing Wizard can also be launched from Control Panel Connections. The wizard does not allow configuration of any options but can get a home network up on the Internet in minutes. What simplifies the configuration is automatic addressing and automatic name resolution through the DHCP allocator, DNS proxy, and WINS proxy components. Each of these components provides a simplified configuration over the full version of DHCP, DNS, and WINS servers.

By enabling ICS on the computer that uses the dial-up connection, you are providing NAT, addressing, and name resolution services for all computers on your home network. After ICS is enabled and users verify their networking and Internet options, home network or small office network users can use applications such as Microsoft Internet Explorer and Microsoft Outlook Express as if they were directly connected to the ISP. The ICS computer then dials the ISP and creates the connection so that the user can reach the specified Web address or resource. To use the ICS feature, users on your home office or small office network must configure TCP/IP on their local area connection to obtain an IP address automatically.

Enabling Internet Connection Sharing

Before you enable ICS, consider the following:

- You should not use the ICS feature in a network with other Windows 2000 Server domain controllers, DNS servers, gateways, DHCP servers, or systems configured for static IP.

- When you enable ICS, the network adapter connected to the home or small office network is given a new IP address configuration. Existing TCP/IP connections on the ICS computer are lost and need to be reestablished.

- To use the ICS feature, users on your home office or small office network must configure TCP/IP on their local area connection to obtain an IP address automatically.

- If the ICS computer is using ISDN or a modem to connect to the Internet, you must select the Enable On-Demand Dialing check box.

▶ **To enable ICS on a network connection**

1. Click Start, point to Settings, then click Network And Dial-Up Connections.

2. Right-click the dial-up, virtual private network (VPN), or incoming connection you want to share, then click Properties.

3. In the Sharing tab, select the Enable Internet Connection Sharing For This Connection check box.

4. If you want this connection to dial automatically when another computer on your home network attempts to access external resources, select the Enable On-Demand Dialing check box.

Installing Connection Sharing

Connection Sharing is configured from within the Routing and Remote Access Manager.

▶ **To install Connection Sharing**

1. In the Routing and Remote Access Manager, open the IP Routing folder and right-click on General.

2. Click New Routing Protocol, as illustrated in Figure 12.5.

   The Select Routing Protocol dialog box appears.

3. In the Select Routing Protocol dialog box, click Connection Sharing.

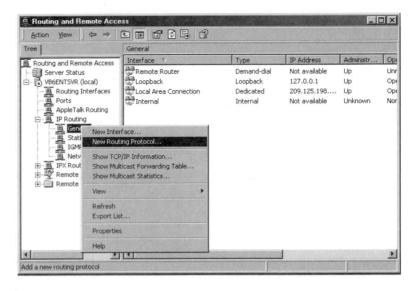

Figure 12.5   Routing and Remote Access Manager IP Routing menu

Configuring Internet Options for Internet Connection Sharing

If you have not previously established an Internet connection, complete the following steps.

► **To establish an Internet connection**

1. Open Internet Explorer.

2. Click I Want To Set Up My Internet Connection Manually or I Want To Connect Through A Local Area Network (LAN), then click Next.

3. Click I Connect Through A Local Area Network (LAN), then click Next.

4. Clear the Automatic Discovery Of Proxy Server [Recommended] check box, then click Next.

5. If you want to set up an Internet mail account now, and know your connection information, click Yes, and provide the e-mail account information for which the wizard prompts you. If you do not want to set up an Internet mail account, click No, click Next, then click Finish.

If you have previously established an Internet connection, you will be prompted to complete the following steps.

► **To configure Internet options for ICS**

1. From the Tools menu, click Internet Options.

2. In the Connections tab, click Never Dial A Connection, then click LAN Settings.

3. In Automatic Configuration, clear the Automatically Detect Settings and Use Automatic Configuration Script check boxes.

4. In Proxy Server, clear the Use A Proxy Server check box.

Internet Connection Sharing and NAT

To connect a small office or home office network to the Internet, you can use either a routed or translated connection. For a routed connection, the computer running Windows 2000 Server acts as an IP router that forwards packets between the internal network and the public Internet. Although conceptually simple, a routed connection requires knowledge of IP addressing and routing. However, routed connections allow for all IP traffic between internal hosts and the public Internet. For more information, see the Small Office/Home Office (SOHO) Network to the Internet online help topic.

For a translated connection, the computer running Windows 2000 Server acts as a network address translator. Translated connections that use computers running Windows 2000 Server require less knowledge of IP addressing and routing, and provide a simplified configuration for hosts and the Windows 2000 router. However, translated connections may not allow all IP traffic between SOHO hosts and Internet hosts.

In Windows 2000 Server, you can configure a translated connection to the Internet by using either the ICS feature of Network and Dial-Up Connections or the NAT routing protocol provided with Routing and Remote Access. Both ICS and NAT provide translation, addressing, and name resolution services to SOHO hosts.

As described in the previous section, ICS is designed to provide a single step of configuration (a single check box) on the computer running Windows 2000 to provide a translated connection to the Internet for all of the hosts on the network. However, once enabled, ICS does not allow further configuration beyond the configuration of applications and services. For example, ICS is designed for a single IP address obtained from an ISP and does not allow you to change the range of IP addresses allocated to hosts.

As you learned in Lesson 1, the NAT routing protocol is designed to provide maximum flexibility in the configuration of the computer running Windows 2000 Server to provide a translated connection to the Internet. NAT requires additional configuration steps; however, each step of the configuration is customizable. The NAT protocol allows for ranges of IP addresses from the ISP and the configuration of the range of IP addresses allocated to hosts.

Table 12.2 summarizes the features and capabilities of ICS and NAT.

Table 12.2   ICS and NAT Features

ICS	NAT
Single check box configuration	Manual configuration
Single public IP address	Multiple public IP addresses
Fixed address range for internal hosts	Configurable address range for internal hosts
Single internal interface	Multiple internal interfaces

ICS and NAT are features of Windows 2000 Server that are designed to connect SOHO networks to the Internet. ICS and NAT are not designed to

- Directly connect separate private networks together
- Connect networks within an intranet
- Directly connect branch office networks to a corporate network
- Connect branch office networks to a corporate network over the Internet

Troubleshooting Connection Sharing (NAT)

You can answer the following questions to troubleshoot configuration problems with Connection Sharing (NAT):

- **Are all of your interfaces (public and private) added to the Connection Sharing (NAT) routing protocol?**   You must add both public (Internet) and private (small office or home office) interfaces to the Connection Sharing (NAT) routing protocol.

- **Is translation enabled on the Internet (external) interface?**   You need to verify that the interface on the Windows router that connects to the Internet is configured for translation. The Enable Translation Across This Interface option in the General tab of the Properties Of The Internet Interface dialog box should be selected.

- **Is Connection Sharing enabled on the private (internal) interface?**   You need to verify that the interface on the Windows router that connects to the internal network is configured for Connection Sharing. The Allow Clients On This Interface To Access Any Shared Networks option in the General tab of the Properties Of The Home Network Interface dialog box should be selected.

- **Is TCP/UDP port translation enabled?**   If you only have a single public IP address, you need to verify that the Translate TCP/UDP Headers check box in the General tab of the Properties Of The External Interface dialog box is selected.

- **Is your range of public addresses set correctly?**   If you have multiple public IP addresses, you need to verify that they are properly entered in the Address Pool tab of the Properties Of The Internet Interface dialog box. If your address pool includes an IP address that was not allocated to you by your ISP, then inbound Internet traffic that is mapped to that IP address may be routed by the ISP to another location.

- **Is the protocol being used by a program translatable?**   If you have some programs that do not seem to work through the NAT, you can try running them from the NAT computer. If they work from the NAT computer and not from a computer on the private network, then the payload of the program may not be translatable. You can check the protocol being used by the program against the list of supported NAT editors.

- **Is Connection Sharing addressing enabled on the home office network?**   If static addresses are not configured on the private network, verify that Connection Sharing addressing is enabled on the interfaces corresponding to the private network. To verify, click Interfaces in the Addressing tab of the Properties Of The Connection Sharing Object dialog box.

Lesson Summary

ICS is a feature of Network and Dial-Up Connections that allows you to use Windows 2000 to connect your home network or small office network to the Internet. ICS can be fully configured and administered from the Routing and Remote Access Manager. By enabling ICS on the computer that uses the dial-up connection, you are providing NAT, addressing, and name resolution services for all computers on your home network.

Lesson 3: Installing and Configuring NAT

The main intent of NAT is to save on the diminishing IP address space. A secondary benefit of NAT is providing network connectivity without the need to understand IP routing or IP routing protocols. The NAT can be used without the knowledge or cooperation of an ISP. Contacting the ISP for the addition of static routes is not required. In this lesson, you will learn how to install and configure NAT.

After this lesson, you will be able to

- Describe some design issues you should consider before implementing NAT
- Enable NAT addressing
- Configure interface IP address ranges
- Configure interface special ports
- Configure NAT network applications

Estimated lesson time: 20 minutes

Network Address Translation Design Considerations

A common use for NAT is Internet connectivity from a home or small network. To prevent problems, there are certain design issues you should consider before you implement NAT. For example, when using a NAT, private addresses are normally used on the internal network. As described in Lesson 1, private addresses are intended for internal networks, meaning those not directly connected to the Internet. It is recommended that you use these addresses instead of picking addresses at random to avoid potentially duplicating IP address assignment. Additionally, you should consider routing instead of a NAT because routing is fast and efficient, and IP was designed to be routed. However, routing requires valid IP addresses and considerable knowledge to be implemented.

IP Addressing Issues

You should use the following IP addresses from the InterNIC private IP network IDs: 10.0.0.0 with a subnet mask of 255.0.0.0, 172.16.0.0 with a subnet mask of 255.240.0.0, and 192.168.0.0 with a subnet mask of 255.255.0.0. By default, NAT uses the private network ID 192.168.0.0 with the subnet mask of 255.255.255.0 for the private network.

If you are using public IP networks that have not been allocated by the InterNIC or your ISP, then you may be using the IP network ID of another organization on the Internet. This is known as illegal or overlapping IP addressing. If you are using overlapping public addresses, then you cannot reach the Internet resources of the overlapping addresses. For example, if you use 1.0.0.0 with the subnet mask of 255.0.0.0, then you cannot reach any Internet resources of the organization that is using the 1.0.0.0 network. You can also exclude specific IP addresses from the configured range. Excluded addresses are not allocated to private network hosts.

▶ **To configure the NAT server**

1. Install and enable Routing and Remote Access.

   In the Routing and Remote Access Server Setup Wizard, choose the options for ICS and to set up a router with the NAT routing protocol. After the wizard is finished, all of the configuration for NAT is complete. You do not need to complete steps 2 through 8. If you have already enabled Routing and Remote Access, then complete steps 2 through 8, as needed.

2. Configure the IP address of the home network interface.

3. For the IP address of the LAN adapter that connects to the home network, you need to configure the following:

   ▪ IP address: 192.168.0.1

   ▪ Subnet mask: 255.255.255.0

   ▪ No default gateway

Note   The IP address in the preceding configuration for the home network interface is based on the default address range of 192.168.0.0 with a subnet mask of 255.255.255.0, which is configured for the addressing component of NAT. If you change this default address range, you should change the IP address of the private interface for the NAT computer to be the first IP address in the configured range. Using the first IP address in the range is a recommended practice, not a requirement of the NAT components.

---

4. Enable routing on your dial-up port.

   If your connection to the Internet is a permanent connection that appears in Windows 2000 as a LAN interface (such as DDS, T-Carrier, frame relay, permanent ISDN, xDSL, or cable modem), or if you are connecting your computer running Windows 2000 to another router before the connection to the Internet, and the LAN interface is configured with an IP address, subnet mask, and default gateway either statically or through DHCP, skip to step 6.

5. Create a demand-dial interface to connect to your ISP.

   You must create a demand-dial interface that is enabled for IP routing and uses your dial-up equipment and the credentials that you use to dial your ISP.

6. Create a default static route that uses the Internet interface.

   For a default static route, you need to select the demand-dial interface (for dial-up connections) or LAN interface (for permanent or intermediate router connections) that is used to connect to the Internet. The destination is 0.0.0.0 and the network mask is 0.0.0.0. For a demand-dial interface, the gateway IP address is not configurable.

7. Add the NAT routing protocol.

   Instructions for adding the NAT routing protocol are described in the next procedure.

8. Add your Internet and home network interfaces to the NAT routing protocol.

9. Enable NAT addressing and name resolution.

▶ **To add NAT as a routing protocol**

1. Click Start, point to Programs, point to Administrative Tools, then click Routing and Remote Access.

2. In the console tree, click General under Routing And Remote Access\Server Name\IP Routing.

3. Right-click General, then click New Routing Protocol.

4. In the Select Routing Protocol dialog box, click Network Address Translation, then click OmK.

▶ **To enable NAT addressing**

1. Click Start, point to Programs, point to Administrative Tools, then click Routing And Remote Access.

2. In the console tree, click NAT.

3. Right-click NAT, then click Properties.

4. In the Address Assignment tab, select the Automatically Assign IP Addresses By Using DHCP check box.

5. If applicable, in IP Address And Mask, configure the range of IP addresses to allocate to DHCP clients on the private network.

6. If applicable, click Exclude, configure the addresses to exclude from allocation to DHCP clients on the private network, then click OK.

Single or Multiple Public Addresses

If you are using a single public IP address allocated by your ISP, no other IP address configuration is necessary. If you are using multiple IP addresses allocated by your ISP, then you must configure the NAT interface with your range of public IP addresses. For the range of IP addresses given to you by your ISP, you must determine whether the range of public IP addresses can be expressed by using an IP address and a mask.

If you are allocated a number of addresses that have a power of 2 (2, 4, 8, 16, and so on), you can express the range by using a single IP address and mask. For example, if you are given the four public IP addresses 200.100.100.212, 200.100.100.213, 200.100.100.214, and 200.100.100.215 by your ISP, then you can express these four addresses as 200.100.100.212 with a mask of 255.255.255.252. If your IP addresses are not expressible as an IP address and a subnet mask, you can enter them as a range or series of ranges by indicating the starting and ending IP addresses.

▶ **To configure interface IP address ranges**

1. Click Start, point to Programs, point to Administrative Tools, then click Routing And Remote Access.

2. In the console tree, click NAT.

3. In the details pane, right-click the interface you want to configure, then click Properties.

4. In the Address Pool tab, click Add.

   If you are using a range of IP addresses that can be expressed with an IP address and a subnet mask, in Start Address, type the starting IP address, and in Mask, type the subnet mask. However, if you are using a range of IP addresses that cannot be expressed with an IP address and a subnet mask, in Start Address, type the starting IP address, and in End Address, type the ending IP address.

Allowing Inbound Connections

Normal NAT usage from a home or small business allows outbound connections from the private network to the public network. Programs such as Web browsers that run from the private network create connections to Internet resources. The return traffic from the Internet can cross the NAT because the connection was initiated from the private network. To allow Internet users to access resources on your private network, you must do the following:

- Configure a static IP address configuration on the resource server including IP address (from the range of IP addresses allocated by the NAT computer), subnet mask (from the range of IP addresses allocated by the NAT computer), default gateway (the private IP address of the NAT computer), and DNS server (the private IP address of the NAT computer).

- Exclude the IP address being used by the resource computer from the range of IP addresses being allocated by the NAT computer.

- Configure a special port. A special port is a static mapping of a public address and port number to a private address and port number. A special port maps an inbound connection from an Internet user to a specific address on your private network. By using a special port, you can create a Web server on your private network that is accessible from the Internet.

▶ **To configure interface special ports**

1. Click Start, point to Programs, point to Administrative Tools, then click Routing And Remote Access.

2. In the details pane, right-click the interface you want to configure, and then click Properties.

3. In the Special Ports tab, in Protocol, click either TCP or UDP, then click Add.

4. In Incoming Port, type the port number of the incoming public traffic.

5. If a range of public IP addresses is configured, click On This Address Pool Entry, and then type the public IP address of the incoming public traffic.

6. In Outgoing Port, type the port number of the private network resource.

7. In Private Address, type the private address of the private network resource.

Configuring Applications and Services

You may need to configure applications and services to work properly across the Internet. For example, if users on your small office or home office network want to play the Diablo game with other users on the Internet, NAT must be configured for the Diablo application.

▶ **To configure NAT network applications**

1. Click Start, point to Programs, point to Administrative Tools, then click Routing And Remote Access.

2. In the console tree, click NAT.

3. Right-click NAT, then click Properties.

4. In the Translation tab, click Applications.

5. To add a network application, in the Applications dialog box, click Add.

6. In the Add Application dialog box, type the settings for the network application, then click OK.

Note   You can also edit or remove an existing NAT network application by clicking Edit or Remove in the Applications dialog box.

Virtual Private Network Connections from a Translated Network

To access a private intranet using a VPN connection from a translated network, you can use the PPTP and create a VPN connection from a host on the internal network to the VPN server within the second private intranet. The NAT routing protocol has a NAT editor for PPTP traffic. Layer 2 Tunneling Protocol (L2TP) over IPSec connections do not work across the NAT server.

Virtual Private Networks and NATs

Not all traffic can by translated by the NAT. Some applications may have embedded IP addresses (not in the IP header) or may be encrypted. For these applications one can tunnel through the NAT using PPTP. PPTP does require an editor, which has been implemented in the NAT. Only the IP and Generic Routing Encapsulation (GRE) headers are edited or translated. The original IP datagram is not affected. This allows for encryption or otherwise unsupported applications to go through the NAT.

The source of the PPTP packets will be translated to a NAT address. The encapsulated IP packet will have a source address assigned by the PPTP server. When the packet is beyond the PPTP server, the encapsulation is removed and the source address will be the one assigned by the PPTP server. If the PPTP server is using a pool of valid Internet addresses, the client now has a valid address and can go anywhere on the Internet. Any application will work, as the original IP datagram is not translated. Only the encapsulation or wrapper is translated by the NAT.

Note   L2TP does not require a NAT editor. However, L2TP with IPSec cannot be translated by the NAT. There cannot be a NAT editor for IPSec.

This method of NAT bypass is only useful if there is a PPTP server to tunnel to. This will be good for branch offices or home users tunneling to a corporate network, as illustrated in Figure 12.6.

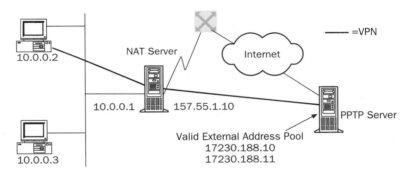

Figure 12.6   Implementing a VPN through a NAT server

Lesson Summary

When using a NAT, private addresses are normally used on the internal network. It is recommended that you use these addresses on a private network instead of picking addresses at random because they are potentially duplicate addresses not valid on the Internet. To prevent problems, you should identify design issues before you implement NAT. Normal NAT usage from a home or small business allows outbound connections from the private network to the public network. You may need to configure applications and services to work properly across the Internet. In addition, remember that not all traffic can by translated by the NAT because some applications may have embedded IP addresses or may be encrypted. For these applications you can tunnel through the NAT using PPTP.

Review

Answering the following questions will reinforce key information presented in this chapter. If you are unable to answer a question, review the appropriate lesson and then try the question again. Answers to the questions can be found in Appendix A, "Questions and Answers."

1. What is the purpose of NAT?

2. What are the components of NAT?

3. If a small business is using the 10.0.0.0 private network for its intranet and has been granted the public IP address of 198.200.200.1 by its ISP, to what public IP address does NAT map all private IP addresses being used on network 10.0.0.0?

4. What must you do to allow Internet users to access resources on your private network?

C H A P T E R   1 3

Implementing Certificate Services

About This Chapter

Certificates are fundamental elements of the Microsoft Public Key Infrastructure (PKI). Certificates enable users to use smart card logon, send encrypted e-mail, and sign electronic documents. Certificates are issued, managed, renewed, and revoked by certificate authorities. In this chapter, you will learn how to install and configure certificates.

Before You Begin

To complete this chapter, you must have

- Installed Microsoft Windows 2000 Server
- Installed Active Directory
- Installed Domain Name System (DNS)

Lesson 1: Introducing Certificates

In this lesson, you will learn about digital certificates and Windows 2000 Certificate Services. Certificates are a very important part of Microsoft's PKI. You will also learn about certificate authorities (CAs) supported by Windows 2000 Certificate Services.

After this lesson, you will be able to

- Define a certificate
- Explain the components of a certificate
- Describe the use of certificates
- Explain the difference between enterprise and stand-alone CAs

Estimated lesson time: 25 minutes

Overview of Certificates

A certificate (digital certificate, public key certificate) is a digital document that attests to the binding of a public key to an entity. The main purpose of a certificate is to generate confidence that the public key contained in the certificate actually belongs to the entity named in the certificate. As illustrated in Figure 13.1, certificates play a fundamental role in the Microsoft PKI.

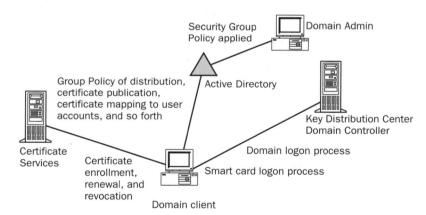

Figure 13.1   Certificate services integrated with Active Directory and distributed security services

A certificate may consist of a public key signed by a trusted entity. However, the most widely used structure and syntax for digital certificates is defined by the International Telecommunications Union (ITU) in ITU-T Recommendation X.509. Figure 13.2 illustrates a certificate that can be used to validate the sender of an e-mail message.

Figure 13.2   Example certificate

An X.509 certificate contains information that identifies the user, as well as information about the organization that issued the certificate, including the serial number, validity period, issuer name, issuer signature, and subject (or user) name. The subject can be an individual, a business, a school, or some other organization, including a CA.

How Certificates Are Created

Certificates are issued by a CA, which can be any trusted service or entity willing to verify and validate the identities of those to whom it issues certificates, and their association with specific keys. Companies may issue certificates to employees, schools may issue certificates to students, and so on. Of course, a CA's public key must be trustworthy or the certificates it issues will not be trusted. Because anyone can become a CA, certificates are only as trustworthy as the authority that issues the underlying keys. The following six steps describe the process of requesting and issuing a certificate.

1. **Generating a key pair.**   The applicant generates a public and private key pair or is assigned a key pair by some authority in his or her organization.

2. **Collecting required information.**   The applicant collects whatever information the CA requires to issue a certificate. The information could include the applicant's e-mail address, birth certificate, fingerprints, notarized documents—whatever the CA needs to be certain that the applicant is who he or she claims to be. CAs with stringent identification requirements produce certificates with high assurance—that is, their certificates generate a high level of confidence. CAs themselves are said to be of high, medium, or low assurance.

3. **Requesting the certificate.** The applicant sends a certificate request, consisting of his or her public key and the additional required information, to the CA. The certificate request may be encrypted using the CA's public key. Many requests are made using e-mail, but requests can also be sent by postal or courier service, for example, when the certificate request itself must be notarized.

4. **Verifying the information.** The CA applies whatever policy rules it requires to verify that the applicant should receive a certificate. As with identification requirements, a CA's verification policy and procedures influence the amount of confidence generated by the certificates it issues.

5. **Creating the certificate.** The CA creates and signs a digital document containing the applicant's public key and other appropriate information. The signature of the CA authenticates the binding of the subject's name to the subject's public key. The signed document is the certificate.

6. **Sending or posting the certificate.** The CA sends the certificate to the applicant or posts the certificate in a directory as appropriate.

How Certificates Are Used

Certificates are used to generate confidence in the legitimacy of specific public keys. A certificate must be signed with the issuer's private key; otherwise, it is not a certificate. Therefore, the issuer's signature can be verified using the issuer's public key. If an entity trusts the issuer, then the entity can also have confidence that the public key contained in the certificate belongs to the subject named in the certificate.

Enterprise and Stand-Alone CAs

Certificate Services includes two policy modules that permit two classes of CAs: enterprise CAs and stand-alone CAs. Within these two classes, there can be two types of CAs: a root CA or a subordinate CA. The policy modules define the actions that a CA can take when it receives a certificate request, and can be modified if necessary.

CAs are usually organized in a hierarchy in which the most trusted CA is at the top. The Windows 2000 PKI assumes a hierarchical CA model. There may be multiple disjointed hierarchies; there is no requirement that all CAs share a common top-level parent.

Enterprise CAs

In an enterprise, the enterprise root CA is the most trusted CA. There can be more than one enterprise root CA in a Windows 2000 domain, but there can be only one enterprise root CA in any given hierarchy. All other CAs in the hierarchy are enterprise subordinate CAs.

An organization should install an enterprise CA if it will be issuing certificates to users or computers within the organization. It is not necessary to install a CA in every domain in the organization. For example, users in a child domain can use a CA in a parent domain. Enterprise CAs have a special policy module that enforces how certificates are processed and issued. The policy information used by these modules is stored centrally in Windows 2000 Active Directory.

Note An Active Directory and a DNS server must be running prior to installing an enterprise CA.

Stand-Alone CAs

An organization that will be issuing certificates to users or computers outside the organization should install a stand-alone CA. There can be many stand-alone CAs, but there can be only one stand-alone CA per hierarchy. All other CAs in a hierarchy are either stand-alone subordinate CAs or enterprise subordinate CAs.

A stand-alone CA has a relatively simple default policy module and does not store any information remotely. Therefore, a stand-alone CA does not need to have Microsoft Windows 2000 Active Directory available.

Types of CAs

The setup requirements for the four types of CAs available from Certificate Services are described in the following sections.

Enterprise Root CA

An enterprise root CA is the root of an organization's CA hierarchy. An organization should set up an enterprise root CA if the CA will be issuing certificates to users and computers within the organization. In large organizations, the enterprise root CA is used only to issue certificates to subordinate CAs. The subordinate CAs issue certificates to users and computers.

The enterprise root CA requires the following:

- Windows 2000 DNS Service
- Windows 2000 Active Directory Service
- Administrative privileges on all servers

Enterprise Subordinate CA

An enterprise subordinate CA is a CA that issues certificates within an organization but is not the most trusted CA in that organization; it is subordinate to another CA in the hierarchy.

The enterprise subordinate CA has the following requirements:

- It must be associated with a CA that will process the subordinate CA's certificate requests. This could be an external commercial CA or a stand-alone CA.
- Windows 2000 DNS Service.
- Windows 2000 Directory Service.
- Administrative privileges on all servers.

Stand-Alone Root CA

A stand-alone root CA is the root of a CA trust hierarchy. The stand-alone root CA requires administrative privileges on the local server. An organization should install a stand-alone root CA if the CA will be issuing certificates outside of the organization's enterprise network, and the CA needs to be the root CA. A root CA typically only issues certificates to subordinate CAs.

Stand-Alone Subordinate CA

A stand-alone subordinate CA is a CA that operates as a solitary certificate server or exists in a CA trust hierarchy. An organization should set up a stand-alone subordinate CA when it will be issuing certificates to entities outside the organization.

The stand-alone subordinate CA has the following requirements:

- It must be associated with a CA that will process the subordinate CA's certificate requests. This could be an external commercial CA.
- Administrative privileges on the local server.
- Certificate enrollment is the process of obtaining a digital certificate.

Lesson Summary

In this lesson, you learned that certificates are fundamental elements of the Microsoft PKI. Certificates enable users to use smart card logon, send encrypted e-mail, sign electronic documents, and so forth. Certificates are issued, managed, renewed, and revoked by CAs.

Lesson 2: Installing and Configuring Certificate Authority

In this lesson, you will explore certificates in more detail by learning how to install and protect your CA. Next, you will be introduced to the process of the enrollment of certificates and the various ways to accomplish it.

After this lesson, you will be able to

- Explain how to use Certificate Authority Manager
- Explain how to install a CA
- Explain how to protect a CA
- Describe the certificate enrollment process

Estimated lesson time: 35 minutes

Deploying a CA

CAs will be installed during the following practice. The Certificate Services Installation Wizard walks the administrator through the installation process. This section discusses key elements that should be considered before beginning the installation process.

- **Establishing a Windows 2000 domain.**   If an enterprise CA is to be deployed, establish a domain before installing Certificate Services.

- **Active Directory integration.**   Information concerning enterprise CAs is written into a CA object in the Active Directory during installation. This provides information to domain clients about available CAs and the types of certificates they will issue.

- **Selecting the host server.**   The root CA can run on any Windows 2000 Server platform, including a domain controller. Factors such as physical security requirements, expected loading, and connectivity requirements should be considered in making this decision.

- **Naming.**   CA names are bound into their certificates and hence cannot change. Renaming a computer running Certificate Services is not supported. Consider factors such as organizational naming conventions and future requirements to distinguish among issuing CAs. The CA name (or common name) is critical because it is used to identify the CA object created in the Active Directory for an enterprise CA.

- **Key generation.**   The CA's public–private key pair will be generated during the installation process and is unique to this CA.

- **CA certificate.**   For a root CA, the installation process will automatically generate a self-signed CA certificate using the CA's public–private key pair. For a child CA, the administrator has the option to generate a certificate request that may be submitted to an intermediate or root CA.

- **Issuing policy.**   The enterprise CA setup will automatically install and configure the default enterprise policy module for the CA. The stand-alone CA setup will automatically install and configure the default stand-alone policy module. Custom policy modules can be substituted if necessary.

After a root CA has been established, it is possible to install intermediate or issuing CAs subordinate to this root CA. The only significant difference in the installation policy is that a certificate request is generated for submission to a root or intermediate CA. This request may be routed automatically to online CAs located by means of the Active Directory, or routed manually in an offline scenario. In either case, the resultant certificate must be installed at the CA before it can begin operation.

The enterprise CA trust model may or may not correspond to the Windows 2000 domain trust model. A direct mapping between CA trust relationships and domain trust relationships is not required. There is nothing that prevents a single CA from servicing entities in multiple domains or even entities outside the domain boundary. Similarly, a given domain may have multiple enterprise CAs.

Protecting a CA

CAs are high-value resources, and it is often desirable to provide them with a high degree of protection. Specific actions that should be considered include:

- **Physical protection.**   Because CAs represent highly trusted entities within an enterprise, they should be protected from tampering. This requirement is dependent on the inherent value of the certification made by the CA. Physical isolation of the CA server in a facility accessible only to security administrators can dramatically reduce the possibility of such physical attacks.

- **Key management.**   The CA's private key provides the basis for trust in the certification process and should be secured from tampering. Cryptographic hardware modules (accessible to Certificate Services through a CryptoAPI cryptographic service provider (CSP)) can provide tamper-resistant key storage and isolate the cryptographic operations from other software running on the server. This significantly
reduces the likelihood of a CA key being compromised.

- **Restoration.**   Loss of a CA—due to hardware failure, for example—can create a number of administrative and operational problems and prevent revocation of existing certificates. Certificate Services supports backup of a CA instance so it can be restored at a later time. This is an important part of the overall CA management process.

Certificate Enrollment

The process of obtaining a digital certificate is called certificate enrollment. The Windows 2000 PKI supports certificate enrollment to the Microsoft enterprise CA, stand-alone CA, or third-party CAs. Enrollment support is implemented in a transport-independent manner and is based on use of industry-standard public

#7 responses containing the resulting certificate or certificate chain. At the time of this writing, certificates supporting RSA keys and signatures, DSA keys and signatures, and Diffie-Hellman keys are supported.

Multiple Enrollment Methods

The PKI supports multiple enrollment methods, including Web-based enrollment, an enrollment wizard, and policy-driven autoenrollment that occurs as part of a user's logon processing. In the future, Microsoft plans to evolve the certificate enrollment process in a manner consistent with the Certificate Request Syntax (CRS) draft currently in the Internet Engineering Task Force (IETF) PKIX working group.

Web-Based Enrollment

The Web-based enrollment process begins with a client submitting a certificate request and ends with the installation of the certificate in the client application. Certificate Services includes a Hypertext Transfer Protocol (HTTP) enrollment control with forms, illustrated in Figure 13.3, for custom certificate enrollment and renewal applications for Microsoft Certificate Services. The enrollment control and its forms are accessed through the Certificate Services Enrollment Page, which is available from the Certificate Services Administrative Tools Web Page, *http://<server_name>/certsrv/ default.asp*. You can customize the Microsoft Certificate Services Web pages to modify user options or provide links to online help, support, or user instructions.

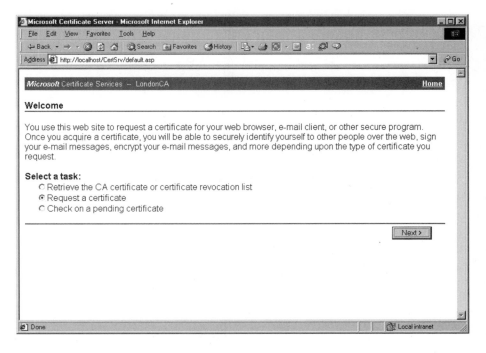

Figure 13.3   Certificate Server Web enrollment

Client Certificate Enrollment

Certificate Services supports client certificate enrollment using Internet Explorer version 3.0 or later. To obtain a client certificate with these browsers, the user opens the client authentication page and submits identification information. After Certificate Services creates the client certificate, it is returned to the browser, which installs the certificate on the client.

Automated Enrollment

The automated enrollment process is controlled by two key elements: certificate types and autoenrollment objects. These are integrated with the Group Policy object and may be defined on a site, domain, organizational unit (OU), computer, or user basis.

Certificate types provide a template for a certificate and associate it with a common name for ease of administration. The template defines elements such as naming requirements, validity period, allowable CSPs for private key generation, algorithms, and extensions that should be incorporated into the certificate. The certificate types are logically separated into machine and user types and applied to the policy objects accordingly. Once defined, these certificate types are available for use with the autoenrollment objects and Certificate Enrollment Wizard.

This mechanism is not a replacement for the enterprise CA issuing policy, but is integrated with it. The CA service receives a set of certificate types as part of its policy object. These are used by the Enterprise Policy Module to define the types of certificates the CA is allowed to issue. The CA rejects requests for certificates that fail to match these criteria.

The autoenrollment object defines policy for certificates that an entity in the domain should have. This can be applied on a machine and user basis. The types of certificates are incorporated by reference to the certificate type objects, and may be any defined type. The autoenrollment object provides sufficient information to determine whether an entity has the required certificates, and enrolls those certificates with an enterprise CA if they are missing. The autoenrollment objects also define policy on certificate renewal. This can be set by an administrator to occur in advance of certificate expiration, supporting long-term operation without direct user action. The autoenrollment objects are processed, and any required actions taken, whenever policy is refreshed (logon time, Group Policy object refresh, and so on).

Practice: Installing a Stand-Alone Root CA

▶ **To install a stand-alone root CA**

1. From within Control Panel, select Add/Remove Programs.
2. Click Add/Remove Windows Components.
3. Check the box next to Certificate Services, then click Next.
4. Select Stand-Alone Root CA, then click Next.
5. Fill in the CA identifying information.

   For CA name, type **ComputernameCA**. Click Next.
6. Use the default data storage locations, then click Next.
7. During the CA installation process, you may need to click OK to stop the World Wide Web Publishing Service, and you will need to give the location of the Windows 2000 installation files (specifically Certsrv.*).
8. Click Finish.
9. Close the Add/Remove Programs window.

▶ **To request and install a certificate from the local CA**

1. Run Certificate Authority Manager.

   Notice that the service is started (check mark), as illustrated in Figure 13.4.

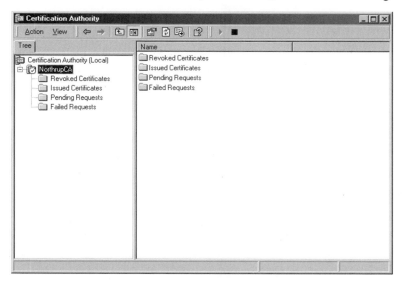

Figure 13.4 Certification Authority Manager

2. Run Internet Explorer and connect to *http://<your_server>/certsrv/default.asp*.

3. Request a Web browser certificate. The request will be pending.

4. Close Internet Explorer.

5. Open Certificate Authority and select the Pending Requests folder. Right-click your request and choose Issue from the All Tasks menu.

   In the left pane select the Issued Certificates folder, and notice that your request has been issued.

6. Run Internet Explorer, connect to *http://<your_server>/certsrv/default.asp*, check on the Pending Certificate Request, then install the certificate.

7. From the Tools menu, click Internet Options, Content, then Certificates.

8. Under Certificates, highlight your certificate, then click View.
   Notice that the certificate was issued by your computer, and close all windows.

Cryptographic Key Storage

Within the Microsoft PKI, cryptographic keys and associated certificates are stored and managed by the CryptoAPI subsystem. Keys are managed by CSPs and certificates are managed by the CryptoAPI certificate stores. The certificate stores are repositories for certificates, along with associated properties. By convention, the PKI defines five standard certificate stores, described in Table 13.1.

Table 13.1   Standard PKI Certificate Stores

Store	Description
MY	This store is used to hold a user's or computer's certificates, for which the associated private key is available.
CA	This store is used to hold issuing or intermediate CA certificates to use in building certificate verification chains.
TRUST	This store is used to hold certificate trust lists. These are an alternate mechanism for allowing an administrator to specify a collection of trusted CAs. An advantage is that they are digitally signed and may be transmitted over nonsecure links.
ROOT	This store holds only self-signed CA certificates for trusted root CAs.
UserDS	This store provides a logical view of a certificate repository stored in the Active Directory (for example, in the userCertificate property of the User object). Its purpose is to simplify access to these external repositories.

These are logical stores that can present a consistent, systemwide view of the available certificates that may reside on multiple physical stores (hard disk, smart cards, and so on). By using these services, applications can share certificates and are assured of consistent operation under administrative policy. The certificate management functions support decoding of X.509 v3 certificates and provide enumeration functions to assist in locating a specific certificate.

To simplify application development, the MY store maintains certificate properties that indicate the CSP and key-set name for the associated private key. Once an application has selected a certificate to use, it can use this information to obtain a CSP context for the correct private key.

Certificate Renewal

Certificate renewal is conceptually similar to enrollment, but takes advantage of the trust relationship inherent in an existing certificate. Renewal assumes the requesting entity wants a new certificate with the same attributes as an existing, valid certificate, but with extended validity dates. A renewal may use the existing public key or a new public key.

Renewal is of advantage primarily to the CA. A renewal request can presumably be processed more efficiently because the existing certificate attributes do not need to be verified again. Renewal is currently supported in the Windows 2000 PKI for automatically enrolled certificates. For other mechanisms, a renewal is treated as a new enrollment request.

Industry-standard message protocols for certificate renewal are not yet defined, but are included in the IETF PKIX CRS draft. Once these standards are ratified, Microsoft plans to implement the associated message formats.

Certificate and Key Recovery

Public key pairs and certificates tend to have high value. If they are lost due to system failure, their replacement may be time-consuming and result in monetary loss. To address this issue, the Windows 2000 PKI supports the ability to back up and restore both certificates and associated key pairs through the certificate management administrative tools.

When exporting a certificate using the Certificate Manager, the user must specify whether to also export the associated key pair. If this option is selected, the information is exported as an encrypted (based on a user-supplied password) PKCS #12 message. This may later be imported to the system, or to another system, to restore the certificate and keys.

This operation assumes that the key pair is exportable by the CSP. This will be true for the Microsoft base CSPs if the exportable flag was set at key generation time. Third-party CSPs may or may not support private key export. For example, smart card CSPs do not generally support this operation. For software CSPs with nonexportable keys, the alternative is to maintain a complete system-image backup, including all registry information.

Roaming

Roaming in the context of this discussion means the ability to use the same public key-based applications on different computers within the enterprise's

Windows 2000 environment. The principal requirement is to make users' cryptographic keys and certificates available wherever they log on. The Windows 2000 PKI supports this in two ways.

First, if the Microsoft base CSPs are used, roaming keys and certificates are supported by the roaming profile mechanism. This is transparent to the user once roaming profiles are enabled. It is unlikely that this functionality will be supported by third-party CSPs, as they will generally use a different method of preserving key data, often on hardware devices.

Hardware token devices, such as smart cards, support roaming, provided they incorporate a physical certificate store. The smart card CSPs that ship with the Windows 2000 platform support this functionality. Roaming support is accomplished by moving the hardware token with the user.

Revocation

Certificates tend to be long-lived credentials. There are a number of reasons these credentials may become untrustworthy prior to their expiration. Examples include

- Compromise, or suspected compromise, of an entity's private key
- Fraud in obtaining the certificate
- Change in status

PK-based functionality assumes distributed verification in which there is no need for direct communication with a central trusted entity that vouches for these credentials. This creates a need for revocation information that can be distributed to individuals attempting to verify certificates.

The need for revocation information, and its timeliness, is dependent on the application. To support a variety of operational scenarios, the Windows 2000 PKI incorporates support of industry-standard certificate revocation lists (CRLs). Enterprise CAs support certificate revocation and CRL publication to Active Directory under administrative control. Domain clients can fetch this information, caching it locally, to use when verifying certificates. This same mechanism supports CRLs published by commercial CAs, or third-party certificate server products, provided the published CRLs are accessible to clients over the network.

Trust

Certificate verification is of primary concern to clients using PK-based applications. If a given end-entity certificate can be shown to "chain" to a known trusted root CA, and if the intended certificate usage is consistent with the application context, then it is considered valid. If either of these conditions is not true, then it is considered invalid.

Within the PKI, users may make trust decisions that affect only themselves. They do this by installing or deleting trusted root CAs and by configuring associated usage restrictions by using the certificate management administrative tools. Within the enterprise, this is expected to be the exception rather than the rule. It is expected that these trust relationships will be established as part of the enterprise policy. Trust relationships established by policy are automatically propagated to Windows 2000 client computers.

Trusted CA Roots

Trust in root CAs may be set by policy to establish trust relationships used by domain clients in verifying PK certificates. The set of trusted CAs is configured using the Group Policy editor. It can be configured on a per-computer basis and will apply to all users of that computer.

In addition to establishing a root CA as trusted, the administrator can set usage properties associated with the CA. If specified, these restrict the purposes for which the CA-issued certificates are valid. Restrictions are specified based on object identifiers as defined for ExtendedKeyUsage extensions in the IETF PKIX Part 1 draft. Currently, these provide a means of restricting usage to any combination of the following:

- Server authentication
- Client authentication
- Code signing
- E-mail
- IP Security Protocol (IPSec) end system
- IPSec tunnel
- IPSec user
- Time stamping
- Microsoft Encrypted File System

Lesson Summary

In this lesson, you learned how to install and protect your CA. CAs are high-value resources and it is important to protect them. You also learned how to provide enrollment of certificates and the various ways to accomplish it. To obtain a client certificate, the user opens the client authentication page and submits identification information. Then, Certificate Services creates the client certificate that is returned to the browser and installed on the client.

Lesson 3: Managing Certificates

Once you start issuing certificates, or clients request that you issue certificates, management of them becomes an important issue. In this lesson, you will learn how to manage certificates, revoke a certificate, and implement an Encrypting File System (EFS) recovery policy.

After this lesson, you will be able to

- Describe the steps to revoke a certificate
- Describe how to issue an EFS recovery policy

Estimated lesson time: 30 minutes

Revoked Certificates

When a certificate is marked as revoked, it is moved to the Revoked Certificates folder. The revoked certificate will appear on the CRL the next time it is published. Certificates revoked with the reason code Certificate Hold can be unrevoked, left on Certificate Hold until they expire, or have their revocation reason code changed. This is the only reason code that allows you to change the status of a revoked certificate. It is useful if the status of the certificate is questionable, and is meant to provide some flexibility to the CA administrator.

Issued Certificates

In the details pane, examine the certificate request by noting the values for requester name, requester e-mail address, and any other fields that you consider critical information for issuing the certificate.

Pending Requests

In the details pane, examine the certificate request by noting the values for requester name, requester e-mail address, and any other fields that you consider critical information for issuing the certificate.

Failed Requests

Failed certificate requests should only occur when a member of the Cert Publishers or Administrators groups denies a certificate request.

How a Certificate Is Issued

When a certificate is presented to an entity as a means of identifying the certificate holder (the subject of the certificate), it is useful only if the entity receiving the certificate trusts the issuing CA. Certificates are issued under the following processes:

- **Key generation.**   The individual or applicant requesting certification generates key pairs of public and private keys. The exception to this is personal digital certificates, in which case the CA generates the public and private keys and sends them to the end user.

- **Matching of policy information.**   The applicant packages up the additional information necessary for the CA to issue the certificate (for example, proof of identity, tax ID number, e-mail address, and so on). The precise definition of this information is up to the CA.

- **Sending of public keys and information.**   The applicant sends the public keys and information (often encrypted using the CA's public key) to the CA.

- **Verification of information.**   The CA applies whatever policy rules it might require to verify that the applicant should receive a certificate.

- **Certificate creation.**   The CA creates a digital document with the appropriate information (public keys, expiration date, and other data) and signs it using the CA's private key.

- **Sending or posting of certificate.**   The CA may send the certificate to the applicant or post it publicly. The certificate is loaded onto the individual's system.

Certificate Revocation

Certificate authorities publish CRLs containing certificates that have been revoked by the CA. The certificate holder's private key may become compromised, or false information may be used to apply for the certificate. CRLs provide a way of withdrawing a certificate after it has been issued. CRLs are made available for downloading or online viewing by client applications.

To verify a certificate, all that is necessary is the public key of the CA and a check against the revocation list published by that CA. Certificates and CAs reduce the public key distribution problem of verifying and trusting one (or more) public keys per individual. Instead, only the CA's public key must be trusted and verified, and then that can be relied on to allow verification of other certificates.

Practice: Revoking a Certificate

▶ **To revoke the certificate from Lesson 2**

1. Open the Certificate Authority Manager.

2. Right-click your request under Issued Certificates, point to All Tasks, then click Revoke Certificate.

3. When prompted for a reason code, select Cease Of Operation. Click Yes.

4. In the left pane, click Revoke Certificates.

   Notice your request has been revoked, as illustrated in Figure 13.5.

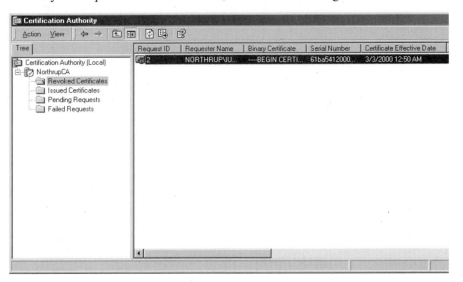

Figure 13.5   Certificate Authority revoked certificates

EFS Recovery Policy

Data recovery is available for the EFS as a part of the overall security policy for the system. For example, if you should ever lose your file encryption certificate and associated private key (through disk failure or any other reason), data recovery is available through the person who is the designated recovery agent. Or, in a business environment, an organization can recover data encrypted by an employee after the employee leaves.

EFS recovery policy specifies the data recovery agent accounts that are used within the scope of the policy. EFS requires an encrypted data recovery agent policy before it can be used, and uses a default recovery agent account (the Administrator) if none has been chosen. In a domain, only members of the Domain Admins group can designate another account as the recovery agent account. In a small business or home environment where there are no domains, the computer's local Administrator account is the default recovery agent account. Only the Administrator account can change local recovery policy for a computer.

A recovery agent account is used to restore data for all computers covered by the policy. If a user's private key is lost, a file protected by that key can be backed up, and the backup sent by means of secure e-mail to a recovery agent administrator. The administrator restores the backup copy, opens it to read the file, copies the file in plaintext, and returns the plaintext file to the user using secure e-mail again.

As an alternative, the administrator can go to the computer that has the encrypted file, import his or her recovery agent certificate and private key, and perform the recovery there. However, this might not be safe and is not recommended because of the sensitivity of the recovery key—the administrator cannot afford to leave the recovery key on another computer.

Practice: Changing a Recovery Policy

In this procedure, you will change the recovery policy for the local computer. Before changing the recovery policy in any way, you should first back up the recovery keys to a floppy disk. In a domain, a default recovery policy is implemented for the domain when the first domain controller is set up. The domain administrator is issued the self-signed certificate, which designates the domain administrator as the recovery agent. To change the default recovery policy for a domain, log on to the first domain controller as an administrator.

Note   To complete this procedure, you must have the appropriate permissions to request the certificate and the CA must be configured to issue this type of certificate.

▶ **To change the recovery policy for the local computer**

1. Click Start, click Run, type **mmc /a**, then click OK.

2. On the Console menu, click Add/Remove Snap-In, then click Add.

3. Under Snap-In, click Group Policy, then click Add.

4. Under Group Policy Object, make sure that Local Computer is displayed, click Finish, click Close, then click OK.

5. In Navigate Local Computer Policy\Computer Configuration\Windows Settings\Security Settings\Public Key Policies, right-click Encrypted Data Recovery Agents, then click one of the following options:

   The Add command designates a user as an additional recovery agent using the Add Recovery Agent Wizard. The Delete Policy command deletes this EFS policy and every recovery agent. The effect of deleting the EFS policy and every recovery agent is that users will not be able to encrypt files on this computer. The computer issues a default self-signed certificate that designates the local administrator as the default recovery agent. If you delete this certificate without another policy in place, the computer has an empty recovery policy. An empty recovery policy means that no one is a recovery agent. This turns EFS off, thereby not allowing users to encrypt files on this computer.

6. To make changes to the File Recovery certificate, start by selecting Encrypted Data Recovery Agents in the left pane, as shown in Figure 13.6. Right-click the certificate in the right pane, then click Properties. For example, you can give the certificate a friendly name and enter a text description.

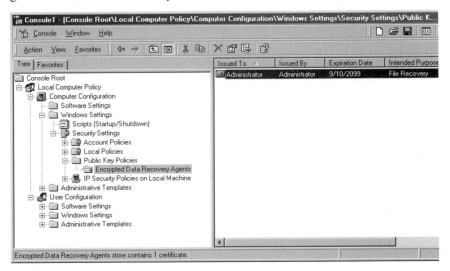

Figure 13.6 Group Policy for EFS recovery

Lesson Summary

You can manage certificates using the Certification Authority snap-in for the Microsoft Management Console. Certificates revoked with the reason code Certificate Hold can be unrevoked. They can also be left on Certificate Hold until they expire or have their revocation reason code changed. Data recovery is available for the EFS as a part of the overall security policy for the system.

Review

Answering the following questions will reinforce key information presented in this chapter. If you are unable to answer a question, review the appropriate lesson and then try the question again. Answers to the questions can be found in Appendix A, "Questions and Answers."

1. What are certificates, and what is their purpose?

2. What is a certificate authority (CA), and what does it do?

3. What are the four types of Microsoft certificate authorities?

4. Name one reason for a certificate revocation.

5. What are the five PKI standard certificate stores?

CHAPTER 14

Implementing Enterprise-Wide Network Security

About This Chapter

In this chapter, you will learn how to implement security on your network and how to properly plan for security. You will also learn how to establish and secure remote access to your network. In addition, troubleshooting and monitoring network resources and remote access is discussed.

Before You Begin

To complete this chapter, you must have

- Installed Microsoft Windows 2000 Server
- Completed Chapters 2 through 10

Lesson 1: Implementing Network Security

As you plan your network, you should implement security technologies that are appropriate for your organization. Addressing these issues early in your Windows 2000 deployment planning ensures that security cannot be breached and that you are ready to provide secure networking facilities when needed. In this lesson, you will learn how to implement security on your network.

After this lesson, you will be able to

- Describe sections of a network security plan
- Identify network security risks
- Describe Windows 2000 security features
- Describe how to secure a connection between your network and the Internet

Estimated lesson time: 35 minutes

Planning for Network Security

Even if you are confident that you have implemented a secure network environment, it is important for you to review your security strategies considering the capabilities of Windows 2000. Some of the new network security technologies in Windows 2000 might cause you to rework your security plan. As you develop your network security plan, you should

- Assess your network security risks.
- Determine your server size and placement requirements.
- Prepare your staff.
- Create and publish security policies and procedures.
- Use a formal methodology to create a deployment plan for your security technologies.
- Identify your user groups and their specific needs and security risks.

Assessing Network Security Risks

Although the ability to share and obtain information is very beneficial, it also presents security risks, described in Table 14.1.

Table 14.1   Network Security Risks

Security Risk	Description
Identity interception	The intruder discovers the user name and password of a valid user. This can occur by a variety of methods, both social and technical.
Masquerade	An unauthorized user pretends to be a valid user. For example, a user assumes the Internet Protocol (IP) address of a trusted system and uses it to gain the access rights that are granted to the impersonated device or system.
Replay attack	The intruder records a network exchange between a user and a server and plays it back at a later time to impersonate the user.
Data interception	If data is moved across the network as plaintext, unauthorized persons can monitor and capture the data.
Manipulation	The intruder causes network data to be modified or corrupted. Unencrypted network financial transactions are vulnerable to manipulation. Viruses can corrupt network data.
Repudiation	Network-based business and financial transactions are compromised if the recipient of the transaction cannot be certain who sent the message.
Macro viruses	Application-specific viruses could exploit the macro language of sophisticated documents and spreadsheets.
Denial of service	The intruder floods a server with requests that consume system resources and either crash the server or prevent useful work from being done. Crashing the server sometimes provides opportunities to penetrate the system.
Malicious mobile code	This term refers to malicious code running as an autoexecuted ActiveX control or Java Applet uploaded from the Internet on a Web server.
Misuse of privileges	An administrator of a computing system knowingly or mistakenly uses full privileges over the operating system to obtain private data.
Trojan horse	This is a general term for a malicious program that masquerades as a desirable and harmless utility.
Social engineering attack	Sometimes breaking into a network is as simple as calling new employees, telling them you are from the IT department, and asking them to verify their password for your records.

Competitors could attempt to gain access to proprietary product information, or unauthorized users could attempt to maliciously modify Web pages or overload computers so that they are unusable. Additionally, employees might access confidential information. It is important to prevent these types of security risks to ensure that your company's business functions proceed undisturbed.

Network Authentication

Authentication is the process of identifying users who attempt to connect to a network. Users who are authenticated on the network can utilize network resources based on their access permissions. To provide authentication to network users, you establish user accounts. This is critical for security management. Without authentication, resources such as files are accessible to unauthorized users.

Network Security Plan

To make sure that only the appropriate people have access to resources and data, you should plan your network security strategies well. This also provides accountability by tracking how network resources are used. Figure 14.1 illustrates the primary steps for determining your network security strategies.

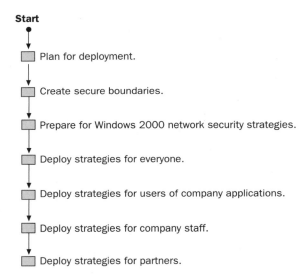

Start

- Plan for deployment.
- Create secure boundaries.
- Prepare for Windows 2000 network security strategies.
- Deploy strategies for everyone.
- Deploy strategies for users of company applications.
- Deploy strategies for company staff.
- Deploy strategies for partners.

Figure 14.1 Primary steps for determining network security strategies

Preparing Your Staff

Security technologies need to be deployed and managed by very capable and trustworthy people. They must integrate the entire network and network security infrastructure so that you can eliminate or minimize weaknesses. As the environment and requirements change, they must continually maintain the integrity of the network security infrastructure.

A critical factor for ensuring the success of your network security staff is to be sure they are well trained and kept up to date as technologies change. The staff needs to take time to learn Windows 2000, particularly its network security technologies. They also need to have opportunities to reinforce their training with experimental work and practical application. Windows 2000 security features are described in Table 14.2.

Table 14.2   Windows 2000 Security Features

Feature	Description
Security templates	Allows administrators to set various global and local security settings, including security-sensitive registry values; access controls on files and the registry; and security on system services.
Kerberos authentication	The primary security protocol for access within or across Windows 2000 domains. Provides mutual authentication of clients and servers, and supports delegation and authorization through proxy mechanisms.
Public key infrastructure (PKI)	You can use integrated PKI for strong security in multiple Windows 2000 Internet and enterprise services, including extranet-based communications.
Smart card infrastructure	Windows 2000 includes a standard model for connecting smart card readers and cards with computers and device-independent application programming interfaces to enable applications that are smart card-aware.
IP Security Protocol (IPSec) management	IPSec supports network-level authentication, data integrity, and encryption to secure intranet, extranet, and Internet Web communications.
NT file system (NTFS) encryption	Public key-based NTFS can be enabled on a per-file or per-directory basis.

Although security technologies can be very effective, security itself combines those technologies with good business and social practices. No matter how advanced and well implemented the technology is, it is only as good as the methods used in employing and managing it.

Planning Distributed Network Security

Distributed network security involves the coordination of many security functions on a computer network to implement an overall security policy. Distributed security enables users to log on to appropriate computer systems and allows them to find and use the information they need. Much of the information on computer networks is available for anyone to read, but only a small group of people is allowed to update it. If the information is sensitive or private, only authorized individuals or groups are allowed to read the files. Protection and privacy of information transferred over public telephone networks, the Internet, and even segments of internal company networks are also a concern. This topic is discussed later in this lesson and in Lesson 2.

A typical security plan includes sections like those shown in Table 14.3. However, you should remember that your network security deployment plan could contain additional sections. The following are suggested as a minimum.

Table 14.3   Network Security Plan Sections

Section in the Plan	Description
Security risks	Enumerates the types of security hazards that affect your enterprise.
Security strategies	Describes the general security strategies necessary to meet the risks.
PKI policies	Includes your plans for deploying certification authorities for internal and external security features.
Security group descriptions	Includes descriptions of security groups and their relationship to one another. This section maps group policies to security groups.
Group Policy	Includes how you configure security Group Policy settings, such as network password policies.
Network logon and authentication strategies	Includes authentication strategies for logging on to the network and for using remote access and smart card to log on. This is discussed in more detail in Lesson 2.
Information security strategies	Includes how you implement information security solutions, such as secure e-mail and secure Web communications.
Administrative policies	Includes policies for delegation of administrative tasks and monitoring of audit logs to detect suspicious activity.

Additionally, your organization might need more than one security plan. The amount of plans you have depends on the scope of your deployment. An international organization might need separate plans for each of its major subdivisions or locations, whereas a regional organization might need only one plan. Organizations with distinct policies for different user groups might need a network security plan for each group.

Testing Your Security Plans

You should always test and revise your network security plans by using test labs that represent the computing environments for your organization. In addition, you should conduct pilot programs to further test and refine your network security plans.

Internet Connection Issues

Today, most organizations want their computer infrastructure connected to the Internet because it provides valuable services to their staff and customers. A connection to the Internet allows your organization's staff to use e-mail to communicate with people around the world and to obtain information and files from a vast number of sources. It also allows your customers to obtain information and services from your organization at any time. In addition, your organization's staff can use company resources from home, hotels, or anywhere else they might be, and partners can use special facilities to allow them to work more effectively with your company. However, the services made available through Internet connection can be misused, which makes it necessary to employ network security strategies.

Implementing a Firewall

To secure your organization's network for access to and from the Internet, you need to put a firewall between the two, as illustrated in Figure 14.2. The firewall provides connectivity to the Internet for company staff while minimizing the risks that connectivity introduces. At the same time, it prevents access to computers on your network from the Internet, except for those computers authorized to have such access.

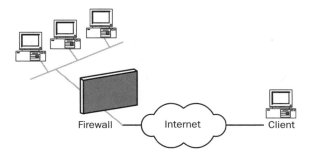

Figure 14.2   Firewall

A firewall employs packet filtering to allow or disallow the flow of very specific types of network traffic. Internet Protocol (IP) packet filtering provides a way for you to define precisely what IP traffic is allowed to cross the firewall. IP packet filtering is important when you connect private intranets to public networks like the Internet. Many firewalls are also capable of detecting and defending against complex attacks.

Firewalls often act as proxy servers or routers because they forward traffic between a private network and a public network. The firewall or proxy server software examines all network packets on each interface to determine their intended address. If they meet specified criteria, the packets are forwarded to the recipient on the other network interface. The firewall may simply route packets, or it may act as a proxy server and translate the IP addresses on the private network.

Microsoft Proxy Server

Microsoft Proxy Server provides both proxy server and some firewall functions. Proxy Server runs on Windows 2000, and both need to be configured properly to provide full network security. If you have a version of Proxy Server earlier than 2.0 with Service Pack 1, you need to upgrade it for Windows 2000 compatibility at the time that you upgrade the server to Windows 2000.

In many cases, the volume of traffic between a company network and the Internet is more than one proxy server can handle. In these situations, you can use multiple proxy servers; the traffic is coordinated among them automatically. For users on both the Internet and intranet sides, there appears to be only one proxy server.

Note Procedures for using Microsoft Proxy Server are included with the product. For more information about Microsoft Proxy Server and for details about Microsoft security technologies, see the Microsoft Security Advisor link on the Web Resources page at *http://windows.microsoft.com/windows2000/reskit/ webresources*.

When you have a proxy server in place, complete with monitoring facilities and properly prepared staff, you can connect your network to an external network. You need to be confident that only the services you have authorized are available, and the risk for misuse is almost nonexistent. This environment requires diligent monitoring and maintenance, but you will also be ready to consider providing other secure networking services.

Lesson Summary

You should plan security strategies to make sure that only the appropriate people have access to resources and data on your network. In addition, you should implement security technologies that are appropriate for your organization. Always test and revise your network security plans by using test labs that represent the computing environments for your organization. You can implement a firewall to secure your organization's network for access to and from the Internet. Microsoft Proxy Server provides both proxy server and firewall functions running with Windows 2000 Server.

Lesson 2: Configuring Routing and Remote Access Security

Remote access enables clients to connect to your network from a remote location through various hardware devices including network interface cards and modems. Once clients obtain a remote access connection, they can use network resources such as files in the same way as they would use a client computer directly connected to your local area network (LAN). In this lesson, you will learn how to configure security for remote access on your network.

After this lesson, you will be able to

- Create a remote access policy
- Configure remote access security
- Configure encryption protocols
- Configure authentication protocols
- Configure and troubleshoot network protocol security

Estimated lesson time: 60 minutes

Overview of Remote Access

As you learned in Chapter 11, Routing and Remote Access is the service that lets remote users connect to your local network by phone. Remote access provides an opportunity for intruders to access your network; therefore, Windows 2000 provides multiple security features to permit authorized access while limiting opportunities for mischief. When a client dials a remote access server on your network, the client is granted access to the network if the following are true:

- The request matches one of the remote access policies defined for the server.
- The user's account is enabled for remote access.
- Client/server authentication succeeds.

After the client has been identified and authorized, access to the network can be limited to specific servers, subnets, and protocol types, depending on the remote access profile of the client. Otherwise, all services typically available to a user connected to a LAN (including file and print sharing, Web server access, and messaging) are enabled by means of the remote access connection.

Configuring Protocols for Security

Consider that someone can intercept a user name and password while a user is attempting to log on to the Routing and Remote Access server using techniques similar to a wiretap. To prevent this, Routing and Remote Access can use a secure user authentication method including

- **Challenge Handshake Authentication Protocol (CHAP).** CHAP is designed to address the concern of passing passwords in plaintext. Historically, CHAP is the most common dial-up authentication protocol used. Because the algorithm for calculating CHAP responses is well known, it is very important that passwords be carefully chosen and sufficiently long. CHAP passwords that are common words or names are vulnerable to dictionary attacks if they can be discovered by comparing responses to the CHAP challenge with every entry in a dictionary. Passwords that are not sufficiently long can be discovered by brute force by comparing the CHAP response to sequential trials until a match to the user's response is found.

- **Microsoft Challenge Handshake Authentication Protocol (MS-CHAP).** MS-CHAP is a variant of CHAP that does not require a plaintext version of the password on the authenticating server. MS-CHAP passwords are stored more securely at the server but have the same vulnerabilities to dictionary and brute force attacks as CHAP. In MS-CHAP the challenge response is calculated with a Message Digest 4 (MD4)-hashed version of the password and the network access server (NAS) challenge. This enables authentication over the Internet to a Windows 2000 domain controller (or a Windows NT 4.0 domain controller on which the update has not been installed).

- **Password Authentication Protocol (PAP).** PAP passes a password as a string from the user's computer to the NAS device. When the NAS forwards the password, it is encrypted using the Remote Authentication Dial-In User Service (RADIUS) shared secret as an encryption key. PAP is the most flexible protocol because passing a plaintext password to the authentication server enables that server to compare the password with nearly any storage format. For example, UNIX passwords are stored as one-way encrypted strings that cannot be decrypted. PAP passwords can be compared to these strings by reproducing the encryption method. Because it uses a plaintext version of the password, PAP has a number of security vulnerabilities. Although the RADIUS protocol encrypts the password, it is transmitted as plaintext across the dial-up connection.

- **Shiva Password Authentication Protocol (SPAP).** SPAP is a reversible encryption mechanism employed by Shiva remote access servers. A Windows 2000 remote access client can use SPAP to authenticate itself to a Shiva remote access server. A remote access client running Windows 32-bit operating systems can use SPAP to authenticate itself to a Windows 2000 remote access server. SPAP is more secure than PAP but less secure than CHAP or MS-CHAP. SPAP offers no protection against remote server impersonation.

Like PAP, SPAP is a simple exchange of messages. First, the remote access client sends an SPAP Authenticate-Request message to the remote access server containing the remote access client's user name and encrypted password. Next, the remote access server decrypts the password, checks the user name and password, and sends back either an SPAP Authenticate-Ack message when the user's credentials are correct, or an SPAP Authenticate-Nak message with a reason why the user's credentials were not correct.

- **Extensible Authentication Protocol (EAP).**   EAP is an extension to Point-to-Point Protocol (PPP) that allows for arbitrary authentication mechanisms to be employed for the validation of a PPP connection. With PPP authentication protocols such as MS-CHAP and SPAP, a specific authentication mechanism is chosen during the link establishment phase. Then, during the connection authentication phase, the negotiated authentication protocol is used to validate the connection. The authentication protocol itself is a fixed series of messages sent in a specific order. Architecturally, EAP is designed to allow authentication plug-in modules at both the client and server ends of a connection. By installing an EAP-type library file on both the remote access client and the remote access server, a new EAP type can be supported. This presents vendors with the opportunity to supply a new authentication scheme at any time. EAP provides the highest flexibility in authentication uniqueness and variations.

Practice: Using Security Protocols for a Virtual Private Network Connection

▶ **To enable your virtual private network (VPN) server to use the CHAP authentication method**

1. Click Start, point to Programs, point to Administrative Tools, then click Routing and Remote Access.

2. Right-click the server name for which you want to enable authentication protocols, then click Properties.

   The Server Properties dialog box appears.

3. In the Security tab, click Authentication Methods.

   The Authentication Methods dialog box appears.

4. In the Authentication Methods dialog box, select Encrypted Authentication, as illustrated in Figure 14.3, then click OK.

5. Click OK to close the Server Properties dialog box.

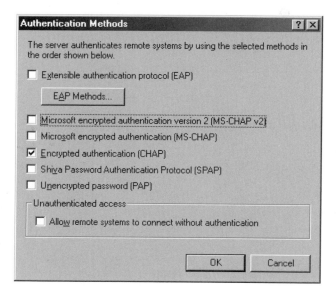

Figure 14.3   Using the CHAP authentication method

Creating Remote Access Policies

Windows 2000 Routing and Remote Access and Windows 2000 Internet Authentication Service (IAS) both use remote access policies to determine whether to accept or reject connection attempts. In both cases, the remote access policies are stored locally. Policy is now dictated on a per-call basis.

With remote access policies, you can grant or deny authorization by time of day or day of the week, by the Windows 2000 group to which the remote access user belongs, by the type of connection being requested (dial-up networking or VPN connection), and so forth.

Local Versus Centralized Policy Management

Because remote access policies are stored locally on either a remote access server or an IAS server, for centralized management of a single set of remote access policies for multiple remote access or VPN servers, you must do the following:

1. Install the Windows 2000 IAS as a RADIUS server on a computer.

2. Configure IAS with RADIUS clients that correspond to each of the Windows 2000 remote access or VPN servers.

3. On the IAS server, create the central set of policies that all Windows 2000 remote access servers are using.

4. Configure each of the Windows 2000 remote access servers as a RADIUS client to the IAS server.

After you configure a Windows 2000 remote access server as a RADIUS client to an IAS server, the local remote access policies stored on the remote access server are no longer used. Centralized management of remote access policies is also used when you have remote access servers that are running Windows NT 4.0 with the Routing and Remote Access Service (RRAS). You can configure the server that is running Windows NT 4.0 with RRAS as a RADIUS client to an IAS server. You cannot configure a remote access server that is running Windows NT 4.0 without RRAS to take advantage of centralized remote access policies.

Using Encryption Protocols

You can use data encryption to protect the data that is sent between the remote access client and the remote access server. Data encryption is important for financial institutions, law-enforcement and government agencies, and corporations that require secure data transfer. For installations where data confidentiality is required, the network administrator can set the remote access server to require encrypted communications. Users who connect to that server must encrypt their data, or the connection attempt is denied.

For VPN connections, you protect your data by encrypting it between the ends of the VPN. You should always use data encryption for VPN connections when private data is sent across a public network such as the Internet, where there is always a risk of unauthorized interception.

For dial-up networking connections, you can protect your data by encrypting it on the communications link between the remote access client and the remote access server. You should use data encryption when there is a risk of unauthorized interception of transmissions on the communications link between the remote access client and the remote access server. There are two forms of encryption available for demand-dial connections: Microsoft Point-to-Point Encryption (MPPE) and IP Security (IPSec).

- **MPPE.**   All PPP connections, including Point-to-Point Tunneling Protocol (PPTP) but not including Layer 2 Tunneling Protocol (L2TP), can use MPPE. MPPE uses the Rivest–Shamir–Adleman (RSA) Rivest's Cipher 4 (RC4) stream cipher and is only used when either the EAP-Transport Layer Security (TLS) or MS-CHAP (version 1 or version 2) authentication methods are used. MPPE can use 40-bit, 56-bit, or 128-bit encryption keys. The 40-bit key is designed for backward compatibility and international use. The 56-bit key is designed for international use and adheres to United States encryption export laws. The 128-bit key is designed for North American use. By default, the highest key strength supported by the calling router and answering router is negotiated during the connection establishment process. If the answering router requires a higher key strength than is supported by the calling router, the connection attempt is rejected.

Note   For dial-up networking connections, Windows 2000 uses MPPE.

- **IPSec.** For demand-dial connections using L2TP over IPSec, encryption is determined by the establishment of the IPSec security association (SA). The available encryption algorithms include Data Encryption Standard (DES) with a 56-bit key, and triple DES (3DES), which uses three 56-bit keys and is designed for high-security environments. The initial encryption keys are derived from the IPSec authentication process.

For VPN connections, Windows 2000 uses MPPE with the PPTP, and IPSec encryption with the L2TP.

▶ **To configure encryption for a dial-up connection**

1. Click Start, point to Programs, point to Administrative Tools, then click Routing And Remote Access.
2. Under the server name, click Remote Access Policies.
3. In the details pane, right-click the remote access policy you want to configure, then click Properties.
4. Click Edit Profile.
5. In the Encryption tab, illustrated in Figure 14.4, specify settings as needed, then click OK.
6. Click OK to close the Policy Properties dialog box.

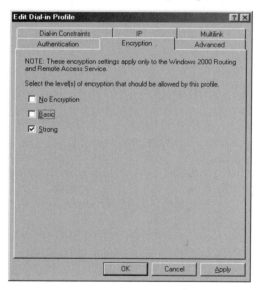

Figure 14.4   Setting the level of encryption

Lesson Summary

Remote access enables clients to connect to your network from a remote location through various hardware devices including network interface cards and modems. Once a client obtains a remote access connection, he or she can use network resources, such as files, as when the client computer is directly connected to the LAN. In Windows 2000 you create remote access policies and then configure them for security. You can set the level of encryption and dial-up permissions for remote access.

Lesson 3: Monitoring Security Events

In Lesson 1, you learned about various sections of a network security plan. Administrative policies for a security plan include policies for delegation of administrative tasks and monitoring of audit logs to detect suspicious activity. In this lesson, you will learn how to monitor security events in Windows 2000 to prevent attacks and intrusion on your network.

After this lesson, you will be able to

- Manage and monitor network traffic
- Manage and monitor remote access

Estimated lesson time: 45 minutes

Monitoring Your Network Security

The network security technologies you implement, such as Microsoft Proxy Server, can meet your security goals only if you plan and configure them carefully. With thorough preparation, this work can be done very successfully. However, anticipating all possible risks can be very difficult because

- New risks develop.
- Systems can break down and the environment in which your systems are placed changes over time.

By continually reviewing your network security strategies, you can minimize security risks. However, you also need to watch the actual network security activity to spot weaknesses before they are exploited, and to stop attempts to break security before they are effective.

To watch your network security activity, you need tools to capture the details about the activities and to analyze the data. For example, Microsoft Proxy Server includes logging at two levels: normal and verbose. Windows 2000 also has event logging, which can be enhanced by enabling security auditing. IAS, discussed later in this chapter, has extensive activity reporting options. Third-party products are also available that can help with monitoring servers and applications, including security servers and applications.

Note   When using security servers and applications, be sure to review the documentation for the systems you use and select the logging options that best meet your requirements.

Using Event Viewer to Monitor Security

Event Viewer allows you to monitor events in your system. It maintains logs about program, security, and system events on your computer. You can use Event Viewer to view and manage the event logs, gather information about hardware and software problems, and monitor Windows 2000 security events. The Event Log service starts automatically when you start Windows 2000. All users can view application and system logs. You can also set up the Windows operating system to audit accesses on specific resources and to have them recorded in the Security Log. Table 14.4 lists various events that you can audit, as well as the specific security threat that the audit event monitors.

Table 14.4   Threats Detected with Auditing

Audit Event	Threat Detected
Failure audit for logon/logoff.	Random password hack
Success audit for logon/logoff.	Stolen password break-in
Success audit for user rights, user and group management, security change policies, restart, shutdown, and system events.	Misuse of privileges
Success and failure audit for file-access and object-access events. File Manager success and failure audit of read/write access by suspect users or groups for the sensitive files.	Improper access to sensitive files
Success and failure audit for file-access printers and object-access events. Print Manager success and failure audit of print access by suspect users or groups for the printers.	Improper access to printers
Success and failure write access auditing for program files (.exe and .dll extensions). Success and failure auditing for process tracking. Run suspect programs; examine security log for unexpected attempts to modify program files or create unexpected processes. Run only when actively monitoring the system log.	Virus outbreak

Practice: Recording Failed Logon Attempts

Security auditing is not enabled by default. You have to activate the types of auditing you require by using the Group Policy snap-in to Microsoft Management Console (MMC). You also must enable auditing for the general areas or specific items you want to track.

▶ **To activate security auditing for failed logon attempts**

1. Click Start, click Run, type **mmc**, then click OK.

2. On the Console menu, click Add/Remove Snap-In, then click Add.

   The Add/Remove Snap-In dialog box appears.

3. Click Add.

   The Add Standalone Snap-In dialog box appears.

4. Select Group Policy, then click Add.

   The Select Group Policy dialog box appears.

5. Click Finish to add the local computer.

   You can also click Browse and then select another computer on your network.

6. In the Add Standalone Snap-In dialog box, click Close.

7. In the Add/Remove Snap-In dialog box, click OK.

8. Under Local Computer Policy\Computer Configuration\Windows Settings\Security Settings\Local Policies, click Audit Policy, as illustrated in Figure 14.5.

9. In the details pane, right-click the Audit Logon Events attribute, then right-click Security.

   The Local Security Policy Setting dialog box appears.

10. Under Audit These Attempts, select Failure, then click OK.

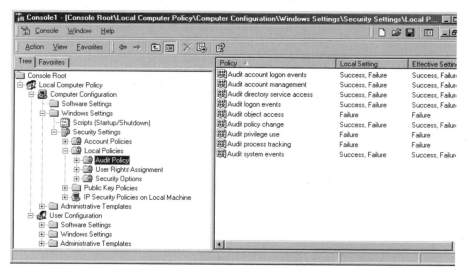

Figure 14.5   Selecting audit policy for the local computer policy

Viewing the Security Event Log

You can specify that an audit entry be written to the security event log whenever certain actions are performed or files are accessed. The audit entry shows the action performed, the user who performed it, and the date and time of the action. You can audit both successful and failed attempts at actions, so the audit trail can show who performed actions on the network and who tried to perform actions that are not permitted. You can view the security log in the Event Viewer.

Recording security events is a form of intrusion detection through auditing. Auditing and security logging of network activity are important safeguards. Windows 2000 enables you to monitor a wide variety of events that can be used to track the activities of an intruder.

The security log records security events, such as valid and invalid logon attempts, and events related to resource use, such as creating, opening, or deleting files or other objects. The security log helps track changes to the security system and identifies any possible breaches to security. For example, attempts to log on to the system might be recorded in the security log, if logon and logoff auditing are enabled. If the security log is examined regularly, it makes it possible to detect some types of attacks, such as password attacks, before they succeed. After a break-in, the security log can help you determine how the intruder entered and what he or she did. The log file entries can serve as legal evidence after the intruder has been identified.

Note   For the highest level of security, monitor the log files constantly.

Practice: Viewing the Security Log

Event logs consist of a header, a description of the event (based on the event type), and, optionally, additional data. Most security log entries consist of the header and a description. Event Viewer displays events from each log separately. Each line shows information about a single event, including date, time, source, event type, category, event ID, user account, and computer name. In this practice, you will view the security event log to detect attempted unauthorized network access. To complete this practice, you must have performed the steps in the previous practice in this lesson.

▶ **To view the security event log**

1. Attempt to log on to the Windows 2000 computer on which you activated security auditing for failed logon attempts using an invalid user name and password.

2. After failing to log on, use a valid user name and password to log on to Windows 2000.

3. Click Start, point to Programs, point to Administrative Tools, then click Event Viewer.

   Event Viewer opens.

4. Click Security Log in the left pane.

   Notice that the failed logon attempt is shown in the right pane of the Event Viewer, as illustrated in Figure 14.6.

5. Double-click the Failure Audit item in the event view to open the Event Properties window.

   Notice that the description section tells you the reason for the failure and the user name entered, but not the password entered.

6. Click OK to close the Event Properties window.

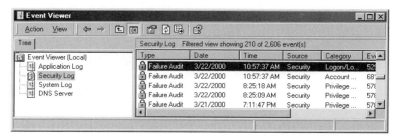

Figure 14.6   Invalid logon entry made in the security event log

System Monitor

System Monitor is a tool that can be used to track system resources usage. System Monitor can be used to test an application's usage of system resources. Common objects that a user can log are memory, CPU, network, and disk activity. Some additional counters, although not performance related, provide useful information about server security. These include

- Server\Errors Access Permissions
- Server\Errors Granted Access
- Server\Errors Logon
- IIS Security

▶ **To monitor security events using System Monitor**

1. Click Start, point to Programs, point to Administrative Tools, then click Performance.

   System Monitor opens in the MMC.

2. In the right pane, click Add.

   The Add Counters dialog box appears, as illustrated in Figure 14.7.

3. In the Performance Object drop-down list box, select Server.

4. Click Select Counters From List.

5. In the Counters list, select a counter, then click Add.

6. Click Close to close the Add Counters dialog box.

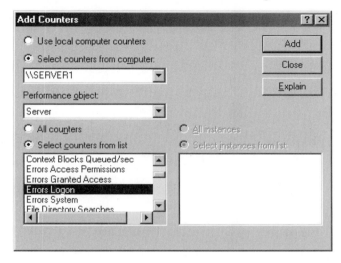

Figure 14.7   Adding the Error Logon counter

The IPSec Monitor Utility

The IPSec Monitor can confirm whether your secured communications are successful by displaying the active SAs on local or remote computers. For example, you can use IPSec Monitor to determine whether there has been a pattern of authentication or SA failures, possibly indicating incompatible security policy settings. IPSec Monitor can be run on the local computer or it can be run remotely if you have a network connection to the remote computer.

▶ **To run IPSec Monitor**

1. Click Start, then click Run.

2. In the Run dialog box, type **ipsecmon <computername>**, then click OK.

   The IP Security Monitor dialog box opens, as illustrated in Figure 14.8. An entry is displayed for each active SA. The information contained in each entry includes the name of the active IPSec policy, the active Filter Action and IP Filter List (including details of the active filter), and the tunnel endpoint (if one was specified).

3. Click the Options button to set the refresh rate.

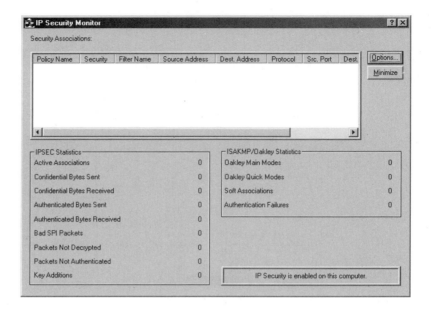

Figure 14.8 The IP Security Monitor interface

IPSec Monitor can also provide statistics to aid in performance tuning and troubleshooting, including the following statistics:

- The number and type of active SAs.
- The total number of master and session keys. Successful IPSec SAs initially cause one master key and one session key. Subsequent key regenerations are shown as additional session keys.
- The total number of confidential (Encapsulated Security Payload) or authenticated (Encapsulated Security Payload or authentication header) bytes sent or received.

Monitoring Security Overhead

Security is achieved only at some cost in performance. Measuring the performance overhead of a security strategy is not simply a matter of monitoring a separate process or thread. The features of the Windows 2000 security model and other security services are integrated into several different operating system services. You cannot monitor security features separately from other aspects of the services. Instead, the most common way to measure security overhead is to run tests comparing server performance with and without a security feature. The tests should be run with fixed workloads and a fixed server configuration so that the security feature is the only variable. During the tests, you should measure

- Processor activity and the processor queue
- Physical memory used

- Network traffic
- Latency and delays

Lesson Summary

You should monitor network security activity to identify weaknesses before they are exploited. You can use Event Viewer to view and manage Windows 2000 security events. The audit entry shows the action performed, the user who performed it, and the date and time of the action. Both System Monitor and Network Monitor can provide useful information about server security. The IPSec Monitor can confirm whether your secured communications are successful. In addition, you can use Routing and Remote Access to monitor remote access traffic in Windows 2000, and enable logging to review this data.

Review

Answering the following questions will reinforce key information presented in this chapter. If you are unable to answer a question, review the appropriate lesson and then try the question again. Answers to the questions can be found in Appendix A, "Questions and Answers."

1. What are some potential security risks you should identify in your security plan?

2. What is authentication and how can you implement it?

3. What are some security features of Windows 2000?

4. How can you secure a connection between your network and the Internet?

5. What are some remote access protocols you can implement for security?

6. Name two forms of encryption available for demand-dial connections.

7. How do System Monitor and Network Monitor provide the ability to monitor security on your network?

8. How is Event Viewer used to monitor security?

9. How do you enable remote access logging in Windows 2000?

APPENDIX A

Questions and Answers

Chapter 1

Review Questions

1. You are currently configuring TCP/IP manually for new computers and computers moving from one subnet to another. You want to simplify management of TCP/IP addresses and assign them automatically. Which Windows 2000 network service should you use?

   Use DHCP to automate and centrally manage TCP/IP addresses.

2. You have an Intel-compatible server with 8 GB of RAM and 8 CPUs. You want to provide file services to over 400 people in your company. Which Windows 2000
   operating system would be most appropriate to deploy, and why?

   In this case, deploy Windows 2000 Advanced Server because it provides network load balancing and enterprise memory architecture. Windows 2000 Server only supports 4 GB of RAM, so it would not satisfy the necessary requirements.

3. You want a Windows 2000 server to connect to and provide routing for AppleTalk-based Macintosh networks. What protocol should you install?

   Windows 2000 supports an AppleTalk protocol stack and AppleTalk routing software so that the Windows 2000 server can connect to and provide routing for AppleTalk-based Macintosh networks.

Chapter 2

Review Questions

1. What is TCP/IP?

2. Which TCP/IP utilities are used to verify and test a TCP/IP configuration?

PING and Ipconfig.

3. What is the purpose of a subnet mask?

To mask a portion of the IP address so IP can distinguish the network ID from the host ID.

4. What is the minimum number of areas in an OSPF internetwork?

An OSPF internetwork always has at least one area called the backbone, whether or not it is subdivided into areas.

5. What is an internal router?

An internal router is a router with all interfaces connected to the same area.

6. What is a border router?

A border router, or ABR, is a router with interfaces connected to different areas.

7. What Windows 2000 administrative tool can you use to manage internal and border routers?

Routing and Remote Access.

Chapter 3

Review Questions

1. What is NWLink and how does it relate to Windows 2000?

NWLink is the Microsoft implementation of IPX/SPX. You must use this protocol if you want to use Gateway Service for NetWare or Client Service for NetWare to connect to NetWare servers.

2. What is SPX?

SPX is a transport protocol that offers connection-oriented services over IPX. SPX is used by utilities that require a continuous connection, and provides reliable delivery using sequencing and acknowledgments and verifies successful packet delivery to any network destination by requesting verification from the destination on receipt of the data. SPX also provides a packet burst mechanism that allows the transfer of multiple data packets without requiring that each packet be sequenced and acknowledged individually.

3. What is Gateway Service for NetWare?

Gateway Service for NetWare allows you to create a gateway through which Microsoft client computers without Novell NetWare client software can access NetWare file and print resources.

4. When choosing between using Client Service for NetWare and Gateway Service for NetWare, what should you consider?

If you intend to create or indefinitely maintain a heterogeneous environment composed of both servers running Windows 2000 and servers running NetWare, consider using Client Service for NetWare. If you intend to migrate gradually from NetWare to Windows 2000 or if you want to reduce administration, consider using Gateway Service for NetWare.

5. What is the NWLink Auto Detect feature?

The Windows 2000 NWLink Auto Detect feature detects the frame type and network number that are configured on NetWare server(s) on the same network. NWLink Auto Detect is the recommended option for configuring both the network number and the frame type. If the Auto Detect feature selects an inappropriate frame type and network number for a particular adapter, you can manually reset an NWLink frame type or network number for that given adapter.

Chapter 4

Review Questions

1. What is the purpose of analyzing frames with Network Monitor?

Analyzing frames allows you to identify client-to-server connection problems, find a computer that makes a disproportionate number of requests, and isolate Application Layer problems.

2. What kind of data does a frame contain?

Each frame contains the source address of the computer that sent the message, the destination address of the computer that the frame was sent to, headers from each protocol used within the frame, and the payload being sent.

3. What is a capture filter, and what is it used for?

A capture filter functions like a database query. You can use it to specify the types of network information you want to monitor. For example, to see only a specific subset of computers or protocols, you can create an address database, use the database to add addresses to your filter, and then save the filter to a file. By filtering frames, you save both buffer resources and analysis time. Later, if necessary, you can load the capture filter file and use the filter again.

Chapter 5

Practice Questions

Lesson 3: Customizing IPSec Policies and Rules

Practice: Building a Custom IPSec Policy

At this point, you still have not configured your custom rule. Only the default response rule properties have been configured.

What is the purpose of the default response rule?

The default response rule enables negotiation with computers requesting IPSec. A default response rule is added to each new policy you create, but it is not automatically activated. A default response rule can be used for any computer that does not require security, but must be able to appropriately respond when another computer requests secured communications. It can also be used as a template for defining custom rules.

Review Questions

1. IPSec is defined by what standards group?

   The Internet Engineering Task Force (IETF) IP Security working group.

2. Define the difference between secret and public key cryptography.

   Secret key cryptography uses a single preshared key. Public key cryptography uses a key pair, one for encrypting data and verifying digital signatures and the second for decrypting data and creating digital signatures.

3. ISAKMP/Oakley provides what functionality?

   ISAKMP/Oakley establishes a secure channel between two computers for communication and establishes an SA.

4. What are rules comprised of?

   Rules are comprised of IP filters, negotiation policies, authentication methods, IP tunneling attributes, and adapter types.

5. When would a public key certificate be used?

   A public key certificate allows a nontrusted domain computer to use IPSec to communicate with a trusted domain computer.

6. What is an IP filter used for?

   IP filters check datagrams for a match against each filter specification. This allows for filtering based on the source and destination address, DNS name, protocol, or protocol ports.

Chapter 6

Practice Questions

Lesson 3: The Hosts File

Practice: Working with the Hosts File and DNS

▶ **To ping your local host name**

1. Type **ping Server1** (where Server1 is the name of your computer) and then press the Enter key.

   What was the response?

   Four successful "Reply from IP address" messages.

▶ **To ping a local computer name**

1. Type **ping computertwo** and then press the Enter key.

   What was the response?

   "Bad IP address computertwo."

▶ **To use the HOSTS file for name resolution**

1. Type **ping computertwo** and then press the Enter key.

   What was the response?

   Four successful "Reply from IP address" messages.

Review Questions

1. What is a host name?

   An alias assigned to a TCP/IP host for the purpose of simplifying access to the host.

2. What is the purpose of a host name?

   To simplify how a host is referenced. Host names are used with PING and other TCP/IP applications.

3. What does a Hosts file entry consist of?

   The host name or names and the corresponding IP address.

4. During the name resolution process, what occurs first: ARP resolution or host name resolution?

   Host name resolution.

Chapter 7

Practice Questions

Lesson 3: Planning a DNS Implementation

Scenario 1: Designing DNS for a Small Network

1. How many DNS domains will you need to configure?

   One (or zero, if they have an ISP to manage the name server).

2. How many subdomains will you need to configure?

   Zero.

3. How many zones will you need to configure?

   One (or zero, if they have an ISP to manage the name server).

4. How many primary name servers will you need to configure?

   One (or zero, if they have an ISP to manage the name server).

5. How many secondary name servers will you need to configure?

   One (or zero, if they have an ISP to manage the name server).

6. How many DNS cache-only servers will you need to configure?

   Zero.

Scenario 2: Designing DNS for a Medium-Size Network

1. How many DNS domains will you need to configure?

   You will need at least one DNS domain that can contain both hosts (computers or services) and subdomains.

2. How many subdomains will you need to configure?

   Three. Your DNS domain includes multiple sites, so you should subdivide the domain to create three subdomains that reflect these groupings.

3. How many zones will you need to configure?

   Four. You can distribute administrative tasks to different groups in the primary sites by configuring four zones. This will also provide more efficient data distribution.

4. How many primary name servers will you need to configure?

   Four. Primary sites will maintain their own equipment and the equipment of the branch offices connected to them. Therefore, you must configure four primary name servers.

5. How many secondary name servers will you need to configure?

   Branch offices have between 25 and 250 users needing access to all four of the primary sites. When a secondary server is configured for a zone, clients can still resolve names for that zone even if the primary server for the zone goes down; therefore, you should configure four secondary name servers.

6. How many DNS cache-only servers will you need to configure?

You should configure 10 cache-only servers (one per branch office). This will speed the performance of DNS resolution, reduce DNS-related query traffic, and improve reliability.

7. Use the following mileage chart to design a zone/branch office configuration based on the geographical proximity between each primary site and branch office. Branch offices should be in the same zone as the nearest primary site.

Zones for each branch office (based on geographical proximity):

Portland, OR	Boston	Chicago	Atlanta
Los Angeles	Montreal	Denver	Dallas
Salt Lake City	Washington, DC	Kansas City	Miami
San Francisco			New Orleans

Mileage Chart	Atlanta	Boston	Chicago	Portland, OR
Dallas	807	1817	934	2110
Denver	1400	1987	1014	1300
Kansas City	809	1454	497	1800
Los Angeles	2195	3050	2093	1143
Miami	665	1540	1358	3300
Montreal	1232	322	846	2695
New Orleans	494	1534	927	2508
Salt Lake City	1902	2403	1429	800
San Francisco	2525	3162	2,187	700
Washington, DC	632	435	685	2700

Scenario 3: Designing DNS for a Large Network

1. How many DNS domains will you need to configure?

Zero (the domain for this company is in Geneva, Switzerland).

2. How many subdomains will you need to configure?

Eleven. Remember that you want to give control of the equipment to each subsidiary, and to have a resource domain in each subsidiary.

3. How many zones will you need to configure?

Each of the regional headquarters' subsidiaries will maintain total control of users within their areas. Therefore, you should configure 11 zones.

4. How many primary name servers will you need to configure?

One of the requirements defined in this scenario is that line of business applications running on your computers will be configured as servers within the domains. Therefore, you should configure 11 primary name servers.

5. How many secondary name servers will you need to configure?

You can configure servers to host as many different primary or secondary zones as is practical. In this case, line of business applications need to be available to all sites within their areas, as well as the other regional headquarters. Therefore, you should configure 11 secondary name servers for redundancy. When a secondary server is configured for a zone, clients can still resolve names for that zone even if the primary server for the zone goes down.

6. How many DNS cache-only servers will you need to configure?

Three or more. At least one per regional headquarter.

Review Questions

1. Name the three components of the DNS.

Resolver, name servers, and domain name space.

2. Describe the differences among primary, secondary, and master name servers.

A primary name server has zone information in locally maintained zone files. A secondary name server downloads zone information. A master name server is the source of the downloads for a secondary name server (which could be a primary or secondary name server).

3. List three reasons to have a secondary name server.

▪ **It operates as a redundant name server (you should have at least one redundant name server for each zone).**

▪ **If you have clients in remote locations, you should have a secondary name server to avoid communicating across slow links.**

▪ **A secondary name server reduces the load on the primary name server.**

4. Describe the difference between a domain and a zone.

A domain is a branch of the DNS name space. A zone is a portion of a domain that exists as a separate file on the disk storing resource records.

5. Describe the difference between recursive and iterative queries.

In a recursive query, the client instructs the DNS server to respond with either the requested information or an error that the information was not found. In an iterative query, the DNS server responds with the best answer it has, typically a referral to another name server that can help resolve the request.

6. List the files required for a Windows 2000 DNS implementation.

Database file, cache file, and reverse lookup file.

7. Describe the purpose of the boot file.

The boot file is used in the Berkeley Internet Name Daemon implementation to start up and configure the DNS server.

Chapter 8

Review Questions

1. How many zones can a single DNS server host?

   A single DNS server can be configured to host zero, one, or multiple zones.

2. What benefits do DNS clients obtain from the dynamic update feature of Windows 2000?

   Dynamic update enables DNS client computers to register and dynamically update their resource records with a DNS server whenever changes occur. This reduces the need for manual administration of zone records, especially for clients that frequently move or change locations and use DHCP to obtain an IP address.

3. Name one benefit and one disadvantage of a caching-only server.

   The benefit provided by caching-only servers is that they do not generate zone transfer network traffic because they do not contain any zones. A disadvantage of a caching-only server is that when the server is initially started, it has no cached information and must build up this information over time as it services requests.

4. List and describe three DNS performance counters.

   - **Dynamic update and secure dynamic update counters, for measuring registration and update activity generated by dynamic clients**

   - **Memory usage counters, for measuring system memory usage and memory allocation patterns created by operating the server computer as a Windows 2000 DNS server**

   - **Recursive lookup counters, for measuring queries and responses when the DNS Server service uses recursion to look up and fully resolve DNS names on behalf of requesting clients**

Chapter 9

Review Questions

1. What are two benefits of WINS?

   - **Automatic name registration and resolution of NetBIOS names**

   - **Provides internetwork and interdomain browsing**

   - **Eliminates the need for a local LMHOSTS file**

2. What two methods can be used to enable WINS on a client computer?

   Manual and automatic with DHCP.

3. How many WINS servers are required in an intranet of 12 subnets?

   Only one is required. It is recommended to have multiple servers for redundancy.

4. What types of names are stored in the WINS database?

NetBIOS unique and group names.

Chapter 10

Review Questions

1. What is DHCP?

   Dynamic Host Configuration Protocol simplifies the administrative management of IP address configuration by automating address configuration for network clients.

2. Describe the integration of DHCP with DNS.

   A DHCP server can enable dynamic updates in the DNS name space for any DHCP clients that support these updates. Scope clients can then use DNS with dynamic updates to update their computer name-to-IP address mapping information whenever changes occur to their DHCP-assigned address.

3. What is a DHCP client?

   The term client is used to describe a networked computer that requests and uses the DHCP services offered by a DHCP server.

4. What is IP autoconfiguration in Windows 2000?

   Windows 2000-based clients can automatically configure an IP address and subnet mask if a DHCP server is unavailable at system start time.

5. Why is it important to plan an implementation of DHCP for a network?

   Either WINS or DNS (or possibly both) is used for registering dynamic name-to-address mappings on your network. To provide name resolution services, you must plan for interoperability of DHCP with these services. Most network administrators implementing DHCP also plan a strategy for implementing DNS and WINS servers.

6. What tool do you use to manage DHCP servers in Windows 2000?

   The primary tool that you use to manage DHCP servers is DHCP Manager, which is a Microsoft Management Console (MMC) component that is added to the Administrative Tools menu when you install the DHCP service.

7. What is the symptom of most DHCP-related problems?

   Most DHCP-related problems are identified as a client IP configuration failure. These failures are most often discovered by clients in one of the following ways:

   ■ **The client might be configured to use an IP address not provided by the server.**

- The server sends a negative response back to the client, and the client displays an error message or popup indicating that a DHCP server could not be found.

- The server leases the client an address but the client appears to have other network configuration-based problems, such as the inability to register or resolve DNS or NetBIOS names, or to perceive computers beyond its same subnet.

Chapter 11

Review Questions

1. What is a VPN?

   A simulated point-to-point connection using encapsulation. This connection can span any underlying network, including the Internet. Security or some form of encryption is usually required to get the "private" part of the definition.

2. Demand-dial filters can screen traffic based on what fields of a packet?

   Source and destination IP address, IP protocol identifier, source and destination ports, ICMP type, and ICMP code.

3. True or false: When setting dial-in user permissions (Allow Access, Deny Access) through the User Property page, RAPs are not used.

   False. In the user interface it appears that RAP is not used. In actuality, the dial-in user settings work in conjunction with RAP.

4. True or False: DHCP packets are never sent over Routing and Remote Access links.

   False. Routing and Remote Access clients do not use DHCP to get an address, but may use DHCPINFORM packets to get other configuration options. The DHCP relay agent must be installed and using the "internal" interface for this to work.

5. What is the function of BAP?

   To bring up or drop modem or ISDN links as needed for bandwidth on demand.

Chapter 12

Review Questions

1. What is the purpose of NAT?

   NAT allows computers on a small network, such as a home office, to share a single Internet connection.

2. What are the components of NAT?

The translation component is the router on which NAT is enabled. The addressing component provides IP address configuration information to the other computers on the home network. The name resolution component becomes the DNS server for the other computers on the home network. When name resolution requests are received by the NAT computer, it forwards the name resolution requests to the Internet-based DNS server for which it is configured and returns the responses to the home network computer.

3. If a small business is using the 10.0.0.0 private network for its intranet and has been granted the public IP address of 198.200.200.1 by its ISP, to what public IP address does NAT map all private IP addresses being used on network 10.0.0.0?

The NAT maps (using static or dynamic mappings) all private IP addresses being used on network 10.0.0.0 to the public IP address of 198.200.200.1.

4. What must you do to allow Internet users to access resources on your private network?

You must configure a static IP address configuration on the resource server including IP address, subnet mask, default gateway, and DNS server. You should exclude the IP address being used by the resource computer from the range of IP addresses being allocated by the NAT computer. Next, you configure a special port, which is a static mapping of a public address and port number to a private address and port number.

Chapter 13

Review Questions

1. What are certificates, and what is their purpose?

A certificate (digital certificate, public key certificate) is a digital document that attests to the binding of a public key to an entity. The main purpose of a certificate is to generate confidence that the public key contained in the certificate actually belongs to the entity named in the certificate.

2. What is a certificate authority (CA), and what does it do?

Certificates are issued by a CA, which can be any trusted service or entity willing to vouch for the identities of those to whom it issues certificates, and their association with specific keys.

3. What are the four types of Microsoft certificate authorities?

Enterprise root CA, enterprise subordinate CA, stand-alone root CA, and stand-alone subordinate CA.

4. Name one reason for a certificate revocation.

- **Compromise, or suspected compromise, of an entity's private key**
- **Fraud in obtaining the certificate**
- **Change in status**

5. What are the five PKI standard certificate stores?

MY, CA, TRUST, ROOT, and UserDS.

Chapter 14

Review Questions

1. What are some potential security risks you should identify in your security plan?

It could be possible for competitors to gain access to proprietary product information, or unauthorized users could attempt to maliciously modify Web pages or overload computers so that they are unusable.

2. What is authentication and how can you implement it?

Authentication is the process of identifying users who attempt to connect to a network. When users are authenticated on your network, they can utilize network resources based on their access permissions. To provide authentication to network users, you establish user accounts.

3. What are some security features of Windows 2000?

- **Security templates**
- **Kerberos authentication**
- **Public key infrastructure (PKI)**
- **IPSec management**
- **NT file system encryption**

4. How can you secure a connection between your network and the Internet?

To secure your organization's network for access to and from the Internet, you can put a firewall between the two networks. The firewall provides connectivity for network users to the Internet while minimizing the risks that connectivity introduces. It also prevents access to computers on your network from the Internet, except for those computers authorized to have such access.

5. What are some remote access protocols you can implement for security?

Routing and Remote Access can use a secure user authentication method including:

- **Challenge Handshake Authentication Protocol (CHAP)**
- **Microsoft Challenge Handshake Authentication Protocol (MS-CHAP)**

- **Password Authentication Protocol (PAP)**
- **Shiva Password Authentication Protocol (SPAP)**
- **Extensible Authentication Protocol (EAP)**

6. Name two forms of encryption available for demand-dial connections.

   Microsoft Point-to-Point Encryption (MPPE) and Internet Protocol Security (IPSec).

7. How do System Monitor and Network Monitor provide the ability to monitor security on your network?

   System Monitor is used to monitor anything from hardware to software, and can also monitor security events such as Errors Access Permissions, Errors Granted Access, Errors Logon, and IIS Security. Network Monitor focuses exclusively on network activity to allow you to understand the traffic and behavior of your network components. If you install the full version available from Systems Management Server, you can capture and view every packet on the network.

8. How is Event Viewer used to monitor security?

   Although you can use Event Viewer to gather information about hardware and software problems, it can also be used to monitor Windows 2000 security events such as valid and invalid logon attempts. The security log can also contain events related to resource use, such as creating, opening, or deleting files or other objects.

9. How do you enable remote access logging in Windows 2000?

   You can enable event logging in the Event Logging tab on the properties of a remote access server in Routing and Remote Access.

Glossary

100VG (Voice Grade) AnyLAN (100VGAnyLAN) An emerging networking technology that combines elements of both Ethernet and Token Ring.

A

access permissions Features that control access to sharing in Windows NT Server. Permissions can be set for the following access levels: No Access—Prevents access to the shared directory, its subdirectories, and its files. Read—Allows viewing of file and subdirectory names, changing to a shared directory's subdirectory, viewing data in files, and running applications. Change—Allows viewing of file and subdirectory names, changing to a shared directory's subdirectories, viewing data in files and running application files, adding files and subdirectories to a shared directory, changing data in files, and deleting subdirectories and files. Full Control—Includes the same permissions as Change, plus changing permissions and taking ownership of files and directories only.

account *See* user account.

account lockout A Windows 2000 security feature that locks a user account if a number of failed logon attempts occur within a specified amount of time, based on security policy lockout settings. Locked accounts cannot log on.

account policy Controls how passwords must be used by all user accounts in a domain or on an individual computer.

Active Directory service The directory service included with Windows 2000 Server. It stores information about objects on a network and makes this information available to users and network administrators. The Active Directory service allows users to use a single logon process to access permitted resources anywhere on the network. The Active Directory service provides network administrators with an intuitive hierarchical view of the network and a single point of administration for all network objects.

Active Directory Service Interfaces (ADSI) A COM-based directory service model that allows ADSI-compliant client applications to access a wide variety of distinct directory protocols, including Windows directory service and Lightweight Directory Access Protocol (LDAP), using a single, standard set of interfaces. ADSI shields the client application from the implementation and operational details of the underlying data store or protocol.

Address Resolution Protocol (ARP) Determines hardware addresses (MAC addresses) that correspond to an Internet Protocol (IP) address.

Administrator A person responsible for setting up and managing domain controllers or local computers and their user and group accounts, assigning passwords and permissions, and helping users with networking issues.

ADSL *See* Asymmetric Digital Subscriber Line (ADSL).

advanced program-to-program communication (APPC) A specification developed as part of IBM's Systems Network Architecture (SNA) model and designed to enable application programs running on different computers to communicate and exchange data directly. *See also* Systems Network Architecture (SNA).

AFP *See* AppleTalk filing protocol (AFP).

agent A program that performs a background task for a user and reports to the user when the task is done or when some expected event has taken place.

American National Standards Institute (ANSI) An organization of American industry and business groups dedicated to the development of trade and communications standards. ANSI is the American representative to the International Organization for Standardization (ISO). *See also* International Organization for Standardization (ISO).

analog Related to a continuously variable physical property, such as voltage, pressure, or rotation. An analog device can represent an infinite number of values within the range the device can handle. *See also* analog line, digital.

analog line A communications line, such as a telephone line, that carries information in analog (continuously variable) form. To minimize distortion and noise interference, an analog line uses amplifiers to strengthen the signal periodically during transmission.

ANSI *See* American National Standards Institute (ANSI).

APPC *See* advanced program-to-program communication (APPC).

AppleShare AppleShare is the Apple network operating system. Features include file sharing, client software that is included with every copy of the Apple operating system, and the Apple-Share print server, a server-based print spooler.

AppleTalk The Apple network architecture that is included in the Macintosh operating system software. It is a collection of protocols that correspond to the OSI model. Thus, network capabilities are built into every Macintosh. AppleTalk protocols support LocalTalk, Ethernet (EtherTalk), and Token Ring (TokenTalk).

AppleTalk filing protocol (AFP) Describes how files are stored and accessed on the network. AFP is responsible for the Apple hierarchical filing structure of volumes, folders, and files and provides for file sharing between Macintoshes and MS-DOS-based computers. It provides an interface for communication between AppleTalk and other network operating systems, allowing

Macintoshes to be integrated into any network that uses an operating system that recognizes AFP.

application programming interface (API) A set of routines that an application program uses to request and carry out lower-level services performed by the operating system.

ArcNet (Attached Resource Computer Network) Developed by Datapoint Corporation in 1977, designed as a baseband, token-passing, bus architecture, transmitting at 2.5 Mbps. A successor to the original ArcNet, ArcNetplus supports data transmission rates of 20 Mbps. A simple, inexpensive, flexible network architecture designed for workgroup-sized LANs, ArcNet runs on coaxial, twisted-pair, and fiber-optic cable and supports up to 255 nodes. ArcNet technology predates IEEE Project 802 standards but loosely maps to the 802.4 document. *See also* IEEE Project 802.

ARP *See* Address Resolution Protocol (ARP).

ARPANET (Advanced Research Projects Agency Network) A pioneering wide area network (WAN) commissioned by the Department of Defense, ARPANET was designed to facilitate the exchange of information between universities and other research organizations. ARPANET, which became operational in the 1960s, is the network from which the Internet evolved.

ASCII (American Standard Code for Information Interchange) A coding scheme that assigns numeric values to letters, numbers, punctuation marks, and certain other characters. By standardizing the values used for these characters, ASCII enables computers and computer programs to exchange information.

Asymmetric Digital Subscriber Line (ADSL) A recent modem technology that converts existing twisted-pair telephone lines into access paths for multimedia and high-speed data communications. These new connections can transmit more than 8 Mbps to the subscriber and up to 1 Mbps from the subscriber. ADSL is recognized as a physical layer transmission protocol for unshielded twisted-pair media.

asynchronous transfer mode (ATM) An advanced implementation of packet switching that provides high-speed data transmission rates to send fixed-size cells over LANs or WANs. Cells are 53 bytes—48 bytes of data with 5 additional bytes of address. ATM accommodates voice, data, fax, real-time video, CD-quality audio, imaging, and multimegabit data transmission. ATM uses switches as multiplexers to permit several computers to put data on a network simultaneously. Most commercial ATM implementations transmit data at about 155 Mbps, but theoretically a rate of 1.2 gigabits per second is possible.

asynchronous transmission A form of data transmission in which information is sent one character at a time, with variable time intervals between characters. Asynchronous transmission does not rely on a shared timer that allows the sending and receiving units to separate characters by specific time periods. Therefore, each transmitted character consists of a number of data bits (that compose the character itself), preceded by a start bit and ending in an optional parity bit followed by a 1-, 1.5-, or 2-stop bit.

ATM *See* asynchronous transfer mode (ATM).

attenuation The weakening or degrading (distorting) of a transmitted signal as it travels farther from its point of origin. This could be a digital signal on a cable or the reduction in amplitude of an electrical signal, without the appreciable modification of the waveform. Attenuation is usually measured in decibels. Attenuation of a signal transmitted over a long cable is corrected by a repeater, which amplifies and cleans up an incoming signal before sending it farther along the cable.

auditing A process that tracks network activities by user accounts and a routine element of network security. Auditing can produce records of list users who have accessed—or attempted to access—specific resources; help administrators identify unauthorized activity; and track activities such as logon attempts, connection and disconnection from designated resources, changes made to files and directories, server events and modifications, password changes, and logon parameter changes.

authentication Verification typically based on user name, password, and time and account restrictions.

authorization A process that verifies that the user has the correct rights or permissions to access a resource.

B

backbone The main cable, also known as the trunk segment, from which transceiver cables connect to computers, repeaters, and bridges.

back end In a client/server application, the part of the program that runs on the server.

backup domain controller (BDC) In a Windows NT Server domain, a computer that receives a copy of the domain's security policy and domain database and authenticates network logons. It provides a backup if the primary domain controller (PDC) becomes unavailable. A domain is not required to have a BDC, but it is recommended to have a BDC to back up the PDC. *See also* domain, domain controller, primary domain controller (PDC).

bandwidth In communications, the difference between the highest and lowest frequencies in a given range. For example, a telephone accommodates a bandwidth of 3000 Hz, or the difference between the lowest (300 Hz) and highest (3300 Hz) frequencies it can carry. In computer networks, greater bandwidth indicates faster or greater data-transfer capability.

baseband A system used to transmit the encoded signals over cable. Baseband uses digital signaling over a single frequency. Signals flow in the form of discrete pulses of electricity or light. With baseband transmission, the entire communication-channel capacity is used to transmit a single data signal.

basic input/output system (BIOS) On PC-compatible computers, the set of essential software routines that test hardware at startup, start the operating system, and support the transfer of data among hardware devices. The BIOS is stored in read-only memory (ROM) so that it can be executed when the computer is turned on. Although critical to performance, the BIOS is usually invisible to computer users.

baud A measure of data-transmission speed named after the French engineer and telegrapher Jean-Maurice-Emile Baudot. It is a measure of the speed of oscillation of the sound wave on which a bit of data is carried over telephone lines. Because baud was originally used to measure the transmission speed of telegraph equipment, the term sometimes refers to the data-transmission speed of a modem. However, current modems can send at a speed higher than 1 bit per oscillation, so baud is being replaced by the more accurate bps (bits per second) as a measure of modem speed.

baud rate Refers to the speed at which a modem can transmit data. Often confused with bps (the number of bits per second transmitted), baud rate actually measures the number of events, or signal changes, that occur in one second. Because one event can actually encode more than one bit in high-speed digital communication, baud rate and bps are not always synonymous, and the latter is the more accurate term to apply to modems. For example, the 9600-baud modem that encodes 4 bits per event actually operates at 2400 baud, but transmits at 9600 bps (2400 events times 4 bits per event), and thus should be called a 9600-bps modem.

BDC See backup domain controller (BDC).

bind To associate two pieces of information with one another.

binding A process that establishes the communication channel between a protocol driver and a NIC driver.

BIOS (basic input/output system) See basic input/output system (BIOS).

BISDN See Broadband Integrated Services Digital Network (BISDN).

bisync (binary synchronous communications protocol) A communications protocol developed by IBM. Bisync transmissions are encoded in either ASCII or EBCDIC. Messages can be of any length and are sent in units called frames, optionally preceded by a message header. Because bisync uses synchronous transmission, in which message elements are separated by a specific time interval, each frame is preceded and followed by special characters that enable the sending and receiving machines to synchronize their clocks.

bit Short for binary digit: either 1 or 0 in the binary number system. In processing and storage, a bit is the smallest unit of information handled by a computer. It is represented physically by an element such as a single pulse sent through a circuit or small spot on a magnetic disk capable of storing either a 1 or 0. Eight bits make a byte.

bits per second (bps) A measure of the speed at which a device can transfer data. See also baud rate.

bit time The time it takes for each station to receive and store a bit.

boot partition The partition that contains the Microsoft Windows 2000 operating system and its support files. The boot partition can be, but does not have to be, the same as the system partition.

bottleneck The limiting factor when analyzing performance of a system or network. Poor performance results when a device uses noticeably more CPU time than it should, consumes too much of a resource, or lacks the capacity to handle the load. Potential bottlenecks can be found in the CPU, memory, NIC, and other components.

bps *See* bits per second (bps).

Broadband Integrated Services Digital Network (BISDN) A consultative committee for the CCITT that recommends definitions for voice, data, and video in the megabit-gigabit range. BISDN is also a single ISDN network that can handle voice, data, and video services. BISDN works with an optical cable transport network called Synchronous Optical Network (SONET) and an asynchronous transfer mode (ATM) switching service. Switched Multimegabit Data Services (SMDS) is a BISDN service that offers high bandwidth to WANs. *See also* Synchronous Optical Network (SONET), asynchronous transfer mode (ATM).

broadband network A type of LAN on which transmissions travel as analog (radio-frequency) signals over separate inbound and outbound channels. Devices on a broadband network are connected by coaxial or fiber-optic cable, and signals flow across the physical medium in the form of electromagnetic or optical waves. A broadband system uses a large portion of the electromagnetic spectrum with a range of frequencies from 50 Mbps to 600 Mbps. These networks can simultaneously accommodate television, voice, data, and other services over multiple transmission channels.

built-in groups One of several group accounts used by Microsoft Windows NT and Windows 2000. Built-in groups, as the name implies, are included with the network operating system. Built-in groups have been granted useful collections of rights and built-in abilities. In most cases, a built-in group provides all the capabilities needed by a particular user. For example, if a domain user account belongs to the built-in Administrators group, logging on with that account gives a user

administrative capabilities over the domain and the servers in the domain. *See also* user account.

byte A unit of information consisting of 8 bits. In computer processing or storage, a byte is equivalent to a single character, such as a letter, numeral, or punctuation mark. Because a byte represents only a small amount of information, amounts of computer memory are usually given in kilobytes (1024 bytes or 2 raised to the 10th power), megabytes (1,048,576 bytes or 2 raised to the 20th power), gigabytes (1024 megabytes), terabytes (1024 gigabytes), petabytes (1024 terabytes), or exabytes (1024 petabytes).

C

CA (certificate authority) *See* certificate authority (CA).

carrier-sense multiple access with collision avoidance (CSMA/CA) access method An access method by which each computer signals its intent to transmit before it actually transmits data, thus avoiding possible transmission collisions.

carrier-sense multiple access with collision detection (CSMA/CD) access method An access method generally used with bus topologies. Using CSMA/CD, a station "listens" to the physical medium to determine whether another station is currently transmitting a data frame. If no other station is transmitting, the station sends its data. A station "listens" to the medium by testing the medium for the presence of a carrier, a specific level of voltage or light—thus the term carrier-sense. The multiple access indicates that there are multiple stations attempting to access or put data on the cable at the same time. The collision detection indicates that the stations are also listening for collisions. If two stations attempt to transmit at the same time and a collision occurs, the stations must wait a random period of time before attempting to transmit.

CCEP *See* Commercial COMSEC Endorsement Program (CCEP).

CCITT (Comité Consultatif Internationale de Télégraphie et Téléphonie) An organization based in Geneva, Switzerland, and established as part of the United Nations International Telecommunications Union (ITU). The CCITT recommends use of communication standards that are recognized throughout the world. Protocols established by the CCITT are applied to modems, networks, and facsimile transmission.

Cellular Digital Packet Data (CDPD) A communication standard that uses very fast technology, similar to that of cellular telephones, to offer computer data transmissions over existing analog voice networks between voice calls, when the system is not occupied with voice communication.

certificate A collection of data used for authentication and secure exchange of information on nonsecured networks, such as the Internet. A certificate securely binds a public key to the entity that holds the corresponding private key. Certificates are digitally signed by the issuing CA and can be managed for a user, computer, or service. The most widely accepted format for certificates is defined by ITU-T X.509 international standards.

certificate authority (CA) An entity responsible for establishing the authenticity of public keys belonging to users or other CAs. Activities of a CA may include binding public keys to distinguished names through signed certificates, managing certificate serial numbers, and revoking certificates.

child domain For Domain Name System (DNS), a domain located in the namespace tree directly beneath another directory name (the parent domain). For example, example.Microsoft.com would be a child domain of the Microsoft.com parent domain. A child domain is also called a subdomain.

codec (compression/decompression) Compression/decompression technology for digital video and stereo audio.

Commercial COMSEC Endorsement Program (CCEP) A data-encryption standard introduced by the National Security Agency. Vendors who have the proper security clearance can join CCEP and be authorized to incorporate classified algorithms into communications systems. *See also* encryption.

console Collections of administrative tools.

contention Competition among stations on a network for the opportunity to use a communication line or network resource. Two or more computers attempt to transmit over the same cable at the same time, thus causing a collision on the cable. Such a system needs regulation to eliminate data collisions on the cable that can destroy data and bring network traffic to a halt. *See also* carrier-sense multiple access with collision detection (CSMA/CD) access method.

CRC *See* cyclical redundancy check (CRC).

crosstalk Signal overflow from an adjacent wire. When a second faint telephone conversation is heard in the background while one is making a phone call, crosstalk is occurring.

cryptography The processes, art, and science of keeping messages and data secure. Cryptography is used to enable and ensure confidentiality, data integrity, authentication (entity and data origin), and nonrepudiation.

CSMA/CD *See* carrier-sense multiple access with collision detection (CSMA/CD) access method.

cyclical redundancy check (CRC) A form of error checking in transmitting data. The sending packet includes a number produced by a mathematical calculation made at the transmission source. When the packet arrives at its destination, the calculation is redone. If the two figures are the same, this indicates that the data in the packet has remained stable. If the calculation at the destination differs from the calculation at the source, this indicates that the data has changed during the transmission. In that case, the CRC routine either drops the packet or signals the source computer to retransmit the data.

D

database management system (DBMS) A layer of software between the physical database and the user. The DBMS manages all requests for database action from the user, including keeping track of the physical details of file locations and formats, indexing schemes, and so on. In addition, a DBMS permits centralized control of security and data integrity requirements.

Data Communications Equipment (DCE) One of two types of hardware connected by an RS-232 serial connection, the other being a data terminal equipment (DTE) device. A DCE device takes input from a DTE device and often acts as an intermediary device, transforming the input signal in some way before sending it to the actual recipient. For example, an external modem is a DCE device that accepts data from a microcomputer (DTE), modulates it, then sends the data along a telephone connection. In communication, an RS-232 DCE device receives data over line 2 and transmits over line 3. In contrast, a DTE device receives over line 3 and transmits over line 2. *See also* Data Terminal Equipment (DTE).

data encryption *See* encryption.

data encryption standard (DES) A commonly used, highly sophisticated algorithm developed by the U.S. National Bureau of Standards for encrypting and decoding data. *See also* encryption.

data frames Logical, structured packages in which data can be placed. Data being transmitted is segmented into small units and combined with control information such as message start and message end indicators. Each package of information is transmitted as a single unit, called a frame. The data-link layer packages raw bits from the physical layer into data frames. The exact format of the frame used by the network depends on the topology. *See also* frame.

data stream An undifferentiated, byte-by-byte flow of data.

Data Terminal Equipment (DTE) According to the RS-232 hardware standard, a device, such as a microcomputer or a terminal, that has the ability to transmit information in digital form over a cable or a communication line. A DTE is one of two types of hardware connected by an RS-232 serial connection, the other being a DCE (Data Communications Equipment) device, such as a modem, that normally connects the DTE to the communication line itself. In communication, an RS-232 DTE device transmits data over line 2 and receives it over line 3. A DCE receives over line 2 and transmits over line 3. *See also* Data Communications Equipment (DCE).

DBMS *See* database management system (DBMS).

DCE *See* Data Communications Equipment (DCE).

DECnet Digital Equipment Corporation hardware and software products that implement the Digital Network Architecture (DNA). DECnet defines communication networks over Ethernet LANs, Fiber Distributed Data Interface metropolitan area networks (FDDI MANs), and WANs that use private or public data transmission facilities. It can use TCP/IP and OSI protocols as well as Digital's DECnet protocols. *See also* Fiber Distributed Data Interface (FDDI), metropolitan area network (MAN).

dedicated server A computer on a network that functions only as a server and is not also used as a client.

DES *See* data encryption standard (DES).

Dfs (Distributed File System) *See* Distributed File System (Dfs).

DHCP *See* Dynamic Host Configuration Protocol (DHCP).

DHCP client Any network-enabled device that supports the ability to communicate with a DHCP server for the purpose of obtaining dynamic leased Internet Protocol (IP) configuration and related optional parameters information.

DHCP scope A range of Internet Protocol (IP) addresses that are available to be leased or assigned to DHCP clients by the DHCP service.

DHCP server In Microsoft Windows 2000 Server, a computer running the Microsoft DHCP service that offers dynamic configuration of Internet Protocol (IP) addresses and related information to DHCP-enabled clients.

dial-up connection The connection to your network if you are using a device that uses the telephone network. This includes modems with a standard phone line, ISDN cards with high-speed ISDN lines, or X.25 networks. If you are a typical user, you may have one or two dial-up connections, perhaps to the Internet and to your corporate network. In a more complex server situation, multiple network modem connections might be used to implement advanced routing.

digital A system that encodes information numerically, such as 0 and 1, in a binary context. Computers use digital encoding to process data. A digital signal is a discrete binary state, either on or off. *See also* analog.

digital line A communication line that carries information only in binary-encoded (digital) form. To minimize distortion and noise interference, a digital line uses repeaters to regenerate the signal periodically during transmission. *See also* analog line.

digital signature A means for originators of a message, file, or other digitally encoded information to bind their identity to the information. The

process of signing information entails transforming the information, as well as some secret information held by the sender, into a tag called a signature. Digital signatures are used in public key environments and they provide nonrepudiation and integrity services.

directory service Provides the methods for storing directory data and making this data available to network users and administrators. For example, Active Directory stores information about user accounts, such as names, passwords, phone numbers, and so on, and enables other authorized users on the same network to access this information.

Distributed File System (Dfs) A single, logical, hierarchical file system. Dfs organizes shared folders on different computers in a network to provide a logical tree structure for file system resources.

DNS *See* Domain Name System (DNS).

domain For Microsoft networking, a collection of computers and users that share a common database and security policy that are stored on a Windows NT Server domain controller. Each domain has a unique name. *See also* workgroup.

domain controller For Microsoft networking, the Windows NT Server-based computer that authenticates domain logons and maintains the security policy and master database for a domain. *See also* backup domain controller (BDC), primary domain controller (PDC).

domain model A grouping of one or more domains with administration and communication links between them that is arranged for the purpose of user and resource management.

domain namespace The database structure used by the Domain Name System (DNS).

Domain Name System (DNS) A general-purpose distributed, replicated, data-query service used primarily on the Internet for translating host names into Internet addresses.

downtime The amount of time a computer system or associated hardware remains nonfunctioning. Although downtime can occur because hardware fails unexpectedly, it can also be a scheduled event, such as when a network is shut down to allow time for maintaining the system, changing hardware, or archiving files.

driver A software component that permits a computer system to communicate with a device. For example, a printer driver is a device driver that translates computer data into a form understood by the target printer. In most cases, the driver also manipulates the hardware to transmit the data to the device.

DTE *See* Data Terminal Equipment (DTE).

duplex transmission Also called full-duplex transmission. Communication that takes place simultaneously, in both directions, between the sender and the receiver. Alternative methods of transmission are simplex, which is one way only, and half-duplex, which is two-way communication that occurs in only one direction at a time.

Dynamic Host Configuration Protocol (DHCP) A protocol for automatic TCP/IP configuration that provides static and dynamic address allocation and management. *See also* Transmission Control Protocol/Internet Protocol (TCP/IP).

E

EBCDIC *See* Extended Binary Coded Decimal Interchange Code (EBCDIC).

EFS (encrypting file system) *See* encrypting file system (EFS).

encrypting file system (EFS) Windows 2000 file system that enables users to encrypt files and folders on an NTFS volume to keep them safe from intruders who have physical access to the disk.

encryption The process of making information indecipherable to protect it from unauthorized viewing or use, especially during transmission or when the data is stored on a transportable magnetic medium. A key is required to decode the information. *See also* Commercial COMSEC Endorsement Program (CCEP), data encryption standard (DES).

Ethernet A LAN developed by Xerox in 1976. Ethernet became a widely implemented network from which the IEEE 802.3 standard for contention networks was developed. It uses a bus topology, and the original Ethernet relies on CSMA/CD to regulate traffic on the main communication line.

EtherTalk Allows the AppleTalk network protocols to run on Ethernet coaxial cable. The EtherTalk card allows a Macintosh computer to connect to an 802.3 Ethernet network. *See also* AppleTalk.

event An action or occurrence to which a program might respond. Examples of events are mouse clicks, key presses, and mouse movements. Also, any significant occurrence in the system or in a program that requires users to be notified or an entry to be added to a log.

Extended Binary Coded Decimal Interchange Code (EBCDIC) A coding scheme developed by IBM for use with IBM mainframe and personal computers as a standard method of assigning binary (numeric) values to alphabetic, numeric, punctuation, and transmission-control characters.

extended partition A portion of a basic disk that can contain logical drives. Use an extended partition if you want to have more than four volumes on your basic disk. Only one of the four partitions allowed per physical disk can be an extended partition, and no primary partition needs to be present to create an extended partition. Extended partitions can be created only on basic disks.

F

FAT (file allocation table) *See* file allocation table (FAT).

fault tolerance The ability of a computer or an operating system to respond to an event such as a power outage or a hardware failure in such a way that no data is lost and any work in progress is not corrupted.

Fiber Distributed Data Interface (FDDI) A standard developed by the ANSI for high-speed, fiber-optic local area networks. FDDI provides specifications for transmission rates of 100 Mbps on networks based on the Token Ring standard.

fiber-optic cable Cable that uses optical fibers to carry digital data signals in the form of modulated pulses of light.

file allocation table (FAT) A table or list maintained by some operating systems to keep track of the status of various segments of disk space used for file storage.

file replication service (FRS) Provides multimaster file replication for designated directory trees between Windows 2000 servers. The directory trees must be on disk partitions formatted with the version of NTFS used with Windows 2000. FRS is used by the Microsoft Distributed File System (Dfs) to automatically synchronize content between assigned replicas, and by Active Directory to automatically synchronize content of the system volume information across domain controllers.

File Transfer Protocol (FTP) A process that provides file transfers between local and remote computers. FTP supports several commands that allow bidirectional transfer of binary and ASCII files between computers. The FTP client is installed with the TCP/IP connectivity utilities. *See also* ASCII (American Standard Code for Information Interchange), Transmission Control Protocol/Internet Protocol (TCP/IP).

firewall A security system, usually a combination of hardware and software, intended to protect a network against external threats coming from another network, including the Internet. Firewalls prevent an organization's networked computers from communicating directly with computers that are external to the network, and vice versa. Instead, all incoming and outgoing communication is routed through a proxy server outside the organization's network. Firewalls also audit network activity, recording the volume of traffic and information about unauthorized attempts to gain access. *See also* proxy server.

FQDN (fully qualified domain name) *See* fully qualified domain name (FQDN).

frame A package of information transmitted on a network as a single unit. Frame is a term most often used with Ethernet networks. A frame is similar to the packet used in other networks. *See also* data frames, packet.

frame preamble Header information, added to the beginning of a data frame in the physical layer of the OSI reference model.

frame relay An advanced, fast-packet, variable-length, digital, packet-switching technology. It is a point-to-point system that uses a private virtual circuit (PVC) to transmit variable-length frames at the data-link layer of the OSI reference model. Frame relay networks can also provide subscribers with bandwidth, as needed, that allows users to make nearly any type of transmission.

front end In a client/server application, front end refers to the part of the program carried out on the client computer.

FRS (file replication service) *See* file replication service (FRS).

FTP *See* File Transfer Protocol (FTP).

full-duplex transmission Also called duplex transmission. Communication that takes place simultaneously in both directions. *See also* duplex transmission.

fully qualified domain name (FQDN) A DNS domain name that has been stated unambiguously so as to indicate with absolute certainty its location in the domain namespace tree. Fully qualified domain names differ from relative names in that they can be stated with a trailing period (.), for example, host.example.microsoft.com, to qualify their position to the root of the namespace.

G

global group One of four kinds of group accounts used by Microsoft Windows NT and Windows NT Server. Used across an entire domain, global groups are created on a primary domain controller (PDC) in the domain in which the user accounts reside. Global groups can contain only user accounts from the domain in which the global group is created. Members of global groups obtain resource permissions when the global group is added to a local group. *See also* group, primary domain controller (PDC).

group In networking, an account containing other accounts that are called members. The permissions and rights granted to a group are also provided to its members; thus, groups offer a convenient way to grant common capabilities to collections of user accounts.

H

half-duplex transmission Two-way communication occurring in only one direction at a time.

handshaking A term applied to modem-to-modem communication. Refers to the process by which information is transmitted between the sending and receiving devices to maintain and coordinate data flow between them. Proper handshaking ensures that the receiving device will be ready to accept data before the sending device transmits.

HDLC *See* High-Level Data Link Control (HDLC).

header In network data transmission, one of the three sections of a packet component. It includes an alert signal to indicate that the packet is being transmitted, the source address, the destination address, and clock information to synchronize transmission.

hierarchical namespace A namespace, such as the Domain Name System (DNS) and Active Directory, that has a tiered structure allowing names and objects to be nested within each other.

High-Level Data Link Control (HDLC) HDLC is a widely accepted international protocol, developed by the International Organization for Standardization (ISO), that governs information transfer. HDLC is a bit-oriented, synchronous protocol that applies to the data-link (message packaging) layer of the OSI reference model. Under the HDLC protocol, data is transmitted in frames, each of which can contain a variable amount of data, but must be organized in a particular way. *See also* data frames, frame.

hop In routing through a mesh environment, the transmission of a data packet through a router.

host name The name of a device on a network. For a device on a Windows 2000 network, this can be the same as the computer name.

HTML *See* Hypertext Markup Language (HTML).

Hypertext Markup Language (HTML) A language developed for writing pages for the World Wide Web. HTML allows text to include codes that define fonts, layout, embedded graphics, and hypertext links. Hypertext provides a method for presenting text, images, sound, and videos that are linked together in a nonsequential web of associations.

Hypertext Transfer Protocol (HTTP) The method by which World Wide Web pages are transferred over the network.

I

IAB *See* Internet Architecture Board (IAB).

IBM cabling system Used in a Token Ring environment. Introduced by IBM in 1984 to define cable connectors, face plates, distribution panels, and cable types. Many parameters are similar to non-IBM specifications. Uniquely shaped, the IBM connector is hermaphroditic.

ICMP *See* Internet Control Message Protocol (ICMP).

IEEE *See* Institute of Electrical and Electronics Engineers (IEEE).

IEEE Project 802 A networking model developed by the IEEE. Named for the year and month it began (February 1980), Project 802 defines LAN standards for the physical and data-link layers of the OSI reference model. Project 802 divides the data-link layer into two sublayers: Media Access Control (MAC) and Logical Link Control (LLC).

incremental backup Backs up only the files created or changed since the last normal (or incremental) backup, and marks the files as having been backed up.

infrared transmission Electromagnetic radiation with frequencies in the electromagnetic spectrum in the range just below that of visible red light. In network communications, infrared technology offers extremely high transmission rates and wide bandwidth in line-of-sight communications.

Institute of Electrical and Electronics Engineers (IEEE) An organization of engineering and electronics professionals; noted in networking for developing the IEEE 802.x standards for the physical and data-link layers of the OSI reference model, applied in a variety of network configurations.

Integrated Services Digital Network (ISDN) A worldwide digital communication network that evolved from existing telephone services. The goal of the ISDN is to replace current telephone lines, which require digital-to-analog conversions, with completely digital switching and transmission facilities capable of carrying data ranging from voice to computer transmissions, music, and video. The ISDN is built on two main types of communications channels: B channels that carry voice, data, or images at a rate of 64 Kbps, and a D channel that carries control information, signaling, and link-management data at 16 Kbps. Standard ISDN Basic Rate desktop service is called 2B+D. Computers and other devices connect to ISDN lines through simple, standardized interfaces.

International Organization for Standardization (ISO) An organization made up of standards-setting groups from various countries. For example, the United States member is the American National Standards Institute (ANSI). The ISO works to establish global standards for communications and information exchange. Primary among its accomplishments is development of the widely accepted OSI reference model. Note that the ISO is often wrongly identified as the International Standards Organization, probably because of the abbreviation ISO; however, ISO is derived from *isos,* which means equal in Greek, rather than an acronym.

International Telecommunications Union (ITU) The organization responsible for setting the standards for international telecommunications.

International Telecommunications Union-Telecommunication (ITU-T) The sector of the ITU responsible for telecommunication standards. Its responsibilities include standardizing modem design and operations and standardizing protocols for networks and facsimile transmission. ITU is an international organization within which governments and the private sector coordinate global telecom networks and services.

Internet Architecture Board (IAB) A body that develops and maintains Internet architectural standards as part of the Internet Society (ISOC). It also adjudicates disputes in the standards process.

Internet Control Message Protocol (ICMP) Used by IP and higher-level protocols to send and receive status reports about information being transmitted.

Internet Information Services (IIS) Software services that support Web site creation, configuration, and management, along with other Internet functions. Microsoft Internet Information Services include Network News Transfer Protocol (NNTP), File Transfer Protocol (FTP), and Simple Mail Transfer Protocol (SMTP).

Internet Protocol (IP) The TCP/IP protocol for packet forwarding. *See also* Transmission Control Protocol/Internet Protocol (TCP/IP).

internetworking The intercommunication in a network that is made up of smaller networks.

Internetwork Packet Exchange/Sequenced Packet Exchange (IPX/SPX) A protocol stack that is used in Novell networks. IPX is the NetWare protocol for packet forwarding and routing. It is a relatively small and fast protocol on a LAN, is a derivative of Xerox Network System (XNS), and supports routing. SPX is a connection-oriented protocol used to guarantee the delivery of the data being sent. NWLink is the Microsoft implementation of the IPX/SPX protocol.

IP *See* Internet Protocol (IP). *See also* Transmission Control Protocol/Internet Protocol (TCP/IP).

IP address A 32-bit address used to identify a node on an IP network. Each node on the IP network must be unique. An IP address consists of a network identifier and a host identifier. This address is typically represented in dotted-decimal notation, with the decimal value of each octet separated by a period, for example, 192.168.7.27. In Microsoft Windows 2000, you can configure the IP address statically or dynamically through DHCP.

ipconfig A diagnostic command that displays all current TCP/IP network configuration values. It is of particular use on systems running DHCP because it allows users to determine which TCP/IP

configuration values have been configured by the DHCP server. *See also* winipcfg.

IPX/SPX *See* Internetwork Packet Exchange/ Sequenced Packet Exchange (IPX/SPX).

ISDN *See* Integrated Services Digital Network (ISDN).

ISO *See* International Organization for Standardization (ISO).

ITU *See* International Telecommunications Union (ITU).

ITU-T *See* International Telecommunications Union-Telecommunication (ITU-T).

K

Kerberos V5 An Internet standard security protocol for handling authentication of user or system identity. With Kerberos V5, passwords that are sent across network lines are encrypted, not sent as plaintext. Kerberos V5 also includes other security features.

L

LAN *See* local area network (LAN).

LAN requester *See* requester (LAN requester).

LAT *See* local area transport (LAT).

Layer 2 Tunneling Protocol (L2TP) An industry standard Internet tunneling protocol. Unlike Point-to-Point Tunneling Protocol (PPTP), L2TP does not require Internet Protocol (IP) connectivity between the client workstation and the server. L2TP requires only that the tunnel medium provide packet-oriented point-to-point connectivity. The protocol can be used over media such as Asynchronous Transfer Mode (ATM), frame relay, and X.25. L2TP provides the same functionality as PPTP. Based on Layer 2 Forwarding (L2F) and PPTP specifications, L2TP allows clients to set up tunnels across intervening networks.

layering The coordination of various protocols in a specific architecture that allows the protocols to work together to ensure that the data is prepared, transferred, received, and acted on as intended.

load balancing A technique used to scale the performance of a server-based program (such as a Web server) by distributing its client requests across multiple servers within the cluster. Typically, each host can specify the load percentage that it will handle, or the load can be equally distributed across all the hosts. If a host fails, the load is dynamically redistributed among the remaining hosts.

local area network (LAN) Computers connected in a geographically confined network, such as in the same building, campus, or office park.

local area transport (LAT) A nonroutable protocol from Digital Equipment Corporation.

local group One of four kinds of group accounts used by Microsoft Windows NT and Windows NT Server. Implemented in each local computer's account database, local groups contain user accounts and other global groups that need to have access, rights, and permissions assigned to a resource on a local computer. Local groups cannot contain other local groups.

LocalTalk Cabling components used in an AppleTalk network, including cables, connector modules, and cable extenders. These components are normally used in a bus or tree topology. A LocalTalk segment supports a maximum of 32 devices. Because of LocalTalk's limitations, clients often turn to vendors other than Apple for AppleTalk cabling. Farallon PhoneNet, for example, can accommodate 254 devices.

M

MAN (metropolitan area network) *See* metropolitan area network (MAN).

media The vast majority of LANs today are connected by some sort of wire or cabling that acts as the LAN transmission medium, carrying data between computers. The cabling is often referred to as the media.

metropolitan area network (MAN) A data network designed for a town or city. In geographic breadth, MANs are larger than local area networks but smaller than wide area networks. MANs are usually characterized by very-high-speed connections using fiber-optic cable or other digital media.

Microsoft Management Console (MMC) A framework for hosting administrative tools, called consoles. A console may contain tools, folders, or other containers, World Wide Web pages, and other administrative items. These items are displayed in the left pane of the console, called a console tree. A console has one or more windows that can provide views of the console tree. The main MMC window provides commands and tools for authoring consoles. The authoring features of MMC and the console tree itself may be hidden when a console is in User Mode.

Microsoft Technical Information Network (TechNet) Provides informational support for all aspects of networking, with an emphasis on Microsoft products.

mixed mode The default domain mode setting on Microsoft Windows 2000 domain controllers. Mixed mode allows Windows NT and Windows 2000 backup domain controllers to coexist in a domain. Mixed mode does not support the universal and nested group enhancements of Windows 2000. The domain mode setting can be changed to Windows 2000 native mode when all Windows NT domain controllers are removed from a domain.

MMC (Microsoft Management Console) *See* Microsoft Management Console (MMC).

N

name resolution The process of translating a name into some object or information that the name represents. A telephone book forms a namespace in which the names of the telephone subscribers can be resolved to telephone numbers. The Microsoft Windows NT file system (NTFS) forms a namespace in which the name of a file can be resolved to the file itself. The Active Directory forms a namespace in which the name of an object in the directory can be resolved to the object itself.

namespace A set of unique names for resources or items used in a shared computing environment. For MMC, the namespace is represented by the console tree, which displays all of the snap-ins and resources that are accessible to a console. *See also* Microsoft Management Console (MMC), resource, snap-in. For DNS, namespace is the vertical or hierarchical structure of the domain name tree. For example, each domain label, such as host1 or example, used in a fully qualified domain name, such as host1.example. microsoft.com, indicates a branch in the domain namespace tree.

NAS (network access server) *See* network access server (NAS).

nbtstat A diagnostic command that displays protocol statistics and current TCP/IP connections using NBT (NetBIOS over TCP/IP). This command is available only if the TCP/IP protocol has been installed. *See also* netstat.

NDIS *See* Network Device Interface Specification (NDIS).

NetBEUI (NetBIOS Enhanced User Interface) A protocol supplied with all Microsoft network products. NetBEUI advantages include small stack size (important for MS-DOS-based computers), speed of data transfer on the network medium, and compatibility with all Microsoft-based networks. The major drawback of NetBEUI is that it is a LAN transport protocol and therefore does not support routing. It is also limited to Microsoft-based networks.

NetBIOS (network basic input/output system) An application programming interface (API) that can be used by application programs on a LAN consisting of IBM-compatible microcomputers running MS-DOS, OS/2, or some version of UNIX. Primarily of interest to programmers, NetBIOS provides application programs with a uniform set of commands for requesting the lower-level network services required to conduct sessions between nodes on a network and transmit information between them.

netstat A diagnostic command that displays protocol statistics and current TCP/IP network connections. This command is available only if the TCP/IP protocol has been installed. *See also* nbtstat.

network access server (NAS) The device that accepts PPP connections and places clients on the network that the NAS serves.

Network Device Interface Specification (NDIS) A standard that defines an interface for communication between the Media Access Control (MAC) sublayer and protocol drivers. NDIS allows for a flexible environment of data exchange. It defines the software interface, called the NDIS interface, which is used by protocol drivers to communicate with the network interface card. The advantage of NDIS is that it offers protocol multiplexing so that multiple protocol stacks can be used at the same time.

network monitors Monitors that track all or a selected part of network traffic. They examine frame-level packets and gather information about packet types, errors, and packet traffic to and from each computer.

Network News Transfer Protocol (NNTP) A protocol defined in RFC 977. It is a de facto protocol standard on the Internet used for the distribution, inquiry, retrieval, and posting of Usenet news articles over the Internet.

NNTP *See* Network News Transfer Protocol (NNTP).

Novell NetWare One of the leading network architectures.

NSLOOKUP A command-line utility that allows you to make Domain Name System (DNS) queries for testing and troubleshooting your DNS installation.

NTFS *See* NTFS file system.

NTFS file system An advanced file system designed for use specifically within the Microsoft Windows 2000 operating system. It supports file system recovery, extremely large storage media, long filenames, and various features for the Portable Operating System Interface for UNIX (POSIX) subsystem. It also supports object-oriented applications by treating all files as objects with user-defined and system-defined attributes.

O

object An entity such as a file, folder, shared folder, printer, or Active Directory object described by a distinct, named set of attributes. For example, the attributes of a file object include its name, location, and size; the attributes of an Active Directory user object might include the user's first name, last name, and e-mail address.

Open Shortest Path First (OSPF) A routing protocol for IP networks, such as the Internet, that allows a router to calculate the shortest path to each node for sending messages.

Open Systems Interconnection (OSI) reference model A seven-layer architecture that standardizes levels of service and types of interaction for computers exchanging information through a network. It is used to describe the flow of data between the physical connection to the network and the end-user application. This model is the best known and most widely used model for describing networking environments.

OSI *See* Open Systems Interconnection (OSI) reference model.

OSPF *See* Open Shortest Path First (OSPF).

P

packet A unit of information transmitted as a whole from one device to another on a network. In packet-switching networks, a packet is defined more specifically as a transmission unit of fixed maximum size that consists of binary digits representing data; a header containing an identification number, source, and destination addresses; and sometimes error-control data. *See also* frame.

Packet Internet Groper (ping) A simple utility that tests if a network connection is complete, from the server to the workstation, by sending a message to the remote computer. If the remote computer receives the message, it responds with a reply message. The reply consists of the remote workstation's IP address, the number of bytes in the message, how long it took to reply—given in milliseconds (ms)—and the length of Time to Live (TTL) in seconds. Ping works at the IP level and will often respond even when higher-level TCP-based services cannot.

packet switching A message delivery technique in which small units of information (packets) are relayed through stations in a computer network along the best route available between the source and the destination. Data is broken into smaller units and then repacked in a process called packet assembly and disassembly (PAD). Although each packet can travel along a different path, and the packets composing a message can arrive at different times or out of sequence, the receiving computer reassembles the original message. Packet-switching networks are considered fast and efficient. Standards for packet switching on networks are documented in the CCITT recommendation X.25.

page-description language (PDL) A language that communicates to a printer how printed output should appear. The printer uses the PDL to construct text, and graphics to create the page image. PDLs are like blueprints in that they set parameters and features such as type sizes and fonts, but leave the drawing to the printer.

PBX Private Branch Exchange (PABX Private Automated Branch Exchange) A switching telephone network that allows callers within an organization to place intraorganizational calls without going through the public telephone system.

PDC *See* primary domain controller (PDC).

PDL *See* page-description language (PDL).

PDN *See* public data network (PDN).

performance counter In System Monitor, a data item associated with a performance object. For each counter selected, System Monitor presents a value corresponding to a particular aspect of the performance defined for the performance object.

performance monitor A tool for monitoring network performance that can display statistics, such as the number of packets sent and received, server-processor utilization, and the amount of data going into and out of the server.

performance object In System Monitor, a logical collection of counters that is associated with a resource or service that can be monitored.

ping *See* Packet Internet Groper (ping).

PKI (public key infrastructure) *See* public key infrastructure (PKI).

pointer (PTR) resource record A resource record used in a reverse lookup zone created within the in-addr.arpa domain to designate a reverse mapping of a host Internet Protocol (IP) address to a host Domain Name System (DNS) domain name.

point-to-point configuration Dedicated circuits that are also known as private, or leased, lines. They are the most popular WAN communication

circuits in use today. The carrier guarantees full-duplex bandwidth by setting up a permanent link from each endpoint, using bridges and routers to connect LANs through the circuits. *See also* Point-to-Point Protocol (PPP), Point-to-Point Tunneling Protocol (PPTP), duplex transmission.

Point-to-Point Protocol (PPP) A data-link protocol for transmitting TCP/IP packets over dial-up telephone connections, such as between a computer and the Internet. PPP was developed by the Internet Engineering Task Force in 1991.

Point-to-Point Tunneling Protocol (PPTP) PPTP is an extension of the Point-to-Point Protocol that is used for communication on the Internet. It was developed by Microsoft to support virtual private networks (VPNs), which allow individuals and organizations to use the Internet as a secure means of communication. PPTP supports encapsulation of encrypted packets in secure wrappers that can be transmitted over a TCP/IP connection. *See also* virtual private network (VPN).

PPP *See* Point-to-Point Protocol (PPP).

PPTP *See* Point-to-Point Tunneling Protocol (PPTP).

primary domain controller (PDC) The server that maintains the master copy of the domain's user-accounts database and validates logon requests. Every network domain is required to have one, and only one, PDC. *See also* domain, domain controller.

primary zone database file The master zone database file. Changes to a zone, such as adding domains or hosts, are performed on the server that contains the primary zone database file.

private key The secret half of a cryptographic key pair that is used with a public key algorithm. Private keys are typically used to decrypt a symmetric session key, digitally sign data, or decrypt data that has been encrypted with the corresponding public key.

protocol The system of rules and procedures that govern communication between two or more devices. Many varieties of protocols exist, and not all are compatible, but as long as two devices are using the same protocol, they can exchange data. Protocols exist within protocols as well, governing different aspects of communication. Some protocols, such as the RS-232 standard, affect hardware connections. Other standards govern data transmission, including the parameters and handshaking signals such as XON/OFF used in asynchronous (typically, modem) communications, as well as such data-coding methods as bit- and byte-oriented protocols. Still other protocols, such as the widely used XMODEM, govern file transfer, and others, such as CSMA/CD, define the methods by which messages are passed around the stations on a LAN. Protocols represent attempts to ease the complex process of enabling computers of different makes and models to communicate. Additional examples of protocols include the OSI model, IBM's SNA, and the Internet suite, including TCP/IP. *See also* Systems Network Architecture (SNA), Transmission Control Protocol/Internet Protocol (TCP/IP).

protocol driver The driver responsible for offering four or five basic services to other layers in the network, while "hiding" the details of how the services are actually implemented. Services performed include session management, datagram service, data segmentation and sequencing, acknowledgment, and possibly routing across a WAN.

protocol stack A layered set of protocols that work together to provide a set of network functions.

proxy server A firewall component that manages Internet traffic to and from a local area network (LAN). The proxy server decides whether it is safe to let a particular message or file pass through to the organization's network, providing access control to the network, and filters and discards requests as specified by the owner, including requests for unauthorized access to proprietary data. *See also* firewall.

public data network (PDN) A commercial packet-switching or circuit-switching WAN service provided by local and long-distance telephone carriers.

public key The nonsecret half of a cryptographic key pair that is used with a public key algorithm. Public keys are typically used when encrypting a session key, verifying a digital signature, or encrypting data that can be decrypted with the corresponding private key.

public key cryptography A method of cryptography in which two different keys are used: a public key for encrypting data and a private key for decrypting data.

public key infrastructure (PKI) The term generally used to describe the laws, policies, standards, and software that regulate or manipulate certificates and public and private keys. In practice, it is a system of digital certificates, certification authorities, and other registration authorities that verify and authenticate the validity of each party involved in an electronic transaction. Standards for PKI are still evolving, even though they are being widely implemented as a necessary element of electronic commerce.

Q

QoS (quality of service) *See* quality of service (QoS).

quality of service (QoS) A set of quality-assurance standards and mechanisms for data transmission, implemented in Windows 2000.

R

RADIUS (Remote Authentication Dial-In User Service) *See* Remote Authentication Dial-In User Service (RADIUS).

RAS *See* Remote Access Server (RAS).

redirector Networking software that accepts I/O requests for remote files, named pipes, or mail slots, and sends (redirects) the requests to a network service on another computer.

Remote Access Server (RAS) Any Microsoft Windows 2000-based computer configured to accept remote access connections.

Remote Authentication Dial-In User Service (RADIUS) A security authentication protocol based on clients and servers and widely used by Internet service providers (ISPs) on non-Microsoft remote servers. RADIUS is the most popular means of authenticating and authorizing dial-up and tunneled network users today.

remote computer A computer that can be accessed only by using a communications line or a communications device, such as a network card or a modem.

remote user A user who dials in to the server over modems and telephone lines from a remote location.

Request for Comments (RFC) The official documents of the Internet Engineering Task Force (IETF) that specify the details for protocols included in the Transmission Control Protocol/Internet Protocol (TCP/IP) family.

requester (LAN requester) Software that resides in a computer and forwards requests for network services from the computer's application programs to the appropriate server. *See also* redirector.

resource Any part of a computer system. Users on a network can share computer resources, such as hard disks, printers, modems, CD-ROM drives, and even the processor.

resource record Standard database record types used in zones to associate Domain Name System (DNS) domain names to related data for a given type of network resource, such as a host Internet Protocol (IP) address. Most of the basic resource record types are defined in RFC 1035, but additional resource record types are defined in other RFCs and approved for use with DNS.

reverse lookup In Domain Name System (DNS), a query process by which the Internet Protocol (IP) address of a host computer is searched to find its friendly DNS domain name.

RFC *See* Request for Comments (RFC).

RIP *See* Routing Information Protocol (RIP).

Routing Information Protocol (RIP) A protocol that uses distance-vector algorithms to determine routes. With RIP, routers transfer information among other routers to update their internal routing tables, and use that information to determine the best routes based on hop counts between routers. TCP/IP and IPX support RIP.

S

SAP (service access point) *See* service access point (SAP).

SAP (Service Advertising Protocol) *See* Service Advertising Protocol (SAP).

SDLC *See* Synchronous Data Link Control (SDLC).

secondary master An authoritative Domain Name System (DNS) server for a zone that is used as a source for replication of the zone to other servers. Secondary masters update their zone data only by transferring zone data from other DNS servers. They do not have the ability to perform zone updates.

security Making computers and data stored on them safe from harm or unauthorized access.

security identifier *or* **security ID (SID)** A unique number that identifies user, group, and computer accounts. Every account on your network is issued a unique SID when the account is first created. Internal processes in Windows 2000 refer to an account's SID rather than the account's user or group name. If you create an account, delete it, and then create an account with the same user name, the new account will not have the rights or permissions previously granted to the old account because the accounts have different SID numbers.

segment The length of cable on a network between two terminators. A segment can also refer to messages that have been broken up into smaller units by the protocol driver.

Sequenced Packet Exchange (SPX) Part of Novell's IPX/SPX protocol suite for sequenced data. *See also* Internetwork Packet Exchange/Sequenced Packet Exchange (IPX/SPX).

Serial Line Internet Protocol (SLIP) Defined in RFC 1055. SLIP is normally used on Ethernet, over a serial line; for example, an RS-232 serial port connected to a modem.

serial transmission One-way data transfer. The data travels on a network cable with one bit following another.

server message block (SMB) The protocol developed by Microsoft, Intel, and IBM that defines a series of commands used to pass information between network computers. The redirector packages SMB requests into a network control block (NCB) structure that can be sent over the network to a remote device. The network provider listens for SMB messages destined for it and removes the data portion of the SMB request so that it can be processed by a local device.

service A program, routine, or process that performs a specific system function to support other programs, particularly at the hardware level. When services are provided over a network, they can be published in Active Directory, facilitating service-centric administration and usage. Some examples of Microsoft Windows 2000 services are Security Accounts Manager service, File Replication service, and Routing and Remote Access service.

service access point (SAP) The interface among each of the seven layers in the OSI protocol stack that has connection points, similar to addresses, used for communication among layers. Any protocol layer can have multiple SAPs active at one time.

Service Advertising Protocol (SAP) Allows service-providing nodes (including file, printer, gateway, and application servers) to advertise their services and addresses.

service (SRV) resource record A resource record used in a zone to register and locate well-known Transmission Control Protocol/Internet Protocol (TCP/IP) services. The SRV resource record is specified in RFC 2052 and is used in Microsoft Windows 2000 or later to locate domain controllers for Active Directory service.

session management Establishing, maintaining, and terminating connections between stations on the network.

shell A piece of software, usually a separate program, that provides direct communication between the user and the operating system. This usually, but not always, takes the form of a command-line interface. Examples of shells are Macintosh Finder and the MS-DOS command interface program COMMAND.COM.

SID (security identifier *or* security ID) *See* security identifier or security ID (SID).

Simple Mail Transfer Protocol (SMTP) A TCP/IP protocol for transferring e-mail. *See also* Transmission Control Protocol/Internet Protocol (TCP/IP).

Simple Network Management Protocol (SNMP) A TCP/IP protocol for monitoring networks. SNMP uses a request and response process. In SNMP, short utility programs, called agents, monitor the network traffic and behavior in key network components to gather statistical data, which they put into a management information base (MIB).

To collect the information into a usable form, a special management console program regularly polls the agents and downloads the information in their MIBs. If any of the data falls either above or below parameters set by the manager, the management console program can present signals on the monitor locating the trouble and notify designated support staff by automatically dialing a pager number.

SLIP *See* Serial Line Internet Protocol (SLIP).

smart card A credit card-sized device used to securely store public and private keys, passwords, and other types of personal information. To use a smart card, you need a smart card reader attached to the computer and a personal identification number for the smart card. In Windows 2000, smart cards can be used to enable certificate-based authentication and single sign-on to the enterprise.

smart card reader A standard device within the smart card subsystem. A smart card reader is an interface device (IFD) that supports bidirectional input/output to a smart card.

SMB *See* server message block (SMB).

SMTP *See* Simple Mail Transfer Protocol (SMTP).

SNA *See* Systems Network Architecture (SNA).

snap-in A type of tool you can add to a console supported by Microsoft Management Console (MMC). A stand-alone snap-in can be added by itself; an extension snap-in can only be added to extend the function of another snap-in.

SNMP *See* Simple Network Management Protocol (SNMP).

SONET *See* Synchronous Optical Network (SONET).

SPX *See* Sequenced Packet Exchange (SPX).

SQL *See* structured query language (SQL).

stand-alone computer A computer that is not connected to any other computers and is not part of a network.

stand-alone server A computer that runs Microsoft Windows 2000 Server but does not participate in a domain. A stand-alone server has only its own database of users, and it processes logon requests by itself. It does not share account information with any other computer and cannot provide access to domain accounts.

start-of-authority (SOA) resource record A record that indicates the starting point or original point of authority for information stored in a zone. The SOA resource record is the first resource record created when adding a new zone. It also contains several parameters used by other computers that use Domain Name System (DNS) to determine how long they will use information for the zone and how often updates are required.

structured query language (SQL) A database sublanguage used to query, update, and manage relational databases. Although not a programming language in the same sense as C or Pascal, SQL can be used either in formulating interactive queries or embedded in an application as instructions for handling data. The SQL standard also contains components for defining, altering, controlling, and securing data.

subdomain A Domain Name System (DNS) domain located directly beneath another domain name (the parent domain) in the namespace tree. For example, example.microsoft.com would be a subdomain of the microsoft.com domain. A subdomain is also called a child domain.

subnet A portion of a network, which may be a physically independent network segment, that shares a classful network address with other portions of the network and is distinguished by a subnet number.

subnet mask A 32-bit value that allows the recipient of Internet Protocol (IP) packets to distinguish the network ID portion of the IP address from the host ID.

SVC *See* switched virtual circuit (SVC).

switched virtual circuit (SVC) A logical connection between end computers that uses a specific route across the network. Network resources are dedicated to the circuit, and the route is maintained until the connection is terminated. These are also known as point-to-multipoint connections.

synchronous A form of communication that relies on a timing scheme coordinated between two devices to separate groups of bits and transmit them in blocks called frames. Special characters are used to begin the synchronization and check its accuracy periodically. Because the bits are sent and received in a timed, controlled (synchronized) fashion, start and stop bits are not required. Transmission stops at the end of one transmission and starts again with a new one. It is a start/stop approach, and more efficient than asynchronous transmission. If an error occurs, the synchronous error detection and correction scheme implements a retransmission. However, because more sophisticated technology and equipment are required to transmit synchronously, it is more expensive than asynchronous transmission.

Synchronous Data Link Control (SDLC) The data link (data transmission) protocol most widely used in networks conforming to IBM's SNA. SDLC is a communications guideline that defines the format in which information is transmitted. As its name implies, SDLC applies to synchronous transmissions. SDLC is also a bit-oriented protocol and organizes information in structured units called frames.

Synchronous Optical Network (SONET) A fiber-optic technology that can transmit data at more than 1 gigabit per second. Networks based on this technology are capable of delivering voice, data, and video. SONET is a standard for optical transport formulated by the Exchange Carriers Standards Association (ECSA) for the ANSI.

System Monitor A tool that allows you to collect and view extensive data about the usage of hardware resources and the activity of system services on computers you administer.

Systems Network Architecture (SNA) A widely used communication framework developed by IBM to define network functions and establish standards for enabling its different models of computers to exchange and process data. SNA is a design philosophy that separates network communication into five layers. Each layer, like those in the similar ISO/OSI model, represents a graduated level of function moving upward from physical connections to applications software.

SYSVOL A shared directory that stores the server copy of the domain's public files, which are replicated among all domain controllers in the domain.

T

TCO *See* total cost of ownership (TCO).

TCP *See* Transmission Control Protocol (TCP).

TCP/IP *See* Transmission Control Protocol/Internet Protocol (TCP/IP).

TDI *See* transport driver interface (TDI).

Technet *See* Microsoft Technical Information Network (TechNet).

Telnet The command and program used to log on from one Internet site to another. The Telnet command and program bring the user to the logon prompt of another host.

Terminal Services Software services that allow client applications to be run on a server so that client computers can function as terminals rather than independent systems. The server provides a multisession environment and runs the Microsoft Windows-based programs being used on the clients.

throughput A measure of the data transfer rate through a component, connection, or system. In networking, throughput is a good indicator of the system's total performance because it defines how well the components work together to transfer data from one computer to another. In this case, the throughput would indicate how many bytes or packets the network could process per second.

Time to Live (TTL) A timer value included in packets sent over TCP/IP-based networks that tells routers when a packet has been forwarded too many times. For DNS, TTL values are used in resource records within a zone to determine how long requesting clients should cache, and use this information when it appears in a query response answered by a DNS server for the zone.

TokenTalk An expansion card that allows a Macintosh II to connect to an 802.5 Token Ring network.

total cost of ownership (TCO) The total amount of money and time associated with purchasing computer hardware and software and deploying, configuring, and maintaining the hardware and software. TCO includes hardware and software updates, training, maintenance, administration, and technical support.

tracert A trace route command-line utility that shows every router interface through which a TCP/IP packet passes on its way to a destination.

Transmission Control Protocol (TCP) The TCP/IP protocol for sequenced data. *See also* Transmission Control Protocol/Internet Protocol (TCP/IP).

Transmission Control Protocol/Internet Protocol (TCP/IP) An industry-standard suite of protocols providing communications in a heterogeneous environment. In addition, TCP/IP provides a routable, enterprise networking protocol and access to the Internet and its resources. It is a transport layer protocol that actually consists of several other protocols in a stack that operates at the session layer. Most networks support TCP/IP as a protocol.

transport driver interface (TDI) An interface that works between the file-system driver and the transport protocols, allowing any protocol written to TDI to communicate with the file-system drivers.

transport layer The fourth layer of the OSI reference model. It ensures that messages are delivered error-free, in sequence, and without losses or duplications. This layer repackages messages for efficient transmission over the network. At the receiving end, the transport layer unpacks the messages, reassembles the original messages, and sends an acknowledgment of receipt. *See also* Open Systems Interconnection (OSI) reference model.

transport protocols Protocols that provide for communication sessions between computers and ensure that data is able to move reliably between computers.

trunk A single cable, also called a backbone or segment.

trust relationship Trust relationships are links between domains that enable pass-through authentication, in which a user has only one user account in one domain, yet can access the entire network. User accounts and global groups defined in a trusted domain can be given rights and resource permissions in a trusting domain even though those accounts do not exist in the trusting domain's database. A trusting domain honors the logon authentication of a trusted domain.

TTL (Time to Live) *See* Time to Live (TTL).

U

UDP *See* User Datagram Protocol (UDP).

UNC (Universal Naming Convention) *See* Universal Naming Convention (UNC).

uninterruptible power supply (UPS) A device connected between a computer or another piece of electronic equipment and a power source, such as an electrical outlet. The UPS ensures that the electrical flow to the computer is not interrupted because of a blackout and, in most cases, protects the computer against potentially damaging events such as power surges and brownouts. Different UPS models offer different levels of protection. All UPS units are equipped with a battery and loss-of-power sensor. If the sensor detects a loss of power, it immediately switches over to the battery so that users have time to save their work and shut off the computer. Most higher-end models have features such as power filtering, sophisticated surge protection, and a serial port so that an operating system capable of communicating with a UPS (such as Windows NT) can work with the UPS to facilitate automatic system shutdown.

Universal Naming Convention (UNC) The standard used for a full Windows 2000 name of a resource on a network. It conforms to the *server**share* syntax, where servername is the name of the server and sharename is the name of the shared resource. UNC names of directories or files can also include the directory path under the share name, with the following syntax: *server**share*\ *directory**filename*.

UPS *See* uninterruptible power supply (UPS).

user account Consists of all of the information that defines a user on a network. This includes the user name and password required for the user to log on, the groups in which the user account has membership, and the rights and permissions the user has for using the system and accessing its resources.

User Datagram Protocol (UDP) A connectionless protocol responsible for end-to-end data transmission.

user groups Groups of users who meet online or in person to discuss installation, administration, and other network challenges for the purpose of sharing and drawing on each other's expertise in developing ideas and solutions.

user name A unique name identifying a user account to Microsoft Windows 2000. An account's user name must be unique among the other group names and user names within its own domain or workgroup.

V

virtual private network (VPN) A set of computers on a public network such as the Internet that communicate among themselves using encryption technology. In this way, their messages are safe from being intercepted and understood by unauthorized users. VPNs operate as if the computers were connected by private lines.

W

WAN *See* wide area network (WAN).

Web server A computer that is maintained by a system administrator or Internet service provider (ISP) and responds to requests from a user's Web browser.

wide area network (WAN) A computer network that uses long-range telecommunication links to connect networked computers across long distances.

Windows 2000 Advanced Server A powerful departmental and application server that provides rich network operations system (NOS) and Internet services. Advanced Server supports large physical memories, clustering, and load balancing.

Windows 2000 Datacenter Server The most powerful and functional server operating system in the Microsoft Windows 2000 family. It is optimized for large data warehouses, econometric analysis, large-scale simulations in science and engineering, and server consolidation projects.

Windows 2000 Professional A high-performance, secure network client computer and corporate desktop operating system that includes the best features of Microsoft Windows 98, significantly extending the manageability, reliability, security, and performance of Windows NT Workstation 4.0. Windows 2000 Professional can be used as a desktop operating system, networked in a peer-to-peer workgroup environment, or used as a workstation in a Windows 2000 Server domain environment.

Windows 2000 Server A file, print, and applications server, as well as a Web server platform that contains all of the features of Microsoft Windows 2000 Professional plus many new server-specific functions. This product is ideal for small- to medium-sized enterprise application deployments, Web servers, workgroups, and branch offices.

Windows Internet Name Service (WINS) A software service that dynamically maps Internet Protocol (IP) addresses to computer names (NetBIOS names). This allows users to access resources by name instead of requiring them to use IP addresses that are difficult to recognize and remember. WINS servers support clients running Microsoft Windows NT 4.0 and earlier versions of Microsoft operating systems.

winipcfg A diagnostic command specific to Microsoft Windows 95 and 98. Although this graphical user interface (GUI) utility duplicates the functionality of ipconfig, its GUI makes it easier to use. *See also* ipconfig.

WINS *See* Windows Internet Name Service (WINS).

workgroup A collection of computers grouped for sharing resources such as data and peripherals over a LAN. Each workgroup is identified by a unique name.

workstation Any networked Macintosh or PC using server resources on the network.

World Wide Web (the Web, WWW) The Internet multimedia service that contains a vast storehouse of hypertext documents written in HTML. *See also* Hypertext Markup Language (HTML).

X

X.25 A recommendation published by the CCITT that defines the connection between a terminal and a packet-switching network. A packet-switching network routes packets whose contents and format are controlled standards such as those defined in the X.25 recommendation. X.25 incorporates three definitions: the electrical connection between the terminal and the network, the transmission or link-access protocol, and the implementation of virtual circuits between network users. Taken together, these definitions specify a synchronous, full-duplex, terminal-to-network connection. Packets transmitted in such a network can contain either data or control commands. Packet format, error control, and other features are equivalent to portions of the HDLC protocol defined by the ISO. X.25 standards are related to the lowest three levels of the OSI reference model.

X.400 A CCITT protocol for international e-mail transmissions.

X.500 A CCITT protocol for file and directory maintenance across several systems.

XNS (Xerox Network System) A protocol developed by Xerox for its Ethernet LANs.

Z

zone In a Domain Name System (DNS) database, a zone is a subtree of the DNS database that is administered as a single, separate entity. This administrative unit can consist of a single domain or a domain with subdomains. A DNS zone administrator sets up one or more name servers for the zone.

zone database file The file where name-to-IP-address mappings for a zone are stored.

zone transfer The process by which Domain Name System (DNS) servers interact to maintain and synchronize authoritative name data. When a DNS server is configured as a secondary master for a zone, it periodically queries another DNS server configured as its source for the zone. If the version of the zone kept by the source is different, the secondary master server will pull zone data from its source DNS server to synchronize zone data.

zones Logical groupings of users and resources in an AppleTalk network.

Index

Note to the reader   Italics are used to indicate references to illustrations.

There's no *substitute* for *experience.*

Now you can apply the best practices from real-world implementations of Microsoft technologies with NOTES FROM THE FIELD. Based on the extensive field experiences of Microsoft Consulting Services, these valuable technical references outline tried-and-tested solutions you can use in your own company, right now.

Deploying Microsoft® Office 2000
(Notes from the Field)
U.S.A. $39.99
U.K.   £25.99 [V.A.T. included]
Canada $59.99
ISBN 0-7356-0727-3

Deploying Microsoft SQL Server™ 7.0
(Notes from the Field)
U.S.A. $39.99
U.K.   £25.99
Canada $59.99
ISBN 0-7356-0726-5

Optimizing Network Traffic
(Notes from the Field)
U.S.A. $39.99
U.K.   £25.99 [V.A.T. included]
Canada $59.99
ISBN 0-7356-0648-X

Managing a Microsoft Windows NT® Network
(Notes from the Field)
U.S.A. $39.99
U.K.   £25.99 [V.A.T. included]
Canada $59.99
ISBN 0-7356-0647-1

Building an Enterprise Active Directory™ Services
(Notes from the Field)
U.S.A. $39.99
U.K.   £25.99 [V.A.T. included]
Canada $61.99
ISBN 0-7356-0860-1

Microsoft®
mspress.microsoft.com

The *intelligent* way to practice for the MCP exam

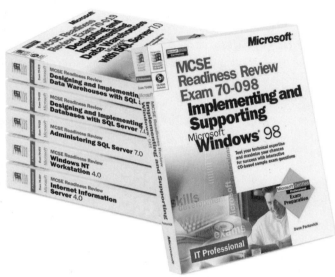

If you took the Microsoft Certified Professional (MCP) exam today, would you pass? With the READINESS REVIEW MCP exam simulation on CD-ROM, you get a low-risk, low-cost way to find out! Use this electronic assessment tool to take randomly generated 60-question practice tests, covering actual MCP objectives. Test and retest with different question sets each time, and then consult the companion study guide to review all featured exam items and identify areas for further study. READINESS REVIEW—it's the smart way to prep!

Ready solutions *for the* IT administrator

Keep your IT systems up and running with ADMINISTRATOR'S COMPANIONS from Microsoft Press. These expert guides serve as both tutorial and reference for critical deployment and maintenance tasks for Microsoft products and technologies. Packed with real-world expertise, hands-on numbered procedures, and handy workarounds, ADMINISTRATOR'S COMPANIONS deliver ready answers for on-the-job results.

Microsoft® Resource Kits— powerhouse resources to minimize costs while maximizing performance

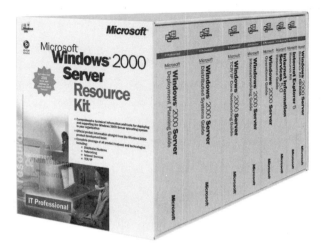

Microsoft® Windows® 2000 Server Resource Kit
ISBN   1-57231-805-8
U.S.A. $299.99
U.K.   £189.99 [V.A.T. included]
Canada $460.99

Microsoft Windows 2000 Professional Resource Kit
ISBN   1-57231-808-2
U.S.A. $69.99
U.K.   £45.99 [V.A.T. included]
Canada $107.99

Microsoft BackOffice® 4.5 Resource Kit
ISBN   0-7356-0583-1
U.S.A. $249.99
U.K.   £161.99 [V.A.T. included]
Canada $374.99

Microsoft Internet Explorer 5 Resource Kit
ISBN   0-7356-0587-4
U.S.A. $59.99
U.K.   £38.99 [V.A.T. included]
Canada $89.99

Microsoft Office 2000 Resource Kit
ISBN   0-7356-0555-6
U.S.A. $59.99
U.K.   £38.99 [V.A.T. included]
Canada $89.99

Microsoft Windows NT® Server 4.0 Resource Kit
ISBN   1-57231-344-7
U.S.A. $149.95
U.K.   £96.99 [V.A.T. included]
Canada $199.95

Microsoft Windows NT Workstation 4.0 Resource Kit
ISBN   1-57231-343-9
U.S.A. $69.95
U.K.   £45.99 [V.A.T. included]
Canada $94.95

Deploy and support your enterprise business systems using the expertise and tools of those who know the technology best—the Microsoft product groups. Each RESOURCE KIT packs precise technical reference, installation and rollout tactics, planning guides, upgrade strategies, and essential utilities on CD-ROM. They're everything you need to help maximize system performance as you reduce ownership and support costs!

Microsoft®

mspress.microsoft.com

System Requirements

To complete the exercises in this book and to use the book's Supplemental Course Materials CD-ROM, you need two computers each equipped with the following minimum configuration:

- 32-bit 166-MHz or higher Pentium-compatible CPU

- Microsoft Windows 95, Windows 98, Windows NT 4.0 or later

- 64 MB of RAM

- 2 GB hard disk with a minimum of 500 MB free space

- 12x or faster CD-ROM drive

- Microsoft Mouse or compatible pointing device (recommended)

- High-density 3.5-inch disk drive, unless your CD-ROM is bootable and supports starting the setup program from a CD-ROM

- SVGA monitor capable of 800 x 600 resolution (1024 x 768 recommended)

To use the online version of this book from the Supplemental Course Materials CD-ROM, you need a computer additionally equipped with the following:

- 24x CD-ROM drive

- Microsoft Internet Explorer 5.0